The
RISE
of
AMERICAN
DEMOCRACY

VOLUME III
SLAVERY AND THE CRISIS OF
AMERICAN DEMOCRACY
1840–1860

Sean Wilentz

W. W. Norton & Company
New York London

Copyright © 2005, by Sean Wilentz
Copyright © 2007 by W. W. Norton & Company, Inc.,
All rights reserved
Printed in the United States of America

For information about permission to reproduce selections from this book, write to
Permissions, W. W. Norton & Company, Inc., 500 Fifth Avenue, New York, NY
10110

ISBN-13: 978-0-393-93008-5(pbk)
ISBN-10: 0-393-93008-4(pbk)

The Library of Congress has catalogued the one-volume edition as follows:

Wilentz, Sean.
The rise of American democracy : Jefferson to Lincoln / Sean Wilentz.—1st ed.
p. cm.
Includes bibliographical references and index.
ISBN 0-393-05820-4 (hardcover)
1. United States—Politics and government—1783–1865. 2. Presidents—United
States—History—18th century. 3. Presidents—United States—History—19th
century.
4. Politicians—United States—History—19th century. 6. Democracy—United
States—History—18th century. 7. Democracy—United States—History—19th
century. I. Title.

E302.1.W55 2005
973.5—dc21

2004029466

W. W. Norton & Company, Inc.
500 Fifth Avenue, New York, NY 10110
www.wwnorton.com

W. W. Norton & Company Ltd.
Castle House, 75/76 Wells Street, London W1T 3QT

1 2 3 4 5 6 7 8 9 0

A NOTE ON THE COLLEGE EDITION

The three-volume College Edition of *The Rise of American Democracy: Jefferson to Lincoln* has two chief goals. First, many students and teachers, as well as many general readers, are mainly interested in one or two phases of the long history covered in the larger work. Publishing each of the book's three major parts as separate volumes allows those readers to focus on their period or periods of special interest. Second, many readers prefer a version without the elaborate scholarly apparatus of the original, but with pointers on further reading. The College Edition includes a list of select additional titles pertinent to each volume, while it eliminates the endnotes in the full edition. Not a word of text from the larger work has been omitted.

To enhance continuity, brief synopses of events covered earlier in the general work appear in volumes II and III.

—S.W

To P.B. and L.W.
& to all my dearest

CONTENTS

LIST OF ILLUSTRATIONS

MAPS

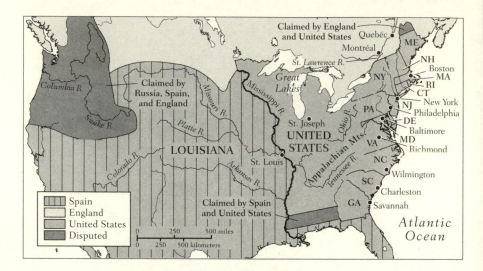

NORTH AMERICA, 1783

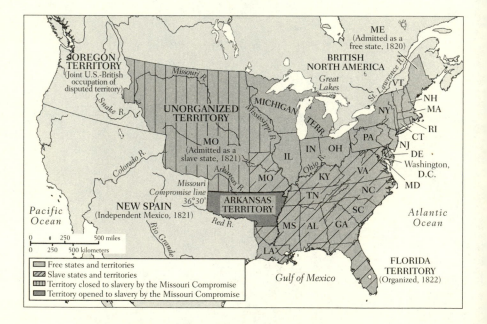

THE MISSOURI COMPROMISE, 1820

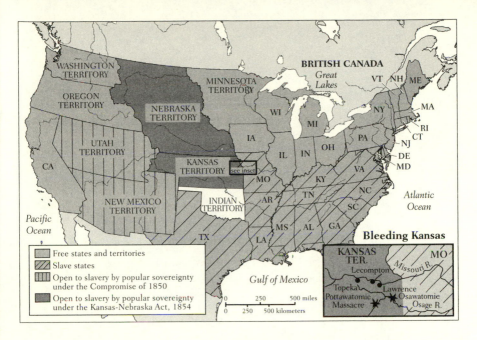

THE KANSAS-NEBRASKA ACT, 1854

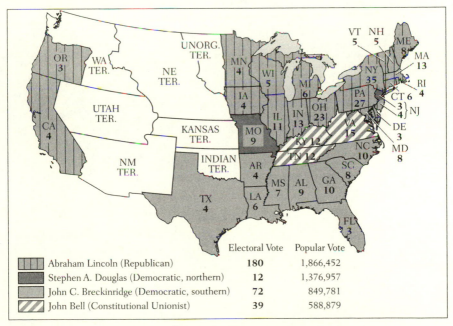

	Electoral Vote	Popular Vote
Abraham Lincoln (Republican)	180	1,866,452
Stephen A. Douglas (Democratic, northern)	12	1,376,957
John C. Breckinridge (Democratic, southern)	72	849,781
John Bell (Constitutional Unionist)	39	588,879

THE ELECTION OF 1860

PREFACE TO VOLUME III

The simple title of the general work from which this volume is drawn, *The Rise of American Democracy*, describes the historical arc of the overall subject. Important elements of democracy existed in the infant American republic of the 1780s, but the republic was not democratic. Nor, in the minds of those who governed it, was it supposed to be. A republic–the *res publica*, or "public thing"–was meant to secure the common good through the ministrations of the most worthy, enlightened men. A democracy—derived from *demos krateo*, "rule of the people"—dangerously handed power to the impassioned, unenlightened masses. Democracy, the eminent political leader George Cabot wrote as late as 1804, was *"the government of the worst."* Yet by the 1830s, as Alexis de Tocqueville learned, most Americans proclaimed that their country was a democracy as well as a republic. Enduring arguments had begun over the boundaries of democratic politics. In the 1840s and 1850s, the arguments centered increasingly on slavery and slavery's expansion, and led to the Civil War.

The change was astonishing, but it was neither inevitable nor providential. American democracy did not rise like the sun at its natural hour in history. Its often troubled ascent was the outcome of human conflicts, accommodations, and unforeseen events, and the results could well have been very different than they were. The difficulties and the contingencies made the events all the more remarkable. A momentous rupture occurred between Thomas Jefferson's time and Abraham Lincoln's, in which the elitist presumptions and institutions of the infant republic gave way to far broader conceptions of popular sovereignty and to new forms of mass political participation, in and out of elections. The polity that emerged contained the lineaments of modern democratic politics. The rise of American democracy is the story of that rupture and its immediate consequences.

Democracy is a troublesome word, and explaining why is one of *The Rise of American Democracy's* larger purposes. A decade before the American Revolution, the early patriot James Otis defined democracy in its purest and simplest form as "a government of all over all," in which "the votes of the majority shall be taken as the voice of the whole," and where the rulers were the ruled and the ruled were the rulers. As fixed descriptions go, this is as good as any, but its abstractness, of course, begs explication. Since the Revolution, citizens, scholars, and political leaders have latched on to one or another particular aspect of government or politics as democracy's essence. For some, it is a matter of widened political rights, usually measured by the extent of the suffrage and actual voting; for others, democracy means greater opportunity for the individual pursuit of happiness; for still others, it is more of a cultural phenomenon than a political one, "a habit of the heart," as Tocqueville put it, in which deference to rulers and condescension for the ruled give way to the ruder conventions of equality.

All of these facets are important, but I think we go astray in discussing democracy simply as a form of government or society, or as a set of social norms—a category or a thing with particular structures that can be codified and measured. Today, democracy means, at a minimum, full enfranchisement and participation by the entire adult citizenry. By that standard, the American democracy of the mid-nineteenth century was hardly a democracy at all: women of all classes and colors lacked political and civil rights; most blacks were enslaved; free black men found political rights they had once enjoyed either reduced or eliminated; the remnant of a ravaged Indian population in the eastern states had been forced to move west, without citizenship. Even the most expansive of the era's successful democratic political reforms encompassed considerably less than half of the total adult population, and at best a bare majority of the free adult population.* But to impose current categories of democracy on the past is to block any understanding of how our own, more elevated standards originated. It is to distort the lives of Americans who could barely have anticipated political and social changes that we take for granted. It is to substitute our experiences and prejudices for theirs.

By democracy, I mean a historical fact, rooted in a vast array of events and experiences, that comes into being out of changing human relations between governors and the governed. Stopping history cold at any particular point and parsing its political makeup negates that historical flow and stifles the voices and activities of actual people attempting to define the operations of government. Only over an extended period of time is it possible to see democracy and democratic government grow out of particular social, intellectual, and political contexts.

Democracy appears when some large number of previously

---

* This is based on the figures gathered in the federal census for 1850, which show that 44.5 percent of the adult population (twenty years and older) and 51.0 percent of the free adult population were white males. Noncitizens and Indians are not included in the calculations. The numbers are crude indicators, but the main point of comparison with the present is obvious.

excluded, ordinary persons—what the eighteenth century called "the many"—secure the power not simply to select their governors but to oversee the institutions of government, as officeholders and as citizens free to assemble and criticize those in office. Democracy is never a gift bestowed by benevolent, far-seeing rulers who seek to reinforce their own legitimacy. It has always to be fought for, by political coalitions that cut across distinctions of wealth, power, and interest. It succeeds and survives only when it is rooted in the lives and expectations of its citizens, and continually reinvigorated in each generation. Democratic successes are never irreversible.

Since Tocqueville, there has been a long tradition of scholarship devoted to understanding the democratic rupture that the general work describes. The rise of American democracy has engaged the attention of great historians who are now forgotten by the general reading public (Dixon Ryan Fox, J. Franklin Jameson), as well as such acknowledged giants as Charles and Mary Beard, Frederick Jackson Turner, Richard Hofstadter, and, most recently, Gordon S. Wood. But modern study of the subject owes the most to Arthur M. Schlesinger Jr.'s *The Age of Jackson*, published in 1945. Before Schlesinger, historians thought of American democracy as the product of an almost mystical frontier or agrarian egalitarianism. *The Age of Jackson* toppled that interpretation by placing democracy's origins firmly in the context of the founding generation's ideas about the few and the many, and by seeing democracy's expansion as an outcome more of struggles between classes than between sections. More than any previous account, Schlesinger's examined the activities and ideas of obscure, ordinary Americans, as well as familiar political leaders. While he identified most of the key political events and changes of the era, Schlesinger also located the origins of modern liberal politics in the tradition of Thomas Jefferson and Andrew Jackson, and in their belief, as he wrote, that future challenges "will best be met by a society in which no single group is able to sacrifice democracy and liberty to its interests." Finally, Schlesinger examined and emphasized the shattering moral and political dilemmas that an expanding southern slavery posed to American democracy, leading to the Civil War.

Since *The Age of Jackson* appeared, a revolution in historical studies has focused scholars' attentions on groups of Americans and aspects of American history that held minor interest at best in the historical profession in 1945. That revolution has altered historians' views of every detail of our past. The tragedy of Indian removal; the democratic activities of ex-slaves and other free blacks; the ease and sometimes the viciousness with which some professed democrats, North and South, championed white racial supremacy; the participation of women in reform efforts (and, in time, in electoral campaigns), along with the ridicule directed at the fledgling woman suffrage movement; the liberal humanitarian impulses that informed important strains of supposedly "conservative," pro-business politics; the importance of ethnicity and religion in shaping Americans' political allegiances—each of these, either ignored or slighted sixty years ago, has generated an enormous scholarly literature.

Yet if the social history revolution has profoundly changed how historians look at the United States, it has not diminished the importance of the questions *The Age of Jackson* asked about early American democracy. On the contrary, it has made those questions—especially about democratic politics, social class, and slavery—all the more pertinent to our understanding of the dramatic events that led from the American Revolution to the American Civil War. Some important recent works have attempted to raise those questions anew, and bridge the so-called new style of history with the older. The most ambitious of them have reinterpreted the connections between society and politics before 1860 as part of a larger market revolution that swept across the country. But these admirable studies have generally submerged the history of politics in the history of social change, reducing politics and democracy to byproducts of various social forces without quite allowing the play of politics its independent existence and importance. *The Rise of American Democracy* offers a different interpretation of these connections with a greater focus on the vagaries of politics, high and low.

The general work's subtitle, *Jefferson to Lincoln*, reaffirms the importance of political events, ideas, and leaders to democracy's rise—once an all-too-prevalent idea, now in need of some rescue and repair. Thomas Jefferson, more than any other figure in the early Republic, established (and was seen to have established) the terms of American democratic politics. Abraham Lincoln self-consciously advanced an updated version of Jefferson's egalitarian ideals, and his election to the presidency of the United States caused the greatest crisis American democracy has yet known. By singling out Jefferson and Lincoln, I certainly do not mean to say that presidents and other great men were solely responsible for the vicissitudes of American politics. One of the book's recurring themes is how ordinary Americans, including some at the outermost reaches of the country's formal political life, had lasting influence on the exercise of power. But just as political leaders did not create American democracy out of thin air, so the masses of Americans did not simply force their way into the corridors of power. That Jefferson and not John Adams was elected president in 1800–01—a fact that nearly did not come to pass—made a vast difference to subsequent political developments. So did the presence of other public officials, elected and unelected, from the top of American public life to the bottom. Featuring Jefferson and Lincoln in the subtitle of the larger work is a shorthand way of insisting on what ought to be a truism: that some individuals have more influence on history than others. The title, by referring to a broader history, insists that these individuals cannot make history just as they please, constrained as they are by a host of forces and persons beyond their control and anticipations.

The Rise of American Democracy can be read as a chronicle of American politics from the Revolution to the Civil War with the history of democracy at its center, or as an account of how democracy arose in the United States (and with what consequences) in the context of its time. Either way, the general work has a few major themes. One, given special attention in the first volume of the College Edition, is that democracy, at the nation's inception, was highly contested, not a given, and developed piece-meal, by fits and starts, at the state and local as well as the national level. A second theme, taken up in the second volume, is that social changes barely foreseen in 1787, chiefly the rapid commercialization of the free labor North and the renaissance of plantation slavery in the South, deeply affected how democracy advanced, and retreated, after 1815.

Third, Americans perceived these social changes primarily in political terms and increasingly saw them as struggles over contending ideas of democracy. Americans of the early nineteenth century lived in a different mental universe from ours with regard to politics. Above all, they inherited from the Revolutionary era a republican perspective that regarded political institutions as the foundation of social and economic relations, and not the other way around. Certain kinds of societies appeared more conducive than others to a just and harmonious government. Americans sharply disagreed about which societies were superior. But if order and happiness abounded, they believed it was because political institutions and the men running them were sound: disorder and unhappiness stemmed from unsound institutions or from the corruption of sound institutions by ambitious and designing men. Across the chasm of the Civil War, the era of high industrialism, and the conflicts of the twentieth century, we are more likely to see economic power and interests as the matrix for politics and political institutions. For Americans of the early Republic, politics, government, and constitutional order, not economics, were primary to interpreting the world and who ran it— a way of thinking that can wrongly look simplified, paranoid, and conspiracy-driven today.

A fourth theme concerns the constancy of political conflict: democracy in America was the spectacle of Americans arguing over democracy. If the word became a shibboleth for new and emerging political parties and movements, it did not on that account become degraded and bland. Precisely because opposing groups claimed to champion the same ideal, they fought all the harder to ensure their version would prevail. There was no end to the possible qualifying labels Americans could devise to illustrate exactly what sort of democrats they were—not just with separate major- and third-party labels (Democratic, Whig, State Rights, Know-Nothing, and so on) but with the blizzard of names for factions within the parties that always bemuse uninitiated readers: Loco Foco, Barnburner, Hunker, Silver Gray.* In part, these labels connoted patronage connections for political insiders. But in an age when elections came to be conducted more or less year-round, they also reflected beliefs and deep commitments above and beyond party machinations—while for a radical such as William Lloyd Garrison they were craven and sinful, and for a corrosive skeptic such as Herman Melville they inspired ambivalence and dread.

Fifth, the many-sided conflicts over American democracy came, in the 1840s and 1850s, to focus on an issue of recognized importance since the republic's birth: the fate of American slavery. Throughout the decades after the Revolution, but with a hurtling force after 1840, two American democracies emerged, the free labor democracy of the North and the slaveholders' democracy of the South—distinct political systems as well as bodies of thought. Although they often praised identical values and ideals, and although they were linked through the federal government and the national political parties, the two were fundamentally antagonistic. The nation's political leaders suppressed those antagonisms, sometimes in the face of powerful protests and schismatic movements, from the 1820s through the early 1850s. By 1860, the conflict could no longer be contained, as a

---

* From 1856: "Thus every party and sect has a daily register of the most minute sayings and doings, and proceedings and progress of every other sect; and as truth and error are continually brought before the masses, they have the opportunity to know and compare. There are political parties under the names of Whigs, Democrats, Know-nothings, Freesoilers, Fusionists, Hunkers, Woolly-heads, Dough-faces, Hard-shells, Soft-shells, Silver-greys, and I know not what besides; all of them extremely puzzling to the stranger, but of great local significance." Isabella Lucy Bird, *The Englishwoman in America* (London, 1856), 422–23.

democratic election sparked southern secession and the war that would determine American democracy's future.

The work's final theme is implied in the others: that the idea of democracy is never sufficient unto itself. Since the Second World War, and even more since the great democratic revolutions of 1989–91, the world has witnessed the continuing resilience and power of democratic ideals. So swiftly have former tyrannies turned into self-declared democratic governments that the danger has arisen of taking democracy for granted, despite its manifest fragility and possible collapse in large parts of the globe. As the early history of the United States shows, the habits and the institutions of modern democracy are relatively new in the larger span of history. Their breakthrough, even in the most egalitarian portions of the New World, required enormous reversals of traditional assumptions about power and legitimacy. As those habits and institutions began taking hold, different American social orders produced clashing versions of democracy, generating enmities so deep that they could only be settled in blood. Thereafter, democratic ideas, both in the United States and elsewhere, have had to be refreshed, fought over, and redefined continually. The rise of American democracy, from Jefferson's era to Lincoln's, created exhilarating new hopes and prospects, but also fierce conflicts and enormous challenges about what democracy can be and should be. Along with democracy's hopes and prospects, its conflicts and challenges persist. So do its vulnerabilities.

This third volume of the College Edition of *The Rise of American Democracy*, entitled *Slavery and the Crisis of American Democracy*, takes the story from the aftermath of the presidential campaign of 1840, which had marked the coming of age of a democratic system driven by mass electoral parties, to the opening shot of the Civil War in 1861.

The previous sixty years had witnessed enormous alterations in American politics, including an uneven enlargement of democratic institutions In 1782, Charles Thompson, an expert in Latin who was helping to design the Great Seal of the United

States, suggested including the motto "Novus Ordo Seclorum." Borrowed from an eclogue by the classical poet Virgil, the phrase translated roughly as "A New Order of the Ages," and signified the belief that a new American era in history had begun in 1776. Yet only five years after Thompson's suggestion, Americans found themselves framing and ratifying a national constitution to replace the Articles of Confederation in force in 1782. Under that new federal framework, fresh conflicts arose over foreign as well as domestic affairs that raised anew an issue asked during the War for Independence: how democratic should the new American republic be?

This crisis of the new order led directly to the so-called Revolution of 1800, which elevated Thomas Jefferson to the presidency and handed control of Congress to Jefferson's Republican allies. Yet the crisis continued, fed by protracted struggles over foreign affairs as well as over the proper structure of American politics and government. In 1812, Jefferson's successor, James Madison, led the country into a war with Britain that would prove a watershed in the nation's history and the unsteady, at times contradictory, history of the expansion of American political democracy. By the war's end, certain democratic propositions and institutions initially distrusted by the Revolutionary generation, including a widened suffrage and the rudiments of mass political parties, had come into being. But the resolution of the crisis of the new order did not quell the continued arguments over American democracy, which became entangled more and more with the future of American slavery. These matters became the subject of heated conflict over the decades to come, undertaken by a new generation of Americans, whose leaders included the greatest military hero of the War of 1812, Andrew Jackson.

The conflicts began to erupt during the brief, so-called "Era of Good Feelings" (more accurately, an "Era of Bad Feelings") that began after the war's conclusion. Rattled by the effects of the first national economic depression after the financial panic of 1819, as well as by congressional debates over whether slavery ought to be extended into Missouri, the postwar mood of nationalist unity quickly evaporated. Within a supposed "one-party" system, bitter ideological as well as personal divisions led to what many deemed dangerous political chaos. Simultaneously, popular movements for expanded political democracy at the state and local levels met with great success, in many important states, especially in the Northeast and Northwest (though, especially with respect to free blacks, these advances were more like defeats). After the election of 1824, settled in the House of Representatives, brought John Quincy Adams to the White House, the stage was set for his defeated opponent, Andrew Jackson, to lay claim to the legacy of Thomas Jefferson. In 1828, Jackson seized the victory he believed had been stolen from him four years before.

In many respects, Jackson's election did not mark the beginning of a new wave of democratic reform as much as the outcome of reforms undertaken for decades. Jackson's presidency, though, undeniably changed the terms of democratic argument. With the motto "the majority is to govern," Jackson set about removing what he considered unconstitutional as well as undemocratic national institutions, above all the Second Bank of the United States. He also pursued, in the name of democracy, policies that, even at the time, seemed to many Americans far from egalitarian, including the coerced removal of eastern Indian tribes and the suppression of rising northern abolitionist radicals. Jackson's chief opponents, meanwhile, objected most strenuously to what they considered his arbitrary and unconstitutional expansion of executive power.

Pulling together a coalition of diverse forces united in their dislike of Jackson, opposition leaders such as Henry Clay, Daniel Webster, and Thurlow Weed invented the Whig Party in 1834–35. By dropping the old-line prejudices against democracy, refining a pro-business populism, absorbing Christian humanitarian themes from the religious revival known as the Second Great Awakening, and adopting mass party campaign techniques, the Whigs swept to power in 1840. Yet in that same election, a tiny collection of anti-slavery radicals, rejecting the more staunch anti-political stand of abolitionist leaders such as William Lloyd Garrison, entered the fray under the banner of the Liberty Party. Although its effect on the outcome in 1840 was minimal, the party's very existence carried portents about the future direction of American democracy.

Slavery and the Crisis of American Democracy opens with a Supreme Court trial. In July of 1839, a cargo of newly imported African slaves on the Spanish schooner *Amistad*, sailing from Havana to another part of Cuba, took over the ship and insisted that it be sailed back to Africa. Misdirected, the ship ended up off Long Island Sound, where the U.S. Coast Guard seized it and arrested the Africans for piracy and murder. The case became a cause célèbre as the Africans' status as slave or free came into question and, due to the Spanish ship's origins, it raised issues relating to international law. By the time the case came before the U.S. Supreme Court, no less a personage than ex-president John Quincy Adams had become involved. After recovering from his defeat by Jackson, Adams had won a seat in Congress, the only former U.S. president ever to win national elective office. By the mid-1830s, having always steered clear of antislavery politics, Adams suddenly became the leading opponent in the House of Representatives to the so-called gag rule, a parliamentary procedure that silenced abolitionist petitioners to Congress. Bidden by his constituents as well as his conscience to vindicate democratic freedom of expression, Adams gradually drew closer to the abolitionists through his efforts to overturn the gag rule. After some hesitation, he agreed to join the *Amistad* defense team and spent the early winter of 1840–41 carefully preparing his arguments.

The

RISE

of

AMERICAN

DEMOCRACY

VOLUME III

SLAVERY AND THE CRISIS OF

AMERICAN DEMOCRACY

1840–1860

1

WHIG DEBACLE, DEMOCRATIC CONFUSION

On March 1, 1841, in the vaulted Supreme Court hearing room at the Capitol just beneath the Senate chamber, seventy-four-year-old John Quincy Adams completed his eight-hour argument in defense of the *Amistad* rebels. The proceedings had been interrupted by the sudden death of Justice Philip Barbour, and by the time he resumed, Adams had been thinking about mortality and the departed great Americans of decades past.* His defense was more political than legal, charging the Van Buren administration with gross interference and moral indifference. Nearing the close of his statement, reverie and politics converged as Adams pointed to two framed copies of Jefferson's Declaration of Independence that hung in the

---

* The day before he finished his argument, Adams heard a sermon from the book of Revelation, to mark the closing of the congressional session. Although the minister was not, according to Adams, up to his task, Adams wrote out the verses in his diary, including Revelation 20:12: "And I saw the dead, small and great, stand before God; and the books were opened; and another book was opened, which is the book of life; and the dead were judged out of those things which were written in the books, according to their works." JQAD, 10: 434–5.

room, in clear view of all the justices: "The moment you come, to the Declaration of Independence, that every man has a right to life and liberty, an inalienable right, this case is decided. I ask nothing more in behalf of these unfortunate men, than this Declaration." The maturing contradictions, for northerners, in the Jackson Democracy's professions of equality and its tolerance of slavery could not have been rendered more dramatically.

Three days later, also at the Capitol, another Whig, the new president, William Henry Harrison, delivered an inauguration address that was a fraction of the length of Adams's *Amistad* argument but seemed to go on forever. Speaking in a driving snowstorm for one hour and forty-five minutes—still the longest presidential inaugural speech in history—Harrison's billowing prolixity expounded little beyond a restatement of Whig precepts of a limited executive and his promise not to seek a second term, assurances that he would not overuse the veto power, and an opaque discussion of economic issues, hostile both to the independent treasury and to the revival of a national bank. It was a fitting commencement for a figurehead president (delivered to throngs of supporters in military finery and Tippecanoe Club gear) whose primary political virtue was his haziness and whose administration was already beset by rival Whig factions, each hoping to manipulate him and elect its own favorite in 1844.

The contrast between the revitalized Adams's performance and Harrison's was stark. (Adams called the inauguration display "showy-shabby.") So was the difference in where the performances led. On March 9, the Supreme Court, in a 7-to-1 decision written by Justice Story, ruled in favor of the *Amistad* defense, declaring that the rebels had never been slaves and ordering them freed once and for all. The same day, and for weeks to come, Harrison, suffering from a severe cold since his swearing-in—he had declined to wear a topcoat despite the snowstorm—was beset by the locusts of Whig office seekers who had poured into Washington. Late in March, his illness was diagnosed as pleurisy. He recovered briefly (and one day slipped off to buy some household provisions at a nearby market), but suffered a relapse. Exactly one month after his inauguration, he died. A vice president of convenience, the state-rights, anti–national bank Virginian John Tyler, was suddenly the president, which plunged the Whig Party and the government into utter confusion.

At the Hermitage, Andrew Jackson did not hide his delight at Harrison's demise. "A kind and overruling providence had interfered," he wrote to Francis Blair, "to prolong our glorious Union and happy republican system which Genl. Harrison and his cabinet was preparing to destroy under the dictation of that profligate demagogue, Henry Clay." Yet if Jackson's Democracy had been spared a fight to the finish, it would not be spared its own confusion. Most Democrats expected that, with Harrison dead, they would continue their struggle over economic issues, await what Martin Van Buren always called "the sober second thought of the people," and reinstall Van Buren with a new Democratic Congress in 1844. But John C. Calhoun—hard at work in his spare time writing what he called "a regular &, I think, I may say scientifick development of my views of gover[n]ment"—had different ideas. So did many others, as growing popular unrest over slavery and democracy shook the Democracy to its core.

THE WHIGS IN DISARRAY

John Tyler—tall and refined, with an aquiline nose that reminded many of an ancient Roman statesman's—greeted Henry Clay graciously when the senator paid his first official visit in May. Tyler and Clay had long been political and personal friends, dating back to their alliance during the Missouri crisis twenty years earlier. Although their principles had since diverged widely, Tyler was considered a Clay man within his adoptive Whig Party. But lately Clay had been on a rampage, seeking to gather not just the Whigs but the entire federal government under his command on Capitol Hill, and the meeting with Tyler was bound to be difficult. The two men conversed in detail about the major current political issues, above all the rechartering of a new national bank, which Clay adamantly favored. Tyler demurred; Clay stood his ground; and the exasperated president finally lost his patience.

"Then, sir," Tyler snapped, "I wish you to understand this— that you and I were born in the same district; that we have fed upon the same food, and have breathed the same natal air. Go you now, then, Mr. Clay, to your end of the avenue, where stands the Capitol, and there perform your duty to the country as you shall think proper. So help me God, I shall do mine at this end of it as I shall think proper."

After the Whig victories in 1840, Clay had determined that even if he was not president, he would run the government and shift power away from the executive branch and back to Capitol Hill. At last, the Whigs could undo President Jackson's supposed theft of Congress's power, but with Clay now eager to become a chieftain every bit as powerful as Jackson had been. Clay's legislative agenda—chartering another national bank, passing a land bill to provide revenues for internal improvements, sustaining a protective tariff—would, he expected, become the agenda for the whole Whig Party, and then the nation. Next would come what Clay considered urgent constitutional reforms: to limit the power of the presidential veto, limit presidential tenure to a single term, and bring the Treasury Department under the exclusive control of Congress.

Clay was always aware that personal rivalries, especially with Daniel Webster, would complicate his plans. Harrison, offended by Clay's imperiousness, had named Webster secretary of state and appeared to favor Webster's friends over Clay's in selecting most of his cabinet. Yet the origins of Clay's new difficulties would prove, as ever, more political and ideological than personal—his failure, in this instance, to understand that his own view of proper Whig government was only one among many, and that even his iron will and disarming wit could not fully suppress the differences. The Whig Party, old Harrison Gray Otis advised Clay, was "a coalition of persons, brought together from the four ends of the earth." There were the Webster Whigs, conservative on economics and on abolitionism, but with some antislavery sympathies; there were the new-school Whigs, like Seward and Weed, uncomfortable with the Bank of the United States and with slaveholder domination; there were the northern Whigs like John Quincy Adams and his little anti–gag rule band, caught up in the slavery and abolition whirligig; and there were the slave-holder Whigs like Tyler and his fellow Virginians Abel Upshur and Henry A. Wise, supremely committed to southern state rights. If Clay failed to find, and then stick to, political ground that all factions could share (as they had during the Log Cabin enthusiasm), then, Otis warned, "the cossacks will be on you in one or two years." Otis was right.

Tyler attempted to create a middle path between Clay's pro-BUS Whiggery and the hard-money radicalism that still dominated the Democracy. Although he had defected to the Whigs in 1835 over what he deemed Jackson's abuses of state rights—he had voted against the Force Bill in 1833—Tyler had always been an opponent of Biddle's BUS and had firmly supported Jackson's bank policies. His willingness to join the Whig ticket in 1840 led some to think that, as president, he could be persuaded to back the Whigs' measures—"including a Bank of the U.S.," Clay wrote hopefully upon hearing of Harrison's death. But Tyler had a stubborn streak of his own. His row with Clay during their initial testy White House interview would degenerate during the summer of 1841 into an all-out war.

Clay had coaxed President Harrison, before his death, into calling a special summertime session of Congress because of the continuing economic depression and the possibility that the federal government would soon go bankrupt, but Clay also desired to pass as much of his program as quickly as he could and consolidate his rule. Working on a punishing daily schedule, he rammed through the Senate his first order of business, repeal of the independent treasury, and by the session's end, Tyler had signed the bill. Other Clay-backed measures won approval after prolonged congressional haggling. Thanks to Tyler, however, Clay did not get his national bank, and after that defeat, the senator made sure that the president lost virtually all connection with the Whig Party.

The bank debacle unfolded in two stages. After close consultations with Secretary of the Treasury Thomas Ewing (a Webster ally), John C. Calhoun backed a carefully crafted administration bank bill with a section that provided for the establishment of branch offices, but only if the states where they were to be located formally approved. The requirement had been added to overcome Tyler's constitutional objections to the Second BUS. Clay would have none of it, declared the people wanted "a real old-fashioned Bank," and rewrote the bill. Eliminating the branching proposal proved politically impossible, so Clay concocted an awkward compromise, enabling the states to disallow branches only immediately after passage of the bank bill, but allowing the bank to overrule those objections whenever it became "necessary and proper" to establish a branch office. The contraption squeaked through the Senate, then passed the House in early August. On August 16, Tyler's veto arrived, objecting to the branching amendment as well the bank's proposed powers to discount notes. Hisses, boos, and groans rained down from the Senate gallery as the message was read. Clay sat at his desk, unperturbed; Thomas Hart Benton, who had joined a small delegation of Democrats at a well-lubricated White House celebration the night after Tyler announced his veto, turned to the galleries and shouted back at the "Bank ruffians."

Tyler's veto was not his final word on the matter. Although he opposed any "old-fashioned" national bank, he could live with some sort of national fiscal institution so long as it passed constitutional muster. With an eye to running for president himself in 1844, and reluctant to be known as a simon-pure antibank man, he agreed to support yet another compromise bill, giving way on the branch office question but insisting that states have the power to disallow the branches' discounting of promissory notes. That bill, too, was destined to pass Congress, but by the time it did, Tyler had changed his mind once more.

Clay, in responding to Tyler's veto of the original bill, could not help veering into sarcasm, referring to the president as "solitary and alone, shivering by the pitiless storm," with nary enough supporters to "compose a decent *corporal's guard.*" With friends like that, Tyler decided, he'd be better off rejoining the Democrats, or perhaps starting a third party to win the presidency. Besides, except for the estimable Webster, he had tired of his scheming, pro-BUS cabinet secretaries and was looking for a way to get rid of them without conducting an ugly public purge. Reversing himself on the bank bill would surely drive them out. And so, in late August, Tyler informed the cabinet that he would not sign the bill and asked them to work for a postponement. "Never, never!" Clay replied when asked to withdraw the bill. "No, not if we stay here till Christmas." On September 9, Tyler announced his second veto. Within forty-eight hours, every cabinet member save Webster and Postmaster General Francis Granger had quit, and Granger resigned soon after. The special session of Congress ended with the Whigs thoroughly demoralized, but with Clay ready to rally the faithful once more. In a speech to the Whig caucus, he commended the members for their efforts and compared the president to Benedict Arnold: "Tyler is on his way to the Democratic camp. They may give him lodging in some outhouse, but they will never trust him. He will stand there, like Arnold in England, a monument of his own perfidy and disgrace."

Clay would return for the next session of Congress, but fatigue and the effects of what may have been a mild heart attack sapped his will. On March 31, 1842, he resigned from the Senate and returned to Ashland, where he would rest in preparation for yet another try for the presidency in 1844. His spirit lingered in Congress, which passed a new protective tariff bill retaining the rates of the 1833 Compromise Tariff, just as Clay had hoped. (Tyler's veto of an earlier tariff bill led to the first serious presidential impeachment investigation in American history, led by John Quincy Adams, over alleged abuse of the veto power.) Clay's old rival Webster, meanwhile, stubbornly kept faith with the administration for as long as he could. In 1842, he concluded negotiations on a major treaty with British foreign secretary Lord Ashburton that resolved the Maine–New Brunswick border dispute and, for good measure, settled the entire length of the U.S.-

Canadian border east of the Rocky Mountains, sparing the nation from what some feared was an inevitable third Anglo-American war. Reveling in an executive office—"[h]aving been without it all his life," George Bancroft observed, "he has a fondness for it, of which you can have no conception"—Webster happily (and injudiciously) attacked Clay's presidential prospects, thereby alienating his own virulently anti-Tyler state party. Webster feigned indifference, yet by 1843 Tyler had begun heeding southern Democratic counsels over a new project that Webster despised, the annexation of Texas. Finally, in May, Webster stepped down, severing the administration's last important tie to the Whigs.

Hundreds of miles to the north, on his estate outside Kinderhook, New York, Martin Van Buren was gloating. With little experience but great common sense, he ran an excellent farm. He also indulged his love of entertaining guests with rich food and French champagne. More dubiously, Van Buren's admiration for European style extended to architecture, which would prompt him years later to deface the fine old Federalist-style mansion he had bought in 1839 by adding gingerbread frills and an Italianate tower. But in the early 1840s, pretension was crowded out by simple country elegance and pleasant conversation, much of it about politics. In his dining room, Van Buren hung portraits of Jefferson and Jackson, and here, and in his private study, he would talk over the Whigs' debacles and the deluge of letters supporting his return to office in 1844. The "eyes of the people" were reopening, he said, just as he had said they would.

Early in 1842, Van Buren took a political tour of the South and West, from Charleston to New Orleans, up to Tennessee, and then, for the month of June, to the Old Northwest. The highlight was a sentimental visit to the Hermitage (Van Buren's first ever), where Jackson, though much reduced and hit by waves of chills and fever, gave him a delighted reception. Van Buren could not have known how at the time, but his journey looked to the future as well as the past. One evening, making his way from St. Louis to Chicago, he stopped in the town of Rochester, outside Springfield, Illinois. As usual, the local Democratic notables turned up to greet and entertain him, and they brought along a young Whig friend, now a former state representative, "Honest" Abe Lincoln. Lincoln had never liked Van Buren's mentor, and he had lately been gripped by a deep and prolonged melancholia that would chronically plague him the rest of his life. A night out would give him a chance to meet an ex-president and might even force him to relax. As it happened, perhaps to his surprise, he and the Little Magician Van Buren hit it off. Kindling to his company, Lincoln was in excellent form, spinning stories and telling jokes with the former president and his party until late at night. Van Buren went to bed aching from his laughter, and later remarked that he had never "spent so agreeable a night in his life."

While Van Buren and Lincoln made merry, John C. Calhoun was plotting. Tyler's accession had frustrated Calhoun's hopes to manipulate the Democracy into becoming the party of southern state rights, with himself at the helm. Now the vindication of state rights lay in the hands of a nominal Whig, elected in a demagogic campaign that the South Carolina legislature had formally denounced as an insult to free men everywhere. The irony might have brought the hint of a smile even to Calhoun's thin lips, but he was never amused for long. In the Senate, Calhoun did what he could to resist Clay's nationalist onslaught while watching Clay and Tyler tear each other apart—a development that gave him hope so long as the South did not break en masse to support the president in 1844. Tyler would fight hard over the state-rights issues connected to the BUS, Calhoun cautioned, but he would be soft on the rest of the Whig program, which would be a disaster for the South. "I go for victory to my own cause, complete victory," he wrote one close associate on the day the special congressional session ended. "My principles now must triumph, or be defeated." The surest way to go for victory was to overtake Van Buren and run for president himself.

The sight of his ancient enemy from New York living it up during his southern tour redoubled Calhoun's resolve. In his speeches to the Senate as well as in his outside political activities, Calhoun began his presidential quest with what for him amounted to a turn to the left, appealing to the Jacksonians' popular base outside the South. He quieted his pro-slavery views and spent most of his time attacking the monied interests that he claimed were still trying to impose Clay's American System. His most arresting effort came in response to one of Clay's impossible projects, a proposed constitutional amendment that would permit Congress to override presidential vetoes by simple majorities in both houses. In attacking the idea, Calhoun might have looked, to a careless viewer, like Andrew Jackson's twin, as he denounced efforts by Congress "to substitute the will of a majority of the people." Although he took the ground that the veto was essential as a check on majority rule—the reverse of Jackson's defense of the presidential veto—the real danger, Calhoun suggested, was Clay and the Whigs' effort to enact the American System, which could expand the illegitimate powers of the federal government. As far as Calhoun was concerned, the speech was virtually a restatement of his theories of nullification, "the premises," he wrote, "from which it irresistibly flows." But Francis Blair, who had denounced Calhoun bitterly in 1832 and 1833, could see only that Calhoun was attacking Clay and the forces of associated wealth, and he lauded the speech as one of the "ablest, most luminous, and unanswerable ever delivered on the nature of this Government."

In the fall of 1842, Calhoun followed Clay's example and retired from the Senate to prepare for the presidential race. His chances, to his managers, looked good, especially if he could attract a reasonable hard-money northern Jacksonian—perhaps Levi Woodbury—to join his ticket. The mistaken belief that Calhoun had turned into a Jacksonian was so widespread that even the normally astute Amos Kendall tried to broker a rapprochement between Calhoun and Old Hickory, which for Calhoun was going much too far. The South Carolinian had strong contacts in New Hampshire and in Massachusetts (where, under Tyler's patronage, David Henshaw was making a political comeback), as well as in the South. To challenge Van Buren at his base, Calhoun tried with some success to make inroads within New York politics, especially in New York City, home to the most radical of those he once disparaged as the "more filthy" democrats. In a campaign managed by Joseph Scoville, a young Manhattan journalist, Calhoun reached out to two distinct constituencies: the city's established salt-water merchant elite, which hated the tariff nearly as much as the southern state-rights men did, and the city's working-class radicals, on the outs, despite some cooperation during the subtreasury struggle, with Van Buren's allies at Tammany Hall, and now aroused by Calhoun's attacks on the monied interests. Keeping up with changing working-class demographics, Calhoun also went out of his way to proclaim his Irish background and, suddenly a proud son of the Auld Sod, joined the New York Irish Immigrant Society.

The one major force sidelined in national politics after Harrison's death was the new-school Whig leadership that had nominated and elected him. Clay had never been the new-schoolers' man (although many of the younger Whigs, such as Lincoln, admired him intensely), and the political misfit Tyler was impossible, a partisan ploy gone fatefully wrong. Thurlow Weed, courted by Tyler and counseling patience with the administration, traveled to Washington to see what soothing influence he might have, but for once even Weed's wizardry was not up to the task. Whig divisiveness in Washington, coupled with the continuation of hard times despite the great political shift of 1840, deeply depressed the party's voting base. Startling defeats in state elections in 1841, and even more devastating losses in the midterm congressional elections a year later, made it appear that the mighty Whig machine of the 1840 campaign had been built out of nothing more substantial than its own trinkets and illuminations. "The Whig Party now seems tota'y broken up and dismembered," one Whig official despaired, less than a year after the Log Cabin frenzy. But these fears were overwrought. The Whigs' disarray would eventually redound to the benefit of Henry Clay, the one man who could undo the damage he himself had helped inflict and reunite the party's disparate elements. And inside the Democracy, new local and national battles over finances and political democracy, barely noticeable before 1842, were wreaking a different kind of havoc, favorable to the Whigs and with worrisome portents for the pro–Van Buren hard-money men, now known as Radicals.

Within a year of the Democratic downfall in 1840, the party faithful were back to the internecine bickering between Radicals and Conservatives that had sharpened in the struggle over the independent treasury. These renewed fights were conducted at the state and local level, chiefly in the North. The most important of them occurred in New York.

RADICALS, HUNKERS, AND CALHOUNITES

In the decade and a half since the completion of the Erie Canal, New York had fully earned its cognomen as the Empire State. Having commandeered the lion's share of commerce from the burgeoning commercial districts of the upper West, from the cotton plantations of the Deep South via New Orleans, and onward across the Atlantic, New York had become the preeminent mercantile and financial state in the Union. By 1840, New York City was the nation's most productive manufacturing center. Along the gigantic ditch connecting the Hudson River to Lake Erie, smaller industrial towns and cities were rising quickly to produce everything from milled flour to milled iron. The state's western rural counties, especially in the hinterlands of the canal towns, formed one of the leading commercial agricultural centers in the world. A new influx of immigrants from Ireland and Germany, settling in amid the old polyglot stock of Yankees, Dutch, and English, was making New York ethnically and religiously the most diverse state in the nation.

One important effect of this growth was to complicate greatly New York's already complicated political scene, fracturing it into an ever-more confusing array of economic and social interests. With power and prestige so divided and so varied, politics was bound to be more turbulent than elsewhere in the country—and political movements from the bottom as well as the top of the system had greater opportunities to shake up the status quo. New York in the 1840s became a hotbed for the political permutations and combinations that would spread elsewhere, with portents for national politics as well. The tumult began with fights over the Erie Canal, the most important catalyst in New York's rise to power.

As early as 1827, the canal's immense profitability had permitted the state legislature to undertake the experiment of ending direct taxation and counting on the revenue from canal tolls to cover state expenditures. The plan proved overly optimistic. In 1835, backed by his comptroller Azariah Cutting Flagg, a flinty Jacksonian from the northernmost reaches of the state, Governor William Marcy announced that unless direct taxation was resumed, the state would slide into heavy debt. Marcy, who had been state comptroller himself in 1827 and had objected to the no-tax plan from the beginning, now pleaded with the legislature, insisting "that internal improvements cannot be long prosecuted on an extensive scale unless sustained by a wise system of finance." But Conservative Democrats friendly to Nathaniel P. Tallmadge joined with the Whigs in preferring debt to taxation, and in pledging the state's credit to extend the canal system even farther, thereby (they predicted) increasing revenues—an early version of what today is known as "borrow-and-spend" conservatism. In 1838, they passed a bill authorizing four million dollars in state borrowing for the canals. Marcy—whose views on canal construction had begun to moderate, and who would soon drift even closer to the Conservatives—did not veto it.

Tensions among Democrats worsened during debates over the legalities of the specie suspension of 1837 (which the Conservatives backed strongly) and over a bill, that same year, to repeal a Radical-inspired law restricting the issue of small notes (a move the Radicals managed to forestall). Public meetings in Manhattan expressed outrage at the Conservatives' treachery over specie suspension and pushed Radical demands ranging from the total eradication of the paper system to more moderate hard-money calls for "a well regulated credit system," including the Loco Foco free banking plan. But after the election of the new-school Whig William Seward as governor in 1838, to go along with a large Whig majority in the assembly elected the previous year, attention shifted back to the canal-funding issue.

Governor Seward's ambitious agenda of liberal Whig reform quickly embroiled him in controversies with his own party's conservative wing as well as with Democrats. Old-guard Whigs and nativists disliked his humanitarian efforts, especially his alliance with New York City Catholic Bishop John Hughes to provide public funds for Catholic schooling. Democrats, meanwhile, hammered away at Seward's canal- and railroad-building proposals, as well as his support for a voter registry law (aimed, the Democrats claimed, to restrict poor and Irish voters) and allegations of systematic voter fraud by the Whigs in the 1839 elections. Seward won a second term in 1840, but his margin of victory was half of what it had been two years earlier. By the spring of 1841, discouraged, he had decided not to run again. Although Seward would, in his final message to the legislature, push for expansion of internal improvements, the only hope for their passage was that the Democrats might splinter and give the antitax, pro-development Conservatives the balance of power. Seward would not get his way, but divisions did appear inside the Democracy that proved deep and lasting.

The Conservative faction came to be known as Hunkers, an obscure label that may have meant they were supposed to "hanker" after office. Their ostensible leader was, in fact, more of a moderate, William C. Bouck, an amiable commercial farmer and former canal commissioner who wore his hair in a peaked pompadour and was known as "Old White Hoss of Schoharie." Defeated by Seward in 1840, Bouck hoped to run again in 1842, with his measured canal-friendly brand of Democracy offering a third position between the Seward expansionists and the Radical Democrats. The Hunkers also counted on the former chief editor for the Albany Regency, Edwin Croswell of the *Albany Argus*; former Utica congressman and violent anti-abolitionist Samuel Beardsley; and Marcy's young protégé, Horatio Seymour, a banker's son from upstate. (Marcy by now had strong Hunker leanings, but he preferred to hold his formal allegiances close to his chest.) Without fully endorsing the Whigs' deficit-spending program, the Hunkers distinguished themselves from their Democratic opponents, the Radicals, by refusing to support a drastic retrenchment of internal improvements.

New York Radical Democrats would in time receive their own nickname, the Barnburners, taken from a Dutch tale about a farmer who chose to burn down his whole barn to destroy the rats. Led in the legislature by Michael Hoffman, an iron-willed, veteran hard-money Jacksonian and former congressman from Herkimer County, the Radicals introduced, in 1842, a "stop-and-tax" bill, imposing an immediate halt to all canal construction projects not deemed absolutely essential and raising new state revenues with a mild direct tax. After a heated debate, the bill passed the legislature and was enacted, reluctantly, by Seward. In support of these efforts, the Radicals mobilized most of what had been known as the Silas Wright wing of the old Albany Regency, including (besides Wright himself) Benjamin F. Butler, William Cullen Bryant, Azariah Flagg, and two rising young men, Van Buren's winsome, Yale-educated son, John, and Preston King, a lawyer from the same part of the state as Flagg, near the Canadian border. (The elder Van Buren, though bound by political necessity to stay above the fray and quite friendly with Bouck, was nevertheless unmistakably partial to the Radicals out of both family loyalty and political principle.)

Although the Radicals carried their point in the legislature, the stop-and-tax measure nearly ripped the party in two at the Democrats' nominating convention in October. Compromising, the delegates nominated the Hunker Bouck for a second try at the governorship but adopted a Radical platform that proposed continued retrenchment, with an understanding that, if elected, Bouck would not obstruct the new retrenchment law. Bouck defeated an overrated, vainglorious Whig, Luther Bradish; the

Democrats retained control of the legislature; and victory temporarily quieted intraparty fighting while leaving the Hunkers in control. The economy also cooperated with the Democrats, as the first signs of a gradual general recovery from the depression heightened the value of the state's bonds. Naturally, both the Conservatives and the Radicals claimed that their respective policies had improved the fiscal situation. But Bouck and the Hunker legislature seized the opportunity to initiate a scaled-down version of Seward's internal-improvement drive. The passage of a new canal bill in 1844, shepherded through the legislature by the Conservative Horatio Seymour, left Hoffman, Flagg, and the Radical minority furious. Once again, the New York Democracy was so divided, one veteran Democrat told Van Buren, that "at Albany [t]here is not only no *harmony*, but no *cordiality* of feeling amongst our Friends."

The divisions in New York, although particularly sharp, were not unique. All across the Northeast and West, equivalents of the Radical-Conservative fights split the state Democratic parties, chiefly over banking issues. In Pennsylvania, soft-money Democrats—abetted by Governor David R. Porter, a former ironmaker and quiet Conservative sympathizer, and Porter's friend, Senator James Buchanan—sustained an uneasy domination over the hard-money men, led by three very different figures: Van Buren's former attorney general, Henry D. Gilpin; the renegade son of Federalism and former Nicholas Biddle supporter, Charles Ingersoll; and Thomas Earle, who in 1840 left the party to run with James G. Birney on the Liberty Party ticket. In Ohio and points west to Missouri, hard-money heroes such as Moses Dawson and Thomas Hart Benton held the upper hand over the "softs." In the Southwest, a general revulsion against the speculative boom mentality after 1837 produced the harshest hard-money reaction anywhere, which included the formal prohibition of commercial banking with constitutional revisions in Louisiana and Arkansas and virtual prohibitions in Alabama and Mississippi. (Somewhat paradoxically, Democrats in the Deep South, where voters had repudiated Loco Foco ideas as late as 1840, were now hailed by eastern hard-money radicals as the nation's leaders in the fight against the banking and paper system.) Only in the Southeast, where the panic and depression had been less wrenching, and where the banks were closely tied to state funds for education and internal improvement, did a significant equivalent of the militant hard-money Radicals fail to materialize.

The implications of these fights were important—and ironic. At both the state and national levels, the depression sparked by the Panic of 1837 had led voters to repudiate the hard-money, antibanking Democrats, in favor of the pro-banking, pro-improvement Whigs. Had President Harrison lived (and had he and Henry Clay managed to keep their rivalry under control), some sort of Third Bank of the United States would almost certainly have been established, and nationally funded internal improvements would have received a great boost. Bolstered by those successes, Whigs and Conservative Democrats in the states would have been far stronger than they were. But the ascension of John Tyler and the disarray among the Whigs in Washington completely changed the political calculus—and Jacksonian-style fiscal retrenchment and hard-money radicalism enjoyed a strong comeback. State governments, either through laws like New York's "stop-and-tax" legislation or through new constitutional bans, took steps to curtail and even outlaw initiatives basic to Whig political economy. The continuing hard times became a rationale for the kinds of economic programs that, in 1840, seemed to have been thoroughly disgraced. In a final irony, the one part of the country where the reversal was least pronounced was the Southeast, where Whig nationalism had long been weakest.

The Democracy's divisions over banking and internal improvements had additional implications for the presidential politics of 1844. Most hard-money Democrats strongly supported renominating Martin Van Buren. In New England, the Bancroft machine, including the old Workie Samuel Clesson Allen and the new governor Marcus Morton, was stalwartly pro–Van Buren. So were the New York Radicals, the Pennsylvania "hards," national hard-money leaders like Gilpin, Benton, and Dawson, and, in Washington, the surviving journalistic standard-bearer for true-blue Jacksonianism, Francis Blair. Conservative Democrats had far less attractive options. The most visible possible candidate, Jackson's former secretary of war, Lewis Cass, found himself (to his own surprise) being touted for the nomination late in 1842 by a combination of Pennsylvania protectionists and Ohio softs. As ponderous as he was vacuous, Cass chiefly had the virtue of availability, which led Philip Hone to remark, not completely disdainfully, that in this "he stands about on a par with General Harrison at the time of his nomination." Richard Mentor Johnson was also available, and he loudly proclaimed as much in a boisterous, saber-rattling western tour in 1843 that sapped some of Cass's support and enraged Andrew Jackson to the point where he was ready to read Johnson out of the Democratic Party. The New Yorker William Marcy, by now a Conservative in all but name, observed that Johnson was not only what he once was, "[i]t may be there was never so much of him as we were formerly led to suppose." The high-tariff centrist James Buchanan rounded out the Hunkers' short and lackluster list. Later, some Conservatives would work up support for Levi Woodbury.

The most surprising development within the Democracy was a growing enthusiasm, among some of the most radical northeastern hard-money advocates, for, of all people, John C. Calhoun. The admixture of ideology and politics that fueled left-wing Calhounism arose from numerous sources. For some labor Jacksonians, the results of 1840 had been deeply disillusioning. Saving democracy, they now believed, required uniting the small disciplined group who understood what democracy really was and upending the demagogic rule of capital by the most direct means necessary—which in 1842, after his own strange left-wing turn, seemed to be Calhoun. The perverse proposal that labor's redemption depended on the slaveholders' triumph must have unsettled some of the new Calhounites, who included at least some antislavery men. But the perversity was smoothed over by repeating the old Jacksonian claim that the abolitionists were just neo-Federalist aristocrats in disguise, and by picking up the pro-slavery ideologues' theme (a favorite of Calhoun's) that southern slaves were exploited far less severely than northern wage-earners. For the New Yorkers, the old animosities against Van Buren and Tammany Hall overcame the rapprochment over the independent treasury and made Calhoun look more attractive. Above all, there was the lure of Calhoun as an antibusiness candidate, pledged to an official platform that included, *"No Debt— No Connection with Banks—Economy—Retrenchment—and a strict adherence to the Constitution."* Squint hard enough and Calhoun might even look like a southern-style hard-money Radical, but without Van Burenism's taint on him.

The largest clutches of left-wing Calhounites appeared in New York City. Some Barnburners and ex–Loco Focos would not, even now, accept the trimmer Van Buren. A Tammany Democrat loyal to the ex-president reported that Calhoun's supporters were confident that "the radical disaffected democrats" could "by judicious management be won for Mr. Calhoun." Leading the agitation was Fitzwilliam Byrdsall, the author of a partisan but informative history of the Loco Focos, whom he served as secretary. Byrdsall was among those in the northern pro-Calhoun ranks who thought slavery was being badly maligned in the North. In 1842, he established something called the Free-Trade Association, which was really a front for the Calhoun campaign, and among those he recruited were hard-core Loco Focos who had refused to rejoin the Democracy even after Van Buren issued his message on the independent treasury. The union leader John Commerford (who had signed an abolitionist petition in 1836) was selected as president, and other veteran Locos, including John Windt, assumed leading roles. George Henry Evans, who had left Manhattan for rural New Jersey and returned, also lent his support.

The most exciting (and excitable) member of New York's pro-Calhoun left was a newcomer, the leader of the so-called shirtless or subterranean Democracy, Mike Walsh. Walsh was born in Ireland in 1810 and, as a toddler, emigrated to America with his father, a cabinetmaker and veteran of the United Irishman uprising of 1798. (A Protestant, Walsh always considered himself a "true American," though as an immigrant he detested nativism.) After apprenticing as an engraver and traveling across the South, he turned up as a journalist in New York at the end of the 1830s, first as a correspondent for the New York *Aurora* (where Walt Whitman was, for a time, his editor), then as editor of his own weeklies, the *Knickerbocker*, followed by, in 1843, the *Subterranean*. Aspiring to a position of power within the Democratic Party, Walsh also founded the Spartan Association, a combination political club and lower-class gang. Kept at a distance by the Tammany leadership, Walsh and his Spartans would storm party meetings, and to shouts of "Go it, Mike!," Walsh would launch into cocky tirades against corrupt office seekers and Tammany power brokers—those "who fawn upon us and call us the bone and sinew of the country . . . and who would use us until there was nothing but bone and sinews left of us." Like the Loco Foco diehards, Walsh reserved special sectarian hatred for Van Burenite Radicals such as Benjamin Butler, who, with their lying rhetoric about the few and the many, supposedly neutered radicalism and propped up wage slavery.

Basking in his reputation as a favorite of the roughneck Bowery B'hoys, Walsh's social radicalism was as sincere as it was vitriolic. In his earliest speeches, he claimed the legacy of the Loco Focos and of William Leggett's war on "feudal corporations." The original rules of the Spartan Association mentioned political reforms such as the abolition of corporation charters as the group's major goals. Walsh's attacks on what he called "the slavery of wages" became increasingly pointed in the early 1840s, as did his attacks on Tammany politicians and those Whigs who worshiped moral reform "on the glutted altars of Mammon." Yet, though it would only become fully evident later in the decade, Walsh's economic radicalism was coupled with a racism that left him vulnerable to slaveholder politicians who in any way attacked northern capital. He greatly admired Tyler (and, in a personal letter to Walsh, Tyler returned the admiration), and he seemed to adore Calhoun, not because of any of Calhoun's ideas about democracy but because Calhoun attacked banks and was Van Buren's sworn enemy. Calhoun, in turn, was so anxious about securing a toehold outside South Carolina that, even more than Tyler, he was willing to flatter and encourage the shirtless democrat, a man he would later privately call the editor of "the organ of what may be called the lowest strata in the New York population."

Calhoun developed closer ties with an uneasy radical who was better suited to his temperament, Orestes Brownson. For Brownson, the consummate rebel logician, the defeat of 1840 was worse than a political setback—it was a philosophical cataclysm. Previously, his skepticism about political democracy and universal suffrage had been based on his certainty that the ruling class would not give up its power without a violent fight. But the Log Cabin campaign showed that the people themselves could not be fully trusted to decide wisely, that they would eagerly hand their political birthright over to whatever threadbare pro-business demagogue came down the pike, so long as he claimed to be democratic. Majority rule could turn out to be tyrannical. Forced to rethink his politics entirely, he turned to Aristotle; more decisively, he turned to Calhoun, the only national statesman with a mind that Brownson respected. The two developed a warm correspondence in which Brownson sought advice on how he might, as he wrote in a despairing piece on the election, "come up with something worth having."

As it happened, Calhoun, between congressional sessions, had begun writing his own summary view of politics, a work he called "Disquisition on Government." Here, Calhoun explained as fully as he ever would his idea of the concurrent majority. Given human imperfection, Calhoun posited, government was not a necessary evil (as the dewy-eyed optimist Jeffersonians believed), but a positive good required to restrain the masses. The majority, by these lights, had no claim to superior wisdom, only to superior force. History had shown that this majority was easily manipulated by the dominant economic force in any society, to prostrate all competing interests and establish its absolute rule. How, then, could that manipulative power be checked? For Calhoun, drawing his own logical conclusions from his nullification doctrines, it could only be done, as he had said in 1833, "by giving to each part [of society] the right of self-protection." Nullification had attempted to establish a mechanism for this protection but had failed. In the "Disquisition," Calhoun devised his alternative.

"Power," Calhoun observed, "can only be resisted by power." He considered each sovereign state the embodiment, in national affairs, of a distinct political interest. And so, under his new theory, he would provide each state concurrent power in the making of national laws, and a veto over their execution. It might be viewed as a radical revision of the Articles of Confederation, which required a dissent from four of the thirteen states to annul a national law. Calhoun, writing at a time when there were twice as many states as there had been in 1778, would reduce that veto number, in perpetuity, to one. He declared, however, that he had borrowed not from some long-discarded federal plan but from the living, breathing elitist republican constitution of South Carolina. Alone of all the states, Calhoun believed, South Carolina had discovered the means to suppress majoritarian democracy while granting universal white manhood suffrage, thereby assuring that all of its citizens—low country and up-country, planter and merchant—had a say in government. Instead of a despotic "democracy," he had said four years earlier, South Carolina was "a republic, a commonwealth" that "protected the feebler interests"—"a far more popular government than if it had been based on the simple principle of the numerical majority." Calhoun wanted to nationalize the political structures of South Carolina, establishing a "Government of the people, in the true sense of the term," he wrote, "and not that of the mere majority, or the dominant interest."

Here lay both the strength and the crippling weaknesses of Calhoun's scheme. His brilliant essential perception was that in modern societies, aggregations of whole interests and classes, and not individuals, had become the basic units of politics. Yet Calhoun was much more attentive to some interests than to oth-

ers. Slaves, naturally, were excluded from any political consideration except as the property of their masters. But even as he was
now flattering northern workers, Calhoun had remarkably little
to say about or to southern nonslaveholders, the preponderance
of the white South. He imagined, as he had told the Whig
Horace Binney years earlier, that the republic rested on just two
pillars, "a slave class and a property class, such white persons as
were not within the property class being wholly ignored," except
as incipient slaveholders. And while that may have been a reasonable simplification in South Carolina, it hardly fit the South as a
whole, where political pressures from the yeomanry had created
Master Race democratic polities far more egalitarian, for white
men, than South Carolina's republic.

Nor was eccentric South Carolina a reasonable model on
which to build a national system of concurrent balanced interests. Peculiarities of geography, economics, and demography had
conspired to create in South Carolina a coherent political elite
that, if not monolithic, was certainly consensual. Interests in
other states were far more complex and divided. Calhoun did not
completely delude himself on this point, for he allowed that the
conditions were far from ripe for his plan to succeed. But until a
concurrent majority system could be established, he believed it
was crucial to uphold in national politics one interest above all
others, the strongest counterweight to majoritarian democracy,
an interest that Calhoun now thought under siege—slavery. The
northern masses had proved their stupidity in giving their oppressors consent to oppress them even further. Only the slaveholders
had the intelligence and the will, as well as the material interest,
to resist this hegemony and keep the northern capitalists at bay.
Out of South Carolina's obsessions—and his own—with the tariff and the abolitionists, Calhoun had built a general theory of
politics that, without prescribing slavery, provided a shield
behind which the slaveholders could dwell securely.

To Brownson, all of this made perfect sense. Recent history
proved, he believed, that the more that suffrage was expanded,
the greater the power of the business class grew. Only a small

minority of the voters was interested in the authentic liberation of labor from business rule and exploitation. Hence, the growing power of the federal government would always be wielded on behalf of the capitalists and against labor. It followed, Brownson argued, that the word *democracy* had to be forsaken in favor of the "old and legitimate appelation of REPUBLICAN," and that labor's surest allies would be the Calhounite South, united to establish "a rigid constitutional order" and check the power of capital. Since a considerable portion of the working class were dupes of the ruling class, it further followed that the enlightened few—including, of course, Brownson himself— would have to guide them to political wisdom. And to this task Brownson applied himself with his customary gusto in 1842 and 1843, writing pro-Calhoun newspaper editorials, churning out addresses for Calhoun public meetings, and considering, for a time, becoming the editor of a pro-Calhoun newspaper in New York City.

The disarming appearance of remorseless logic can always obscure mere facts. Brownson's abstractions looked muscular and sounded plausible, except that they could not account for any number of basic political realities. How, for example, could Brownson explain that, in 1840, the major party of the great slaveholders and of strident pro-slavery state-rights leaders such as Henry A. Wise had been the Whigs—the party Brownson himself, in "The Laboring Classes," had denounced as the party of business? Much as he and Calhoun might have wished it so, neither Calhoun nor Calhoun's South Carolina represented slaveholders en masse in 1840, something that Calhoun at least recognized. Whig planters were more than happy to ally with northern capitalists, so long as the arrangement promised them sound and stable cotton prices and improved means to get their crop to market. Perhaps slaveholders were as susceptible to false consciousness as the workers who had voted Whig; perhaps, then, they were not such reliable anticapitalist allies of labor after all. In any event, Brownson's faith in the planter minority in protecting the good of the entire country looks more like a product of desperation than of logic. Although he instinctively recognized basic differences between workers and slaveholders (he called the first "democrats" and the second "anti-democrats"), he said nothing of substance about slavery itself, about how it contributed to "anti-democracy," and about why northern workers might regard it as a threat to their own dignity.

There was far more to American politics than was ever dreamt of in Brownson's philosophy. By the end of 1844, Brownson himself would come to recognize this, as he quickly moved on to a philosophical system he at last found irrefutable, fastened to an organic order and religious faith beyond political uncertainty: the Roman Catholic Church. Calhoun, meanwhile, would continue his work as the self-appointed vanguard leader of the slaveholding South against the hated abolitionists and their apologists—a South that Calhoun loved but still thought was politically too soft on democracy outside of his great practical model, the people's republic of South Carolina.

The deepening divisions among Radicals, Hunkers, and Calhounites presented new challenges to Martin Van Buren and to the unity of the Democracy. As he traveled through the South in 1842, the former president had good reason to believe that he would also be the next president, given the Whigs' collapse. But the renewed clashes among Democrats over fiscal policy threatened to capsize Van Buren's candidacy in some crucial states, including New York. The Southeast was sorely lacking in the kinds of hard-money men who would form the backbone of his campaign. President Tyler might well exploit that weakness, launch a disruptive third-party bid, steal Virginia away from the Democrats, and throw all electoral calculations into chaos. Even worse, Calhoun might succeed in building a new version of the old coalition between the planters of the South and the plain republicans of the North, this time between South Carolina slaveholders and New York labor radicals (with Brownson pitching in up in Boston). All of these possibilities suggested that the Democratic national convention could become a logjam that would deny Van Buren the nomination.

Some of these matters would appear to be resolved by the outcome of yet another great fight at the state level in 1842 and 1843—the final northern struggle for white manhood suffrage in the small but economically dynamic state of Rhode Island. The so-called war over Rhode Island's constitution has sometimes been portrayed as a comic opera conflict in a comic opera of a state, and it certainly had its absurd moments. But for those who followed into battle the Rhode Island rebel leader, one Thomas Dorr, and for those who bitterly opposed him, the conflict was a deadly serious test of democracy's meaning and democracy's future. Reactions to the Rhode Island events, in turn, destroyed Calhoun's quest for a slaveholder-labor alliance.

DEMOCRACY IN RHODE ISLAND: THE DORR WAR

There exists a daguerreotype portrait, attributed to the studio of Mathew Brady and dated between 1844 and 1854, of a frowning man with a forelock who is almost certainly Thomas Wilson Dorr. His suit, a bit tight in the shoulders, dignified and black, is that of a businessman or lawyer or political leader; nearly as black are the brows and shadowy bags around his eyes. The frown is enigmatic, projecting either defeat or determination, maybe both. The forelock could be an insouciant touch or just a matter of carelessness. It all fits with Dorr's career and personality. Some experts have demurred and said that the man in the picture is not Dorr but either the Whig orator and governor Edward Everett or the Prince Bonaparte. The claims are unlikely, but also oddly fitting, for there were bits of Everett and Bonaparte in Thomas Dorr as well.

Dorr was born in Providence in 1805, the son of a wealthy Federalist family, and went on to graduate from Exeter and Harvard before studying law with the sturdiest pillar of the New York Federalist bar, Chancellor James Kent. Elected to the state's House of Representatives in 1834, he gravitated to a group of younger new-school Whigs, who shared liberal concerns about slavery issues and, even more, the state's continued governance under the colonial charter of 1663. Dorr was especially critical of the stiff property requirements for voting, and of the underlying social theory (still propounded by Kent) that justified it. "Enough has been said in vague and general terms, about *'unwholesome citizens,'* 'persons not to be *safely* trusted,' 'without property and vicious'—about 'protecting the *sound* part of the community against those who have nothing at stake in society' . . . ," Dorr declared. "Let those who use this language come out and say, if they will venture the assertion, *that the body of traders and mechanics, and professional men, and sons of landholders, are the base and corrupt persons who are aimed at in these sweeping denunciations."* In another state, Dorr might have ended up a liberal Whig, but there was no room for such heresies among the Whigs of Rhode Island. In 1837 Dorr formed his own heavily Democratic Constitutionalist Party and then defected in full to become head of the state's Democracy.

Rhode Island's anomalous clinging to its colonial charter testified to the singular consolidated power of the state's old landed and mercantile elite, dating back to the eighteenth century. So jealous were Rhode Island's rulers of their peculiar privileges that they had refused to send a delegation to the constitutional convention in Philadelphia in 1787, and the state did not ratify the Constitution until 1790, the last of the original states to do so. But that tenacious order grew increasingly unstable as Rhode Island became a key manufacturing center, with a new working class that included thousands of Irish Catholic immigrants. The 1663 charter enfranchised only those who owned $134 in land or paid $7 in rent, which meant that by 1840 well over half of the adult male population could not vote, a proportion that was increasing as the number of factory workers swelled. Representation under the charter was severely malapportioned in favor of the older rural and seashore counties in the southern half of the state and at the expense of manufacturing towns like Pawtucket. The charter also lacked a bill of rights and other guarantees of personal liberties, and it failed to provide an independent judiciary. Popular agitation to replace it with a more liberal constitution had begun in 1817 (and was led, in the 1830s, by the ubiquitous workingman orator Seth Luther) but had always fizzled out because of the landowner legislature's adamance. In 1841, when agitation renewed with the emergence of a working class–based Rhode Island Suffrage Association, the reformers decided to bypass the legislature completely and proclaim their own constitution in the name of the sovereign people. At their head was Thomas Dorr.

The insurgency quickly led to a crisis over who would govern Rhode Island. Dorr and the Suffrage Association called a state convention, based on what they claimed was the revolutionary "constituent power." The convention drafted a so-called People's Constitution establishing universal white manhood suffrage and an independent judiciary. In December 1841, a referendum conducted through the state's town meetings ratified the Dorrite plan by an enormous margin. The legislature then called its own convention, which drafted its own so-called Freemen's constitution granting the most begrudging minor concessions on the franchise and none at all on legislative apportionment. The town meetings rejected it resoundingly in March 1842.

On May 3, Dorr, who had been voted in as governor in elections held under the People's Constitution, started to organize his government in Providence and called for the new state legislature, already at work, to convene on July 4 at Sprague's Tavern in his hometown of Chepachet. The conservative pro-charter government held on fiercely, declared Dorr's regime illegitimate, and started arresting Dorrite leaders under newly enacted and highly punitive treason laws (measures that the reformers began denouncing as the "Algerine" laws, in reference to the tyrannical dey of Algiers). Dorr escaped to Washington, where he received an indifferent reception from government officials, and then journeyed to New York, where the Radical Democrats, including Ely Moore and Churchill C. Cambreleng, embraced him as the greatest hero of the day. Alexander Ming Jr., the old Loco Foco leader, offered to provide Dorr with an armed escort back to Providence; Levi Slamm, editor of the *New Era*, said he had hired a steamboat to carry a thousand citizen soldiers up to

Rhode Island should the Tyler administration try to interfere against Dorr; and Mike Walsh, never to be outdone, promised to take along his shirtless Democrats and, if need be, personally lay Providence to waste on Dorr's behalf.

Emboldened, Governor Dorr planned a military strike. At his side, providing continuity with the Workie and labor agitation of the past decade, was his organizational secretary, Seth Luther, but more important, he had pledges of support from most of the state's local militia companies. On the evening of May 17, Dorr and a force of 234 men stormed the Providence Arsenal, demanding control as the duly constituted government of Rhode Island. Backers of the Freemen's constitution, taking the name of the Law and Order Party, had occupied the arsenal and refused to hand it over to the rebels. When the Law and Order men would not budge, Dorr, near dawn, ordered two cannons wheeled forward and gave the order to fire; the cannon powder flashed but the cannons did not shoot, and the defenders stood their ground. Suddenly, all the bells of Providence began ringing the alarm, and an awakened citizenry stumbled into the streets, wondering what was happening. Dorr's men, beaten back and discouraged, returned home, and Dorr retreated to New York.

A month later, Dorr returned to Rhode Island, accompanied by Walsh and a few of his Spartan Association roughnecks, planning to link up with a larger force in Chepachet. Entrenched atop Acote's Hill, the Dorrites learned of a large and well-equipped force headed their way in response to a general call to arms from the pro-charter governor Samuel King. After a brief standoff with King's troops, the rebels dispersed once more. Dorr left the state, discouraged by the Tyler administration's decision, at King's request, finally to send federal troops. A savage repression followed, as state officials declared martial law for six weeks, searched hundreds of homes, arrested hundreds of real and suspected Dorrites, and scattered sullen working-class crowds with live-round rifle fire. Among those jailed, on a charge of high treason, was Seth Luther, who spent a dispiriting few months writing an epic poem and finally tried, unsuccessfully, to escape by setting fire to the jailhouse. Recommitted to jail for arson, then released in 1843, he would return to his labor agitation and, in 1846, volunteer for service in the Mexican War—but judged insane, he instead wound up in the East Cambridge lunatic asylum in 1846 and would remain in Rhode Island and Vermont asylums until his death in 1863.

The conservatives now devised a new draft constitution that combined significant reform with provisions that fractured the working-class electorate along ethnic and racial lines. Suffrage property requirements were drastically reduced to a token tax-paying requirement, bringing Rhode Island in line into conformity with most of the other states. Thomas Dorr's pleas to uproot the old stake-in-society principles had been largely heeded. But only native-born male taxpayers were included under the new liberalized rules. Naturalized immigrants had to meet the old charter's property requirements, as well as a new and lengthy residence requirement. As a result, virtually all of Rhode Island's rapidly growing Irish immigrant working class was disenfranchised. Regarding race, the new draft constitution incorporated a deft and divisive political payback to the state's relatively tiny proportion of black voters. Dorr himself was friendly to the abolitionists and defended equal rights for blacks. But during the Dorrite convention, reformers' fears of appearing too radical, coupled with the racist disdain shared by some delegates, led to the exclusion of blacks from voting under the supposedly radical People's Constitution. A number of black abolitionists who had been drawn to the cause immediately denounced the Dorrites, and black Rhode Islanders were thereafter conspicuous in their non-support of the reformers. In part out of gratitude, the new conservative constitution enfranchised black males who met the same minimal taxpaying requirements as native-born whites. The point was clear: blacks, supposedly, were more trustworthy citizens than naturalized Irishmen. Black voters rightly considered the constitution a great advance, whereas the Irish felt as if their wounds had been salted.

Suppressed, exhausted, and divided against itself, the Dorrite movement collapsed, and the new constitution was approved (with most Dorrite voters abstaining) in November 1842. But Rhode Island's Law and Order Whigs were not quite finished wreaking their revenge. After the Chepachet fiasco, Thomas Dorr spent a year in wandering exile, living in nearby Democratic states whose governors refused to send him back to Rhode Island to face charges stemming from the rebellion. Once the new constitution was ratified, Dorr announced he would return home after the fall elections, which he did—only to be arrested shortly after his arrival in Providence under indictment for high treason. Four months later, a jury of twelve Whigs in Newport instantly found him guilty, and Dorr was sentenced to life imprisonment at hard labor in solitary confinement. In his incensed final remarks to the court, Dorr called the entire proceeding a travesty and, acting the hero, retorted that it "does not reach the man within."

The spiteful severity directed at Dorr backfired. All of Dorr's old supporters, including Mike Walsh, protested both the trial and the sentence. Rhode Island Democrats and Dorr supporters, including the newly elected governor Charles Jackson, made obtaining Dorr's freedom their major political demand. In June 1845, after a year's imprisonment, Dorr was released by an act of a new Democratic-controlled legislature. Six years later, Dorr regained his political and civil rights, and three years after that, his treason conviction was voided. But it all came as cold comfort to the People's Governor and to his erstwhile supporters. In 1855, broken by his experiences, Dorr died at the age of forty-nine. The restrictions in the new Rhode Island Constitution of 1843 so demoralized the electorate that after a few years the state plunged into a profound political apathy.

The final important incident of the Dorr War did nothing to console the rebels. In 1842, during the Algerine law crackdown, a Rhode Island military official named Borden was ordered to arrest a Dorrite sympathizer named Luther. Luther sued Borden for breaking and entering, claiming that the government that had ordered the arrest had been supplanted when the People's Constitution was ratified. Article IV, Section 4 of the U.S. Constitution guaranteed to every state in the Union "a Republican Form of Government"; hence, the defense claimed, the Dorrite Constitution, replacing the manifestly unrepublican Charter of 1663, was fully legitimate. In effect, Luther's attorneys were reasserting the Dorrites' claim that the majority in any state had the right to overthrow its government and install a new one. The case wound its way to the U.S. Supreme Court, which in the landmark decision of *Luther v. Borden* in 1848 affirmed a lower-court ruling that Borden had not trespassed, and stated that the judiciary had no authority to offer a definition of a republican form of government. Luther's suit had acquired a strong political charge: Benjamin Hallett, the prominent Massachusetts Democrat, argued before the Court on Luther's behalf, while Senator Daniel Webster argued for Borden. And although Chief Justice Taney and the Court majority were evasive on the most explosive issue at hand, Borden's release strongly suggested that they had rejected the Dorrites' thinly veiled claims about the majority's right to revolution.

The Dorr War was a striking, exceptional case in the history of American democratization before the Civil War. In no other state did a landed elite square off so sharply or so violently against a growing manufacturing working class and its liberal sympathizers. Elsewhere in the early industrializing North, the multiplicity of interests at the top of society and politics cracked open enough space for disenfranchised white men to win expanded political rights without resorting to firearms and revolutionary conventions. By comparison, tiny Rhode Island was more like Chartist Britain—indeed, in some ways, an even starker case than Britain—with an obstinate gentry that thought more like bygone ultra-Federalists than like Whigs and fought to keep the industrial masses at bay before granting carefully calculated reform. Without question, the pro-charter conservatives were formally correct in claiming that the Dorrites' revolutionary majoritarianism threatened constitutional guarantees and augured turning the will of the majority into merely the will of the strongest. Yet substantively, the Dorrites were also in the right, for they had been pushed into their rebellion by an atavistic ruling class that would brook no compromise until it was forced to do so. Without the uprising of 1842, it is impossible to imagine that the conservatives would have stopped stalling and proffered their constitution of 1843. Except for the exceptional rigidity and irresponsibility of Rhode Island's united rulers, constitutional reform could have come much earlier, with some faction of the old elite—led by someone like the young Whig Thomas Dorr—gaining the credit as friends of the people. That it had not was, in America, a strange story.

Unique though it was, the Dorr Rebellion had a significant impact on national politics. Although some Democratic leaders expressed private reservations about the rebels' conduct, most of them, as well as of the rank and file, thought the Dorrites had conducted a straightforward battle for democracy against aristocratic oppression. Shortly after Dorr's installation as governor, Senator Levi Woodbury sent him a private letter, counseling caution but stating emphatically that if his cause was unjust, then "the whole fabric of our American liberty rests on sand and stubble." Andrew Jackson, also in private, cheered the Dorrites' defense of majority rule. Martin Van Buren went further, publicly offering his "most hearty sympathy" for the Dorrites' labors. Francis Blair's *Globe* warned that any effort to suppress the Dorr government by force would be met with force. The same message came thundering from the Democratic governors who, during Dorr's exile in 1842 and 1843, refused to turn him over. "If the views of those who oppose the course, *be right*," New Hampshire Governor Henry Hubbard declared, "then, in my judgment, our revolution which was to secure to free men, just and equal rights . . . *has proved a solemn mockery*."

The national Whigs were just as united in pronouncing Dorr a disloyal desperado. The most reactionary elements of the party's old guard, represented by Rhode Island's own Senator James F. Simmons, hailed the wisdom of the old charter's narrow property restrictions on suffrage, arguing they created "a feeling of cherished regard to home and to country." Other conservatives focused on Dorr's offenses against constitutional order and claims to majority sovereignty, likening the Dorrites (in the words of Connecticut's leading Whig paper) to "the Fanny Wrights, Robert Dale Owens, O.A. Brownsons, and their fellow laborers against the social system of our country." The most liberal of Whigs were no less condemnatory, recognizing the justice of expanding the suffrage but excoriating the rebels' methods. William Seward, while still New York's governor, flatly called the uprising "treason" and pledged to cooperate with Rhode Island officials should Dorr set foot in his state. Henry Clay, speaking on behalf of the broader Whig national coalition, called the events "a wanton defiance of established authority." Much as the rebellion blurred the factionalism within the Democracy, so it stimulated a primordial political unity among the Whigs.

Coming amid the crack-ups of the Tyler years, the polarized reactions to the Dorr War reminded everyone that there truly were fundamental political differences between Democrats and Whigs. The reflexive return to partisan first principles, if only momentary, boded well for the preeminent established leadership of the national parties, and especially for Martin Van Buren and Henry Clay, preparing for the 1844 elections. It boded extremely ill for John C. Calhoun.

No one who had attended closely to Calhoun's writings and speeches could have doubted where he would stand on the Dorr War. For years, he had specifically criticized majoritarianism on the ground that it meant a mere majority might at its pleasure subvert the constitution. This is precisely what the Dorrites were attempting, and although Calhoun favored an expansion of the white male suffrage, he could never approve the Dorrite movement. Yet the rebellion also put Calhoun in a terrible bind, for if he were to denounce it openly, he would put at risk his fledgling alliance with northern labor, which firmly supported Dorr. Pro-Calhoun editors in New York demanded that he speak out, while his close southern political friends begged him to keep quiet lest he scuttle his own candidacy. Calhoun, at first, remained circumspect—although when Dorr visited Washington in search of support, Calhoun abruptly dressed him down in a private interview at Calhoun's boardinghouse. Finally, in July 1843, Calhoun publicly declared that the success of movements like the Dorrites' would be the "death-blow of constitutional democracy, to admit the right of the numerical majority, to alter or abolish constitutions at pleasure."

Pro-Calhoun northerners now faced an even greater problem. Orestes Brownson had actually been something of a Dorrite, having addressed a meeting of the Rhode Island Suffrage Association, at Dorr's invitation, in 1841, and having written Dorr a letter of strong encouragement when Dorr was sworn in as governor a year later. Only later in 1842 did he change his mind, denouncing the Dorrites and ridiculing what he called "the virtue and intelligence of the people" as "all a humbug." Although a few other pro-labor Calhounites joined Brownson in his political line rectification (notably Theophilus Fisk, who had moved to Virginia and was editing a pro-Calhoun paper), others either ignored the matter or grew noticeably colder. Thereafter, all efforts by Calhoun's northern friends and loyalists to advance beyond their small beachheads were doomed.

THE GLIMMERING OF NORMAL POLITICS

In January 1844—having lost a bid to obtain voting rules at the nominating convention favorable to his candidacy, and having watched his supporters in New York and elsewhere flounder—Calhoun publicly withdrew his name from consideration for the presidency. By binding the Democracy ever closer to its majoritarian democratic ideals, the Dorr War had isolated him once again and demonstrated sharply that he was no democrat. Having suffered, then won a highly compromised victory, and then suffered again in Rhode Island, the Dorrites could claim that they had helped reconfigure national politics—a greater triumph, in some respects, than could ever have been achieved in a single state.

As the elections of 1844 neared, the major parties appeared to be pulling through the confusion in Washington, laying aside their factional divisions, and settling into their familiar partisan postures. Van Buren, although not the most exciting personality, would almost certainly be the Democratic presidential nominee, calling for a return to hard-money policies. Clay would most likely prevail among the Whigs, ending the aberrant interregnum of "His Accidency," John Tyler, and proclaiming the full enactment of the American System, including the establishment of the Third Bank of the United States. More clearly than ever, the nation would get to choose between the democratic commerce favored by the Democrats and the capitalist democracy favored by the Whigs.

But political normality would prove short-lived, when fate and John Tyler intervened to disrupt national politics once again in 1844. This new turn would transpire over slavery, territorial expansion, and the continuing activities of the antislavery movement. At the center of all the rearranging, ever on the alert, was the implacable John C. Calhoun. On the margins, but with a growing sense of purpose, were the equally implacable Liberty Party abolitionists and the antislavery Whigs led by John Quincy Adams.

2

ANTISLAVERY, ANNEXATION, AND THE ADVENT OF YOUNG HICKORY

In 1840, the leaders of the fledgling Liberty Party assessed their showing in the presidential election with equanimity, even optimism. "The fewer we have now," Joshua Leavitt observed in his newspaper, the *Emancipator*, "the more we have to gain before we carry our point. That's all.'" The slaveholder Tyler's subsequent unexpected rise to the presidency, a disappointment to northern antislavery Whigs, reinforced the case for independent antislavery politics. By the end of 1841, the party's growing influence in antislavery districts caused the high-spirited Alvan Stewart to exult: "The matter is absolutely settled that we must abolish slavery, & as sure as the sun rises we shall in 5 or 6 years run over slavery at full gallop unless she pulls herself up & gets out of the way of Liberty's cavalry." Stewart's ally Gerrit Smith speculated, two years later, that northern Whigs and Democrats would cut their party ties to the slaveholders and "identify themselves with our great doctrine of impartial and universal liberty"—a more reasonable, if premature forecast.

Liberty Party activity alone, of course, would never be sufficient to convert sympathetic Whigs and Democrats and make slavery the central issue of national politics. The two major parties would have to divide from within, and the glimmering of political normality early in 1844 made that prospect seem unlikely. The normality would quickly dissipate, though, over the spring and summer, when pro-slavery forces attempted, once again, to bully the Democratic Party. At year's end, the collapse of the major parties over slavery still lay well in the future. But the crack-up had commenced.

ANTISLAVERY GOES POLITICAL

Lest anybody think it had given up, the Liberty Party held a convention in New York City only six months after the 1840 election, renominated James Birney for the presidency, and substituted the prominent former Jacksonian Thomas Morris for Thomas Earle in the vice presidential slot. The delegates then approved an ambitious plan of organization similar to those of the Democrats and Whigs. A national party committee would handle party matters between elections and oversee a chain of command leading down to state, county, district, city, town, and ward committees. The city and town committees would each keep a roll of voters who had pledged to back only abolitionist candidates. Two established newspapers with national audiences—Leavitt's *Emancipator* and, in Cincinnati, the continuation of Birney's *Philanthropist*, edited by Gamaliel Bailey—would spread the party's message.

What that message ought to be was the subject of rich and sometimes sharp internal debate. The party's twin goals—to propagandize on behalf of abolition and to grapple for power within the political system—always caused divisions over how best to pursue the second without diluting the first. Some of the original Liberty Party leaders, including Thomas Earle, worried that by restricting itself to a "one-idea" antislavery program, the party would never gain credibility with the voters. The radical one-idea concept nevertheless prevailed, out of concerns that abandoning it might make the party look too much like a mere extension of one of the major parties, while exposing it to infiltration and co-optation.

Tensions remained over the party's political direction. Former Democrats and Democratic sympathizers, including the hard-money man Bailey and ex-Whig Ohio lawyer Salmon P. Chase, counseled drawing a distinction between the party's moral and political functions. While they proclaimed their hatred of slavery and racial inequality, they urged that the party bow to the Constitution's protection of slavery where it already existed and confine itself to practical issues like the abolition of slavery in the District of Columbia and the territories. The point, as Thomas Morris said, was to achieve "the deliverance of the government from the control of the slave power"—luring Democrats and Whigs into the party and forcing a divorce of slavery and government akin to the Jacksonians' divorce of banking and government. Abolitionist evangelicals such as Joshua Leavitt, centered in the eastern states, countered that the effacement of universal abolition would cost the party its essential idealistic fervor. "What are we? . . . ," one Ohio Liberty man complained of the party's pragmatic turn. "We look upon it as a direct and bold attempt to sell the abolitionist . . . to one of the political parties, and we cry, Beware!!" The purists preferred to fight for the idea that the Constitution's provisions about habeas corpus, due process of law, and republican government overrode its compromises over slavery and rendered bondage illegal throughout the land.

Through the mid-1840s, the pragmatic position held sway without causing any major splits in the party. Liberty men agreed to agitate over various issues that would hasten what they called the "de-nationalization of slavery." Congress could abolish slave labor on public works projects and in all federal facilities, including forts and navy yards, as well as in the District of Columbia. More important, by keeping slavery out of the federal territories, the government could halt the expansion widely deemed essential to slavery's survival, and accelerate slavery's total demise, without challenging the widely accepted claim that the Constitution protected slavery in the states where it already existed. "It is a more important object to prevent a million of human beings from being made slaves," argued the Milwaukee *American Freeman* (later the *Wisconsin Free Democrat*), "than it is to free an equal number who have already been half destroyed by being reared and long retained in the condition of slavery."

These arguments directed attention to what Morris had called the Slave Power and at how it had twisted the nation's political institutions. The mails controversy, the gag rule, and the *Amistad* prosecution were only the most recent manifestations of the Slave Power's domination. Behind these events lay the Constitution's anomalous three-fifths clause, which, paradoxically, had become more oppressive with the rise of mass democratic parties. Without the added representation given the South under the clause, the gag rule almost certainly could not have survived. And because both the Whigs and the Democrats apportioned their national convention delegates on the basis of representation in the House, southern slaveholders exerted an inflated influence over party rules, platforms, and presidential nominations. That influence further augmented the Slave Power's ability to demand preference in federal appointments, from members of the cabinet down to the lowliest deputy postmaster. Even though they represented a tiny minority of the American population, the slaveholders and their northern lackeys could, it seemed, rule forever.

In framing these arguments, the Liberty Party appealed directly to the Jacksonians' principles about majority rule and the illegitimacy of artificial combinations that thwarted it. In 1841, a Michigan Liberty paper sounded the theme urgently, pointing to the "overwhelming political ascendancy of the slave power." Slavery, the paper observed, was a moral excrescence—and it was also "an overwhelming political monopoly, in the hands of an oligarchy of 250,000 slaveholders, which by holding the balance of political power in the nation, has long rigidly controlled its offices, its finance and all its great interests, and has thus tyrannically subverted the constitutional liberties of more than 12,000,000 of nominal American freemen." Although hard-core Democrats would resist the idea that their beloved Jackson had bent to the Slave Power's control, the Liberty Party's reformulation of Jacksonian ideas and rhetoric offered an antislavery idiom attractive to northern Jackson supporters. While they drew heavily on antislavery Whig alienation, the Liberty men also aimed to outdemocratize the Democrats.

Because of local peculiarities in election procedures, the first significant Liberty Party victories occurred in New England. In Massachusetts, Liberty Party legislative candidates across the state drew just enough support in 1841 to prevent Whig or Democratic nominees from winning the absolute majority required by law, thereby leaving more than eighty seats in the state legislature unfilled. A year later, Liberty Party backers spoiled the election of nearly all of Massachusetts's congressional representatives and threw the gubernatorial election to the legislature. All across the North, Liberty Party support, although still small, grew steadily. State-by-state returns in 1841 showed a threefold increase over what the Birney-Earle ticket had received in 1840. A year later, the total jumped another 50 percent. At that rate, the Michigan editor Theodore Foster computed, the party would win 160,000 votes in 1844 and gain a huge majority in the nonslaveholding states by 1848.

Where the Liberty men could not immediately grab the balance of power, they harassed vulnerable officeholders, invariably Whigs, in antislavery districts. The most famous case involved Joshua Giddings of Ohio. Giddings's district, in the Western Reserve around Ashtabula, recorded the largest support for the Liberty Party of any in the state, and the district also delivered the heaviest Whig majorities. Safe from any charges that they were aiding the Democrats, the Liberty men targeted the strongly antislavery Giddings, demanding that he defend his membership in a slaveholders' party. Gamaliel Bailey's *Philanthropist* hit Giddings hard for belonging to a party that upheld "capitalists, large manufacturers and farmers . . . and monied interests"—the

Money Power as well as the Slave Power. The Liberty men also established an ably produced local weekly, and attracted Edward Wade, brother of Giddings's law partner, to run against him for Congress. Giddings insisted that the Whig Party offered the only practical vehicle for antislavery politics, and that the Whig leadership was quietly friendly to antislavery measures—an exaggeration that only harmed Giddings further by alarming southern Whigs as well as conservative downstate Ohio Whigs, who began to regard him as a dangerous man.

Behind the scenes, the Liberty men exchanged the stick for the carrot. Even as he was lambasting Giddings and other antislavery Whigs for their subservience to the Slave Power, Bailey was writing privately to several of them, including John Quincy Adams, beseeching them to keep up their pressure on eliminating the gag rule, and offering his aid. Late in 1841, Joshua Leavitt, who had relocated to Washington as the *Emancipator's* capital correspondent, helped to organize an informal antislavery Whig caucus—a "select committee," he called it—which met at the boardinghouse of a Mrs. Ann Spriggs, across the street from the Capitol, where many of the younger men had taken up residence. Early in 1842, Theodore Dwight Weld joined the group, offering his services as a researcher. While pressing the antislavery Whigs from without, the Liberty men also did their best to ensure that the Whigs' national leadership would not excommunicate the party's antislavery wing, as Ohio's Democrats had eliminated Thomas Morris from the Senate in 1838.

The presence of the Garrisonian Weld in the Whigs' small meetings signaled an additional important development—the softening of some hard-core abolitionists' objections to political abolitionism. In 1843, Lewis Tappan, influenced by both the suffrage agitation of the British Chartists and the parlous state of his American & Foreign Anti-Slavery Society, set aside his misgivings and endorsed the Liberty Party. ("Rallying under this banner will be bearing a testimony against the two great political parties," he wrote to Elizur Wright, "& encourage people to regard moral principle in their political act &c. &c.") Other abolitionists, like

Weld, managed to shuttle easily between the different factions of the movement. Even William Lloyd Garrison—who called the ballot box "a pro-slavery argument," and who was rapidly coming to the disunionist conclusion that the U.S. Constitution was ineluctably pro-slavery—covered Liberty Party activities in the *Liberator*.

Most striking were the connections between black abolitionists and the Liberty men. Black antislavery activists, dating back to the formation of the American Anti-Slavery Society in 1833, had always felt a special kinship and admiration for Garrison, the most prominent and immovable white foe of slavery and racism in the country. Dispiriting events in the North in the 1830s and early 1840s had deepened that respect, just as it deepened the blacks' alienation from the rest of white America. The reaffirmation of white-male-only suffrage, between 1830 and 1845, in Connecticut, Delaware, and New Jersey, the admission of Michigan on the same basis in 1837, and, most alarming of all, the wholesale disenfranchisement of blacks in Pennsylvania in 1838 blasted black hopes about improving their situation through political action. ("We can never force our constituents to go peaceably to the polls, side by side with the negro," one Pennsylvania convention delegate declared.) The Dorrites' exclusion of blacks from their People's Constitution reinforced black antipathy to the Democracy. Throughout the North, an intensification of racial discrimination, in schooling, transportation, and other areas of public life, made the initial abolitionist hopes of the early 1830s seem naive.

The Supreme Court's ruling in 1842 in the case of *Prigg v. Pennsylvania* reinforced the northern siege on black rights and antislavery. In 1826, the Pennsylvania legislature passed a "personal liberty law," forbidding state authorities from aiding in the capture and return of runaway slaves. Six years later, a slave named Margaret Morgan escaped with her children from their Maryland master and fled to Pennsylvania, where a slave catcher named Edward Prigg tracked them down and demanded they be handed over under the terms of the federal Fugitive Slave Act of

1793. The local constable refused, but Prigg seized them anyway, touching off a case that tested the constitutionality of the Pennsylvania law. Writing for the majority, Justice Story ruled that although states were not required to aid in the enforcement of the federal law, neither were they entitled to block that enforcement. In dissent, Justice Taney concurred on the law's unconstitutionality, but argued that individual masters were entitled to seize their human property wherever they might find it. For northern blacks and antislavery whites, the Court's split decision offered a choice between bad and even worse.

The racist turn in northern laws pushed black activists to take an ever-greater concern in movements and organizations of their own for collective self-improvement and protection. The former included the black convention movement begun in the 1830s, as well as church groups, benevolent societies, and a plethora of local voluntary associations—like the vigilance committees already established in the seaboard cities to protect runaway slaves, and even free-born blacks, from being seized. Most famous of all was the New York Vigilance Committee and its secretary and general agent, David Ruggles. In 1837, two years after its formation, the New York committee reported that it had protected 335 persons from enslavement, and in time Ruggles himself would be credited with assisting in the escapes of upwards of one hundred slaves. Compared to such urgent matters, the idea of supporting a marginal, white-led third party in a period of black disenfranchisement could easily have looked like a distracting will-o'-the-wisp, and perhaps a dangerous one.

Liberty Party leaders, however, purists and pragmatics alike, made clear from the start that they supported black rights throughout the country as well as the destruction of southern slavery. Northern oppression of blacks, they argued, was the sturdiest prop to the continued toleration of slavery by northern whites, and to what one Liberty convention called the "proslavery spirit" of the major parties. Negro heroes such as Toussaint L'Ouverture, Liberty men pointed out, proved that both races could produce valiant figures, and if there were not more blacks in that category at present, it was only because they were kept enthralled by ignorance and poverty. Party members became important advocates in numerous battles against northern racist laws and proscriptions, including discriminatory voting laws. Just as firmly as the Garrisonians, they repudiated the colonization movement as irredeemably racist, based on what one Liberty paper called the groundless assumption "that the blacks"—whose forefathers had helped secure American independence—"can never be so elevated as to enjoy their rights in this country."

Thanks to this steadfastness, the Liberty Party, despite its sometimes patronizing tone, won wide and sometimes enthusiastic appreciation from northern black activists. The contrast, to blacks, between the Liberty men—who actually welcomed blacks into their ranks—and the Democrats and Whigs was obvious. The nation's leading black paper, Samuel Cornish's fiercely abolitionist *Colored American*, loudly trumpeted the party's virtues before the paper published its final issue in December 1841. The gifted ex-slave and minister Henry Highland Garnet took to the stump on behalf of Liberty Party candidates, as did the ex-slave abolitionist lecturer Henry Bibb. The National Convention of Colored Men, held in Buffalo in 1843, gave the party its overwhelming endorsement. The party even managed to gain the respect of an ex-slave who had begun making a name for himself as an uncompromising Garrisonian abolitionist—Frederick Douglass.

Born Frederick Bailey in 1818 on Maryland's eastern shore, the son of a slave woman and unknown white father, Douglass had escaped from slavery in 1838, winding up in New York City, where he was taken in as one of David Ruggles's refugees (and married his betrothed, who escaped by prearranged plan shortly after he did). Moving to New Bedford, Massachusetts (where, to avoid detection, he took the name Douglass, after the hero of Sir Walter Scott's novel *The Lady of the Lake*), he found work as a common laborer and a ship's caulker and, upon reading the *Liberator*, became a quick convert to Garrison's cause. In 1839, Garrison published some of Douglass's anticolonizationist statements in the *Liberator*, and in April 1841, the two finally met when they both addressed the annual meeting of the Massachusetts chapter of the AA-SS. Impressed with the young man's bearing and sonority, Garrison immediately hired him as an AA-SS traveling lecturer, charged with telling audiences the story of his life and gathering up subscriptions to the *Liberator*.

Douglass's powerful performances—there is no other word for them—were the finest example of what was to become the Garrisonians' most potent antislavery weapon in the 1840s, publicizing the testimony of escaped ex-slaves. For decades, southern slaveholders and their defenders had talked soothingly of slavery's mild, patriarchal hierarchy, so unlike the harsh free-labor system of the North. The fugitive slave lecturers were there to say it was all a grotesque lie, and nobody put truth to the lie better than Douglass. Introduced to his listeners as "a piece of property," or as "a graduate of that peculiar institution, with his diploma written on his back," Douglass would commence a horrifying recollection of his life as a slave—of the brutal beatings he had endured and seen inflicted on women, children, and elderly people, of the systematic "breeding" of female slaves, and more. He always reminded his listeners that his experiences in Maryland would seem idyllic to the vast majority of slaves in the cotton fields of the Deep South. The horror was not unrelieved: Douglass used wit and sarcasm to his advantage, taking special pleasure in telling how he beat up a "breaker" overseer named Covey, secure in the knowledge that Covey's pride would keep the embarrassing story under wraps. And while Douglass's words touched his listeners, his elegant manner and diction—still in formation, but already considerable—impressed upon them all the harder the basic human absurdity as well as the injustice of slavery.

Douglass was an immediate hit on the Garrisonian circuit. In 1842, he traveled through New York and Massachusetts to lecture alongside Garrison himself. He also traveled to Rhode Island, where he denounced the Dorrites over black suffrage. The following year, he spoke before more than one hundred meetings in a tour that took him from New England through upstate New York, Ohio, and Indiana. In late July, he broke off from his travels to attend, with his fellow lecturer Charles Remond, the National Convention of Colored Men, and heard Garnet and others laud the Liberty Party. As a disciple of Garrison's, Douglass was bound to repudiate politics and insist that slavery had to be attacked as morally wrong, that it could be ended only by moral suasion. Yet the Buffalo convention was the first sizable gathering of black men Douglass had ever attended, and Garnet's forceful address impressed him (even though he delivered a sharp riposte). Without abandoning Garrison, at least for the moment, Douglass began defending the Liberty Party to antislavery audiences, on the ground that any and all attacks on slavery were worth supporting.

Slowly but surely, the antislavery movement was investing its most consequential energies within the political realm. And those energies began making an impact in Washington—chiefly through the actions of the small knot of antislavery northern Whigs who had taken John Quincy Adams as their grand old man.

Aside from the dramatic *Amistad* affair, antislavery politics in Washington in the early 1840s focused on the continuing battle over the gag rule. In 1840, as the presidential campaign was getting started, southern Whigs led by Waddy Thompson and William Cost Johnson of Maryland, out to embarrass the Van Buren administration, passed a version of the rule much closer to James Hammond's severe original proposal than to the compromise measure Van Buren helped to maneuver through the House four years earlier. Under the new rule, antislavery petitions would not even be received. With the formerly united, pro–gag rule northern Democrats now split down the middle, the vote was nowhere near as decisive as that on the earlier, softer gag rule—but thanks to the extra seats given the South by the three-fifths rule, the revised "hard" gag rule squeaked through by a margin of 114 to 108.

Adams and his coterie—above all Joshua Giddings, William Slade, and Seth Gates—remained undaunted. Early in the special congressional session of 1841, Adams and his allies managed on three separate occasions to have the newly installed hard gag rule voted down in the House—only to see the southern members, Whig and Democrat, regroup to demand a revote and reinstitute the rule. Six months later, on January 25, 1842, Adams pushed the matter to the wall. He had in his hand, he announced, a petition from one Benjamin Emerson and forty-five other citizens of Haverhill, Massachusetts, complaining of intolerable sectional imbalances in political power and praying for "measures peacefully to dissolve the Union." Adams moved that the petition be accepted and sent to committee, with instructions to inform the petitioners why their request ought not be granted.

The reaction was a virtual reprise of the verbal brawl that Adams had instigated in 1838. One southern Whig demanded that the petition not only be rejected but publicly burned. Thomas Marshall, the Kentucky Whig and nephew of the late Chief Justice John Marshall, offered a resolution of censure, charging that Adams was complicit in "high treason." Adams, perhaps recalling his summation in the *Amistad* case a year earlier, asked the clerk to read the opening paragraphs of the Declaration of Independence, to remind his colleagues of the people's right to alter governments that denied their inalienable rights—then demanded the right to defend himself like any other American accused of a capital crime. Debate over the censure motion lasted several days, the high points coming when Henry A. Wise accused Adams of trying to foment disunion, and when Adams, taking advantage of the situation, accused the slaveholders of endangering every element of American liberty in order to suppress anything "that might not be pleasing to the members of the 'peculiar institution.'" Finally, as in 1838, the censure failed, though now with northern Democrats as well as Whigs voting to table the motion. But the southerners' attack on the antislavery Whigs was not over. Having once again failed to bring down Old Man Eloquent, they set their sights on his young abettor, Joshua Giddings, who had recently offended southern honor over an incident eerily similar to the *Amistad* affair.

In late October 1841, the American brig *Creole* set sail from Hampton Roads, Virginia, bound for New Orleans, with a cargo of 135 slaves. Unlike the *Amistad* captives, the bondmen and women on the *Creole* were indubitably enslaved, and they were enslaved to Americans—chattel, by American law, being shipped southward in the fully legal coastal trade in slaves that operated between the southeastern seaports and New Orleans. On November 7, as the ship prepared to enter the harbor at Abaco Island in the Bahamas, a preorganized band of nineteen slaves, led by the ship's cook, Madison Washington, overpowered the crew and forced one of the white overseers to steer the ship to Nassau. One crew member and one slave were killed in the fighting, and when the *Creole* landed in the Bahamas on November 9, British colonial authorities arrested the nineteen rebels. The rest of the slaves were freed, partly at the insistence of locals who surrounded the brig with their small boats. The *Creole* finally arrived in New Orleans, slaveless, on December 2. The rebels were imprisoned in Nassau for five months, then also freed.

Previously, when smaller American ships bearing slaves had wrecked or accidentally run aground on British shores, the local authorities had liberated the slaves, under the 1833 British Emancipation Act that ended slavery in the empire. But the decision to free summarily some of the *Creole*'s slaves, and then lightly punish the others, touched off predictably impassioned reactions in the United States. Southern newspapers denounced British interference with the coastal trade in slaves. Northern abolitionist and evangelical papers called the rebels saintly, above all the propitiously named Madison Washington, whom they praised (fancifully) for ministering Christ-like to wounded members of the *Creole*'s crew. According to Elizur Wright, the rebellion was an act of God in the truest sense. William Goodell, the Liberty Party leader, noted that the uprising had occurred four years to the day after Elijah Lovejoy's martyrdom, which could not have been a coincidence.

The case would in time be settled diplomatically by Secretary of State Daniel Webster, assisted by the British, as part of his treaty negotiations with Lord Ashburton (although compensation for the slaveowners only came in 1853). Well before then, the *Creole* rebellion helped make Joshua Giddings into an antislavery hero. Ambitious, intrepid, and resourceful, Giddings exemplified the young new-school men who had revitalized the Whig Party. Having pulled himself up from next to nothing to become a lawyer in the Ohio Western Reserve, he had entered politics in the early 1830s espousing the National Republican views of his mentor and patron, Congressman Elisha Whittlesey. Financial difficulties and a personal crisis of faith in 1837 pulled Giddings away from his nominal Congregationalism and conventional Whiggery and into evangelical holy benevolence and abolitionism. Siding with the more politically oriented abolitionists—"the wisdom of providence is . . . manifestly to be seen in any subject" debated in Congress, he later told a friend—he ran as a Whig and replaced Whittlesey in the House when the older man retired in 1838. Arriving in Washington (where he had his first direct, devastating contact with the slave trade), Giddings gravitated to John Quincy Adams and then to the small circle of young antislavery Whigs headquartered at Mrs. Sprigg's. Giddings took up lodgings there and aided in the battle against the gag rule, until the *Creole* case gave him the opportunity to step forward on his own.

Inspired by Adams, Giddings was determined, as he put it, to "spring" additional matters on the southern members, "when they think not of it." On February 28, a few days after the move to censure Adams failed, Giddings tried to reintroduce the Haverhill remonstrance, and in early March, he helped beat back an effort for compensation for slaves lost to the British during the War of 1812. Finally, on March 21, Giddings introduced nine resolutions, drafted earlier by Weld, asserting that the laws of slavery had no effect outside of the southern states, and that the *Creole* rebels were fully justified in their violent strike for freedom. Isaac Holmes, a South Carolina Democrat, quickly arose and delivered a biting remark about fools rushing in where angels fear to tread. But revenge, and not mere bluster, was now on the southerners' agenda. In a maneuver led by Virginia Whig John

Minor Botts and Ohio Democrat John Weller, Giddings's opponents sprang their own trap, demanding an instant vote on a motion censuring Giddings without giving Giddings the chance to reply as Adams had done so effectively. Giddings did try to defend himself the next day, but was ruled out of order, and the censure resolution passed by a margin of 125 to 69. Unlike in the Adams vote, virtually all of the northern Democrats turned against the younger, hotter antislavery Whig. Almost all of the southern Whigs also supported censure, splitting the party along sectional lines.

Giddings curtly resigned his seat and returned home, determined to win reelection. Four years earlier, the Ohio legislature, still in control of the state's Senate selections, had been able to remove the unruly antislavery man Thomas Morris without consulting the voters. But the fate of Giddings's House seat could only be determined by the citizens of Ohio's fervently antislavery Sixteenth District—and so Giddings stood in the special election called for late April, expecting not simply to win but to turn the attack on him and the antislavery Whigs into a vindication for the antislavery cause. A Giddings victory, Seth Gates wrote, would be "of the very highest importance to the cause of freedom."

Giddings received no aid whatsoever from Washington, either from the national Whig leadership in Congress or from the Whigs in his own state's House delegation. The largest Whig paper in the Western Reserve attacked him as a "firebrand" and urged Whittlesey to come out of retirement. But within Giddings's district, a combination of antislavery fervor and repugnance at having their elected representative chastised brought him overwhelming support. Every Whig paper in the district supported Giddings, as did the Liberty Party papers, as did Garrison's *Liberator*. Popular, nonpartisan conventions of local voters endorsed him and requested that he reintroduce his *Creole* resolutions in the House. The result was never in doubt, but the magnitude of Giddings's triumph—a 7,469 to 393 majority over a mocking Democrat—surprised even his friends.

Giddings's triumph was of crucial significance in several ways.

Once he returned to Washington, he was more passionate than ever in his antislavery floor speeches, attracting audiences eager to hear his fire and brimstone—and eliciting only occasional outbursts from southern members. Although the gag rule would not be formally voted down until December 1844, it had, as Giddings later related, "morally ceased to operate" after the moves to censure Adams and permanently remove Giddings failed. Killing the gag rule in turn dramatically increased the likelihood of additional sectional wrangling in Congress. When the pro-slavery stalwart Henry A. Wise told Giddings that his reelection was "the greatest triumph ever achieved by a member of this House," he was both expressing his respect for Giddings's political fortitude and anticipating the opportunity to reply in kind to the antislavery minority's attacks. Agitation over slavery, on both sides, was now fair play.

The manner of Giddings's victory was just as important as the fact that he won. By taking his campaign back to the voters of the Sixteenth District of Ohio, Giddings turned the affair into one of majority rule at odds with the Slave Power, including its northern Whig allies. The special election in April 1842 left no doubt that the voters wanted Giddings to represent them, in defiance of what the political abolitionists had called the "pro-slavery spirit" of state and national leaders of both parties. Giddings's victory was, incontestably, a democratic victory. As never before, antislavery radicals had successfully mobilized the principles of majoritarian democracy and many of its techniques—campaign newspapers, public conventions, the entire machinery of popular electioneering—while attacking the great compromise over slavery on which the Democrats and Whigs based their survival, and its constrictions of free speech and conscience. A special election for a single congressional seat in Ohio cracked open a fearsome issue: Could American democracy coexist with American slavery?

The Giddings affair also illuminated how even the lowliest of Americans, far outside the broadened terrain of national politics, continued to shape the course of political events. Giddings was on the lookout for some way to advance antislavery agitation beyond organizing yet again against the gag rule, but he found it only after the *Creole* rebellion. Earlier black rebels and abolitionists had hammered at the contradictions between American slavery and American equality. Their actions had pushed southern slaveholders to reply with their own arguments that there was no contradiction at all, that American democracy depended on the existence of American slavery and white supremacy. Now, with the Giddings affair and the repeal of the gag rule, the conflict moved closer to becoming a permanent issue in national politics. And at the bottom of these new developments was a rebellion led by a slave with a name suited to the ironies and importance of his impact—Madison Washington.

For Joshua Giddings's unfaithful Whig Party allies, the heightening of sectional tensions in Congress made it imperative that they find some compromise middle ground in the 1844 campaign, a situation that further strengthened the presidential aspirations of the Great Compromiser, Henry Clay. The same intersectional logic held true for the Democrats but would prove difficult for the Democrats to heed. By early 1844, Martin Van Buren and the Radical Democrats controlled the party's nominating machinery—to the intense displeasure of Calhounites and Hunkers alike, and to the trepidation of other Democrats who feared that the uncharismatic Van Buren could never unite the party and win the election. Calhoun's departure from the presidential race in January 1844 appeared to seal Van Buren's nomination. The New Yorker would, once again, have to find a way to placate the South if he were to defeat the Whigs' nominee, but Van Buren had been playing that game successfully for decades. The key question seemed to be whether candidate Van Buren could heal the divisions within the party over banking and internal improvements.

Suddenly, only weeks after Calhoun's withdrawal, the entire political calculus changed. Deep inside the Tyler administration, the departure of Daniel Webster and the severing of the president's last surviving tie to the Whigs had already brought a sharp swerve in American foreign policy, under the new secretary of state, Calhoun's admirer, the conservative Abel Parker Upshur of Virginia. With Tyler's approval, Upshur had begun moving aggressively to promote the annexation of Texas, a polarizing policy that the president hoped might revive his own fading political hopes. Then, in February 1844, an accidental shipboard explosion accelerated a chain of events that would make Texas annexation the overriding issue in the fight for the Democratic nomination.

"A DEEP, DEEP, DEEP INTEREST": MANIFEST DESTINY AND TEXAS ANNEXATION

That Judge Upshur ended up in a position of great national importance in 1843 was one of the oddest elevations in the entire history of early American politics—and one of the sharper ironies of the Tyler presidency. Not that Upshur would have realized as much, for as far as he was concerned he had been born and bred to greatness. A native of Accomack County on Virginia's Eastern Shore, he had matriculated at Princeton (which threw him out for leading a student rebellion), then moved to Yale (where he failed to graduate), then studied law in Richmond with the superior Federalist William Wirt. Elected to the Virginia legislature in 1812 and to the post of commonwealth attorney in 1816, he served as a delegate to the state's constitutional convention of 1829–30, where he joined John Randolph and Benjamin Watkins Leigh in calling on his more wobbly colleagues to stand up against the western peasantry who, whatever their present disposition, might some day plunder the eastern slaveholders. After that moment of glory, Upshur withdrew to his Eastern Shore plantation and a seat on the Virginia Supreme Court. Inside his little world, he cut quite a figure, a large man with an imposing bald head, never without a malicious quip that his fellow squires thought the height of drollery. But that world was getting pushed aside, even in the Commonwealth of Virginia, by the vulgar Jackson Democracy and its contemptible agents like Thomas Ritchie.

On the fringes of power, Upshur had time to write, and he was prolific, churning out political essays, reviews, pamphlets, and reams of private letters to, among others, his old friend Congressman John Tyler. Although he was formally a Whig (he bitterly opposed government regulation of banks), his principal views might best be described as orthodox Calhounite. Like his South Carolina hero, Upshur had little faith in the Whig Party as a vehicle for true conservatism, which upheld the virtuous rule of patrician whites over slaves and plebeian whites. The Whigs' victorious Log Cabin campaign only further depressed Upshur's hopes for himself as well as his country. After the election, he pathetically wrote to one associate that he "frequently had occasion to remark that for the last half of my life I have been almost something." Then, suddenly, Upshur's close friend Tyler was president; soon after, Tyler lost most of his cabinet and began casting about for loyal friends to stock a new one; and late in 1841, Judge Upshur traveled to Washington to take up his duties as Tyler's new secretary of the navy.

Upshur's tenure at the Navy Department, which lasted less than two years, brought needed reorganization and modernization to the service, the construction of new sail and steam warships, and the establishment of both the Naval Observatory and the Hydrographic Office—a record of solid achievement that was all the more creditable given Upshur's lack of federal government experience. His efforts as a policy adviser were more frustrating. He certainly had the president's ear, perhaps more than any other person in Washington. And he had plenty of advice to give, about how Tyler could and should form a party of his own, "of which the St[ate] Rights Party may form a nucleus." But finding a way to launch the enterprise was next to impossible, given that Henry Clay (and, after Clay's departure, his supporters) were setting the Whig agenda at the other end of Pennsylvania Avenue. By the spring of 1843, Upshur sounded as if he had given up. Still, he did have ideas about one issue, the annexation of Texas, that might prove the galvanizing force he had been looking for—and, astonishingly, when Tyler named him to succeed the retiring

Webster as secretary of state in June, Upshur suddenly had the power to press the issue forward.

Texas annexation had long been a taboo subject for Whigs and Democrats alike. Ever since the formation of the independent Lone Star Republic in 1836, its new government had expressed interest in joining the United States. The newly elected Texas president, Sam Houston, backed the idea in his inaugural address in October, and in August 1837, a proposal favoring Texas annexation was laid before Congress. But the idea instantly ran into trouble in Washington. Although Jackson had been happy to recognize the new Texas Republic, annexing it as a state could well lead to war with Mexico, which both Jackson and Van Buren wanted to avoid. Moreover, northern antislavery opinion, riveted by Benjamin Lundy's account of the Texas revolution as a slaveholders' uprising, saw annexation as the latest southern subterfuge to augment slavery's control of the federal government. "[T]he whole people of the United States," John Quincy Adams told the House, have "a deep, deep, deep interest in the matter." Adams was convinced that a very large portion of the citizenry, "dearly as they loved the Union, would prefer its total dissolution to the act of annexation of Texas." He proceeded to filibuster the annexation resolution for more than three weeks. In late August 1837, Secretary of State John Forsyth informed Texas officials that the effort would fail.

Under Houston's successor, the Georgia émigré Mirabeau Buonaparte Lamar, Texas renounced annexation and turned inward, removing Indians by force, planning a state education system, and raising hopes that one day the Lone Star Republic would extend to the Pacific—all while its treasury virtually collapsed. There the annexation issue rested (even after Houston's return as president) until 1843, when rumors began feeding fears that the British government had designs on the floundering republic. "I anticipate an important movement in regard to Texas," Upshur wrote, months before he took over from Webster. Texas also had become ripe for reconquest by Mexico, which had never conceded its loss. The British, so the stories ran, would be happy to step in and prevent it, and get Mexico at last to recognize Texas's independence—so long as the Texans, respectful of the authority of Her Majesty's government, freed their slaves. From one angle, Upshur and other Tidewater conservatives reasoned, the British interference might be beneficial if it prevented the further draining away of eastern slaves westward and thereby helped the old-line eastern patricians to rebuild their former glory. But from another angle, the prospect of establishing a huge free territory (and potential haven for runaway slaves) on the borders of Louisiana and Arkansas was frightening.

For Upshur, raising the specter of slavery besieged looked like the best way to break through the demagogy of low political party managers and initiate the great southern-led state-rights party. Prodded by word from Calhoun's right-hand man Duff Green, and then from Calhoun himself, that the British government, with assistance of British abolitionists, was on the verge of striking a deal with the Texans, Upshur pressed Tyler to secure the only practical check on Britain's ambitions, Texas annexation. By September, administration officials were engaged in secret talks with Sam Houston. On October 16, Upshur met with the Texas chargé d'affaires Isaac Van Zandt and began preliminary discussions toward negotiating an annexation treaty.

The pursuit of Texas was bound to cause some sectional disagreements among the Whigs, but they were not nearly as sharp as those sparked by incidents like the Giddings censure. Since 1836, most old-guard and new-school northern Whigs had opposed annexation, some fearing a further expansion of slavery and southern power, others fearing that the nation was expanding too quickly ahead of the civilizing hand of moral progress and the American System, and still others hoping to make life more complicated for Webster's rival Clay. (Pro-expansionist Democrats added charges that pro-business Whigs opposed westward expansion in order to create a glut in the eastern labor market and suppress workers' wages.) Although some influential northern Whigs, above all Tyler's minister to England, Edward Everett, strongly backed annexation, they were in the decided minority.

And if state-rights southern Whigs were more receptive to Tyler's plans, a significant number of Whig planters, mainly in the older southeastern states, opposed them in order to halt the diffusion of the slave population—and what they feared was their imminent abandonment to their depleted land and unpaid debts. Annexation's impact on the Democracy would be even more complicated. Southern Democrats, as expected, generally lined up with the administration, but the northern Democracy was deeply divided. Some leading New York Radicals took a dim view of annexation. Other northern Democrats loudly supported it, shouting new slogans about Manifest Destiny.

The Manifest Destiny impulse fed off a mixture of crassness, truculence, and high idealism. Without question, there were those who proclaimed America's providential mission to expand as a eulogistic cover for speculation in land and paper. But those were hardly the motives of John L. O'Sullivan, the writer who coined the term, or the other writers, loosely referred to as Young America, in and around O'Sullivan's *Democratic Review* (which had relocated from Washington to Manhattan over the winter of 1840–41). For O'Sullivan and his allies, the expansionist imperative was essentially democratic—not simply in the old Jeffersonian tradition of enlarging the empire of liberty, but in a supercharged moral sense, stressing America's duties to spread democratic values and institutions to a world still dominated by monarchs and deformed by ignorant superstition. The grand national mission, O'Sullivan wrote as early as 1839, was to spread four great freedoms around the globe: freedom of conscience, freedom of person, freedom of trade, and what he called "universality of freedom and equality." The mission was even more precise closer to home, where, O'Sullivan claimed six years later, America enjoyed "the right of our manifest destiny to overspread and to possess the whole of the continent which Providence has given us for the . . . great experiment of liberty."

In retrospect, this posturing can look like the most arrogant form of imperial bullying. Certainly it was arrogant, and Mexicans, including Mexican liberals, had ample reason to consider it imperialist. But there was a deeply idealistic democratic side to Manifest Destiny that, to be understood, requires an appreciation for the situation facing democrats around the world, and especially in Britain and Europe, in the early 1840s. That situation was terrible. In Britain, the Reform Bill of 1832 had left the vast majority of urban and rural workingmen disenfranchised. Radicals from William Cobbett (who wrote an admiring brief biography of Jackson) to the Chartists were struggling through one setback after another, on the road to Chartism's collapse in 1848. In France, the hopeful revolution of 1830 had produced a stockjobber monarchy that hesitated not at all to repress popular republican stirrings in blood—and that inspired, in Paris, Honoré Daumier's brilliant pictorial satires and indictments. In Ireland, Daniel O'Connell's nonviolent mass movement for repeal of the union with Britain was stirring great crowds, but getting nowhere fast against the obdurate ministry of Sir Robert Peel. Across the face of Europe, nationalist as well as democratic aspirations remained stifled by Metternichian reaction. In all of these places, but especially in England and Ireland, intellectuals and agitators looked to the United States for practical as well as spiritual inspiration—and, when the repression at home got too great, looked to the United States for asylum.

Manifest Destiny was rooted in its proponents' allegiance to the beleaguered forces of democracy outside the United States. The name ascribed to and then embraced by the O'Sullivan circle, Young America, had been borrowed from the insurgent liberals of Giuseppe Mazzini's Young Italy, initiated in the 1830s. (There were, in time, many others in the international movement, including Young Germany, Young England, Young Ireland, Young France, Young Poland—and even, one writer tried to claim during the Dorr Rebellion, a Young Rhode Island.) Democracy, the expansionists asserted, was a universal value that should—and could—rule the world. "Why should not England be republican?" the *Democratic Review* queried in a typical article on the Chartists. "Are her lower classes unfit for the burden of government?" And what of Ireland, her lifeblood drained for centuries by the British monarchy: "[I]s Ireland incapable of entering upon the simple task of self-government, because for so long she has been unused to it?" What of the French, the Hungarians, the Italians, the much-abused Greeks?

There were, of course, large omissions from this expansionist idealism: black slaves along with, as ever, displaced Indians. O'Sullivan and his admirers sharply denied that their intentions were pro-slavery. (On the Texas question, O'Sullivan agreed with southerners, most prominently Senator Robert J. Walker of Mississippi, who argued that annexation would lead to a dispersal of the slave population through the West and into Latin America, hasten slavery's demise, and leave behind an all-white United States—a rehashing of the old Jeffersonian "diffusion" idea.) But neither were they capable of expanding their democratic radicalism to endorse antislavery. Like the centrist mainstream of their party, the Manifest Destiny Democrats took an agnostic position on slavery. With regard to race, they candidly but clumsily evaded even considering the possibilities of equality between blacks and whites. "Strong as are our sympathies in behalf of liberty, universal liberty, in all applications of the principle not forbidden by great and manifest evils," O'Sullivan wrote in the *Democratic Review*, "we confess ourselves not prepared with any satisfactory solution of the great problem of which these questions present various aspects." After 1845, this moral indifference about slavery and race would leave the Young America movement and the slogans of Manifest Destiny vulnerable to capture by pro-slavery ideologues. But until then, Young America could electrify masses of northern Democrats, for whom enlarging on what O'Sullivan called the "gigantic boldness" of the American Revolution was the greatest idea in the world.

O'Sullivan and Young America won support from a diverse collection of northern Radicals, Hunkers, and Calhounites, including Churchill Cambreleng and Mike Walsh. But there were other Democrats, including the flickering taper that was once Andrew Jackson, who desired Texas for defensive reasons, to block the unending treachery of Great Britain. For Jackson, the Texas

maneuverings created the imminent danger of a British reconquest of America. With a base in Texas, Jackson predicted, the
British would gather up hordes of Indians as well as slaves to
attack the nation's borders, then send in their own troops to
march on New Orleans and seize control of both the lower Mississippi Valley and the Gulf of Mexico. Reversing that course,
even if successful, would spill oceans of American blood and cost
untold fortunes. Texas, Jackson told Francis Blair in 1844, was
"the important key to our future safety—take and lock the door
against all danger of foreign influence."

Contrary to both Young America and Jackson, however, a significant portion of the northern Democracy strongly objected to
Texas annexation. Theodore Sedgwick III, the party's leading
anti-annexation voice, had been writing antislavery Democratic
pieces for the *Evening Post* for several years. In 1840—while he
was working on the *Amistad* case and putting through the press a
two-volume posthumous edition of William Leggett's collected
writings—he sustained Leggett's Jacksonian abolitionism in
terms that spoke directly to the Democracy: "Give us the real
issue," he bellowed. "*Is Slavery a good or an evil to the free citizens
of these States?*" Three years later, Sedgwick composed a fresh
series of articles (which he eventually collected under the dis-
armingly calm title *Thoughts on the Proposed Annexation of Texas*)
laying out the case that the admission of Texas to the Union was
just "another name for '*the perpetuity of slavery*,'" which threatened the dignity of northern labor and thus democracy itself.
Sedgwick's articles caused a stir among the New York Barnburners, which in turn reinforced Democratic antislavery opinion
elsewhere. Silas Wright came out strongly against annexation, as
did Wright's protégé, the one-time radical Jacksonian hotspur
and now congressman from St. Lawrence County Preston King.
They were joined by Marcus Morton of Massachusetts and
another hard-money Radical Democrat, New Hampshire Senator
John Parker Hale.

Antislavery Democrats had long been a submerged element
within the party, harassed by party officials and, in some cases,

subdued by their own self-censorship in order to keep up a united front against the Whigs. By 1844, some had finally defected in disgust to the Liberty Party. Others had either died, fallen by the political wayside, or, like Nat Turner's defender George Henry Evans, embarked on the strange journey that took them temporarily into Calhounism. The fight over Texas, however, revived the antislavery intellectual strain with the Democracy, and it gave antislavery a new and potentially disruptive political urgency among party leaders. It was one thing for Sedgwick's Manhattan friends (including William Cullen Bryant) to oppose Texas annexation; it was quite another when the opposition came to include Silas Wright. Once Wright and other Radical worthies joined the anti-annexationists, questions inevitably arose about their boss and mentor, the Democracy's prospective presidential nominee, Martin Van Buren. Would Texas annexation enter into the campaign of 1844? If it did, how would the preternaturally cautious Van Buren handle it? And no matter how Van Buren acted, could a Democratic Party that included proslavery southerners, Manifest Destiny enthusiasts, and anti-annexationist northerners possibly unite as long as the Texas question was on everybody's mind?

Secretary of State Upshur was intent on forcing the issue, and he was not alone. At the end of 1843, Calhounites all across the South began exploiting Texas annexation to revive their man's fading presidential chances. Only "the immediate calling up of the Texas question," Calhoun's Maryland friend Virgil Maxcy wrote in December, could unite the South, weaken Henry Clay, and bring a true southern candidate to power. (Maxcy was already plotting with the South Carolina extremist Robert Barnwell Rhett on how to kill Van Buren's chances at the Democratic convention.) Upshur had a different script in mind: the South should nominate Calhoun as a third-party presidential candidate on a pro-annexation platform; that candidacy would throw the election into the House of Representatives; and the southern members, by refusing to vote for Van Buren, would at the very least hold the balance of power in selecting the next administra-

tion. Calhoun dampened speculation when he formally abandoned his quest for the Democratic nomination in January 1844,
but he remained open to using Texas as a political bludgeon on
behalf of the South and did not rule out a third-party presidential
run. President Tyler, meanwhile, hoping to become the South's
tribune, tried with his usual ineptness to get Van Buren out of the
way by offering him a seat on the Supreme Court. Tyler's mes-
senger brought back the derisive reply that Van Buren's nomination to the Court would give the nation "a broader, deeper,
heartier, laugh than it ever had."

On the diplomatic front, Upshur's steady labor was proving,
tortuously, successful. He was well aware that gaining the two-
thirds' majority in the Senate necessary to ratify any annexation
treaty with Texas would be an uphill fight. The quicker he could
conclude the treaty itself, the quicker he and his friends could go
to work convincing Anglophilic southerners that the English
emancipation threat had become an emergency. The southerners
could then force the northern congressional Democrats to heel—
or, failing in that, could form their own party along the lines
Upshur favored and elect either Tyler or, even better, Calhoun as
president. But getting a treaty out of the Texans proved difficult.
President Sam Houston truly was interested in the British option
and was pursuing it vigorously and openly. Only by applying all of
the political pressure on Houston it could think of—including a
plea from his old friend, Andrew Jackson—did the administration
finally get him to come around. Finally, late in February 1844,
Houston gave way. But by the time news of Houston's agreement
arrived in Washington, on March 5, Secretary Upshur was dead.

Six days earlier, Upshur had joined a large presidential party
aboard the battleship USS *Princeton*, anchored in the Potomac.
The *Princeton* was the pride of the fleet, carrying the largest
naval gun ever built, called "The Peacemaker." The day's highlight was to be a demonstration firing of the massive weapon, but
something went terribly wrong and instead it exploded, blasting
the dignitaries and sailors on deck to pieces. Tyler's life was
spared, but Upshur, along with Secretary of the Navy Thomas

Gilmer, Calhoun's close friend Virgil Maxcy, and five others were killed, and nine persons, including Senator Thomas Hart Benton, were injured. The president, although stunned and grief-stricken, acted swiftly to shore up his shaken government. At his Fort Hill plantation, in the same mail that carried an eyewitness description of the tragedy from his son Patrick (who was nearly killed himself), John C. Calhoun received word that Tyler would nominate him as Upshur's successor. Suddenly, the southern sectionalists' hero, who had figured so greatly in the plotting over Texas annexation, would be back in Washington as the chief officer of the cabinet, overseeing the entire Texas matter. And Martin Van Buren's renomination to the presidency was no longer a sure thing.

DIVIDED DEMOCRATS AND THE ELECTION OF 1844

Calhoun's accession augured little change in the broad lines of administration policy on Texas; indeed, Upshur's maneuverings had closely followed a letter of advice Calhoun had sent him six months earlier. But Calhoun's iron-willed personality and reignited political ambitions could not help but affect the tone of the annexation effort. On April 12, after only two weeks in office, Calhoun signed a treaty that would bring Texas into the Union as a territory—then added a political stinger in the form of an extraordinary letter to Richard Pakenham, the British minister to the United States. Two days before Upshur's death, Pakenham had forwarded Upshur a message from the British foreign minister, Lord Aberdeen, explaining that although his government supported the end of slavery throughout the world, it would support an independent Texas with or without slavery, a reassuring grace note that denied Britain was pursuing an abolitionist agenda. Calhoun, however, took offense at what he perceived as Aberdeen's moral smugness, and suggested to Pakenham undertaking an exchange of letters on slavery and emancipation. When Pakenham turned him down, Calhoun struck back with a long letter that defended not just annexation but American slavery.

Calhoun had several motives for writing what soon became notorious as the Pakenham letter. At bottom he was following the same course he had outlined to Upshur the previous summer, though with an aggressiveness and moral indignation all his own. To Aberdeen's assertion that Britain had no intention of interfering with the internal affairs of Texas or the United States, Calhoun replied that Britain had in fact been interfering for a long time, always with the stated hope that slavery in both places would one day disappear. Unable to stop there, though, he added a long paternalistic defense of slavery based on the supposed inherent inferiority of blacks. In every state where slavery had been abolished, Calhoun claimed, blacks had sunk into wretchedness and depravity. Under slavery, blacks enjoyed levels of health and happiness on a par with any working population in the Western world—"and it may be added, that in no other condition or in any other country has the negro race ever attained so high an elevation in morals, intelligence or civilization" as in the slave South. British abolitionist philanthropy would consign freed slaves to misery, while throwing the rest of the world into confusion. Texas annexation—in Calhoun's formulation, an explicitly pro-slavery enterprise—would benefit all mankind.

It is inconceivable that Calhoun did not comprehend his letter's political implications. Had he taken precautions to guarantee his remarks would not see print, his defense of slavery might be ascribed merely to his desire to upbraid Pakenham and Aberdeen. Instead, he sent the letter along with the other official documents pertaining to Texas to the Senate—the "Texas bombshell," Benton called it—thereby assuring that an antislavery senator would release it to the press (as Benjamin Tappan of Ohio swiftly did). Instantly, the letter became a public litmus test for national Democrats and Whigs: support Texas annexation and its pro-slavery rationale and alienate the North, or oppose it and forever lose the South. With one master stroke, Calhoun managed, in a presidential election year, to polarize national politics along sectional lines—the objective of all of his planning since at least 1833.

Even before the release of the Pakenham letter, Van Buren had come under intense scrutiny over Texas. On March 20, a pro-annexationist Tennessee Democrat, Aaron Brown, arranged publication of a letter that Brown had received a year earlier from Andrew Jackson supporting annexation. After Blair refused it for the *Globe*, Thomas Ritchie reprinted the letter in the *Richmond Enquirer*, accompanied by a warning that unless Van Buren followed Jackson's lead, he would ruin his chances to win their party's nomination. From every section of the country, Democratic leaders wrote to Van Buren making the same point. At the same time, the anti-annexationist Barnburners implored him, in Silas Wright's words, "to take boldly the side of truth and principle, [rather] than to temporize with a matter which may prove so vital to the perpetuity of our institutions." The release of Calhoun's Pakenham letter made the political cross-pressures on Van Buren almost unbearable.

Van Buren responded by acting deliberately. Knowing that delay would be fatal, he decided to announce his position in reply to a letter he had received from Congressman William Hammett of Mississippi, but to keep on the safe side he sent a draft to his Regency friends for comments. When Benjamin Butler told him that he could imagine supporting annexation, provided Texas was admitted as a territory and not a state and provided Mexico consented, Van Buren sensed a possible compromise and dispatched Butler to the Hermitage to sound out Jackson. But before Butler could send back word from Tennessee, Van Buren changed his mind and decided to side as much as he could with truth and principle.

Van Buren's reply to Hammett, dated April 20, was the most courageous act of his political career. Not that he failed to hedge his bets: in a vague concession to the South, he allowed that as president he would annex Texas if the people showed they strongly favored it. But the letter's thrust was strongly anti-annexation, criticizing Tyler for his secret and sudden negotiations and asserting that admitting Texas would be an act of aggression against Mexico—born of a "lust for power, with fraud and violence in the train" that would stain the nation's honor. After more than twenty years of doing all that he could to appease the slaveholders, Van Buren would appease them no longer. Without question, the letter was designed partly to solidify support among his Radical base. But in doing so, Van Buren knowingly courted the vehement hatred of the South, which had distrusted him in the best of times. Following, he said, "the path of duty," he would resist the expansion of slavery even if it meant jeopardizing his chances of winning the Democratic nomination.

By coincidence, on the same day that Van Buren's letter appeared in the *Globe*, the *National Intelligencer* printed a letter from Henry Clay, also opposing annexation. Since retiring from the Senate, Clay had taken several tours around the country to build support for his presidential race. Reluctantly, he had given up on his quixotic quest for a new national bank. But the Texas issue struck him as a gigantic distraction from the real issues that remained: internal improvements, the tariff, and the rest of the American System. After the Pakenham letter appeared, Clay's political friends begged him to say nothing. He ignored them, arguing that annexation would inevitably lead to a costly and dishonorable war with Mexico over territory that a "considerable and respectable portion of the Confederacy" did not want to see brought into the Union anyway.

Clay's so-called Raleigh letter (named after the place where he wrote it) took few of the political risks that Van Buren's letter to Hammett did. Clay had already, years earlier, made public his opposition to Texas annexation, so he had comparatively little to lose by reiterating it. Unlike Van Buren, he faced no formidable opposition from within his own party over Texas, and none was likely to arise before the Whigs held their nominating convention in early May, barely a week after the two letters appeared. Although some southern state-rights Whigs would oppose Clay's stance, his break with Tyler had already alienated them; northern Whigs would applaud him warmly. By contrast, Van Buren, by opposing annexation, held his Radical northern base, but repelled pro–Manifest Destiny northerners and infuriated southern Democrats. While Van Buren talked of doing his duty, Clay remained blandly confident that, for himself, going public was perfectly safe: "The public mind is too fixed on the Presidential question, the current is running too strong and impetuously to be now affected by Texas," he wrote to John J. Crittenden, who, aghast, had agreed to have the Raleigh letter published anyway.

The Whig convention in Baltimore, which assembled on May 1, was a thoroughly joyous and exciting affair. The delegates unanimously approved Clay's nomination and then ratified a four-point unity platform that restated Clay's positions on the American System and did not even mention Texas. The one surprising development was the convention's selection of the venerable "Christian Statesman," Theodore Frelinghuysen of New Jersey, as Clay's running mate. More than most Whig leaders, Frelinghuysen, with his past opposition to Jackson's Indian removal policy and his solicitations for Yankee moral reform, might put off some southern voters. But his impeccable rectitude would also offset Clay's reputation for moral laxity and would reinforce the Whigs' chances in the evangelical strongholds of the middle states, above all New York. "The nomination of Mr. Frelinghuysen was no doubt unexpected by you," Clay wrote to Thurlow Weed, "as it certainly was by me. I think nevertheless it is a most judicious selection." Weed agreed.

The Democratic convention met four weeks later, also in Baltimore, and was filled with sourness, division, and backroom recriminations. The timing of the meeting had been pushed back at the Calhounites' insistence in 1843, before their man withdrew, and the delay had a corrosive effect, allowing the delegates more than four weeks to absorb the implications of Van Buren's Hammett letter. The Democratic Richmond Junto had already denounced Van Buren over annexation; there was serious trouble brewing in the Tennessee delegation; and when the convention, prodded by Robert J. Walker of Mississippi, readopted the rule (first established in 1832 to benefit Van Buren) requiring a two-thirds' majority to win nomination, Van Buren's chances sharply dwindled. The Hunker-backed presidential hopefuls who had stayed the course—Lewis Cass, James Buchanan, and Levi Woodbury—had once seemed doomed to win no more than the honorific designation as their respective states' favorite son. But now, Butler reported, pro-annexationists cooked up endless "plots and counterparts," pledging to support one Hunker candidate or another in exchange for standing firm on the two-thirds rule. Van Buren's supporters, holding a majority of the delegates but not two-thirds of them, argued themselves white in the face to suspend the supermajority rule, to no avail. One inconclusive ballot followed another, and Van Buren's support collapsed piece by piece, as Vermont, Connecticut, Illinois, and finally Pennsylvania deserted him.

On the eighth ballot, following a leaders' caucus involving Butler, George Bancroft, and a Tennessean, Gideon Pillow, the New Hampshire and Massachusetts delegations announced thirteen votes for a candidate new to the field who had the personal endorsement of Andrew Jackson: the pro-annexation ex-Speaker of the House of Representatives and former governor of Tennessee, James K. Polk. The Tennessee, Alabama, and Louisiana delegations followed suit (conventions at the time voted in geographical, not alphabetical order), and although the stalemate remained unresolved when the voting ended, a stampede had begun. In a hopeless fury, Samuel Young, New York's secretary of state and a Van Buren ally for decades, denounced the annexationists for denying the former president the nomination and demanded, one last time, a suspension of the two-thirds rule. Southern delegates tried to shout him down; fistfights broke out on the floor; and the New York delegates left the meeting room to caucus. When they returned, with the ninth ballot already started, Benjamin Butler, awash in tears, took the podium, officially withdrew Van Buren's name from consideration, called for party unity, and announced that he was switching his vote to Polk. The convention duly nominated the Tennessean in a unanimous vote.

Mindful of the blow struck to sectional accord, the delegates tried to nominate Silas Wright for vice president. In Washington, Wright received word via the newly invented telegraph machine—and just as quickly, he wired back word declining the offer. To do otherwise, Wright believed, would have been a renunciation of both his personal loyalties and his highest principles. (The convention settled instead on the conservative Pennsylvanian George M. Dallas.) Later, Wright wrote Van Buren that, though defeated, they had upheld their individual honor and character as well as that of their state and party. Van Buren, for his part, vowed to stick by his position on Texas lest he look like exactly what his critics had long unfairly accused him of being, a trimmer, who adjusted his sails "to catch the passing breeze."

What had the Democrats done? At first glance, they seemed to have succumbed to Calhoun's plotting and, by rejecting Van Buren, capitulated to the pro-slavery South. So thorough was the reversal, even southern Democrats reacted with dismay at what Justice Peter V. Daniel—a conservative pro-slavery Virginian whom Van Buren had named to the Supreme Court—called the "selfish avarice and ambition" of Calhoun and his henchmen. The outcome was actually more complicated, as the campaign to come would reveal. Above all, the party's aggressively pro-expansionist platform pressed not only for the annexation of Texas but for a favorable settlement of outstanding disputes over the Oregon border as well. Since 1842, westward migrants along the newly blazed Oregon Trail had swarmed into the fertile Willamette Valley and put increasing pressure on American authorities to secure the territory's borders as far north as the Russian-occupied area at latitude 54°40'. The Webster-Ashburton Treaty of 1842 had settled the U.S.-Canadian boundary only as far west as the Rockies, leaving the Oregon dispute open for agitation by westerners and Manifest Destiny propagandists, who raised the cry of "Fifty-four Forty or Fight!" In Baltimore, the Democrats linked the Oregon issue with Texas as "great American measures." To the Whigs, it was mere sugarcoat-

ing of the bitter Texas pill; to Democrats, it was an effort to sur-
mount sectionalism with democratic nationalist expansionism
and to achieve equilibrium after what looked like the Calhounites' coup.

James K. Polk was also an excellent choice to lead the Democrats out of their difficulties. Although he had benefited from
Calhoun's plotting, he was not a Calhoun man. Less well known
to the electorate than either Van Buren or Clay—prompting the
Whigs to chant derisively, "Who is James K. Polk?"—he was well
known in Washington as one of the most capable of the younger
border-state Jacksonians, whose abilities had won him two terms
as Speaker of the House of Representatives from 1835 to 1839.
Polk had been a Democratic hero of the Bank War, serving as
Jackson's congressional point man during the struggle over the
removal of the deposits. Less prominent during the nullification
controversy, he had nevertheless backed Jackson's Force Bill and
denounced the South Carolina insurgency as heretical. On
Texas, his support of annexation, like Jackson's, had to do with
protecting the United States from British encroachments, and
not the pro-slavery pretensions proclaimed by Calhoun's Pakenham letter.

In other respects, Polk embodied some of the spirit of the
Jackson Democracy in its glory days, as carried forth by its
younger generation. Born in 1795 in the North Carolina backcountry, the grandson of a blacksmith, he had worked hard to
improve himself, graduating with honors from the newly established public University of North Carolina before turning to law
and then to politics. A short, dignified, unfailingly courteous
man with a high forehead and long swept-back hair, he was also
an excellent party worker in the Van Burenite mold, known for
his amazing skill at remembering names and faces. His personality was, to be sure, prim compared to Old Hickory's. A somewhat
long-winded campaigner, known in Tennessee as "the Napoleon
of the Stump," he had a formal, staid demeanor that served him
poorly once the Whigs had mastered the demagogic arts. Still,
Jackson himself, who had done more than anyone to initiate the

boom that won Polk the nomination, saw him as a strong successor. Polk, combining the Young America nickname with his mentor's, became known as "Young Hickory."

If any pro-annexationist could reach out to the Van Burenites, it was Polk. Apart from its plank on Oregon and Texas, Polk's platform was a straight Van Burenite Jacksonian document, calling for, among other things, restoration of the independent treasury. Polk pledged early in the campaign to serve only one term, giving Van Buren hope for 1848. Above all, Polk stood for annexation as an opportunity to expand not slavery but the freedom of American democratic institutions, coupled with the acquisition of more land for settlement by independent farmers who would not be forced to work for wages. Some committed antislavery Radicals considered Polk's nomination, Theodore Sedgwick III wrote, a "rascally fraud . . . a complete surrender by the Majority to the slaveholding Minority." But others—including Michael Hoffman, Silas Wright, and Churchill Cambreleng, who had served with Polk in the House—respected the candidate's record and concluded that if they could not have Van Buren, Polk was the next best man. Polk in turn worked closely with the Van Burenites to persuade Wright to leave the Senate and run for governor, in order to maximize the New York Democratic turnout. New York City Radicals, including Sedgwick and William Cullen Bryant, eventually composed a privately circulated letter that repudiated the Baltimore platform's annexationist plank and called for the defeat of pro-annexationist congressmen, but endorsed Polk for president. Van Buren himself wrote to friends who had threatened to boycott the election, and urged them strongly to back Polk and Dallas.

Henry Clay reacted to Polk's candidacy with his usual nonchalant contempt for the opposition. "Are our Democratic friends serious in the nominations which they have made in Baltimore for President and Vice President?" he asked one associate. Yet Clay also knew that by naming Polk, the Democrats had wounded, perhaps mortally, the Whigs' electoral hopes in the South, where support for Texas annexation ran deepest. Only by carrying the border states along with New York, Pennsylvania, and New England would Clay's campaign stand a chance. With large blocs of voters in those states already committed one way or another, the surest strategy was to chip away at the margins, seeking to capture enough minor constituencies to add up to a majority. It was the same strategy that the Democrats would follow, making for a campaign that, in retrospect, looks jumbled and weirdly inconsistent.

In the South, Democrats played racist politics and smeared Clay as a "niggar"-loving abolitionist, while in the North, they defamed him as a debauched, dueling, gambling, womanizing, irreligious hypocrite whose reversal on the bank issue proved he had no principles. They also pitched their nominees to particular local followings, having Polk hint preposterously, in a letter to a Philadelphian, that he favored "reasonable" tariff protection for domestic manufacturers, while they attacked the pious humanitarian Frelinghuysen as an anti-Catholic bigot and crypto-nativist enemy of the separation of church and state. To ensure the success of their southern strategy, the Democrats also muffled John Tyler. Still hopeful that he might ride the Texas issue to another four years as president, Tyler had his corporal's guard of supporters hold a third-party convention in Baltimore at the same time as the Democrats' meeting. Polk's surprise nomination ruined Tyler's plans, but the president continued his stumbling run through the early summer, until Democratic entreaties, including a respectful coaxing letter from Andrew Jackson, persuaded him to withdraw.

The Whigs countered the Democratic attacks by revving up the Log Cabin electioneering machinery and redeploying it on behalf of the man they now celebrated as "Ol' Coon" Clay. They also attacked former House Speaker Polk as a political nobody who was, deep down, a dangerous Loco Foco radical. To mollify southern outrage at his Raleigh letter, Clay wrote two additional letters, both to Whig editors in Alabama, attempting to soften his stance on annexation, but succeeding only in looking like the prevaricator he had always accused Van Buren of being. ("Things look blue," Thurlow Weed wrote to Francis Granger after Clay's second missive appeared. "Ugly letter, that to Alabama.") With greater success, the Whigs linked up with a resurgent nativist anti-Catholic movement that was strongest in New York and Pennsylvania, and planted stories that as president Clay would tighten up immigration and naturalization laws. (Too late, Clay tried to distance himself from the nativists.)

The Liberty Party campaign added to the confusion. Excited by the mere fact of their survival, the abolitionists greeted the Texas controversy as a godsend and concentrated their attack on Clay, the alleged antislavery candidate who, in their eyes, was as big a fraud as ever. Polk, they claimed, was "too small a man, too openly committed, body and soul to the Slave-Interest, to seduce any anti-slavery voter into his support." But Clay was a gifted leader whose northern managers were successfully depicting as someone "anti-slavery in his feelings." And so, Clay became the object of nasty abolitionist attacks. One notorious handbill, widely reprinted, by an abolitionist minister named Abel Brown, denounced Clay as a *Man Stealer, Slave-holder, and Murderer,* and accused him of "Selling Jesus Christ!" because he dealt in slaves. With the campaign to be decided at the electoral margins, Whig managers grew so concerned that, late in the campaign, they concocted a fraudulent letter that supposedly proved James Birney was secretly working in league with the Democrats, and circulated it in New York and Ohio.

Polk won, narrowly. Clay held eleven states that Harrison had won in 1840: Tennessee, Kentucky, and Ohio in the West; North Carolina, Maryland, Delaware, and New Jersey in the East; and, in New England, Connecticut, Rhode Island, Massachusetts, and Vermont. But Polk, the candidate of democratic (and not merely slave) expansionism, vastly increased the Democratic vote over the figures from 1840 in the Northwest and the middle Atlantic states, carried the entire Deep South as well as Virginia, won Pennsylvania for the Democrats, and, most important, carried New York by a scant 2,106 votes out of nearly one-half million cast. Had only a modest proportion of the Liberty Party's

New York vote of nearly 16,000 gone instead to the Whigs, Henry Clay would have been elected president. Hurt by the Whigs' forged letter campaign, the abolitionists did less well overall than they had expected, winning only 2 percent of the vote nationwide. But they could claim that they had decided a presidential election—an outcome that sent new-school antislavery Whigs into paroxysms. "[T]he false representations of Birney, Leavitt & Co. that *Clay was as much for Annexation as Polk, and more likely to effect it, &c. &c.*," Horace Greeley's *New-York Daily Tribune* cried, "have carried all these votes obliquely in favor of Annexation, War, and eternal Slavery."

Of course, things were not that simple. John Quincy Adams, a great maker of enemies' lists when provoked, better described the manifold reasons behind the Whigs' defeat, first and foremost the three-fifths clause that inflated Polk's electoral vote, but much more as well: "The partial associations of Native Americans, Irish Catholics, abolition societies, liberty party, the Pope of Rome, the Democracy of the sword, and the dotage of the ruffian"—Andrew Jackson—had undone Henry Clay. Adams's ire took him overboard, but his basic point was correct: in the 1844 presidential election, as in any close national race, numerous factors determined the outcome. Among those factors, which Whigs admitted only reluctantly, was that the orchestrated pandemonium of 1840 proved less effective the second time around, especially when mounted on behalf of genuinely substantive and thus controversial candidates. "Hurrah! Hurrah! The country's risin'/For Henry Clay and Frelinghuysen" sounded forced and tinny compared to the old roar for Tippecanoe and Tyler, too. In the crucial state of New York, the gubernatorial candidacy of anti-annexationist Silas Wright helped augment the Democratic totals, perhaps enough to swing the election. Overall, the northern Democrats' ability to get its voters to the polls, including new voters and a large number of Catholic immigrants offended by the Whigs' nativism, turned the electoral tide.

The issues of annexation and slavery—interjected so methodically by Upshur and Tyler and then inflamed by Calhoun—had hovered over the election and shaped its larger significance. Without them, it is unclear whether Van Buren or Clay would have been the victor; but with them, it was perfectly clear that the sectional harmony crucial to both the Democratic and Whig Parties was coming under tremendous strain. The congressional results only worsened the strain, as the Democrats slightly increased their majority in the House and recaptured the Senate in spectacular fashion, turning a six-seat deficit into a twelve-seat majority and effectively wiping out the southern Whigs. To Adams, whose war against the gag rule had done so much to dissolve sectional comity, the result and the prospect looked grim, "sealing the fate of this nation, which nothing less than the interposition of Omnipotence can save." But the Omnipotent moved in mysterious ways. The nation's fate would also hinge on the shifting political calculations and loyalties of the Van Burenite Radical Democrats, who had swallowed their pride and voted for Polk but still smoldered over the betrayals of 1844.

NORTHERN DEMOCRACY, SOUTHERN DEMOCRACY

On June 8, 1844, while the Democracy and the nation were recovering from the shock of Polk's nomination, the Senate rejected the Texas annexation treaty, 35 to 16. Only five northerners—two each from Pennsylvania and Illinois, and Levi Woodbury from New Hampshire—voted aye. Even after the fall elections, and the Democratic gains in the Senate, it remained highly unlikely that a two-thirds' majority could ever be won; in any case, that new body would not assemble until December 1845, which gave the skittish Sam Houston plenty of time to change his mind again. Tyler and Calhoun, determined to win their goal before leaving office, arrived at the alternative, albeit constitutionally dubious strategy, of immediately annexing Texas by joint congressional resolution, which would require a mere simple majority in both houses of Congress. The move would gain support from lame-duck southern Whigs who were eager to shed Democratic charges that they were soft on Texas. More important, it would achieve Texas annexation in ways open to the pro-slavery justification laid down by Calhoun instead of the nationalist grounds favored by Polk. According to the White House plan, up to four new states—three of which were almost certain to be slave states—could eventually be carved out of the annexed territory and admitted to the Union.

The proposal touched off a political scramble. In the House, southern Whigs attempted, unsuccessfully, to pass an annexation resolution they deemed even more favorable to the slaveholders' interests. In the Senate, Thomas Hart Benton, the only Democrat from a slaveholding state who had voted against annexation, offered his own plan, which would split the annexed Texas into two equal districts, one slave and one free, and require Mexico's consent. When his proposal failed, Benton offered a second that authorized the president to send a five-member commission to negotiate all the terms of annexation with the Texans. With the support of the Radicals as well as Andrew Jackson, Benton's plan reconciled most northern Democrats to annexation. On February 27, six days before Polk's swearing-in, the Senate voted 27 to 25, along party lines, to admit Texas, leaving open the decision on what would become of the enormous new American dominion. The next day, on even stricter party lines, the House added its assent, which gave Tyler the option of signing the resolution or passing it on to his successor.

Although laced with compromise, the annexation of Texas was the latest indignity for the Van Burenite northern Democrats. Once again, the southern minority had thrown a firebrand into national politics; once again, the northern majority had ended up giving way. Even worse for northern Democratic pride, antislavery Whigs seemed to have claimed the mantle of egalitarianism. The protracted fight over the gag rule, the Joshua Giddings affair, the Calhounite coup at the Democratic convention—all made the northern antislavery Whigs appear more consistent than the Democrats in championing the democratic rights of ordinary citizens. In Washington, the most inspired outcries to vindicate free speech and Jefferson's Declaration of Independence came not from any Jacksonian Radical but from the original object of the Jacksonians' ire, the newly revived John Quincy Adams. In the strange convulsions of American politics, the man who had forged the notoriously aristocratic corrupt bargain two decades earlier had become, in his resistance to the repressive southerners, a stalwart advocate of democracy.

Or, rather, of one version of democracy. In the Deep South and in the border slaveholding states, an alternative Master Race democracy remained strong in the 1840s, run at the state level almost entirely by slaveholders and dedicated to the proposition that white men's equality depended on black enslavement. Through the early 1840s, the intersectional alliances within the Whig and Democratic Parties had muted fundamental and growing contradictions between the two democracies, northern and southern. Now those alliances had been damaged, thanks to the political designs and will of southern extremists who were barely democrats at all, led by John C. Calhoun—their power suddenly increased far beyond their numbers by the advent of "His Accidency," John Tyler. How firmly the Calhounites could sustain their influence, over southern as well as national politics, would depend on how the issues connected with slavery and westward expansion played themselves out. In the short run, those matters depended on the presidency of James K. Polk.

3

THE BITTER FRUITS OF
MANIFEST DESTINY

Goaded by John C. Calhoun, John Tyler would not depart the White House until he had squeezed the last bitter drops out of the Texas controversy. On the advice of Calhoun that delay might prove fatal, the outgoing president signed the joint congressional resolution on annexation three days before James K. Polk's inauguration. He then dispatched an envoy to Texas with orders to instruct the American diplomatic agent in Houston City, Jackson's nephew Andrew Jackson Donelson, to arrange for annexation on the pro-slavery terms favored by the House southern Whigs. Van Burenite Democrats complained that, at the last minute, Tyler had taken actions that should have been left to his successor. Polk conferred with his designated cabinet but mostly kept his own counsel, while putting the finishing touches on his inaugural address.

In the address, Polk presented a full-throated defense of Manifest Destiny, celebrated the impending admission of Texas to the Union, and called America's claims to Oregon "'clear and unquestionable.'" Yet as George Bancroft remembered forty years later, Polk had much more on his mind. In a private meeting, Polk pledged to the politician-historian—whom he had just named to the cabinet as secretary of the navy—that he would gain four great measures during his four-year term: the settlement of the Oregon question; the reduction of the protectionist tariff of 1842; reestablishment of the independent treasury; and, astonishingly, the acquisition of California from Mexico. As for Texas, Polk would soon reveal that he, like Tyler and Calhoun, believed that the quicker the matter was concluded, the better. On March 10, Polk ordered Tyler's Texas envoy to offer annexation to the Texans according to Tyler's instructions. Thomas Hart Benton and his Radical allies immediately challenged Polk about repudiating his agreements to pursue Benton's plan. Polk claimed he had no idea what they were talking about: "if any such pledges were made," he said disingenuously, "it was in a total misconception of what I had said or meant."

Other unsettling signs appeared throughout the transition and the early days of the new administration. In making his key appointments, Polk tried to satisfy all factions, but he tacked more heavily toward Hunker-style conservatives than even the most disappointed northern Radicals had feared. Having apparently agreed on the names of cabinet members with Jackson at the Hermitage, Polk tore up his list as soon as he got to Washington and had surveyed the political situation. Out of the running was the old hard-money veteran Amos Kendall, who had campaigned hard on his behalf. Out as well was Jackson's close friend Major William Lewis. Instead, Polk named a group that included the exasperating James Buchanan as secretary of state, Robert J. Walker of Mississippi as secretary of the Treasury, and the New York quasi-Hunker William Marcy as secretary of war. George Bancroft at the Navy Department was the one solid concession to the northern Radicals. Only the Calhounites received less than the Van Burenites.

Even more outrageous to the Van Burenites was Polk's decision to remove Francis Blair from his editorship of the *Globe*. Polk feared, with reason, that because Blair had insulted so many important Democrats over the years, including Calhoun, he would now impair party unity. Polk also thought, again with reason, that Blair's political inclinations were dangerously close to Van Buren's. As Blair's replacement, Polk chose Thomas Ritchie of the *Richmond Enquirer*, who renamed the administration organ the *Union*. Andrew Jackson called the removal "the most unexpected thing I ever met with," and warned Polk that it might actually "result in injury to the perfect unity of the democracy." But Young Hickory seemed intent on remaking the Democracy to fit the political circumstances of a new age, one he hoped would quickly witness the growth of the United States into a transcontinental republic. Although the closeness of the electoral vote might have dictated that he proceed with caution, Polk would govern as if he had a magnificent popular mandate. He was determined, he wrote, "to be *myself* President of the U.S."

Ten weeks later—his body bloated, his eyes sunk deep into his head—Andrew Jackson died. Toward the end, he wrote to another aging War of 1812 veteran of how "[t]rue virtue" could only reside "with the people, the great laboring and producing classes, that form the bone and sinew of our confederacy." It was a fitting valedictory, the straight Jackson line of the 1830s, but now the line was snagged and tangled around issues of expansion and slavery that raised disturbing questions about both true virtue and the people. The Jacksonian revolution, and the revolution of conservatism that followed in its train, had run their course. New revolutions, already underway, would blast the old politics to pieces once Polk pushed the nation westward to California.

"A NEW AGE, A NEW DESTINY"

Polk was better than his word. Not only did he get his way on his four major measures; he largely completed his work during the first session of the Twenty-ninth Congress. In part, Polk's extraordinary diligence explained his efficiency. ("How he manages to perform so great an amount of labor as he accomplishes every twenty-four hours is a mystery too deep for our comprehension," one observer commented. "He is most justly entitled to the honorable appellation of *Workingman*.") His penchant for secrecy and disingenuousness, along with his audacity, helped him impose his will on a fractious, albeit heavily Democratic Congress. His greatest limitations—his lack of curiosity, his literal-mindedness—in some ways freed him to pursue his programs unburdened by the troubled moral imagination that afflicted other men. All of these qualities would enrage Polk's adversaries, not least within the Democratic Party, who came to regard him as not just misguided but mendacious. Yet while his critics fumed, Polk racked up one policy victory after another.

Nothing indicated more clearly the passing of the Jacksonian era under Polk than the relative importance attached to domestic and foreign affairs. Jackson and Van Buren certainly had foreign policies; Jackson even came close to instigating a Franco-American war. But foreign affairs in the 1830s paled in importance compared to the Bank War, nullification, Indian removal, and the Jacksonians' pursuit of reform. For the expansionist Young Hickory, hoping to spread the blessings of American democracy, widen the sphere for American settlement, and soothe sectional differences with a great patriotic endeavor, the agendas were reversed. Still, Polk did care deeply about his own domestic goals, and with the help of the large Democratic majorities in Congress, he reversed the policies of the Harrison-Tyler years.

Lowering the tariff posed the greatest political difficulties. In his inaugural address, Polk reiterated his earlier statements that he opposed "a tariff for protection merely," and he suggested that some sort of "revenue limit" might be legislated to allow for incidental protection. During the following summer, Secretary of the Treasury Walker, overturning doubts that he was not up to his job, supervised a massive survey of customs officials and importers in every major port and ascertained the rates at which duties on particular items would bring maximum revenue without discouraging imports. Secretary of State Buchanan, the in-house spokesman for Pennsylvania's protectionist interests, urged major upward modifications on tariffs for iron, coal, and a few other items, but efforts at compromise failed and Polk went to Congress with Walker's proposals.

Along with eastern free traders, western congressmen, their districts now clamoring for foreign markets, strongly backed the Walker bill. Some antislavery Democrats and Whigs dissented, calling it, in John Niles's formulation, an act to "favour the slave labour of the south." But the sternest opposition came from the pro-tariff Pennsylvanians, who maneuvered this way and that in Congress, picking up support where they could about rates on specific items that they deemed too high or too low. Polk responded with a full political offensive, directing Ritchie's *Union* to chastise wayward Democrats, dispatching cabinet members to Capitol Hill to buttonhole waverers, and vowing not to let the congressional session end without a vote. Finally, at the end of July 1846—with Vice President Dallas casting a decisive tie-breaking ballot in the Senate—the Walker Tariff passed.

The reestablishment of the independent treasury (or, as Polk preferred to call it, the "constitutional treasury") occasioned less struggle and excitement, a result of the Democrats' firm control of Congress but also proof positive that the Jackson–Van Buren era had ended. When the House took up the administration's bill in April 1846, Democratic congressmen demanded a hard-money amendment requiring that all payments to the government be made in gold and silver coin. Thus altered, the bill passed the House in a strict party-line vote. Immediately, consternation hit the nation's banking and financial circles, but it was nothing like the uprising of the 1830s. Although the old radical Benton–Van Buren forces raised suspicions of their own when the Senate amended the House bill, those objections were quickly stifled, and the measure passed the Senate, once again along strict party lines. A bill for the graduation of public land prices was the only major administration measure that failed to win congressional approval—and it fell short only because the House and Senate could not reconcile differences on various amendments.

In foreign affairs, the Oregon boundary question was settled well before Congress adjourned, after a strange diplomatic dance with the British. Despite the expansionist bluster about "Fifty-four Forty," American settlement lay well to the south of the Russian border, and Polk was willing, like Tyler before him, to extend to the Pacific the forty-ninth-parallel border established east of the Rockies by the Webster-Ashburton treaty. The British insisted that the line be drawn at the Columbia River, leaving in dispute most of the present state of Washington. When Polk took office, he learned that the British were interested in a compromise devised by the outgoing American minister, Edward Everett, that would hand the bulk of the area below the forty-ninth parallel to the United States—a deal put in temporary jeopardy by Polk's belligerent inaugural address. The British minister in Washington, poorly informed about the situation, summarily rejected a renewed American offer to make the forty-ninth parallel the border. Considering himself insulted, Polk withdrew the proposal, demanded all of Oregon south of 54°40', and made menacing moves toward war. Polk's saber-rattling broke the impasse, and in June 1846, the two nations signed a treaty setting the boundary along the line that Everett had proposed a year earlier. After only fifteen months in office, Polk had reached half of his ambitious foreign policy goals.

The other half, acquiring California, would take longer—but more than a month before the Oregon settlement was signed, Congress gave Polk the war with Mexico that his still-secret California project eventually required. As he entered office, the president could not be as candid in public about California as he had been with Bancroft. Yet he did make an issue of the Mexican government's continuing failure to recompense millions of dollars owed private Americans for various alleged seizures and spoliations of property. With Texas preparing to assent to annexation, Polk had the staging ground he needed to intimidate the Mexicans with the threat of armed conflict should peaceful pressure fail. Early in his presidency, Polk assured the Texans that he would support their most grandiose territorial claims, embracing the area from the Nueces River (the traditional Tejas border) to the Rio Grande, and following the latter northwest as far as the ancient settlements in the Mexican department of New Mexico. Then, in June 1845, the Washington *Union* let the troublesome word slip out in public: should the Mexicans resist the manifest destiny of the United States regarding the Texas border, a corps of American volunteers would invade and occupy Mexico, and "enable us not only to take California but to keep it."

Polk followed up with what he called a peace initiative, but which was in fact an effort to bully Mexico into granting new territorial concessions and, failing in that, to persuade the American public of the need to go to war. Early in his term, Polk had secretly sent a diplomatic agent to Mexico City to begin negotiating additional American claims against Mexico. The Mexican government, under heavy pressure from its own war party, finally agreed to receive a formal emissary, and in September, Polk dispatched a Spanish-speaking, former Louisiana congressman and arch-expansionist, John Slidell. The *Union*, meanwhile, whipped up American public opinion by focusing on the "swaggering and gasconading" of the Mexican war party. And Polk, in response to reports about an impending Mexican invasion, backed up Slidell's mission in mid-October by ordering the U.S. Army under General Zachary Taylor to approach the Rio Grande.

In November 1845, with Taylor's troops in no-man's-land, Slidell arrived at Vera Cruz bearing instructions from Secretary of State Buchanan to demand Mexican recognition of the Rio Grande boundary (giving the United States eastern New Mexico), the sale of the rest of New Mexico for three million dollars, and the sale of California for twenty-five million—all in exchange for American assumption of the outstanding private claims against the Mexican government. Already in crisis, the sitting government in Mexico City crumbled, and the war party took power. Polk immediately ordered Taylor's forces, who had not budged in October, to move all the way to the east bank of the Rio Grande, where they established a fortification with cannons aimed directly at the plaza of the Mexican border town of Matamoros. When the new Mexican government formally spurned Slidell on March 12, the White House had all the justification it thought necessary to declare war.

Negotiations with the British over Oregon delayed matters, but five days after the Senate voted to approve the Oregon treaty, Polk asked Buchanan to begin drafting a war message to be sent to Congress. Slidell, taking his time traveling east to allow the Oregon matter to be settled, finally arrived in Washington on May 8; the next day, the cabinet approved Polk's plan to forward the war message to Capitol Hill. Four hours after the cabinet meeting ended, word arrived that a detachment of Americans had skirmished with Mexican cavalry on the Rio Grande, resulting in sixteen American casualties and forty-seven captured and adding emotionally charged patriotic gore to the outrage over Slidell's rejection. After a sharply curtailed debate in the House and a brief delay in the Senate, Congress overwhelmingly approved Polk's war bill on May 12—not a formal declaration of war, but a recognition that, at Mexico's instigation, a state of war already existed.

Massive displays of patriotic fervor followed the vote. Twenty thousand Philadelphians turned out for a pro-war rally. An even larger crowd assembled in New York to hear speeches and patriotic singing by, among others, the famed blackface minstrel George Washington Dixon. Newspapers around the country blared that the war, as the *New York Herald* put it, would "lay the foundation of a new age, a new destiny, affecting both this continent and the old continent of Europe." Northerners and southerners, Whigs and Democrats, all seemed caught up in the enthusiasm. (In Illinois, Abraham Lincoln, preparing for a congressional run on the Whig line, encouraged the nation's "citizen soldiery, to sustain her national character [and] secure our national rights" by volunteering to fight in Mexico.) Yet beneath the surface, there were grave misgivings about what would soon become known as Mr. Polk's War.

The strongest dissent came from fourteen antislavery Whigs, led by John Quincy Adams and Joshua Giddings, who were the only House members to vote against the war bill. (Two Senate Whigs also voted nay.) All of the House dissenters except Adams and Giddings were little-known men, and they hailed from widely scattered constituencies that stretched from Maine to Ohio. All were considered "ultraists" on slavery issues. All believed that the war was an extension of the Slave Power's thinly veiled plot to extend its territory and power. Just as important, all were from districts that expected their representatives to take such ultraist positions or face political reprisals. The process that had begun with the Giddings affair two years earlier had gradually expanded beyond the antislavery redoubts of western New York and the Western Reserve of Ohio. There now existed a sectional Whig caucus consisting of men whose entire political raison d'être was to agitate over slavery at every turn—not a large caucus, but enough to stand as a beacon of conscience to antislavery northerners. In time, they would be joined by other Whigs who, though they voted for war, felt extremely uneasy doing so. Garrett Davis, representing Henry Clay's home district, exemplified these wary Whigs. Before the vote, Davis complained that the Democrats were rushing the bill through without sufficient consideration and debate, and that, though a state of "informal war" certainly existed, to blame Mexico was untrue: "It is our own president who began this war."

The other most outspoken opponent of the war, surprisingly to some, was John C. Calhoun. Although gratified at the final acquisition of Texas, Calhoun (who returned to the Senate in 1845) dreaded the prospect that the United States might find itself at war with both Britain and Mexico over lands he deemed unfit for slavery. He was pleased by the Oregon treaty, and the settlement of the dispute short of war—a stance that brought him unlikely praise from some quintessential Yankee reformers, including Elihu Burritt, the outspoken Massachusetts antislavery and universal peace movement leader, and Arnold Buffum, a former principal lecturer for the American Anti-Slavery Society. Calhoun broke with Polk over Mexico, arguing that the full story of the skirmish on the Rio Grande had not been told, and that the administration's effort to evade a formal congressional declaration of war was unconstitutional. When the war vote finally came in the Senate, Calhoun along with two Whigs abstained. In the debate, Calhoun declared that he would no sooner vote for the war bill than "plunge a dagger into his own heart." Most of his political friends believed that, politically, it was his opposition that was lethal to his own political standing—"perfectly suicidal," one of them remarked.

Most Democrats, including northern Radicals, initially backed the war, often with boisterous shouts affirming Manifest Destiny and national honor. "YES: Mexico must be thoroughly chastised—," the Radical Walt Whitman, now the editor of the *Brooklyn Daily Eagle*, wrote on the eve of the war bill's enactment. "We have reached a point in our intercourse with that country, when prompt and effectual demonstrations of force are enjoined upon us by every dictate of right and policy." Yet privately, Radical Democrats in Congress, already angry with Polk, were queasy over his latest maneuvers and suspicious that the war had been manufactured to please expansionist slaveholders. "I am too sick of the miserable concern here to write or say anything about it . . . ," New York's Senator John Dix told Azariah Flagg. "I should not be surprised if the next accounts should show that there is no Mexican invasion of our soil." The war, Dix asserted, "was begun in fraud last winter and I think will end in disgrace." After reading the documents concerned with the Slidell mission, Francis Blair concluded that Polk "has got to lying in public as well as in private." Antislavery and anti-Polk discontent was even stronger among select groups of grassroots Democrats.

The greatest Democratic antislavery convulsions, touched off by Texas annexation and intensified by the war with Mexico, occurred in New Hampshire. Home to the Jacksonian machine originally built by Isaac Hill, New Hampshire was, in national politics, the most reliably Democratic northeastern state. In every presidential election since 1832, it had broken for the Democrat. (In 1840, along with Illinois, it gave Martin Van Buren his only electoral votes from north of the Mason-Dixon Line.) The party's state chairman, Franklin Pierce, a former U.S. senator who had returned home in 1842 after renouncing an allegedly fierce drinking habit, commanded his troops with an iron hand. Early in 1845, the antislavery congressman John P. Hale upset party decorum by violating instructions from the state legislature and publicly condemning Texas annexation. Enraged, Pierce had Hale censured for "treachery" and arranged for his excommunication from the party at a special convention held in Concord in mid-February. Thrown off the Democratic ticket with the election for his seat less than a month away, Hale made tentative plans to move to New York City and practice law in partnership with Theodore Sedgwick III.

Ten days after the convention, however, Hale's rank-and-file supporters, now organized as the Independent Democrats, assembled in Exeter to launch a reelection campaign. Liberty Party men and abolitionists throughout New England—including nonvoting Garrisonians—rallied to Hale's cause, and the irregular campaign gained enough votes to block his replacement on the Democratic ticket from winning the absolute majority required to win. Twice again in 1845 and once more in March 1846, there were fresh canvasses for the seat; each time Hale won enough votes to keep the seat open. Over the winter of 1845–46, Hale's group merged with New Hampshire's Liberty men and antislavery Whigs to form the New Hampshire Alliance, and swept to victory in the March 1846 legislative elections, gaining a large enough majority to elect an antislavery Whig as governor and to elect Hale as U.S. senator the following June. John Greenleaf Whittier, who had become antislavery's unofficial poet laureate, rejoiced in a brief ode, "New Hampshire,—1845": "Courage, then, Northern hearts!—Be firm, be true:/ What one brave State hath done, can ye not also do?"

The Hale alliance was not interested simply in winning elections. One legislative resolution, drafted by Hale himself, condemned the Polk administration's war with Mexico as well as Texas annexation and pledged the state's support for "every just and well-directed effort for the suppression and extermination of that terrible scourge of our race, human slavery." A second resolution called on New Hampshire's congressional delegation to demand abolition of slavery in the District of Columbia, exclusion of slavery from all federal territories, suppression of the domestic slave trade, and the prohibition of the admission of any new slave states. The Liberty Party program for the divorce of slavery and government had become the official policy of the Democratic state of New Hampshire.

The New Hampshire uprising did not come as a complete surprise to the Van Burenites. As early as 1840, when the Liberty Party made its modest debut, New York Democrats were concerned about the rise of antislavery sentiments among their own followers. Those concerns had redoubled in the ensuing five years. In February 1845, Van Buren himself had cautioned the Polk administration, in a letter to George Bancroft, that any further expansionist moves deemed favorable to slavery would force northern Democrats to choose between deserting their southern and western colleagues and facing "political suicide" back home. Holding their tongues during the war bill crisis, the Radicals asked Polk for guarantees during the early months of the fighting that the war would lead to no further acquisition of territory from Mexico. Polk, in his usual ambiguous way, placated them with assurances that he had no such designs.

Meanwhile, the fighting in Mexico began in earnest. By August 1846, Taylor's troops had beaten Mexican forces back across the Rio Grande, occupied Matamoros, and then, after frustrating delays, moved upriver to a new staging ground in the little Mexican town of Camargo. To the north, another force of U.S. volunteers gathered at San Antonio de Bexar near the ruins of the Alamo; farther west, a force consisting mainly of Missouri volunteers secured the New Mexico settlement of Santa Fe without firing a shot and prepared to undertake a long march to Chihuahua. On the Pacific coast, American naval forces captured the ports of Monterey, Yerba Buena (San Francisco), Sonoma, and Los Angeles, as well as Nueva Helvetia, a fortified American settlement in the Sacramento River Valley owned by a Swiss emigrant named Johann Sutter.

These victories, Polk hoped, would silence his carping critics, especially the antislavery northerners. Polk emphatically did not seek California to spread slavery and enlarge the slaveholders' political power. "Slavery," he would write, "was one of the questions adjusted in the compromises of the Constitution. It has, and can have no legitimate connection with the War with Mexico." On the contrary: in expanding American democracy to the Pacific, he wanted to supplant sectional jealousies with nationalist unity. Like Jackson (and unlike Calhoun), Polk had never presented any brief on behalf of slavery as a blessing, and he believed, in any event, that New Mexico and California would never prove hospitable to slavery. Rather, he expected his efforts to acquire new territory would unite men of goodwill in a national endeavor. Patriotism would overcome the designs of those he later described as "demagogues and ambitious politicians"—sectionalists who would pursue personal gain "even at the hazard of disturbing the harmony if not dissolving the Union itself." Polk's vision of Manifest Destiny was as an emollient on sectional discord, and not a sectional ploy.

Polk's insistence on his nationalist goals badly aggravated what was becoming a huge and destructive political paradox—that efforts to eradicate sectionalism through expansion only inflamed sectional antagonisms. Responses to the war, pro and con, were based on clashing views of American government—about whether slavery's expansion did more to uphold the nation's supreme political values or erode them. To antislavery Whigs and Radical Democrats, Polk's spread-eagle nationalism looked increasingly like an apology for the South, and for those pro-slavery southern Democrats who saw the war as a means to extend the slaveholders' democracy. In this Polk's adversaries misjudged the president and went on to slander him as a willing tool of the Slave Power, charges that Polk understandably thought outrageous. Calhoun and his coterie certainly proved, in their opposition to the war, that pro-slavery and expansion were hardly synonymous, and the president despised the Calhounites' criticisms as much as he did the antislavery northerners. Yet Polk, with his cramped moral imagination, could never understand that the sectionalists, northern and southern, had their own views of patriotism and that they held those views as sincerely as he did. This lack of comprehension between Polk and his critics would in time widen the divisions within his own party, moving beyond the lingering political resentments from 1844 and later fights over appointments to more fateful matters about slavery and its spread.

The war fever of 1846 initially blurred those divisions. News of the early American military victories produced a rapid outpouring of books, pamphlets, illustrations, and newspaper dispatches, glorifying the bravery and sacrifice of America's gallant soldiers who were avenging the nation's honor on exotic battlefields that might as well have been in Mesopotamia as in northern Mexico. "[C]old must be the pulse, and throbless to all good thoughts . . . ," Walt Whitman wrote in the spring of 1847, "which cannot respond to the valorous emprise of our soldiers and commanders in Mexico." Yet even as he wrote those words, Whitman, like many other northern Democrats, was having second thoughts about the administration's intentions. The Hale insurgency had planted doubts; even more consequential was a revolt in the House in the late summer of 1846, led by a band of antislavery Van Buren Democrats. That revolt would transform both the politics of the war and, in time, the politics of antislavery. It was rooted in state and local, as well as national events, dating back before the war began.

SLAVERY AND DEMOCRACY IN THE STATES

The conclusion of the Dorr Rebellion in Rhode Island did not end conflicts elsewhere over the basic structures of democratic government. Between 1844 and 1848, three new states, Texas, Iowa, and Wisconsin, adopted constitutions, while reformers either succeeded or campaigned hard in Connecticut, New York, Virginia, and Louisiana. (Florida, admitted as a state in 1845, adopted its territorial constitution drafted in 1838, which strongly endorsed slavery, provided for adult white male suffrage, and barred bankers, clergymen, and anyone who had participated in a duel from holding public office.) The general thrust of these movements, and other developments in state politics in the mid-1840s, advanced what had become a dialectic of democratic reform, in which changes at the local level had widening national implications, and vice versa. They also affirmed the growing divide between the South, largely committed to racist democracy with slavery as its foundation, and the North, committed to white male democracy and divided over black male participation but hostile to slavery.

The new constitutions in the Southwest—Louisiana's revised document and the first Texas state constitution, both adopted in 1845—brought those states in line with the slaveholders' Master Race democracies of Alabama, Mississippi, and Arkansas. In Louisiana, the arrival of large numbers of small farmers in the northern and central portions of the state had put enormous pressure on the downstate Creole elite to revise the highly restrictive original constitution adopted in 1812. Elections, one reformer declared, had "become a sort of monopoly" under the existing charter, and that monopoly, radical Jacksonians charged with increasing fervor after 1837, propped up an artificial moneyed class headquartered in New Orleans. Calling itself the Red River Democracy, the reformers' movement, led by the lawyer and planter Solomon Downs of Ouachita Parish, broke through the Whigs' resistance in 1841 and compelled Governor André Bienvenu Roman to sign a resolution approving a convention to revise the existing organic law.

The Louisiana convention, held in 1845, discarded the existing constitution and wrote a new one. The key change was the abolition of all property requirements for voting and officeholding—a reform, Downs assured the Whig delegates, that would not endanger the sanctity of private property and was essential to protect the dignity of white men in a slave society. ("There is no necessity, no true wisdom, in degrading the poorer classes and placing them on an equality with slaves, by denying them the most important privilege of freemen," Downs told the conven-

tion.) Other successful reforms, above all the abolition of monopolies and incorporated banks, infuriated Whig delegates, and in
1852, these stipulations would fall in another round of constitutional revision. But the principle of formal white male equality as
a buttress to slavery was beyond discussion. The same principle
was enshrined in the Texas constitution, based explicitly on both
the draft Tejas constitution proposed at San Felipe in 1833 and
the new Louisiana constitution.

To the east, Virginia—still the least democratic southern polity
outside South Carolina—felt some delayed aftershocks from its
constitutional showdown of 1829–30. Representation was again
the key issue. Despite the drastically reduced condition of its
tobacco economy, Virginia's free population rose by nearly 10 percent between 1830 and 1840, with the largest increases occurring in the Shenandoah Valley and the counties west of the
Alleghenies, where slavery was relatively unimportant. According
to the 1840 census, the numbers of whites residing west of the
Blue Ridge now exceeded those living east of the mountains by
more than two thousand. The constitution of 1830 had provided
for reapportionment in 1841 and every ten years thereafter, and
in August 1841, a group of citizens in heavily Whig western
Kanawha County, led by local Whig leaders, petitioned the legislature for the required adjustment. When the legislature ignored
them, the old divisions reopened.

The fight was chiefly sectional and not partisan. Pro-
improvement Whigs who had come to dominate the western
counties were more numerous than Democrats in the leadership
of the reform movement. But eastern Whigs allied with eastern
Democrats in resisting reapportionment. As in 1829 and 1830,
only a few leading eastern Democrats, above all Thomas Ritchie,
backed reform, as much to win the loyalty of Richmond workers
as to appeal to western farmers; yet one of the leading western
voices deploring the easterners' domination belonged to a young
Democrat, John Letcher, the editor of the Lexington *Valley Star*.
Along the sectional divide, reformers once again linked their
cause to the Revolution, while assuring easterners that basing

representation on the white population would do more to strengthen slavery than to weaken it. After the eastern-dominated state senate rejected reform in 1841–42 and 1842–43, the westerners escalated their rhetoric, charging that the easterners had made "slaves" of free western citizens, and threatening separation from the rest of the state if their demands were not met. In 1845, Governor James McDowell, a Democrat from Lexington, asked the legislature in his annual message to consider calling a constitutional convention, but the eastern planters killed reform yet again.

By 1847, western Virginians had become so aggrieved that a few revived the antislavery ideas that had been defeated in the unsettling debates of 1832. The new controversy began modestly enough at a forum sponsored in Lexington by the Franklin Society and Library Company, a local organization that had begun as one of the late-forming Democratic-Republican societies in 1800 and was now devoted to literary uplift and political discussion. The topic—"Should the people of Western Virginia delay any longer steps to bring about a division of the state?"—drew several notable speakers, including Reverend Henry Ruffner, president of Washington College. Ruffner, a Whig slaveholder, caused a stir by linking his support for separation with his contention that slavery hurt the white population of the West and ought to be gradually eliminated, followed by the colonization of the freed blacks outside of the United States—a reprise of Thomas Jefferson Randolph's proposals fifteen years earlier. Shortly after the Lexington debate, a group of westerners, including John Letcher, asked Ruffner to expand his remarks into a pamphlet and to lay his "not only able but unanswerable" observations before the general public.

Although Ruffner offered old arguments, he modified them with a Whiggish economic utilitarianism that was also appearing in northern antislavery newspapers and pamphlets. Slavery, Ruffner charged, not only propped up the artificial minority rule of the eastern planters; it was pernicious because it dishonored all labor and hampered economic development. Armed with the latest federal census statistics, Ruffner showed that based on all important indices—free population growth, agricultural productivity, commercial prosperity, the spread of common schools and public education—the slaveholding states lagged far behind the free states. "What has done this world of desolation? Not war; not pestilence," Ruffner declared, "not oppression of rulers, civil or ecclesiastical;—but *slavery*, a curse more destructive in its effects than all of them." In the impending struggle for her rights and prosperity, Ruffner concluded, western Virginia had to press beyond constitutional reform and get to the root of its oppression by completing slavery's gradual destruction. Yet while Ruffner's pamphlet gained wide circulation, it only won acceptance in the West. More than ever, Virginia consisted of two societies encompassed within a single border.

While southern conventions and legislatures reinforced their commitment to slavery, some key northern legislatures affirmed a growing popular opposition to slavery. The most direct response, prior to the Hale Alliance uprising, was the enactment of personal liberty laws in the wake of the *Prigg* decision of 1842. The first of these laws, passed in Massachusetts in 1843, arose directly from a fugitive slave case. In October 1842, a fair-skinned runaway Virginia slave named George Latimer, who had reached the North with his wife, was arrested in Boston at the request of his owner, James Gray. The next day, a crowd of nearly three hundred angry blacks gathered at the county courthouse where Latimer was being held, to prevent his summary release into Gray's custody, thereby forcing the authorities to move Latimer to the city jail. Instantly, the case became a cause célèbre for the city's abolitionists, black and white. In November, a group of prominent whites (including William Ellery Channing's son, William Francis Channing) formed a Latimer Committee and founded a new newspaper, the *Latimer Journal and North Star*, to publicize Latimer's plight and "meet the urgency of the first enslavement in Boston."

After a month of difficult negotiations with the state supreme court, the abolitionists succeeded in getting the charge against

Latimer dropped and in gaining his manumission in exchange for a four-hundred-dollar fee, paid by a local black clergyman. But the most radical abolitionists, led by the Garrisonians, were not satisfied, and they demanded (according to the resolutions of one protest meeting) that Massachusetts never again "allow her soil to be polluted by the footprints of slavery." On November 19, an abolitionist convention assembled in Boston and approved the "Latimer and Great Massachusetts Petition," with three demands: a law forbidding all state officers from aiding in the capture or detention of any fugitive slave, a law forbidding the use of jails or any other public property for detaining fugitives, and amendments to the U.S. Constitution (the details left unspecified) that would "forever separate the people of Massachusetts from all connection with slavery." The Latimer Committee distributed thousands of copies of the petition to local postmasters and "every person who wishes to free Massachusetts."

In February 1843, with the petition campaign in full swing and the Texas annexation issue heating up, John Quincy Adams's son, Charles Francis Adams, appeared at a large public meeting at Faneuil Hall and agreed to advocate the petition in the state legislature, where he was a member. The political outlook of this enlarged pro-petition movement, and of the report that it produced, was decidedly moderate compared to the Garrisonians', yet the joint committee that drafted the report preserved antislavery unity. More than sixty-five thousand persons in Massachusetts ended up signing the petition before Adams presented it and his personal liberty bill to the state legislature. In late March, the bill passed the lower house without debate and virtually without opposition. The next day, it passed the state senate by a vote of 25 to 3, and Governor Marcus Morton immediately signed it into law.

By respecting the limits laid down by Justice Story and the Court majority in the *Prigg* decision, the Massachusetts Personal Liberty Law of 1843 struck a blow against slavery without in any way challenging the legitimacy of the U.S. Constitution. The law's practical effect was to place the burden for rounding up fugitive slaves on already overtaxed federal officials. Its political effect was to give fresh impetus to the political abolitionist movement. Not surprisingly, the New England legislatures reacted first: Vermont passed its own personal liberty law in 1843, New Hampshire (as an outgrowth of the Hale Alliance struggle) followed suit three years later, and Rhode Island did likewise in 1848. More strikingly, in Pennsylvania, where antiblack sentiment had led to wholesale black disenfranchisement in 1838, an intense petition campaign pushed the legislature into approving its own personal liberty law, even tougher than the Massachusetts version, in February 1847.

Other northern states proved less liberal on issues connected to slavery and race through 1848. In 1845, Connecticut removed the minimal taxpaying suffrage requirement left over from its reforms of 1818, but sustained the disenfranchisement of blacks. Despite the Giddings uprising in the Western Reserve and the fervent activities of Salmon Chase and the Liberty Party elsewhere in the state, Ohio retained its notorious black codes dating back to 1804, as well as its disenfranchisement of blacks. Wisconsin, another site of growing antislavery activity, nevertheless barred blacks from voting under its new 1848 constitution, just as Iowa had under its new constitution two years earlier. By the end of 1848, black men could vote on the same basis as whites in only five northern states—one fewer than had been the case a decade earlier. Still, even outside New England, the northern politics of democracy, race, and antislavery were neither simple nor static in the mid-1840s. Pennsylvania's personal liberty law was one example of movement. Far more complicated were constitutional debates that rocked New York, originating not in controversies over black rights but in factional politics and a rebellion by white tenant farmers.

Temporarily muted by the party's electoral successes in 1842, the fierce divisions among New York's Democrats soon reemerged, which led to calls for a complete overhaul of the state's constitution. Anticipating the end of the prolonged economic depression and a rise in canal revenues, the newly elected

Hunker governor William Bouck caught the Radicals by surprise by proposing to spend surplus state monies on enlarging the Erie Canal and on two other pending canal projects—a direct violation of the platform on which he had run. Michael Hoffman, the Radical leader in the state legislature, was one of the few who had predicted Bouck's reversal, and he had vowed to push for a new state constitutional convention if new spending and borrowing were in the offing. "Monopoly may hiss and locality may yell," Hoffman wrote to Azariah Flagg shortly after Bouck's nomination, "but a convention of the people must be called to sit in judgment on the past and command the future." Soon thereafter, however, the Radicals' counteroffensive ran into complications caused by an upsurge of rural plebeian turmoil.

The great Anti-Rent war that wracked New York in the 1840s was a social equivalent of the Dorr Rebellion, aimed at eliminating the antiquated remnants of the quasi-feudal leasehold tenure system that still governed large portions of the state. The epicenter of the uprising, the Manor of Rensselaerwyck, included the upper Hudson River Valley counties of Albany and Rensselaer, although in time the struggle moved farther south and west. In 1839, the longtime great landowner of Rensselaerwyck, Stephen Van Rensselaer III, died. Known as the "Good Patroon" because of his willingness to allow long overdue rents to go uncollected, Van Rensselaer left behind immense tracts of tenant-occupied land with their payments long in arrears. His heirs, less enamored of manorial paternalism, began demanding back payments and full compliance with the tenant-lease arrangements. The tenants immediately drafted an "Anti-Renters' Declaration of Independence" and began forcibly resisting landlord agents and sheriffs who attempted to serve writs on them.

The Anti-Renters' campaign of intimidation and rent strikes continued on and off over the next five years, with no settlement forthcoming. Suddenly, in 1844, unrest flared, as resisters disguised as Indians preyed on any authority bold enough to enforce the hated tenure laws. Events reached a crisis in August 1845, when a crowd of Anti-Renters killed a deputy sheriff in Delaware

County, prompting newly elected Radical Governor Wright to declare the entire county in a state of insurrection and have scores of Anti-Renters arrested and imprisoned. Normally, Radical Democrats, including Wright, could be expected to sympathize with the rebels, and the Whigs with the landowners, but the degeneration of the contest into violence under a Democratic governor and the attendant politics played havoc with expectations. Following the Delaware County killing, Bryant's *Evening Post* likened the Anti-Renters to the South Carolina nullifiers of 1832–33, and declared that "[a] free people cannot subsist in a state of violence and anarchy." Governor Wright refused to grant clemency to the men later convicted of the deputy's murder, and he told the state legislature to accede to none of the Anti-Renters' demands until farmers throughout the state laid down their arms. Angry tenant sympathizers—supported by a new land reform group called the National Reform Association, headed by the old Workie George Henry Evans—named independent Anti-Renter tickets in the state legislative elections in the fall of 1845, then bombarded the new legislature with requests to free the convicted men and abolish the existing land tenure system.

Liberal new-school Whigs saw in the Anti-Rent agitation a political opportunity for themselves and for the state's disenfranchised blacks. Like the Democrats, New York's Whig Party remained badly divided between its progressives and conservatives. The majority Seward-Weed progressives, having expressed their sympathy for New York's black population in the struggles over state education and having pushed unsuccessfully to uphold a New York personal liberty law, wanted to expand the black electorate by revising the state constitution—thereby, they calculated, adding thousands of mostly Whig black voters to the election rolls and undercutting the Liberty Party's appeal. Horace Greeley, among others, made the case for black suffrage (and against the Democrats) on moral and democratic grounds: "On the one side," he wrote, "stand Equality, Reason, Justice, Democracy, Humanity; on the other are a base, slavery engendered prejudice and a blackguard clamor against "Niggers.'" Seward conceded, freely, that hardheaded motives were also at work, explaining to Gerrit Smith that "the obvious interests of the Whig party" dictated that it lead the way "for a convention to extend the Right of Suffrage." Whig conservatives, however, opposed any effort to make the party appear friendly to blacks, and preferred to strengthen the nativist connections they had forged in 1844.

The Anti-Rent disturbances heightened the rift among the Whigs and gave the Seward progressives another constituency to cultivate. Whig conservatives despised the Anti-Renter movement as the latest example of home-grown Jacobinism, whose true aim, the stiff-necked Daniel D. Barnard declared in a long denunciation, was "the utter overthrow of all social order, and the ruin of the whole social fabric." But the Weed-Seward Whigs had long regarded the tenant-rent system as an obsolete anomaly and fetter on economic freedom, and they now thought they could win over traditionally Democratic voters in the disturbed counties who had been estranged by Governor Wright's opposition. Risking a party rupture, the liberal Whig press, preeminently Greeley's *Tribune*, took up the Anti-Renter cause, and the Sewardites suddenly found themselves in strange alliance with the pro-retrenchment Radicals, favoring the calling of a convention to draft a new state constitution. Expecting they could sustain their predominance within their own party, the Whig liberals hoped that Democratic factionalism over economic issues and over statewide patronage would clear a path to revising the 1821 constitution to their own advantage.

The Whig progressives failed, although not completely. Voters overwhelmingly approved a referendum calling for a new constitutional convention, but selected a body so heavily dominated by Radicals that the liberal Whigs had to change their strategy abruptly. Dropping their demands for equal black suffrage, Weed-Seward delegates quietly allied with the Hunkers, helping to moderate the more radical Democratic economic proposals at the convention while gaining the Hunkers' agreement to sit out the fall elections. Ultimately, the Radicals succeeded in democratizing the state court judiciary and placing some constitutional restrictions on canal funding; the Anti-Rent movement won a prohibition of the controversial land-contract system and of land leases over twelve years; and the Whigs, with their new links to the Hunker Democrats, put themselves in a strong position to defeat Silas Wright in the autumn election. The biggest losers were New York's blacks, who failed to gain any revision of the 1821 suffrage property qualifications, and who saw the old discrimination upheld in the autumn's popular referendum on the new constitution by a margin of greater than 2 to 1.

Although the New York state convention did not expand black rights, the political fallout from it, especially the renewed division between Hunkers and Radicals (by now known as the Barnburners), helped aggravate the growing sectional discord in Washington and the nation at large. Over the summer of 1846, anger at the administration and at the South finally began to boil over among northern Democrats generally, and especially among the Van Burenites. On Capitol Hill, the Polk administration's willingness to compromise with Britain over Oregon but not with Mexico over Texas and California gnawed at northern Democrats. Polk's veto of a major river-and-harbor improvement bill in August 1846 convinced northwestern Democrats that the South had the president in its pocket. In Pennsylvania as well as New England, the rising popular sentiment behind resisting the South over the issue of fugitive slaves had made an impression on northern Democratic as well as Whig officials; so had the Hale uprising in firmly Democratic New Hampshire. And in New York, Barnburner Democrats found themselves suddenly embroiled in a desperate fight to reelect Silas Wright, fully aware that the Hunkers (with, they surmised, the backing of the White House) were now allied with the Whigs. As factional, partisan, and sectional pressures reached the bursting point, Radical Democrats throughout the North were coming to agree with the sturdy Connecticut Jacksonian Gideon Welles that "[t]he time has come . . . when the Northern democracy should make a stand."

That stand would take the form of a surprise effort by dissenting congressional Democrats to clarify the administration's aims in the war with Mexico with respect to slavery. Growing popular anxiety about Polk's ulterior motives played as great a role as factional calculations in persuading the northern dissidents to act; indeed, the two reinforced each other to the point where the northerners' political self-preservation now seemed to require a definitive challenge to both the South and the Polk administration. "[T]hroughout the entire northern portion of this country," one frustrated New York Radical congressman, Martin Grover, remarked early in 1847,

> it was the topic of conversation and discussion, and of earnest investigation, what was to be the result of the war. The charge was iterated and reiterated that the war was undertaken on the part of the Administration, aided by the South, for the purpose of extending the area of slavery. . . . I wished a declaration on that subject for the purpose of satisfying the northern mind: the northern mind was in doubt, was halting. . . . Satisfy the northern people—satisfy the people whom we represent—that we are not to extend the institution of slavery as the result of this war.

By the time Grover offered these reflections, attempts to satisfy the northern mind had made a famous man out of a hitherto undistinguished freshman Democratic congressman from Pennsylvania.

"THE FIRST ELEMENT OF DEMOCRACY": THE WILMOT PROVISO AND THE TRANSFORMATION OF POLITICAL ANTISLAVERY

David Wilmot was, in his own humble way, every bit as devoted a Jacksonian Democrat as James K. Polk was. Born and raised in rural Bethany, Pennsylvania, he had studied law, resettled one hundred miles west in the town of Towanda in 1834, and become one of the most active Democrats in Bradford County. Wilmot supported hard money, the abolition of imprisonment for debt, the independent treasury—and, enthusiastically, the reelection of Martin Van Buren in 1840 and 1844. Elected to the House in the 1844 contest, he was the only member of the Pennsylvania delegation to vote in favor of the Walker Tariff; with the rest of the Van Burenites, he went along with Texas annexation and voted in favor of the Mexico war bill.

Wilmot looked as well as acted the part of a self-made man of the people, eternally vigilant about protecting the rights of labor. Unkempt in dress, his plump face distended by a chaw of tobacco that seemed permanently lodged in one cheek, he had the rough-hewn presence of a soldier in the army of unprepossessing Jacksonians that had been arriving in Congress since the 1830s—marked for dutiful service but not for distinction. His early career gave no indication that he would one day be regarded as an antislavery hero. That reputation began when he gravitated to a small group of restive antislavery Democrats informally headed by the New York Radical, Preston King.

King, who had arrived in Congress in 1843, was well suited politically and personally to unite the gathering insurgency. Although prone to periodic depression—a breakdown in 1838 had required his confinement in an asylum—King at his best was an outwardly calm and eminently sensible man, with a gift for influencing others and achieving consensus among like-minded colleagues. His record of hard-money Jacksonianism was beyond reproach among party loyalists, and his long-standing objections to southern influence in the party made him a natural leader among House antislavery Democrats. Gideon Welles later wrote that the modest and unsung King "more than . . . any other one man" deserved the credit for "boldly meeting the arrogant and imperious slaveholding oligarchy and organizing the party which eventually overthrew them." Thoroughly estranged from the Polk administration, King faced the additional pressure in the summer of 1846 to aid his mentor, Silas Wright, in Wright's difficult gubernatorial reelection campaign. Handled carefully, a measured Democratic strike in Congress against the Polk administration over the issue of slavery and the war would give tactical aid to Wright among antislavery New York voters and lift the burden of southern collaboration from the northern Democracy as a whole. Yet King himself, as Wright's acknowledged spokesman in Washington, could not be too assertive in public lest he make Wright look like the mastermind of a Democratic antislavery plot.

King led a band of roughly a dozen kindred spirits, including his fellow New York Barnburners Timothy Jenkins, Martin Grover, and George Rathbun; Hannibal Hamlin of Maine; Jacob Brinkerhoff of Ohio; Paul Dillingham of Vermont; and James Thompson and David Wilmot of Pennsylvania. Quite apart from their politics, they had much in common. Most were younger men in their thirties. (King, at forty, was one of the older rebels, while Wilmot, thirty-two, was the youngest.) All were serving either their first or second term in the House. Several shared lodgings at Madam Masi's rooming house on Pennsylvania Avenue. None was interested in renouncing the war with Mexico or in burning all the northern Democrats' bridges to the South. (King, in particular, had hopes of gaining the presidential nomination in 1848 for Silas Wright, which would have been impossible without some southern support.) But as a group, they represented a junior cohort of Radicals, a full generation younger than Martin Van Buren and nearly two generations younger than the departed Jackson. Having come of political age after the Jackson Democracy had been formed, they were less reflexively beholden to the intersectional rules drawn up at the party's inception, less sensitive about a possible reprise of the Missouri crisis, and more capable of enlarging on the example of the antislavery Whigs.

How and why Wilmot came to deliver the antislavery Democrats' signal blow remains obscure. Wilmot himself, in the glare of his sudden celebrity, later claimed that the idea was entirely his, although he conceded that he consulted beforehand with his friends. Jacob Brinkerhoff claimed that he, and not Wilmot, was the true author of the proposal, but that he allowed Wilmot to present it to Congress because his own antislavery views were so well known that he would have difficulty gaining the House floor to move the matter. More likely, several members, including Wilmot, came up with the idea independently and the proposal was hastily drafted by committee, with each of the drafters writing down a copy of the approved wording and agreeing that whoever got the first opportunity would have the honor of introducing it to the House. The lot fell to the unremarkable Wilmot.

Polk provided the insurgents with their opening in August 1846 by asking Congress—on the eve of its adjournment, with many of its members having already departed—for a two-million-dollar appropriation for negotiations with Mexico. The request divulged that Polk planned to obtain additional territory, which he had been telling northern Democrats he had no intention of doing. Antislavery Whigs, delighted to be handed an election issue near the close of the congressional session, immediately pointed out the bill's not-so-hidden motive. Hugh White of New York demanded that, as a show of good faith, "gentlemen on the other side of the House" offer an amendment to the bill barring any extension of slavery into any newly acquired territory. Whether White was apprised of what the antislavery Democrats had planned, or whether he was merely taunting them, remains unclear. Either way, the Democrats were ready.

Shortly after White delivered his challenge, with the House well into the evening session and with only a bare quorum present on the floor, one of the New York antislavery freshman Democrats, Bradford Ripley Wood, announced that he would not vote for the appropriation bill unless it was substantially amended "as proposed by the gentleman [Mr. Wilmot] from Pennsylvania." Wood then ceded his time to Wilmot, who, after some procedural interruptions, offered his amendment, its language based on the Northwest Ordinance of 1787, stipulating that "neither slavery nor involuntary servitude shall ever exist" in any territories acquired from Mexico as a result of the war. Pro-administration Democrats tried to have Wilmot ruled out of order, then tried to water down his amendment, but failed. The amendment—soon and forever after to be known as the Wilmot Proviso—passed 83 to 64, as did (more narrowly) the amended appropriations bill. Congress adjourned before the Senate could make a decision on the matter, temporarily shelving the administration proposal. But in January, soon after the new congressional session opened and the White House proposed a new and even larger appropriations bill, the antislavery Democrats' leader, Preston King (freed from his earlier constraints by Silas Wright's defeat for reelection), presented the Proviso once again, in an expanded form. Once again, the House passed it.

The roll call on the original Proviso vote went unrecorded, but the results over the amended appropriations bill were startling. Virtually every northern Whig on hand supported the amended bill, while every southern Whig and Democrat opposed it. The most telling division occurred among the northern Democrats, fifty-two of whom supported the bill and only four of whom voted nay. The bonds of party had broken down. The House was almost perfectly divided along sectional lines, much as it had been during the Missouri crisis more than a quarter of a century earlier. Anti-administration, antislavery sentiments had spread through the entire congressional northern Democracy. Southern hard-liners took note, and as soon as the House passed the Proviso a second time, John C. Calhoun introduced in the Senate what amounted to an anti-Proviso: two resolutions denouncing any congressional law that would "make any discrimination between the States of this Union" or "deprive citizens of any of the States of this Union from emigrating, with their property, into any of the territories of the United States." The resolutions would never be debated or come up for a vote, but they offered the basis for later southern resistance.

Outside of Congress, initial reaction to the Wilmot vote was mild. When the press mentioned the Proviso at all, it was as a mere procedural motion, covering an eventuality that had not yet come to pass. The administration's *Union* left the impression that it would happily accept the appropriations bill, with or without Wilmot's amendment. Apart from a few isolated cases, the Proviso appears to have had no effect on the 1846 congressional races (in which the Whigs regained, narrowly, the House majority), not even in Wilmot's successful reelection campaign. Only after the second session of the Twenty-ninth Congress assembled—after four months of letting its purport sink in, and with the distractions of an impending election gone—did the Wilmot issue explode.

To understand that explosion, it is crucial to understand what the Wilmot Proviso was not, as well as what it was. It was not, by any means, either an antiwar or an anti-expansionist measure. Despite their misgivings about the war's origins and the hidden agenda of the slaveholders, the antislavery Democrats warmly supported Polk's war policies in 1847. David Wilmot himself, who considered California the rightful possession of the United States, declared his support for the "necessary and proper war" only minutes before he first moved his amendment. In this respect, the sectional solidarity between northern Whigs and Democrats was illusory. Antislavery liberal Whigs did rejoice at the Proviso as, in Horace Greeley's words, *"a solemn declaration of the United North against the further extension of Slavery."* But the antislavery Whigs, like the rest of their party, were opposed to any territorial conquest of Mexican lands and not just to the expansion of slavery. By the end of 1847, many moderate and conservative northern Whigs would find themselves backing off of the Wilmot Proviso and instead joining with southern Whigs under the slogan of "No Territory," a temporarily successful reassertion of intersectional party regularity over sectional loyalties.

Neither was the Proviso a blow for the elevation and equality of blacks, as favored by the Liberty Party and some of the hardcore antislavery Whigs. Steeped in the Jacksonian tradition of protecting the rights of free labor, the antislavery Democrats made it clear that in trying to halt slavery's spread, they were chiefly interested in preventing the degradation and dishonor of white workingmen. "If slavery is not excluded by law," Preston King proclaimed when he reintroduced the Proviso in January 1847, "the presence of the slave will exclude the laboring white man." Unlike antislavery Whigs—who took more liberal stances

on black rights and more conservative stances on economic policies—antislavery Democrats, radicals on economic matters, were
primarily concerned with the future of white workers.

Some Democrats' arguments also included the racist claim
that by barring slavery from new territories, those territories
could be kept lily-white. Jacob Brinkerhoff remarked at the
height of the Proviso controversy that he had "selfishness enough
greatly to prefer the welfare of my own race, and vindictiveness
enough to wish to leave and keep upon the shoulders of the
South the burden of the curse which they themselves created
and courted"—the "curse" being a large black population.
Wilmot took a similar view, declaring that he had "no morbid
sympathy for the slave," and that the proposal bearing his name
aimed to "preserve to free white labor a fair country, a rich inheritance" in the West, where "the sons of toil, of my own race and
own color" could live free of blacks. The New York Barnburners
had an especially baleful record of exploiting racial prejudice,
having voted solidly against extending black suffrage at the 1846
state constitutional convention, and raised cries of "Nigger Party,"
"Amalgamation," and "Fried Wool" against the liberal Whigs who
supported reform.

Yet if racism abounded in their ranks, the antislavery Democrats were neither morally indifferent to black enslavement nor
driven chiefly by racism. No matter how deep their Negrophobia,
few if any accepted claims that racial differences justified slavery.
"To hold a human being in bondage; to buy and sell his body,"
Radical John Van Buren stated, "was and must be repugnant to
the ordinary sensibilities of every intelligent man." The Van
Burenite *Seneca Observer*, in a typical Barnburner editorial,
announced that it could not countenance a victory over Mexico if
the result "would be to deprive one human being of those rights
which are his natural inheritance." In backing the Proviso, antislavery Democrats also picked up the widely held argument that
by restricting slavery's spread, they were helping to ensure its
eventual doom where it already existed—not in the lunatic manner favored by the most radical abolitionists, but within the limits

of the U.S. Constitution. Lacking fresh lands to exploit, so the argument went, slave-based staple agriculture would eventually deplete the soil of the newer southern states just as it had along the seaboard—and then slavery would collapse under the weight of its own inefficiency. "What does the past teach us?" the political abolitionist Gamaliel Bailey's newspaper, the *National Era*, asked in 1847. "That slavery lives by *expansion.*" Accordingly, antislavery Democrats reasoned, the Proviso's effort to quarantine slavery also was an effort to hasten slavery's abolition—or, as Wilmot declared in 1847, to "insure the redemption, at an early day, of the negro from his bondage and chains."

The Democratic antislavery argument embodied in the Wilmot Proviso was above all an attack on the authority of the aristocratic Slave Power. At one level, the attack was factional, a settling of scores with southern Democrats going back at least to the Baltimore convention of 1844 and continuing through Polk's deceptions and perceived betrayals. But the outpouring of pent-up Democratic outrage in 1846 and after, inside and outside Washington, brought into the open far more than grudges over petty political matters and a thirst for revenge. The South, antislavery Democrats declared, was ruled by an oligarchy that would stop at nothing to get its way. That oligarchy degraded white labor while living off the labor of black slaves; it throttled free discussion of public matters in the North as well as the South; it retarded economic and mental progress; and now, insatiable as ever, it wanted still more territory "because," George Rathbun charged, "where slavery exists, the slave power prevails."

In sum—and this was the Wilmot Democrats' crowning argument—slavery and the Slave Power were at war with democracy itself. Bradford Ripley Wood, the Radical who helped Wilmot introduce the Proviso, made the point cogently on the floor of the House in February 1847. "This is a national question," Wood observed.

> It is not a question of mere dollars and cents. It is not a
> mere political question. It is one in which the North has

a higher and deeper stake than the South possibly can have. It is a question whether, in the government of the country, she shall be borne down by the influence of your slaveholding aristocratic institutions, that have not in them the first element of Democracy. It is a question whether this Republic shall be weakened, cramped, and degraded by an institution doomed of God and man. . . . Hug this institution to your own bosom, if you choose, until it eats out your very vitals; but let it not blast, and blight, and curse, with the mildew of heaven, any other portion of God's heritage, save where, by leave of the Constitution, it now exists.

Jacksonian antislavery arguments that, a decade earlier, were grounds for excommunication from the Democracy now galvanized virtually every northern Democrat in the House.

The rulers of South Carolina and their champion John C. Calhoun—who, now that American troops were under fire, had said he was prepared to give the war "a quiet but decided support"—responded swiftly. The Wilmot Proviso, the *Charleston Mercury* exclaimed, drew *"a line of political and social demarcation around the Slave States"* that would leave the South "on every side girt round with those who will continually excite our slaves to insubordination and revolt, which it would be folly to suppose would forever be resisted." Other southerners, Whig and Democratic, regarded the Proviso as more of a symbolic issue than a substantive one—a northern effort to insult and then humiliate the South by denying slaveholders rights that they actually did not intend to exercise. Calhoun dismissed the Proviso as an unconstitutional ploy to win over the small number of abolitionist voters who held the balance of power in many of the northern states. Still, Calhoun calculated that Wilmot's amendment might have its uses in finally realizing his dream of uniting southerners across party lines. "I am of the impression," he wrote, "that if the South acts as it ought, the Wilmot Proviso, instead of proving to be the means of successfully assailing us and our peculiar institution, may be made the occasion of successfully asserting our equality and rights by enabling us to force the issue on the North." By March 1847, Calhoun had launched a movement for southern rights and unity, which inspired anti-Proviso mass meetings across the South. One of these gatherings, in Lowndes County, Alabama, pledged to support no national candidate who favored the Proviso, noting that, on the subject of slavery, "among ourselves we know of no party distinctions and never will know any."

In the North, the Proviso became a rallying point for diverse strands of antislavery opinion that augured the enlargement of political antislavery into a major force in national politics. Liberty Party men, recovering from their weaker-than-expected showing in 1844, took heart from the disruption of the Democracy and saw the Proviso's restrictionism as a powerful new weapon for denationalizing slavery. Among Democrats, rank-and-file support for the Proviso was so strong that even some pro-administration Hunkers felt it necessary to declare their repugnance for slavery (although they remained cool to the Proviso itself). Antislavery new-school Whigs, especially in Massachusetts—where they were coming to be known as "Conscience Whigs"—likewise regarded the Proviso as a boost, giving them needed ammunition against the still-predominant old-guard "Cotton Whigs," who counseled tact and restraint in dealing with their southern Whig allies. The Garrisonian radicals alone expressed skepticism about the Proviso as a political snare—a stance that raised further doubts about Garrisonian tactics in the mind of Frederick Douglass who, along with most black abolitionists, applauded Wilmot's amendment. Increasingly, antislavery northerners began contemplating building a northern democratic counter to what Calhoun was trying to create in the South.

A GRAND PARTY OF FREEDOM?

At the end of 1846, while the political implications of Wilmot's Proviso were beginning to sink in, a young Massachusetts antislavery Whig, the lawyer Charles Sumner, predicted what he called "a new crystallization of parties, in which there shall be one grand Northern party of Freedom." Something resembling that party would emerge in late 1847 and 1848. Mr. Polk's War, although begun with an outpouring of popular patriotism, was becoming a source of intense sectional division. The elements of an extraordinary democratic antislavery uprising were beginning to cohere.

The odds against the success of such an uprising remained formidable. Although the partisan bonds of the Jacksonian era had begun to fray, intersectional organizations and loyalties forged during the intense political conflicts of the 1830s and early 1840s were not easy to disrupt. The meager, if improved, Liberty Party turnout in 1844 suggested that third-party antislavery politics had yet to find anything approaching a northern mass base. Indeed, the outcome of the 1844 elections illustrated the perils of third-party politics and the large possibility that any such effort in 1848 would elect the less desirable of the major-party candidates. The patriotic fervor surrounding the war carried over into 1847 and 1848, in curious counterpoint to the rising discontent, further limiting the appeal of sectional politics. But the struggles that the war provoked and that led to the fight over Wilmot's Proviso were also forcing a redefinition of what it meant to be a Democrat or a Whig—or an American. Those struggles would continue even after the nation's troops had returned from Mexico covered with glory, and after Polk had achieved his dream of a transcontinental republic.

4

WAR, SLAVERY, AND THE
AMERICAN 1848

A long with the War of 1812 and the Vietnam intervention, the war against Mexico generated more dissent than any major military conflict in U.S. history through the twentieth century. Yet unlike the other two, the Mexican War was a rousing military success. The doubts and misgivings that turned into repulsion arose not from American setbacks, but from American victories, culminating in the capture of Mexico City in September 1847. The result was a schizophrenic experience on the home front, filled with both exhilarated celebration of our troops and embittered criticism of the war and its goals.

The schizophrenia carried over into national politics. After David Wilmot introduced his proviso, war and its immediate aftermath intensified factional discord and sectional divisions, leading to a burst of antislavery political activity that created the Free Soil Party. Over the summer and early fall of 1848, as the Free Soil revolt reached its peak, some of its leaders and supporters persuaded themselves that American politics was hurtling toward a crash. Given the frenzy that surrounded the Free Soil effort, those assessments are understandable; antislavery politics would never

be the same. But the immediate outcome of the American struggles of 1848 was the election to the White House of a southern
Whig war hero with no political record, hailed chiefly for his
exploits against the cruel Mexican foe. Cracks appeared in the
nation's political system, but mainstream party leaders, drawing
on patriotic attachment to the Union as well as partisan attach-
ments, papered them over. Most voters appeared to reject sectional schisms and favor moderation—at least for the moment.

"THE DEVIL'S THANKEE": VICTORY'S DIVISIVE GAINS

The American defeat of Mexico occurred in three separate the-
aters of operations. In late February 1847, Zachary Taylor's
army won a bloody but decisive victory over a much larger force
commanded by Santa Anna outside the hacienda of Buena
Vista, near Monterrey. At virtually the same moment, Colonel
Alexander Doniphan's Missouri volunteers, having occupied El
Paso del Norte (what is now Ciudad Juárez), defeated a large
Mexican army in Chihuahua. The victories effectively ended the
north Mexican campaign. In California, despite the defeat of an
American rebellion that declared a Bear Flag Republic, and
despite powerful, temporarily successful uprisings by conquered Mexicans in Los Angeles, American force prevailed by
the end of January 1847, leaving the leader of the Bear Flag
rebels, the explorer John C. Frémont, to negotiate the Treaty of
Cahuenga that secured Upper California for the United States.

The most important campaign, commanded by Winfield Scott,
occurred in central Mexico and led to the fall of Mexico City.
The plan, in the works after November 1846, involved approaching the capital from the Gulf Coast, along the same route Cortés
took in his conquest of the Aztecs three hundred years earlier.
Early in 1847, Scott assembled an invasion force on an island off
the Mexican coast. Following several frustrating delays, he set off
for the port city of Vera Cruz, and after a siege and bombardment

of nearly three weeks, the city surrendered in late March. Scott immediately headed inland. Enduring ferocious combat at Cerro Gordo, San Antonio, Contreras, and Churubusco, the Americans finally stormed the fortress of Chapultepec, overlooking Mexico City, in mid-September. After brief engagements at the city's gates, Scott's army marched into the Main Plaza and hoisted the American flag above the National Palace, the so-called Halls of the Montezumas. A mopping-up operation ensued against refractories led by Santa Anna, but by the end of October, the Americans were digging in at Mexico City, to await the negotiation of a peace treaty. Inside of only eighteen months, Mr. Polk had won his war.

The news of victory after victory set Americans agog—an effect made more stunning by the nation's expanding commercial culture. "People here are all in a state of delirium about the Mexican War. A military ardor pervades all ranks . . . and 'prentice-boys are running off to the wars by scores," the new literary celebrity Herman Melville wrote to his Democratic brother Gansevoort from a small town in upstate New York, early in the conflict. "Nothing is talked of but the 'Halls of the Montezumas.'" Melville had just published his first novel, *Typee*, a picturesque, sexually frank tale based on his experiences in the South Seas. He found the patriotic fervor confusing—though proud of the soldiers' valor, he thought the war was "nothing of itself"—and later wrote a series of satirical articles about General Taylor, "Authentic Anecdotes of Old Zach," and a wild allegorical novel, *Mardi*, with a thinly veiled attack on John C. Calhoun. But the preponderance of the nation's authors, songwriters, playwrights, illustrators, and editors enlisted in the war effort and helped deepen the public's delirium through 1847—enlarging the culture of mass celebration beyond anything Americans had ever known.

The aging James Fenimore Cooper—a critic of the war's management but a celebrator of its sublime uplift of American power—contributed a novel, *Jack Tier; or, The Florida Reef*, about the foiling of a traitorous plot to supply the oppressive Mexicans with gunpowder. George Lippard, an author of highly popular lurid Gothic romances, wrote the rhapsodic *Legends of Mexico: The Battles of Taylor* and a war novel, *'Bel of Prairie Eden*. The best the war could stimulate in the way of poetry, William Gilmore Simms's collection *Areytos: or, Songs of the South*, depicted the invading armies as latter-day chivalric knights. More typical were the blood-and-thunder novelettes churned out by Edward Zane Carroll Judson (later known as the father of the dime novel), and the patriotic lyrics and melodies of George Pope Morris, George Washington Dixon, and lesser-known composers (including such numbers as "General Taylor's Encampment Quickstep" and "The Rio Grande Quick March"). The public also sang adaptations of old patriotic tunes, including a rewrite of "Yankee Doodle" called "Uncle Sam's Song to Miss Texas," with the verse: "If Mexy, back'd by secret foes,/Still talks of taken you, gal,/Why we can lick them all, you know,/An' then annex 'em too, gal." Playwrights, actors' companies, and impresarios mounted several hastily written but grandly produced theatrical melodramas: Joseph C. Foster's "The Siege of Monterey" won rave reviews and played to capacity crowds at New York's Bowery Theater.

War fever created a new American pantheon: democratic variants of the romantic great man described by the Scots poet and critic Thomas Carlyle in his widely read *Of Heroes and Hero Worship*, which had been published in 1841. Zachary Taylor best filled the bill. A career soldier but not a West Point graduate, Taylor had gained a modicum of fame as a resolute, even brutal Indian fighter during the War of 1812 and the second Seminole War (where he won his nickname, "Old Rough and Ready," for his unceremonious manner and his toughness under fire). Yet to most Americans, Taylor appeared to come out of nowhere in 1846, when Polk ordered him to lead his troops to the Rio Grande in the operation that led to war—and his quick victories in northern Mexico made him an instant idol of the new penny press. Admirers likened him to Alexander, Caesar, Napoleon, and (greatest of all) George Washington, and one journalist described him as "the American whom Carlyle would recognize as 'a hero' worthy of his pen's most eloquent recognition: THE MAN OF DUTY in an age of Self!" Talk started of making Taylor president. But there were other new action heroes, including the pompous yet effective Winfield Scott, gently mocked by his men as "Old Fuss and Feathers" but nevertheless the conqueror of Mexico City, and once again a possible presidential nominee. There were many smaller heroes as well, like Major General Samuel Ringgold and Captain George Lincoln, gloriously killed in action and symbolic of all the martyred dead.

Curiously, most of the younger literary lights affiliated with the *Democratic Review* and Young America, previously so belligerent in support of Manifest Destiny and creating a new native literature, either said little about the war publicly or began openly expressing doubts. Nathaniel Hawthorne, who supported the war, wrote nothing of value about it. Walt Whitman tempered his initial enthusiasm after Wilmot introduced his Proviso, and took a strong Radical Democrat stance against allowing slavery into any newly annexed territory. The young writer who made the greatest popular reputation out of the war was not a Young American at all but the twenty-eight-year-old Boston abolitionist James Russell Lowell, whose antiwar dialect satire verses, collected as *The Biglow Papers*, lampooned the conflict as a crusade for slavery. "They jes want this Californy/ So's to lug new slave states in," Lowell's fictional Hosea Biglow proclaimed:

> To abuse ye, an' to scorn ye,
> An' to plunder ye like sin,
>
> Aint it cute to see a Yankee
> Take such everlastin' pains
> All to get the Devil's thankee,
> Helpin' on 'em weld their chains?
> Wy, it's jest ez clear ez figgers,
> Clear ez one an' one makes two,
> Chaps that make black slaves o' niggers
> Want to make wite slaves o' you.

Beside the militarist clamor, antislavery sentiments like Biglow's (including, sometimes, his racism) intensified among northerners after 1846, eliciting predictable angry responses from the South—and creating political confusion in and out of the nation's capital.

The politics of Wilmot's Proviso became the focus of conflict in Congress. President Polk had been injured and angered by the failure of his two-million-dollar appropriations bill after the House saddled it with the amendment. As soon as the new session of Congress assembled in December 1846, he went to work on muffling the slavery issue by lining up support from conservative Democrats including Michigan Senator Lewis Cass. But Preston King's introduction of an enlarged version of the Proviso, the House's affirmation of King's version, and John C. Calhoun's angry resolutions in response seemed to rip the Democratic Party to shreds and forestall any future war appropriations. King's speech in January on the revised Proviso, criticized by some as a ploy to promote Silas Wright for the presidency, placed the New York Barnburners squarely behind the free-soil effort for the long haul. In the House, with the aid of other northerners, the Van Burenites defeated a proposal to extend the Missouri Compromise line of 36°30' that would have ensured the introduction of slavery into all of New Mexico and into Upper California as far north as San Luis Obispo. In Albany, at King's prompting, the Democratic-controlled legislature endorsed both annexation and congressional prohibition of slavery. By mid-February, similar resolutions had passed the legislatures of four other states, including Pennsylvania and Ohio, and five more states followed suit over the succeeding weeks and months. Calhoun could not have been more delighted. "You will see," Calhoun wrote to an associate, "that I have made up the issue between North and South. If we flinch we are gone, but if we stand fast on it, we shall triumph either by compelling the North to yield to our terms, or declaring our independence of them."

The polarization of Van Burenites and Calhounites was complete, but with the help of Senator Cass, Polk managed to hold together the political center and get his way yet again. Cass, the old Jacksonian and anti–Van Buren Conservative, had backed the Wilmot amendment earlier on but had not been required to vote on it. Now, with his presidential aspirations still burning, he charged that the Proviso was causing needless sectional conflict and could prevent the acquisition of a single foot of Mexican territory. With help from the White House, Cass won over northern Democrats from Illinois and Indiana, as well as the Hunker Daniel S. Dickinson of New York, and the Senate approved the administration's unamended appropriations bill, 31 to 21. Sent back to the House, the bill finally passed without the Proviso on March 3, the very last day of the session, when seven northern Democrats changed their votes and six others abstained.

Over the nine-month interval between the close of the Twenty-ninth Congress and the opening of the Thirtieth, partisans in all camps of the Wilmot controversy tried to build support at the political grassroots. In July, President Polk undertook a goodwill tour of the northeastern states. Although he did not explicitly mention the territorial issue, he stressed the need for national harmony. "I would recommend in all parts of our beloved country," he told the Maine state legislature, "cultivation of that feeling of brotherhood and mutual regard between the North and the South, and the East and the West, without which we may not anticipate the perpetuity of our free institutions." Polk did not need to add that he thought the chief offenders against brotherhood and mutual regard included David Wilmot, Preston King, and their presumed commander-in-chief, Silas Wright.

Sectional agitators also worked hard during the recess, sometimes achieving more success than met the eye. Calhoun's movement for southern unity ran into resistance from southern Democratic Party leaders who were willing to extend the Missouri Compromise demarcation to the Pacific and were wary of Calhoun's presidential aspirations. But Calhoun did gain support from important southern Whigs who appreciated his criticisms of the war as well as his stand on the territories. ("[T]he people of the South are now anxiously waiting to see what direction you will give it," Robert Toombs of Georgia, one of the leading Whig congressmen from the Deep South, told him.) And among ordinary southern Democrats, Calhoun's pro-slavery stance was increasingly popular outside his home state. In Virginia, for example, a Democratic faction known as "the Chivalry" won unanimous votes in both houses of the legislature in favor of resolutions based on Calhoun's anti-Wilmot proviso—resolutions henceforth called the "Platform of the South."

Even more strikingly, in Alabama, a young rising Democratic star, the transplanted up-country South Carolinian William Lowndes Yancey, began exercising considerable influence inside the state party. In August 1846, even before Wilmot introduced his amendment, the mild-mannered but strong-willed Yancey, now certain that the northern Democracy was useless to the South, resigned from his House seat. Respecting no party at all and no interest other than slavery, Yancey moved about as he pleased. In the spring of 1847, he persuaded Alabama's Democrats to nominate the man he favored as governor and, later, to back the Platform of the South. After the election (with his man safely in office), Yancey dickered with state Whigs over whom to support for the presidency in 1848. "If this foul spirit of party which thus binds and divides and distracts the South can be broken, hail to him who shall do it," he proclaimed in one speech. Gradually, pro-slavery sectionalism that would surpass Calhoun's was gaining a wider purchase on southern minds.

The political situation in the North was even more ominous, as the battle over slavery extention moved alarmed conservatives and moderates in both parties to restore soundness and caution. Among northern Whigs, divisions between antislavery men and conservatives deepened over how best to oppose the administration and terminate the war. At issue was the "No Territory" position hammered out in response to Wilmot's Proviso. To conservatives, who had initially supported the Proviso but who now had the 1848 elections in mind, "No Territory" looked like the only viable way to end the war, finesse the slavery issue, and preserve national party harmony. "We want no more territory,

NEITHER WITH NOR WITHOUT THE WILMOT PRO-
VISO," proclaimed the *Ohio State Journal*, which only months
earlier had backed the Proviso. The antislavery Whig minority
considered this a political as well as a moral evasion. Anything
less than a ban on slavery, Joshua Giddings told the House,
would encourage the slavocrats: "a revolution after the example
of Texas will take place, and annexation to this Union, with a vast
increase in the slave power in the councils of the nation, will be
the result."

The breach in the Whigs' ranks became particularly severe in
Massachusetts, where the conservative so-called Cotton Whig
faction (themselves split by a long-time feud between the allies
of Daniel Webster and those of Abbott Lawrence) predominated
over the minority antislavery Conscience Whigs. At the Whig
state convention in 1846, Webster and Lawrence had paraded
into the meeting hall for one session arm in arm, in a display of
unity against the antislavery insurgents. A year later, however, the
conservatives were divided over presidential politics—the Webster forces wanting to nominate their man, the Lawrence faction
favoring Zachary Taylor—thereby handing Conscience Whigs
the balance of power. Webster finally received the Conscience
Whigs' backing, although it came so grudgingly that the prize was
not worth the candle. But with that business done, Lawrence rallied the conservatives to defeat a resolution pledging all Whig
candidates to support the Wilmot Proviso, thereby creating enormous bitterness among the minority. Soothing words from Webster at the convention's conclusion could not undo the damage.
Never again would the Massachusetts antislavery men attend a
Whig state convention.

The fights between New York's antislavery Barnburner and
conservative Hunker Democrats created an even more involved
and fateful division. The entire history of the Polk administration
had alienated the Barnburners from the White House and
widened the old split in the New York Democracy. The Whigs'
victory over Radical Governor Silas Wright in 1846—achieved,
as even Polk angrily noted, with the malign connivance of the

Hunkers—was a prelude to all-out war. By the spring and early summer of 1847, the undaunted congressional antislavery Democrats, including Preston King and David Wilmot, looked to Wright, the Hunkers' victim, as their candidate for the Democratic presidential nomination in 1848. So did a number of men in the pragmatic wing of the Liberty Party, including Salmon P. Chase, who promised Wright that the party would support him if he ran on a pro–Wilmot Proviso platform. A series of Democratic antislavery mass meetings in New York State, beginning in January 1847, augured a convergence of Liberty men and dissident Barnburners.

Wright was a shrewd as well as a popular choice for the antislavery forces. A charter member of Van Buren's Albany Regency, he had complete credibility as a professional politician who had always submerged his personal interests on behalf of the Democratic Party: honest, unselfish, and affable, if much too fond of alcohol. Wright also had strong antislavery credentials, dating back to his opposition to Texas annexation. His defeat in 1846, at the hands of the Whigs and the Hunkers—and, it was wrongly assumed, President Polk—had only elevated his stature among antislavery Democrats. After his loss, Wright returned to his plebeian rural origins in northern New York, quit drinking, and worked hard on his farm, with his public life, he thought, behind him. Apparently he was uninterested when, in 1847, his name began appearing atop newspaper mastheads as the people's choice for president. But none of it would matter, for in August, Wright keeled over from a heart attack and died, at age fifty-two.

"Burnt out at last," Calhoun reveled when he heard of Wright's passing. Barnburners and other antislavery Democrats were disconsolate. "Ah, it has a crashing effect, still!" Walt Whitman wrote soon after hearing the news, adding that all Radical Democrats "were so identified with this man—relied so upon him in the future—were so accustomed to look upon him as our tower of strength, as a shield for righteous people—that we indeed feel pressed to the very earth by such an unexpected blow." The Barnburners were still grief-stricken when New York's Democrats gathered in Syracuse for their state convention two weeks later. Even without Wright's death, they would have fought hard with the Hunkers over state economic policy and national policy on slavery, but now the Barnburners also had a martyr. "The great chiefs of both factions were on the ground," the visiting Liberty Party abolitionist Henry B. Stanton observed, "and never was there a more fierce, bitter and relentless conflict between the Narragansetts and the Pequods than this memorable contest between the Barnburners and the Hunkers." A Barnburner delegate called on the convention to do justice to Silas Wright; a Hunker sneered in reply that it was too late, Wright was dead; whereupon another Barnburner leapt atop a table and declaimed that, though it might be too late to do Wright justice, "it is not too late to do justice to his assassins." The Hunkers, controlling a small majority of the delegates, defeated resolutions endorsing the Wilmot Proviso and seized the state party machinery. The embittered Barnburners left the convention and, led by John Van Buren, called for a meeting of their own in October in the nearby town of Herkimer.

United in their outrage, the Barnburners differed over strategy and tactics. Many of the older heads, as well as Van Buren's sympathetic father, thought an overtly disloyal breakaway movement would prove self-defeating, and tried to head off the dissidents' meeting. But to the younger schismatics, all of the injuries since the 1844 national convention had begun to dissolve into a revolt against Polk, the Slave Power, and their Hunker servants. The events of August and September also touched an antislavery nerve among rank-and-file Barnburner Democrats that no call to party regularity could relieve. More than four thousand persons turned up in tiny Herkimer and gathered at the railroad station, the largest building in town. The old radical Jacksonian and Loco Foco sympathizer Churchill Cambreleng was brought in to lend a sense of continuity with the past, and named president of the assembly. David Wilmot proclaimed that the party's abiding mission was "to elevate man, to vindicate his rights, to secure his happiness"—a mission that "Slavery commands halt." The main speaker, John Van Buren, held the crowd rapt with his enthusiastic oratory—a skill his father had never commanded—and demanded no further extension of slavery, "in behalf of the free white laborers of the North and the South." The convention summarized the antislavery Democracy's outlook with a credo that would resound in American politics over the next dozen years: "Free Trade, Free Labor, Free Soil, Free Speech, and Free Men."

"I know of no event in the History of Parties in this Country, at all approaching, in sublimity & moment, the Herkimer Convention," Salmon Chase wrote to Charles Sumner. Regular Democrats, as well as older Barnburner sympathizers like Martin Van Buren, took a different view, as the party's division led directly to Whig triumphs in the fall election. (Pro-Herkimer Democrats, determined to defeat the Hunker candidate for governor, handed in spoiled ballots, inscribed "REMEMBER SILAS WRIGHT!") But as autumn gave way to winter, antislavery insurgents began pleading with old Van Buren to try once again for the presidency, this time on a pro–Wilmot Proviso platform. "You, Sir, are the only man left for us in the North, to whom we can look for advice," Wilmot wrote to the former president. Van Buren, who steadfastly refused publicly to endorse the Wilmot Proviso, kept Democrats guessing until late December, when he suddenly departed Lindenwald and took up quarters in New York City, at Julien's Hotel on Washington Square. There he would begin a new political venture.

In Washington, debates over the war issue dragged on. The new Congress that assembled in December included an enlarged number of antislavery Whigs—part of the new Whig majority in the House of Representatives elected in 1846. These new arrivals were not as radical on the slavery issue as the Joshua Giddings hard core, but they were likely to raise uncomfortable partisan issues about Polk's handling of the war. Outside Washington, antislavery men in both parties were angrier than ever at their respective party establishments. Yet even in the North, conservative Democrats and conservative Whigs controlled the state parties' machinery, and as the presidential election year dawned, it seemed likely that they and their southern colleagues would control the national parties as well. Among antislavery men, there was no consensus on whether to fight the good fight from within or to take the politically risky course of allying with the Liberty men and forming a party of their own. And in the South, there remained the perpetual puzzlement over what John C. Calhoun would do, and what difference it would make.

THE AMERICAN 1848: BACKGROUND TO REVOLT

Revolutions tore across Europe in 1848, proclaiming a new age of liberal democracy—until reaction overtook the revolutionaries and installed a revised version of the post-Napoleonic conservative order. A similar, if far less violent dynamic unfolded in the United States. While Whigs viewed the European revolutions with dismay—"Poor France," Henry Clay said when he heard the news of the Paris uprising—Democrats of all factions hailed the demise of despotism and the vindication of the rights of man. Antislavery Democrats took the uprisings as a spur to their own labors. *"Shall we, in view of these struggles of all Europe, with our model before them,"* the Barnburner O. C. Gardiner wrote in one pamphlet, *"renounce the doctrine of our fathers, and the sentiments of the civilized world, that slavery is an evil?"*

General Scott's victory at Mexico City had ended the military phase of the war, but the diplomatic phase that followed proved politically nearly as difficult. As long as the dispatches of military triumph had flowed in, patriotic fervor helped offset sectional divisions. But when weeks passed with no final treaty, political fights took precedence. Although vanquished on the field, the Mexican government refused to negotiate a settlement—suspicious, Polk's opponents claimed, that the administration now intended to swallow up most or even all of Mexico. "We should have had peace in September, but for the inexorable determination of the Executive to acquire a large slice of Mexico by conquest," Greeley's *Tribune* charged. Those charges gained credence in December when Polk, in his annual message, requested additional monies and troops to conclude the war, denounced the No Territory doctrine as an acknowledgment of American guilt, and claimed that the only alternative left to Mexico was "an adequate cession of territory" to the United States. Some took this to mean, despite Polk's explicit denials, that the "adequate cession" ought to be the entire country of Mexico.

The "All Mexico" movement, which the president supposedly supported in secret, caught fire amid the frustrations of the autumn of 1847, and it assembled some strange bedfellows. Its leading proponents were the Manifest Destiny Democrats of the eastern penny press, who saw the total absorption of the foe as a blow for universal freedom. But a small number of antislavery advocates, led by Gamaliel Bailey, came up with their own version of the plan, whereby any or all of Mexico's nineteen states could voluntarily choose to join the United States. Like the antislavery Whigs, Bailey had denounced the war as unchristian and a threat to American democracy (although he ridiculed Whigs who criticized the conflict yet continued to vote in favor of war appropriations). Yet, Bailey also approved of the expansionist drive to acquire new territories, so long as it was done, as he put it, "by the natural process of colonization and assimilation." Now that Mexico was conquered, the United States had a duty to widen republicanism's ambit, and not leave its defeated foe in disarray. Above all, Bailey assumed that as the Mexican states had already abolished slavery, they would remain free states under the American flag, and send a large new crop of antislavery senators and representatives to Washington—a complete inversion of what most antiwar Whigs and abolitionists believed was the war's underlying evil motive.

How much the All Mexico movement actually influenced the Polk administration is questionable, although within the cabinet both Secretary Buchanan and Secretary Walker were known to be sympathetic. But the strong perception that it had gained the initiative reinforced the Whig Party's solidarity across sectional lines. Among moderate and conservative northern Whigs, the idea, to them repugnant, of grabbing all of Mexico, slave or free, strengthened support for the No Territory position. Among southern Whigs, the All Mexico proposal had the additional repellent aspect of adding new states that were unfit for slavery and populated by antagonistic racial inferiors, unfit for enlightened free government. "Do you wish to be placed at the mercy of ten millions," one Georgia Whig paper asked, "hostile to you, as enemies and conquerors, in the first place, and as supporters of [slavery] in the next?" With their slender majority in the new House, the Whigs could cause Polk significant political trouble if they unified behind No Territory.

The antiwar Whigs also had enough southern sectionalist allies to thwart a few of Polk's grander initiatives. On January 4, 1848, Calhoun delivered a major speech reiterating the defensive line strategy he had proposed a year earlier. Going further with the war, he warned, would turn the United States into an "imperial power" and would only compound the nation's racial difficulties. "I protest against the incorporation of such a people," Calhoun observed of the Indian and "mixed blood" Mexicans: "Ours is the government of the white man." The alliance of Calhounites and Whigs blocked an administration appropriations bill to fund the raising of ten new regiments, and stymied the president's requests for twenty thousand new volunteers to fight the war and for duties on coffee and tea to help pay for it.

These anti-administration victories hardly signaled the rise of a unified and all-powerful antiwar opposition. Even for the No Territory Whigs, the largest group, articulating an agreed-upon policy proved easier than acting on it when faced with practical choices. Most shared the view that Congress ought to reject Polk's requests for more appropriations, but others, wanting to avoid looking unsupportive of American troops, agreed to ordinary requests for supplies. Still others, eager to end the war and fearing that Polk could successfully seize all of Mexico no matter how much Congress objected, announced their willingness to compromise and accept new territory short of what one editor called "the line where indemnity ends and conquest begins," usually meaning New Mexico and California. Divided among themselves, as well as against the pro-Wilmot minority, the No Territory Whigs had to fall back on whatever ingenious maneuvers they could to embarrass the Polk administration and the Democrats.

One of the most partisan of these Whig schemers was the ambitious ex-state legislator from Illinois whom Martin Van Buren had run across in 1842: Abraham Lincoln. In 1846, Lincoln finally overcame his melancholia and won election to Congress. The sole Whig representative from heavily Democratic (and heavily pro-war) Illinois, Lincoln went along with the administration's supply requests. But as if to prove his Whig bona fides, he also introduced a series of resolutions demanding that the administration provide evidence that the spot on which American blood was first shed over Texas was indeed on American soil. Lincoln pronounced Polk guilty of deception in getting the war started, and attacked him personally as "a bewildered, confounded, and miserably-perplexed man." His so-called spot resolutions earned their author the derisive nickname "Spotty" Lincoln but accomplished little else. After stepping aside to make way for another Whig candidate, he returned home to Springfield in 1849, the latest congressional one-term wonder.

Suddenly, in late February, news arrived that a peace treaty had been concluded in Mexico and been sent to Polk for his consideration and agreement. The president's negotiator, Nicholas Trist, had accompanied Scott's army into Mexico City and, after being snubbed repeatedly by the Mexicans, received orders from Polk to return home. But Trist disobeyed, reopened talks with a newly elected Mexican regime, and, on February 2, signed a treaty in the village of Guadalupe Hidalgo, near the capital. Compared to what Polk had envisaged in 1845, the deal turned out to be a bargain: the United States would secure all of Texas above the Rio Grande and receive Upper California and New Mexico in exchange for $15 million plus American assumption of all outstanding private American claims against Mexico, which totaled about $3.25 million. Polk at first hesitated, unclear about the agreement's legitimacy, but after recognizing that Trist had negotiated under the terms originally set for him, and that any prolongation of the war would be even more politically disastrous, Polk sent the treaty to the Senate for ratification. A war begun under dubious circumstances would end with dubious authority.

Senate approval of the treaty was not assured. Several members of the Foreign Relations Committee, of both parties, objected that Trist had had no powers to negotiate on behalf of the government once he had been recalled. Some Democrats thought the agreement gave the United States far too little territory; some Whigs, including the die-hard No Territory man Daniel Webster, thought it gave the United States far too much. But as secret deliberations continued, the prospect of finally ending the war overcame all other considerations. "The desire for peace," Calhoun wrote, "& not the approbation of its terms, induces the Senate to yield its consent." After two weeks of discussion, the Senate approved the treaty in a lopsided vote of 38 to 14 that cut across both partisan and sectional lines. The political press, although not uniformly pleased with the result, expressed relief that wonderful peace had returned.

In antislavery circles, the relief was mixed with sorrow. On February 21, the same day the Senate received the treaty with Mexico, the House was debating one of the honorific resolutions of gratitude to the military that antiwar forces routinely voted against, but that always passed. Suddenly, Washington Hunt of New York interrupted the Speaker, and several members rushed over to the desk of eighty-year-old John Quincy Adams, who, after attempting to rise to make some remarks, had toppled nearly to the floor, his face flushed. Carried from the airless chamber into the Speaker's room, Adams lay, barely conscious, for two days. In a passing moment of alertness, he asked to have Henry Clay brought to him, and the old battlers bid each other a tearful goodbye. "This is the end of earth—I am composed,"

Adams is said to have murmured, and then he was dead.

Adams had been the last link in American politics to the era of the American Revolution. In death, he received the public acclaim he had longed for, and never quite received, in his lifetime. Masses of Americans mourned him, both in the Capitol where he lay in state and alongside the railroad tracks over which his body returned to Boston, where thousands lined up to catch a glimpse of the funeral train. Thomas Hart Benton and Daniel Webster wrote tributes; Isaac Holmes of South Carolina, who had supported Adams's censure in 1842, put politics aside to mourn the passing of "the PATRIOT SAGE." (Henry A. Wise had already complimented Adams, backhandedly, as "the acutest, the astutest, the archest enemy of Southern slavery that ever existed.") Little of this would have been imaginable had Adams died before his return to Congress: it was Adams's second career, and his canny fight against the Slave Power, that brought him popular adulation. Although Old Man Eloquent Adams remained too set in his independent ways to endorse political abolitionism outright—or to give more than qualified support to the Wilmot Proviso—he had opened a path that younger antislavery politicians had followed and would follow over the years to come. They included three men present on the floor of the House when he was stricken: the political abolitionist Henry B. Stanton, the radical Whig Joshua Giddings, and the moderate Whig Abraham Lincoln.

The conclusion of the Mexican War—celebrated on July 4, when President Polk formally declared the Treaty of Guadalupe Hidalgo in effect—ended debate over the extent of American expansion, but brought the slavery extension issue to the fore once again, now entangled in presidential politics. Either the national parties and their candidates would support the principles of the Wilmot Proviso or they would not—a matter some would raise insistently and others would do their utmost to evade.

Among the Democrats, who would hold their nominating convention first, attention focused on the badly divided New Yorkers. In February, the Barnburners met in Utica to select their own slate of delegates to the Baltimore nominating convention and adopt a pro–Wilmot Proviso platform. (The Hunkers had held their own meeting in late January.) Passions had cooled slightly since the Herkimer convention, and to prove their party loyalty, the Barnburners dropped the demand that any Democratic presidential candidate support nonextension of slavery. But the growing insurgency had also won over some of the older Barnburners, above all Martin Van Buren. Later that winter, with the help of his son John and Samuel Tilden, Van Buren composed an address, soon to be known as the Barnburner Manifesto, to be read to the Democrats of the state legislature. Although it backed no national candidate, the document emphatically endorsed the Wilmot Proviso and insisted that the Barnburner delegation alone be seated at the Baltimore convention.

At last, the elder Van Buren had taken an unequivocal stance on the extension of slavery. "Free labor and slave labor . . . cannot flourish under the same laws," the manifesto asserted. "The wealthy capitalists who own slaves disdain manual labor, and the whites who are compelled to submit to it . . . cannot act on terms of equality with the masters." If he still refused to allow his own name to be put forward as a pro-Wilmot candidate at the Democratic national convention, Van Buren was eager to put his hard-fought wisdom in service to the dissidents' cause. To his son John, he stressed the importance of blending firmness with common sense. A "single rash and unadvised step" would make them look "indifferent to the general success of the party," motivated by a desire "to revenge past injuries or indulge personal piques." If not admitted to the convention on a full and equal footing with the other delegates, he counseled, the Barnburners should depart the proceedings, making clear that they did so "upon the ground of opposition to the extension of Slavery to free Territories." If admitted, they should make their case to the convention, but be prepared to support whatever candidate won the nomination— unless it was the now intolerable James K. Polk. In late May, the Barnburners traveled to Baltimore full of Van Buren's advice. They would insist on their legitimacy as the sole voice of the New

York Democracy and fight to uphold nonextension of slavery—
two matters that were now one and the same.

The convention, starting on May 22, could not have gone
worse for the Barnburners. After a day of preliminaries, the delegates took up the Barnburners' and Hunkers' rival credentials
claims, and the hall turned into a cacophonous confusion. First
the credentials committee attempted summarily to award New
York's seats to the Hunkers. Led by the Barnburners' bitter opponent, William Lowndes Yancey of Alabama—who may have
feared such a precedent might some day be used against pro-
slavery men—the convention allowed the Barnburners to make
their case. For four hours, the delegates listened to each side.
Yancey then moved a resolution that denounced the Barnburners
as "factious Whigs in disguise and abolitionists" and awarded the
seats to the Hunkers, but after a break for dinner, he withdrew
his motion. Finally, the convention decided, by a tiny majority, to
allow both delegations to be seated and cast New York's votes
jointly. The next day, both sides refused the offer but resolutely
held on to their seats in the convention hall.

Unable to resolve the New York impasse, the delegates proceeded to the nominations. Polk, true to his original pledge, had
decided not to try again, and the three top contenders were
familiar: the conservatives James Buchanan and Lewis Cass, and
the moderate Levi Woodbury. After an eight-ballot battle—with
all of the New Yorkers looking on glumly—the nomination went
to Cass, the uninspiring Michigander who had initially supported
the Wilmot Proviso and then led the fight in Congress against it.
Tumultuous applause greeted the announcement of Cass's triumph—then, suddenly, one of the sidelined Barnburner delegates, M. J. C. Smith, arose to speak. With the hall hushed,
Smith denounced the convention and its candidate, and when he
finished, all of the Barnburner delegates angrily walked out. They
had not followed Van Buren's advice to the letter: by bolting the
convention after the convention had selected its candidate, and
not immediately upon being denied their full credentials, they
invited accusations (as Van Buren had predicted) of an unpar-

donable breach of party decorum. Soon, however, the Barnburners and their allies would be planning an even larger rebellion—and Van Buren would wind up heading it.

The loyalist Democrats completed their work by naming the anti-Wilmot military hero and former congressman William O. Butler of Kentucky as Cass's running mate, and by approving a platform that condemned those who would "induce Congress to interfere with questions of slavery, or to take incipient steps in relation thereto." This was not good enough for Yancey and the more militant pro-slavery southerners. Although mostly satisfied with the platform, they understood that Cass had endorsed an alternative to the Wilmot Proviso which had gained currency among northern moderate and conservative Democrats—the idea of "popular sovereignty," whereby, at some undetermined date, the inhabitants of a territory could decide for themselves whether slavery would be permitted. As the platform was unclear on the matter, Yancey moved an amendment that would have committed the party to the core idea of the Platform of the South, that all territories be opened to slaveholders and their property. The convention resoundingly defeated the motion, whereupon Yancey and another Alabaman along with the Florida delegation walked out amid loud jeers.

Two weeks later, the Whigs opened their convention in Philadelphia. Both of the party's grand old men, Henry Clay and Daniel Webster, had announced for the nomination, but Webster enjoyed only the lukewarm endorsement of his own state's delegation and was nearly forgotten; and Clay, although still revered, was a two-time loser who remained suspect on all sides of the slavery question. The really exciting prospect to the party insiders was General Zachary Taylor. Apart from being the most celebrated man in America, Taylor owned slaves and a large Louisiana cotton plantation, which made him safe enough for the South, especially compared to the Yankee Democratic nominee, Lewis Cass. Taylor had also disagreed with Polk about the conduct of the war, and at one point asked to be relieved of his command, which softened his image among some northerners. Best of all, Taylor's own politics were so indistinct that on the eve of the presidential contest, it was not entirely clear which party he favored, making him an ideal figure in a divisive time. (When he finally chose the Whigs, he hastened to add that he was "not an ultra Whig," sustaining his useful ambiguity.) Taylor stood for national glory as opposed to sectional or partisan division. Indeed, more than Whig managers understood or would have preferred, Taylor, the professional soldier, would come to regard nonpartisanship as a fundamental principle, in government as well as in electioneering.

Taylor's bandwagon of diverse supporters came to Philadelphia well prepared. (They included Abraham Lincoln who, though he worshipped Henry Clay, had decided Clay could never win.) A strong plurality went to Taylor on the first ballot, including several delegates previously pledged to Clay; two ballots later, Clay's forces nearly broke; on the fourth ballot, Taylor was nominated. After selecting the conservative New Yorker Millard Fillmore as Taylor's running mate, and not bothering to approve a platform, the convention adjourned. (After the fact, the Whigs issued a platitudinous simulacrum of a platform, affirming little more than that Taylor, "had he voted in 1844, would have voted the Whig ticket," and promising "Peace, Prosperity, and Union.") The antiwar and anti-annexation party had nominated the greatest hero of the war for the presidency of the United States.

As Old Zach's energized supporters returned home to campaign, other Whigs stood aghast. Horace Greeley, a pro-Clay New York delegate, called the convention "a slaughterhouse of Whig principles." Fifteen other northern delegates and alternates asked a group of Ohio antislavery men led by Salmon Chase (who had already scheduled a Free Territory Convention in Columbus later in the month) to convene an additional anti-extension convention in Buffalo, New York, early in August, in order to forge some sort of merger. The Columbus meeting, one thousand strong, approved the idea, while all across the North, antislavery Whigs repudiated the Philadelphia convention. "This is the cup offered by the slaveholders for us to drink," one Ohio paper protested. "We loathe the sight." The stage was nearly set for the Free Soil revolt.

"THE GREATEST QUESTION OF THE DAY": THE FREE SOIL REVOLT

Two weeks after Taylor's nomination, the New York Barnburners held their own meeting, once again in Utica. After their walkout at the Democratic convention, there was intense pressure on the rebels to curb their anger—or at least direct it solely against the New York Hunkers. But there were also great public outbursts of antislavery support. A large crowd greeted the mutinous Barnburner delegates at the Manhattan train station when they returned from Baltimore, whence the Barnburners went to City Hall Park to deliver defiant speeches before an even larger crowd of twelve thousand. "A clap of political thunder will be heard in this country next November that will make the propogandists of slavery shake like Belshazzar," exclaimed the old Regency man and Barnburner Samuel Young (the same man who had led the fight against black suffrage in 1821). A few days later, the delegation formally asked the New York party to repudiate Cass's nomination— "the price of the most abject subserviency to the slave power"—and then to select its own presidential candidate in Utica on June 22. The insurgency spread among Democrats in New York State, then throughout the North. Hundreds of Barnburners turned up in Utica, along with a small number of antislavery New York Whigs and about twenty antislavery Democratic representatives from Massachusetts, Connecticut, Ohio, Illinois, and Wisconsin. Letters and telegrams pledging support poured in from across the North. The delegates resolved to form what they called Jeffersonian Leagues to fight for "Free Soil and free principles."

All that the movement lacked was a candidate. Benton turned the rebels down; so did New York's more conservative senator John Dix and (the unlikeliest selection) John Hale's persecutor in New Hampshire, Franklin Pierce. It was almost inevitable that the antislavery organizers would return to Martin Van Buren—and, to his friends' dismay, Van Buren seemed increasingly willing at least to leave the possibility open. Only Benjamin Butler of all the old Regency men encouraged Van Buren, envisaging a "northern Democratic party" that might "bring the despots & ingrates of the South & their obsequious satellites of the North, to their senses." ("I consider the prohibition of Slavery in the territories now free, the greatest question of the day," Butler wrote. "[A]s soon as the Mexican war is ended, it will be the only question . . . and fifty years hence, those who took a firm stand for the prohibition will be regarded as the greatest of public benefactors.") When asked to reconsider and allow his name to be put forward at Utica, Van Buren wrote two lengthy drafts before composing a nineteen-page reply. After claiming he did not wish to run, Van Buren called slavery inconsistent with the "principles of the Revolution," and declared that it should be kept out of the territories. Butler read the document to the Barnburners at Utica, who, swept away, inferred, correctly, that Van Buren actually would consent to run, and nominated him for president as a pro-Wilmot Democrat. Their platform defended the walkout in Baltimore, endorsed a number of traditional Democratic positions, upheld the Wilmot Proviso, and denounced slavery "as a great moral, social, and political evil—a relic of barbarism which must necessarily be swept away in the progress of Christian civilization."

The Utica outcome was as disturbing to mainstream national Democrats as it was suspect to many antislavery veterans. President Polk called it "more threatening to the Union" than anything since the Hartford Convention. One southern Democrat attacked Van Buren's Utica letter as "the fierce war-cry of a new and formidable party," headed by a crafty politician reborn as "a bold, unscrupulous and vindictive demagogue." At the other end of the spectrum, Liberty men had strong misgivings about Van Buren from his days when he endorsed the gag rule, opposed abolition in the District of Columbia, and otherwise deferred to the slaveholders. Salmon P. Chase said he would have preferred John Van Buren to his father as the nominee. Others, including antislavery Whigs, sought assurances about Van Buren's sincerity.

The momentum of the Utica meeting, however, pushed both political abolitionists and antislavery Whigs into the pro–Van Buren Democratic camp. John Parker Hale, who had received the Liberty Party's presidential endorsement the previous year, was willing to stand aside for the sake of unity. Preparatory to the grand antislavery meeting in Buffalo, now scheduled for August 9, the practical good sense of rallying behind Van Buren and the Barnburners began to dawn on political antislavery advocates. "[T]hings tend to Van Buren as our candidate," Charles Sumner remarked. "I am willing to take him. With him we can break the slavepower; that is our first aim." There was even a new name being bandied about as the antislavery label: either the Free Democracy or, even better, the Free Soil Party.

Van Buren's decision to join a schism, let alone lead one, was obviously difficult, but it cannot be explained as an act of revenge, as many of his critics and later historians alleged. Van Buren's resentment of the Hunkers and the Polk administration, and his concerns over who would control both the state and national parties, had certainly worsened since 1844. The downfall of the now-martyred Silas Wright had been the last straw. But Van Buren's anger was controlled and purposeful, and it involved basic principles about slavery and antislavery as well as factional loyalties. If he was far from the most outspoken or radical of the Barnburners on the slavery-extension question, Van Buren had long been sympathetic to men like Theodore Sedgwick III and Silas Wright. His momentous letter on Texas annexation in 1844 was hardly calculated to advance his standing in the South, where he had always been suspect, and he had never renounced it. Van Buren's calm and measured correspondence in 1847 and 1848, and his steadily solidifying support for the principle of nonextension, betray no sense of vengefulness; indeed, he took pains to warn the younger Barnburners to avoid such impulses or even the appearance of them. Van Buren's intensely political side and his sense of principle had merged into a mistrust of the increasingly aggressive pro-slavery forces that had apparently grabbed the helm of the Democratic Party—forces, he told Francis Blair, that had "grossly humiliated" northern Democrats in order to expand slavery. Whereas in the 1830s, Van Buren had accommodated southern demands while trying to temper the Calhounite extremists, he now hoped that a show of force would knock some sense back into the southern Democrats and restore the balance of sectional forces on which the party had been built—after which it would be safe to rejoin the party he had helped to found. If pushing back the Slave Power was the only way to redeem the Democracy, then Van Buren was willing to lead the way.

Other unexpected events accompanied the Barnburner revolt, including another democratic uprising in central New York—one very different from and far smaller than the Barnburners', but encouraged by the atmosphere of rebellion that pervaded the politics of 1848. Henry B. Stanton, the abolitionist and Liberty Party activist, kept in close touch with the antislavery Barnburners, whom he admired as the "Girondists of the Democracy." Stanton had attended the 1847 Syracuse convention as an interested spectator. He would go on to play a leading role at the Buffalo meeting in August 1848 and win a seat in the New York state senate as a Free Soiler in 1849. Also in 1848, he moved with his wife Elizabeth and their three sons from the clatter of Boston to the small, drab mill town of Seneca Falls, New York, in the heart of the reformist region that had successively spawned evangelical revivals, abolitionist campaigns, and utopian experiments—and was now roiled by the Barnburner insurgency.

Elizabeth Cady Stanton, at age thirty-three, was an accomplished woman. The daughter of the prominent Federalist jurist, law teacher, and, eventually, state Supreme Court justice Daniel Cady, she had been educated at Emma Willard's pioneering Troy Female Seminary and had been well schooled informally in legal affairs by her father. Encounters with fugitive slaves while visiting the home of her wealthy cousin, Gerrit Smith, led Cady to the abolitionist movement, where she met Henry Stanton, whom she married (against her father's wishes) in 1840. It was a match of tireless reformers. Less than two weeks after their wedding, the couple embarked for London, where, along with other leading American abolitionists including William Lloyd Garrison, they attended a momentous World Anti-Slavery Congress—a meeting notable for the Americans' refusal to heed the convention rule separating male from female delegates with a curtain.

Living on the outskirts of Boston, Henry and Elizabeth Stanton were at home in the most active abolitionist circles, which included the already legendary Philadelphia Quaker Garrisonian, Lucretia Mott, whom Elizabeth had befriended at the London congress in 1840. Yet while she participated in various lobbying efforts to reform laws discriminatory to women, Stanton stepped back from full-time engagement to attend to her growing family. The withdrawal brought enormous personal satisfactions, but also frustrations, which became intolerable after the move to isolated Seneca Falls. With her husband nearly always gone on his antislavery work, with three sons to look after and no household help, Stanton began to suffer, she later recalled, from "mental hunger which, like an empty stomach, is very depressing." Overwhelmed, she retreated for a time to her parents' home in Johnstown. A daguerreotype of Stanton from these years shows an attractive, slightly disheveled young mother entwined with two of her sons—but with an arresting, searching stare.

In July 1848, James and Lucretia Mott, on a journey through upstate New York, paid their annual summer visit to see Lucretia's sister Martha and Martha's husband, David Wright, in Auburn. A Quaker neighbor in nearby Waterloo, Jane Hunt, invited Lucretia and Martha to tea, with the happy news that Elizabeth Stanton, now living only a few miles down the road, would be joining them, along with another friend, Mary Ann McClintock. The table talk quickly turned to politics—and to a promise that Stanton and Mott had made to each other, at the conclusion of the London convention eight years earlier, to form a society to advocate the rights of women. Soon, Elizabeth was pouring out her personal dissatisfactions with such vehemence that, she later recalled, "I stirred myself, as well as the rest of the party, to do and dare anything." The next day, a notice appeared in the *Seneca County Courier*, announcing that a two-day Woman's Rights Convention would be held the following week at the Wesleyan Chapel in Seneca Falls, featuring a speech by none other than the celebrated Lucretia Mott.

To the organizers' delighted surprise, upward of three hundred persons crowded the Seneca Falls chapel on the convention's first day. (Originally, the first session was supposed to be open to women only, but after a hasty caucus, the organizers decided to allow the men, including Mott's husband, to stay.) For two days, the participants were treated to a heady mixture of history, reportage, and satire on the oppressed status of women in the United States and around the world. Lucretia Mott, not surprisingly, dominated the proceedings. But Stanton and McClintock also addressed the convention, and Stanton, the lawyer's daughter, had taken on the job of composing a declaration of sentiments. She wrote the document as a self-conscious adaptation of Jefferson's Declaration of Independence, altered to proclaim that all men and women were created equal—with the demand that women be accorded "the sacred right of elective franchise." The most celebrated man in attendance, Frederick Douglass, Mott's fellow Garrisonian, helped persuade the group to approve a suffrage resolution, which passed by a narrow margin. At the conclusion, Mott took the floor again to give a spirited address that lasted nearly an hour, exhorting women to press on with their fight. One hundred of those present, one-third of them men, signed Stanton's manifesto.

The backlash was immediate. Conservative Whig newspapers served up particularly savage commentary. "[A] dreadful revolt," the *Oneida Whig* proclaimed, adding that the convention was "the most shocking and unnatural incident ever recorded in the history of womanity." At the *New York Herald*, James Gordon Bennett handled the story as if it were a farce, and took special pleasure in smearing Lucretia Mott as a misfit full of "old maid-ish crochets and socialist violations of Christian dignity." Only the antislavery press took the convention at all seriously.

The Seneca Falls convention drew on more than the sudden inspiration of Mott, Stanton, and their friends. Legal reformism, free-thought radicalism, Quaker piety, and abolitionism all had an influence, and would create the foundations of the American women's rights movement for the next half century. But the meet-ing was certainly connected closely, in spirit as well as timing, to the Barnburner revolt—an indication of how the rifts over slavery were opening up new democratic possibilities. The greatest com-mon political identification of the participants at Seneca Falls—including eighteen of the twenty-six separate families with members who signed the Declaration of Sentiments—was with the emerging Free Soil alliance, including the most radical Barn-burner Democrats, antislavery Whigs, and the pragmatic wing of the Liberty Party. It was not that most Free Soilers were also women's rights advocates. (If they had been, the meeting at Seneca Falls would have been far larger than it was.) Nor did Stanton, Mott, and the others act to advance the Barnburners' or the Liberty Party's political fortunes. Still, a highly disproportion-ate number of those who turned up at Seneca Falls were tied in one way or another to the Free Soil milieu. For them, as for Stan-ton, women's rights was a logical extension of the fight for liberty, equality, and independence being waged by the antislavery forces that, during the Seneca Falls convention, were preparing to take their stand three weeks later in Buffalo.

The antislavery forces generated a mass movement in late June and July, proclaiming America's version of the revolution of 1848—a revolution fought not at the barricades but in conven-tion halls, village greens, and city streets across the North. Less than a week after the Barnburners' Utica meeting, five thousand Conscience Whigs, along with a handful of Massachusetts Democrats, assembled in Worcester, listened to speeches attack-ing what Charles Sumner called the unholy alliance between "cotton planters and flesh mongers of Louisiana" and "cotton

spinners and traffickers in New England," and selected six delegates to attend the upcoming Buffalo convention. Smaller antislavery meetings assembled throughout New England and New
York, organized by Whigs and Democrats alike. Antislavery activity in the Northwest amazed observers. "We cannot find room for
even brief notices of all the Free Soil meetings in Ohio," the
National Era reported. "The people there seem to be cutting
loose *en masse* from the old party organizations." In Indiana—
previously cold to third-party antislavery politics—and in Michigan, statewide and local gatherings selected delegations to
Buffalo and resolved to end all partisan differences in order to
unite "for the one great cause of Free Soil and Free Labor." In
Chicago, processions of antislavery Democrats and Whigs
snaked through the city, chanting Martin Van Buren's name.

The Buffalo National Free Soil Convention was multifarious
and boisterous. Barnburners, Whigs, and Liberty men predominated, with a substantial portion of the latter two groups still
uneasy about nominating Van Buren. But there were many other
elements present, each holding some grievance against one or
both of the major political parties: Democrats indifferent to the
slavery issue but still rankled by Van Buren's snubbing in 1844;
Clay Whigs furious at the nomination of Zachary Taylor; antislavery Whigs "breathing the spirit of the departed John Quincy
Adams" (as Henry Stanton later put it); northwesterners, chiefly
Democrats, angry at Polk's veto of river and harbor improvements; and land reformers allied with George Henry Evans, who
now thought cheap homesteads were the workingman's salvation.
Gathered beneath a massive tent erected in the city's public park,
the army of political pilgrims, no fewer than twenty thousand
persons, reminded observers of a gigantic religious revival.

Among the crowds was a delegate from Brooklyn, the pro-
Wilmot Democrat Walt Whitman, recently returned from an
extended stay in New Orleans. Whitman's outspoken views on
politics and slavery had cost him his job as editor of the *Brooklyn
Daily Eagle*, whose owner was an unforgiving Hunker. They had
also begun shaping his poetic imagination: "I go with the slaves of

the earth equally with the masters," he wrote in his notebook in 1847, among the first recorded lines in what would become his mature style. But the poet was still in the middle of what Ralph Waldo Emerson would later call his "long foreground," and politics came first. Fired up by the mounting agitation and the Buffalo proceedings, Whitman would return to Brooklyn and begin editing a new paper he had started planning months earlier, in service to the cause: "Free Soilers! Radicals! Liberty Men! All whose throats are not rough enough to swallow Taylor or Cass! Come up and subscribe to the Daily Freeman!"

The most politically awkward presence was a small group of black abolitionist leaders, including Charles Remond, Samuel Ringgold Ward, Henry Bibb, Henry Highland Garnet, and, most prominently, Frederick Douglass. Douglass had written a powerful autobiography, *Narrative of the Life of Frederick Douglass, An American Slave*, which became an immediate best-seller in 1845. After a two-year sojourn lecturing in Britain and Ireland, he settled with his wife, Anna, in Rochester, New York, an antislavery hotbed, and took up a new career as editor of the *North Star*, intended as a western equivalent of Garrison's *Liberator*. Throughout, Douglass remained, at least outwardly, a Garrisonian, upholding ideals of moral suasion and nonresistance that set him apart from Ward, Bibb, Garnet, and other black members of the Liberty Party. Yet Douglass was also in political and intellectual transition. Although wary of all party politicians—let alone one with hands as dirty as Martin Van Buren's—he attended the Buffalo gathering, curious to see how the invigorated antislavery political agitation would play itself out.

Simply by showing up, Douglass and the other black leaders caused consternation—a sign of important racial divisions that distinguished the more Negrophobic of the antislavery Democrats from the Liberty Party men and antislavery Whigs. Although the convention formally recognized and accepted Douglass and the others, the acceptance was not universal. One delegate later wrote that the Barnburners had not wanted Douglass admitted because "they didn't want a 'nigger' to talk to them."

Others appear to have been willing to tolerate Douglass—who was, after all, famous—but not the other black men. Racist pro-Wilmot Democrats, who despised blacks as well as slavery, wanted to keep their Free Soil convention as lily-white as they hoped to keep the federal territories. It was a portent of the convention's eventual decision to avoid the question of black rights in its national platform, a retreat from the racial egalitarianism propounded by the Liberty Party in 1840 and 1844.

The most remarkable thing about the Buffalo meeting, however, was not its racism but its success in submerging political differences in the common cause—creating a program, heavily influenced by the antislavery Jacksonians' and pragmatic Liberty men's ideas, that the proud Douglass would regard as an imperfect but "noble step in the right direction." A torchlit rally in the park on the eve of the convention set the tone, as a dozen speakers called for a united effort against slavery and the Slave Power. "This Convention must be a self-sacrificing Convention," one Barnburner speaker inveighed the next day at the convention's opening. "A crisis has arrived where old prejudices [have] got to be laid aside." With the turnout much larger than expected, Preston King devised a plan whereby each state delegation would appoint six delegates to form a committee of conferees, which would deliberate on the main issues before the convention and then refer their decision to the tented masses for ratification. The arrangement worked smoothly. Meeting behind closed doors at the Universalist Church, the conferees, chaired by Salmon Chase, appointed a subcommittee on resolutions, headed by Benjamin Butler. The main body of delegates settled in for long hours of militant speechmaking, presided over by the convention's permanent chairman, Charles Francis Adams. (Among the speakers were Frederick Douglass and Henry Bibb, who overcame the racists' objections, received respectful applause, and wished the party well.) In time, the delegates would be asked to approve a platform, as drafted by the resolutions subcommittee and the conferees; then they would vote on the conferees' choice of national candidates.

The platform, chiefly the work of Chase, Butler, and King, was an unambiguous call for the divorce of slavery and state. Its key plank demanded that the federal government "relieve itself of all responsibility for the existence and continuance of slavery" wherever it possessed the constitutional authority to do so. This committed the new party to abolishing slavery in the District of Columbia as well as the territories, and to any additional action the antislavery men might decide was within the national government's purview—thereby pushing the Democratic delegates well beyond the terms of the Wilmot Proviso. The conferees added an assortment of other proposals, ranging from cheaper postal rates and a lower tariff to river and harbor improvements (the last thrown in to attract Whigs and western Democrats), but the party's main purpose was unmistakable. The platform concluded with an abbreviated version of the Barnburners' battle cry from the Herkimer meeting a year earlier: "We inscribe on our banner, 'Free Soil, Free Speech, Free Labor, and Free Men,' and under it will fight on, and fight ever, until a triumphant victory shall reward our exertions." The general assembly approved each plank in the platform with a roar.

The choice of a presidential candidate presented greater difficulties. Some Liberty men and antislavery Whigs still could not stomach the idea of supporting Van Buren. (When Butler, in a speech extolling his friend, went on at length about the former president's skills as a farmer, a delegate interrupted: "D——n his turnips! What are his opinions about the abolition of slavery in the District of Columbia?") But a sense of greater purpose prevailed. "In common with my Whig associates, I had all along felt that I could not support Mr. Van Buren under any circumstances," George Julian of Indiana later recalled, "but the pervading tone of earnestness in the Convention, and the growing spirit of political fraternity, had modified our views. We saw that several of the great leaders of the Liberty party were quite ready to meet the 'Barnburners' on common ground."

The Barnburners' favorite candidate was just as ready to find common ground with the more radical political abolitionists, even if it meant giving up the Utica nomination and abandoning the Democratic Party, at least for this election. In a letter read to the committee of conferees by Benjamin Butler, Van Buren explained that although he had acquiesced in the Barnburners' nomination to help sustain "the ever faithful democracy of New York," the Buffalo convention was of far greater importance— greater, perhaps, than any before it "save, only, that which framed the Federal Constitution." Van Buren affirmed his dedication to keeping "human slavery . . . that great evil" out of the territories. (He would go on to reverse his old stance and pledge that he would sign a bill to abolish slavery in the District of Columbia.) And if, in the spirit of unity, delegates thought it better that he run solely as a Free Soiler, and not as a Democrat, he would happily do so. Deafening cheers followed Butler's reading of the letter, and Van Buren was quickly nominated over the radicals' favorite John Hale, winning the support of about half the Whigs and a small but influential group of Liberty men including Salmon Chase and Henry Stanton. After a brief adjournment, the conferees named Charles Francis Adams, still grieving for his father, as Van Buren's running mate.

The proposed ticket—uniting Andrew Jackson's right-hand man with the son of the man Jackson had overthrown—won the general assembly's approval with one more roar; then the assembled marched and celebrated in a torchlight parade, behind a giant banner:

'87 and '48
JEFFERSON AND VAN BUREN
No Compromise

The atmosphere of spiritual as well as political revival had converted even adamant radicals. Before the convention, Joshua Leavitt, the veteran evangelical, immediatist abolitionist, and Liberty Party man, contended dismissively that Van Buren was acting more "to avenge his old quarrel with the Hunkers than for sympathy for the cause" of free soil and antislavery. Near the convention's close, after Van Buren had won his majority, Leavitt obtained the floor and addressed the convention in a voice choked with emotion. "Mr. Chairman," he began, "this is the most solemn experience of my life. I feel as if in the immediate presence of the Divine Spirit." Then he moved that Van Buren's nomination be made unanimous, and concluded with a shout: "The Liberty party is not dead but TRANSLATED."

Between them, Van Buren and Leavitt had aptly summarized the surpassing importance of the Free Soil convention. Although the new nominee flattered the delegates with his exaggerated comparison to the 1787 federal convention, he was correct to see the gathering as an important turn in American politics, the first deliberate effort to create from the grass roots, out of the disintegration of old party ties, a new political party that would seriously contend for the presidency. When Van Buren had helped cobble together the Jackson Democracy twenty years earlier, he operated from the top down; the Free Soil Party, by contrast, arose seemingly by spontaneous combustion amid the emergency over slavery in 1848. The Liberty Party had taken years to move beyond the political margins; in "translating" those efforts, the Free Soilers represented a wide-ranging political coalition from across the North, with a particularly heavy influx of pro-Wilmot Democrats. Nothing like it had been seen before, the product of a great shudder of popular revulsion and democratic organizing that united men who, all their lives, had opposed each other in politics. "The political table is now turning . . . ," one Ohio Free Soiler wrote, "and by a little effort now great changes can be wrought."

Joshua Leavitt, meanwhile, although somewhat carried away by his enthusiasm, recognized correctly that the Free Soil Party had preserved the essentials of the Liberty Party's crusade, especially as it had been conducted by Salmon Chase, Gamaliel Bailey, and the pragmatic western political abolitionists. The new party did contain its share of open racists, who chiefly wanted to keep blacks out of the territories—although even they declared slavery a moral and political evil. Some spokesmen seemed to go out of their way to distance themselves from abolitionists of any variety. ("The question is not, whether black men are to be made free," one Barnburner bolter declared at the second Utica convention, "but whether we white men are to remain free.") The Free Soil platform's silence about fugitive slaves, the three-fifths clause, and racial discrimination diluted the egalitarian principles of the Liberty Party and hard-core antislavery Whigs—as, to many, did the party's nomination of Martin Van Buren. There would be those who, like William Goodell, believed that the Free Soilers betrayed political abolitionism by placing "its claim to liberty on the lowest possible ground, that of the non-extension of slavery." Many historians have agreed, and portrayed the Free Soil Party as an inglorious step backward for the antislavery movement, sacrificing the goal of black equality in a cynical effort to win votes.

Leavitt and the majority of Liberty Party leaders and supporters knew better. By going beyond the Wilmot Proviso and calling for the complete divorce of slavery and the federal government, and by denouncing the moral enormity of black slavery, the Free Soil Party endorsed what had long been the primary objective of the Liberty men, and in a manner that might actually get masses of voters to listen. "It pledges the new party against the addition of any more Slave States, and to employ the Federal Government not to limit, localize, and discourage, but to abolish slavery wherever it has Constitutional power to do so," one political abolitionist said of the Buffalo platform. "This is all the Liberty party, as such, ever demanded." Whatever their constitutional scruples about interfering with the rights of slave states, observed Owen Lovejoy, brother of the abolitionist martyr Elijah Lovejoy, the two parties' "ultimate object is identical—the extinction of slavery." At those who said they could not abide the thought of voting for Martin Van Buren, Gamaliel Bailey leveled a stark retort: "It is folly to talk to us of the conduct of this man in 1836–40. You say it was subservient of slavery—grant it—what is his course now? . . . You stone Van Buren for his sins committed twelve years ago, though *you* yourself now fall far below the well-doing to which he has since attained!"

Enthused by the drama of the Buffalo convention, the Free Soilers leapt into the 1848 campaign barely organized and short of time and money, but confident that their cause would sweep through the northern states. Huge majorities in the Western Reserve, Chase informed Van Buren, would swing Ohio into the Free Soil column. George Fogg, an ex-Democrat Free Soiler, thought New York would break for Van Buren, as would enough smaller northern states to throw the election into the House of Representatives. Even William Lloyd Garrison found himself caught up in the whirlwind. Although he thought the party's anti-extension, pro-Wilmot position weaker than a spider's web, Garrison called it "gratifying to see the old parties dissolving, 'like the baseless fabric of a vision,'" and he duly reported on the Free Soilers' "eloquent appeals."

"PARTY CONNEXIONS STILL RETAIN MUCH OF THEIR FORCE"

The Free Soil fever broke in November.

Early in the campaign, the Whig candidate, Zachary Taylor, began looking like a poor choice. By repeating professions about the weakness of his party ties, his campaign alienated genuine Whigs. Exasperated party managers finally prevailed on him to write a public letter stating that although he was not an "ultra" Whig, at least he was a "decided" one. It was sufficient to bring wary party members back into the fold, including antislavery men such as William Henry Seward, who were aghast at the possibility that Lewis Cass might be president. The Democrats hammered away at Taylor as two-faced and unprincipled. Cass also tried to square the circle of anti-slavery politics by promoting "popular sovereignty"—the somewhat vague, supposedly democratic solution that would allow the settlers in each territory to decide the slavery issue for themselves. (Taylor even more vaguely announced that he would leave the entire question up to Congress, while some of his northern supporters assured their constituents that he would never veto the Wilmot Proviso.)

The Free Soilers, short on funds but long on enthusiasm, deployed dozens of "stumpers" who fanned out across the North to denounce Cass as a doughface and Taylor as a slaveholding political nonentity. The usual name-calling and campaign hoopla dominated the run-up to the election, although the electorate seemed, overall, less engaged than in the previous two elections.

The Whig strategy worked. In part because of his military glory, but mainly on the strength of his being a large slaveholder, Taylor reversed the Whigs' southern setbacks in 1844, carried Georgia and Florida as well as his home state, Louisiana, and came within a whisker of winning Alabama and Mississippi. Overall, Taylor gained more than half of the total popular vote in the slave states. He also won convincingly in Pennsylvania and New Jersey. New York appeared to decide the election: by capturing more than one out of four New York voters and running second statewide, the Free Soilers took enough Democratic votes away from Lewis Cass to hand New York's thirty-six electoral votes to Taylor. Yet the Free Soilers also took enough votes away from Taylor in Ohio and, possibly, Indiana to give those states to Cass, virtually wiping out the New York advantage. Ultimately, Taylor's convincing victories in the Upper South states of Kentucky, Tennessee, and North Carolina gave him the presidency.

The Van Buren–Adams ticket, meanwhile, won just 10 percent of the national popular vote and just 15 percent of the vote in the free states. The Free Soilers managed to best Cass in New York, Vermont, and Massachusetts, but failed to win a single electoral vote; in only one state, Vermont (and there just barely), did their popular vote come within 10 percentage points of doing so. Had the Free Soilers not run a presidential ticket, Taylor would probably have been elected anyway. As in Europe, it seemed the American 1848 had ended in the rebels' defeat.

Why had the antislavery excitement produced what looked and felt to so many like an anticlimax? Nobody had expected the Van Buren–Adams ticket to prevail outright, but the outcome was still a letdown after the high hopes of August, when antislavery optimists had forecast a deadlocked election. Some Free Soilers who had come over from the Whigs or the Liberty Party blamed their disappointment on Van Buren's nomination, which certainly cost the party support in northeastern Ohio and other parts of greater New England. Yet the magnitude of the Free Soilers' presidential defeat cannot be explained so easily. (Nor did this explanation account for the Radical Democrats who voted Free Soil *because* Van Buren was the nominee.) Plainly, the frenzy at Buffalo unrealistically inflated expectations of the party's organizers, especially those like the exuberant Charles Sumner who had relatively little prior experience in national politics. As the election neared, Charles Francis Adams, who understood national politics well, arrived at more realistic expectations, later borne out by the result. "Enough is visible" to confirm, Adams wrote in mid-October, "that the people of the Free States are not yet roused so fully as they should be to the necessity of sustaining their principles."

The party stumbled over obstacles that confront any third-party effort under the American constitutional system. Before the entry of the Free Soilers, the 1848 campaign had been a dreary affair, filled with the now-familiar spectacles staged by the party managers and focused on personal innuendo. After August, the Free Soilers enlivened the election—but at the cost of having the major parties blast them as dangerous zealots and enemies of the white man. George W. Julian later vividly recalled the abuse:

> I was subjected to a torrent of billingsgate which rivaled the fish market. Words were neither minced nor mollified, but made the vehicles of political wrath and the explosions of personal malice. The charge of abolitionism was flung at me everywhere. I was an "amalgamationist" and a "wooly head." I was branded as the "apostle of disunion" and the orator of "free dirt." It was a standing charge of the Whigs that I carried a lock of Frederick Douglass, to regale my senses with its aroma when I grew faint. . . . I was threatened with mob violence by my own neighbors.

In northern areas strongly influenced by antislavery ideas, Democrats stressed the Free Soilers' disloyalty; Whigs called the new party a bunch of Loco Foco radicals in disguise; and each party bid its old supporters not to waste their votes on a will-o'-the-wisp that would only help their old enemies. In other northern areas and in the slaveholding states (where the Van Buren ticket did not even appear on the ballot), the major parties tried to outdo each other in presenting their man as the eternal foe of Yankee "nigger"-loving heresy.

On the flip side of these attacks, antislavery Whigs who might have been expected to join the Free Soil effort (and some who had appeared supportive early on) decided to stick with the Whig Party, chiefly because they saw in Old Zach a winner at last. Both leading and middle-level Whigs who either claimed to be or were viewed as being opposed to slavery's extension spurned and sometimes harshly attacked the Van Buren–Adams ticket. Daniel Webster, Thurlow Weed, and Horace Greeley (who veered toward the Free Soilers but got pulled into line partly with a one-session replacement appointment to Congress), as well as less celebrated but highly effective campaigners like Thaddeus Stevens and Abraham Lincoln, all honored Whig unity and political self-preservation over the anti-extension principle in 1848. (Lincoln, a strong speaker, enthusiastically stumped in antislavery areas in Massachusetts and Illinois, and said with a straight face that "the self-named 'Free Soil' party" was far behind the Whigs with regard to the Wilmot Proviso.) Except in Massachusetts and Ohio, Whig support for the Free Soilers was negligible. More than 80 percent of the Free Soil vote in New York, New Jersey, and Pennsylvania came from erstwhile Democrats, while at best only 10 percent came from the Whigs. If, from the vantage point of 1848, a seer had predicted that one of the major parties was doomed to collapse over slavery, the Democrats would have seemed the more likely of the two.

Overall, the results bore out Charles Francis Adams's contention that "[p]arty connexions still retain much of their force." Outside New York, seat of the Barnburner schism, the great preponderance of Democratic voters who went to the polls voted Democratic, and the great preponderance of Whigs voted Whig. Party identities born of the political clashes of the 1830s remained stubborn, as did fears of letting the other side prevail. To the extent that the major parties lost support in 1848, it was due more to absenteeism by an apathetic electorate who disliked all of the candidates than to defections. The most pronounced switching of parties in the country involved a surge to the Whigs in the Deep South states of Alabama and Mississippi, which the Democrats managed to win anyway; otherwise, the key to the outcome appears to have been that the Whigs did a better job of keeping their voters from staying at home than the Democrats did. The chief message from the voters was that most of them did not care for the sectional bitterness that at times seemed to have engulfed the nation's capital, and wanted a moderate solution to the issues connected with slavery.

None of which meant, however, that the former status quo had been restored, or that the political dramas of 1848 had not affected the dynamics of American politics. Disappointment was not the same thing as repudiation. Martin Van Buren, over-looking his own inflated rhetoric of 1848, realized as much, and later expressed this sober second thought: "Everything was accomplished by the Free Soil movement that the most sanguine friend could hope for and much that there was no good reason to expect." The total vote for the Van Buren–Adams ticket marked a fivefold increase over the Liberty Party vote for Birney and Morris in 1844—a major advance for antislavery politics, even if it was smaller than the most fervent Free Soilers had expected. The Free Soilers also enjoyed some important victories in congressional contests as well as in races for local offices, electing eight men to the House and helping to elect four others in coalitions with antislavery Whigs. In 1849, an alliance of Democrats and Free Soilers in the Ohio legislature would select Salmon P. Chase for the U.S. Senate, where he would join sitting Senator John P. Hale, who had switched his affiliation to the Free Soil Party. (Simultaneously, Democratic state legislators switched their previous positions and helped finally abolish Ohio's notorious black codes.) In New York, Thurlow Weed brokered the election to the Senate of William Henry Seward—a Whig and not a Free Soiler, but a man of established antislavery convictions. More than ever, Congress would include northern members whose political careers were now linked to agitation over slavery. And, more than ever, erstwhile northern Democratic voters, by the tens of thousands, had voted for candidates of an avowedly antislavery party. The contradictions between equality and slavery that had begun hampering the old Jackson Democracy in the late 1830s were now splitting apart the northern Democracy.

Nor had the election eliminated the sectionalist pro-slavery southerners as a force to be reckoned with in the future. The schismatic Alabaman William Lowndes Yancey, having been hooted out of the Democrats' Baltimore convention, did not fare much better thereafter, outside South Carolina, in trying to rally southerners behind pro-slavery principles; even the South Carolina legislature wound up handing the state's electoral votes to the Democratic ticket. Old Calhoun, now afflicted by the tuberculosis that would kill him, took a public stance of neutrality between what he said had become "two miserable factions." But in his personal correspondence, Calhoun's fury at the Democrats outweighed other considerations. "In my opinion, the best result, that can take place," he wrote from Washington in July, "is the defeat of Gen Cass, without our being responsible for it." Calhoun's wish came true—and in December, with the election safely over, he prevailed upon the South Carolina legislature to approve, unanimously, an ominous resolution, announcing its readiness "to cooperate with her sister states" in resisting any application of the Wilmot Proviso "at any and all hazards." In time, the lawmakers of Alabama, Virginia, Florida, and Missouri would endorse Calhoun's position.

Above all, even if most voters seemed to favor moderation, after 1848 it was far from clear what a successful moderate program would look like with regard to the slavery and territorial issues. The composition of the new Thirty-first Congress—where Democrats held an eight-seat majority in the Senate, but where the House was evenly divided—gave no indication of what was to come. Each of the various compromise proposals that were making the rounds—ranging from the popular sovereignty idea, to keeping the territories free of slavery until the enactment of a positive law permitted its existence, to leaving the entire matter up to the Supreme Court—was open to clashing interpretations. Sectional animosities were swollen and sore. Although it had defeated the uprisings of 1848, the political center was fragile. And more than any other American, the responsibility for preserving it fell on an old soldier who had never even voted for president until he voted for himself—and who, more than anyone realized, was determined to be his own man.

5

POLITICAL TRUCE, UNEASY CONSEQUENCES

Early in January 1849, Henry Clay crossed paths with President-elect Taylor aboard a steamship at Baton Rouge. Clay was on his way to spend the winter in New Orleans, where, in February, he would learn that the Kentucky legislature had returned him to the U.S. Senate. At first Clay did not recognize the man who had defeated him for his party's presidential nomination. It was an understandable gaffe: the two did not know each other well at all, and the diminutive, poorly educated General Taylor emanated no authority off the battlefield. But Clay was embarrassed. After he found Taylor still on board, Clay extended his hand, saying that the general "had grown out of my recognition." Taylor was at least superficially gracious. "You can never grow out of mine," he replied, shaking Clay's hand vigorously. There the conversation politely but pointedly ended. Ten years after his struggles with William Henry Harrison and John Tyler, Clay would find himself back in Washington, dealing with an unfriendly Whig in the White House.

Taylor's critics, including Clay, who considered him a dithering political figurehead, were in for a surprise. Not only did Taylor want to take charge of the government; he wanted to remake the Whig Party completely by throwing aside Clay's and Webster's "ultra" orthodoxies on economics and by luring Free Soil Whigs back into the fold. Having declared, long before his election, that he would never be "the slave of a party instead of the chief magistrate of the nation," Taylor patterned himself after another general-turned-president, George Washington, by attempting to govern above sordid partisan designs. But democracy had rendered the nonpartisan ideals of the Federalist era obsolete, so Taylor instead tried to build his own nationalistic, moderate party, soon to be known as the Taylor Republicans.

Taylor surrounded himself mainly with unimaginative if unobjectionable men on whom he could rely for personal loyalty. (The major exceptions, in the cabinet, were the talented secretary of state, John Clayton of Delaware, and, in the new post of secretary of the interior, Thomas Ewing of Ohio.) Southern Whigs, presumably Taylor's political base, were conspicuously scarce in his inner counsels. Taylor replaced the staid old official Washington Whig paper, the *National Intelligencer*, with the *Republic*, geared to promoting his personal ambitions and his new party of no-party. Most alarmingly to Whig supporters, Taylor made little effort to ensure that government jobs went to party loyalists.

Taylor also turned out to have strong views about territorial policy, a matter made even more urgent by a great unearthing in California. In January 1848, construction laborers were building a sawmill for Johann Sutter, the German-Swiss emigrant whose settlement near Sacramento, Nueva Helvetia, had been secured by American forces early in the war with Mexico. One of Sutter's men noticed gold flakes shimmering in the bed of the American River. News of the find quickly arrived in San Francisco, then headed eastward, and finally turned up in President Polk's final annual message, in a reference to the "extraordinary" California discoveries. The California gold rush was on. By the end of 1849, some eighty thousand Americans, a larger population than either of the states of Delaware or Florida, had arrived in what beckoned as the new El Dorado.

Gold fever added to the pressure to bring California into the Union. The size of the area's new population foretold California's admission sooner rather than later; the roughneck lawlessness of the gold rush camps demanded the creation of some kind of accountable American authority; and the overwhelming dispro-portion of free-state emigrants to the region all but guaranteed that any new territorial or state constitution would exclude slav-ery. But if California demanded attention, so did the rest of the newly acquired Mexican cession, including an unusual American religious settlement over the western slope of the Wasatch Mountains, in the wasteland abutting Great Salt Lake.

The Church of Jesus Christ of Latter-day Saints was one of the most successful of the spiritual enthusiasms that swept through the Yankee Northeast in the 1820s and 1830s—and it was by far the most daring. In 1823, in Palmyra, New York, a young Vermont-born farmer named Joseph Smith Jr. received a visitation in his log cabin from the angel Moroni, who, after severe testing, led him to golden plates atop the hill Cumorah that translated into the Book of Mormon. After Prophet Smith guided a troop of followers westward to Ohio and later to Illinois (where a mob killed him in 1844), his command fell to an extraordinary organizer, Brigham Young, who completed the church's hegira to Salt Lake in 1847 and was named its second prophet. By 1849, thousands of other Mormon converts had set-tled in the region (the total would reach twenty thousand by 1852), holding to their American-inspired scripture and following the practices, above all polygamy, that had helped make them so despised back East. In his headquarters at Salt Lake, Young mapped out a sprawling new Mormon Zion, which he called Deseret, and began negotiating for control with the American government, which had formally obtained the land from Mexico shortly after Young and his pioneer Mormon party had settled there.

President Polk, exhausted and prematurely aged—he would die three months after leaving office, probably of cholera—tried to persuade the lame-duck session of the Thirtieth Congress to admit California and New Mexico as territories and solve the slavery issue by extending the Missouri Compromise line of 36°30' to the Pacific. The proposal was dead on arrival at Capitol Hill. Antislavery members of the House reintroduced the Wilmot Proviso, drafted a constitution for California barring slavery, and passed a resolution calling for the abolition of the slave trade in Washington, D.C. Southerners fought back, some now warning of outright secession. A pro-slavery caucus asked Calhoun to draft a formal response, and Calhoun complied with his "Address of Southern Delegates in Congress to their Constituents." The address denounced a string of alleged northern abuses dating back to the Missouri crisis of 1819–21 and charged that the addition of new states without slavery would lead the North to force the South into total submission. Inspired by grand theories as well as changing political realities—he had completed his "Disquisition on Government" begun six years earlier and started working on an even longer manuscript about the American Constitution—Calhoun stopped short of disunionism but bid the South to unite on a "course of policy that may quietly and peaceably terminate this long conflict between the two sections."

Calhoun's manifesto received a mixed response from southern congressmen—favorable from the great majority of Democrats, but hostile from Whigs who, as Alexander Stephens put it, felt "*secure* under General Taylor." The southern Whigs' confidence would soon disappear. Although a slaveholder and an expansionist, Taylor cared little about the introduction of slavery into the newly acquired territories, where, he believed, the institution would never take root. Taylor's nationalism, born of his lifelong military career, persuaded him that the southern insistence on slaveholders' rights was a divisive conceit that might destroy the Union in the name of legalistic abstractions. As much like a general as a politician, he planned an audacious field maneuver, proposing to bypass the territorial stage altogether (and thus render the Wilmot Proviso moot) and admit California and New Mexico directly as free states. Over objections at what one southern Democrat called his "monstrous trick and injustice," Taylor sent agents to Monterey and Santa Fe to urge settlers to begin drafting state constitutions. Sparsely settled New Mexico would be slow to act, but the Californians were at work even before Taylor's man arrived. In October 1849, California ratified a new state constitution barring slavery and, a month later, elected a governor and a legislature that petitioned Congress for statehood.

By the time the Thirty-first Congress assembled in December 1849, Taylor's combination of nonpartisanship and nationalism had thoroughly demoralized Whig leaders of both sections and enraged southerners of both parties. Jefferson Davis, the former army officer and now a Democratic senator from Mississippi—and Taylor's son-in-law—denounced Taylor's territorial plans as the final step in destroying the balance of power between the sections. "If, by your legislation, you seek to drive us from the territories of California and New Mexico, purchased by the common blood and treasure of the whole people . . . ," the Georgia Whig Robert Toombs roared early in the new Congress's first session, "*I am for disunion.*" In October, a bipartisan meeting in Jackson, Mississippi, called for a southern rights convention to assemble in Nashville the following June "to devise and adopt some mode of resistance to northern aggression." Not surprisingly, southern Whigs took a terrible beating in the off-year state elections.

Some old party loyalties and rivalries further complicated national politics, and to a degree they mitigated the sectional rancor. Although independent antislavery opinion remained strong in New England and northwestern areas, Barnburner Democrats, having made their point during the Free Soil revolt, largely returned to the Democratic Party. Some were confident they had taught the Slave Power a lesson; others were chastened by the Free Soilers' indifferent showing in the presidential tallies of 1848. "We can exercise more influence with our friends—with our own party—than we can standing outside as antagonists," one antislavery New York Democrat later observed. Important northern conservative Whigs, including Daniel Webster, were still allied with southern Whigs, who were gravitating to the idea of popular sovereignty detested by southern Democrats. Internal party splits in New York over patronage and slavery divided the Whigs between the old "progressive" forces of Thurlow Weed and newly elected Senator William Seward and the more conservative Whigs, now headed by Taylor's new vice president, former congressman Millard Fillmore. (Eventually, the latter would be nicknamed the "Silver Grays" after the hair color of one of their number, Francis Granger.) Caught in the crosswinds of party and section, the political system had broken down into a myriad of factions, no one of which held anything close to a working majority. Success would belong to those skilled parliamentarians, dedicated to keeping slavery out of national politics, who could fashion coalitions out of the confusion.

THE EVASIVE TRUCE OF 1850

Two basic misconceptions have marred understanding of the congressional bargain known as the Compromise of 1850. The first stems from the familiar story of how the surviving disinterested wise men of the Senate, led by the Great Compromiser Henry Clay, stepped in one last time to broker national peace over slavery. In fact, the older heads, far from disinterested, stirred enormous conflict and left much of the difficult backroom work to younger men, whose motives were partisan as well as patriotic. Second, the very idea that the bargain was a compromise is misleading. A genuine compromise involves each side conceding something in order to reach an accord. What occurred in 1850 was very different: the passage of a series of separate laws, some of them purposefully evasive on crucial issues, with the majority of congressmen from one section voting in each case against the majority of congressmen from the other. The phrase "Compromise of 1850"—like the "Missouri Compromise" of 1820–21, which in many ways the deal resembled—has been so routinely repeated by generations of historians and schoolteachers that it is unlikely ever to be replaced. But the bargain was actually more of a balancing act, a truce that delayed, but could not prevent, even greater crises over slavery.

The difficulties facing sectional and partisan peacemakers became obvious when the newly elected House of Representatives tried to pick a Speaker in December 1849. Although the Democrats held a marginal plurality of seats, the presence of twelve Free Soilers and one nativist member, along with divisions within the major parties, made a hash of partisan regularity. The Whigs put up their incumbent, an aristocratic but well-liked conservative Massachusetts Cotton Whig, Robert Winthrop. The Democrats countered with the planter Howell Cobb of Georgia, a genial veteran of the House (though only thirty-four years old) who had refused to sign Calhoun's "Address." After three weeks of jostling and more than sixty ballots, neither candidate had won the required absolute majority. Free Soil Whigs failed to back Winthrop because he had abandoned his initial support for the Wilmot Proviso; a half dozen southern Whigs refused to support him because he once *had* supported the Proviso; and several southern Democrats deemed Cobb insufficiently reliable. "The house is not yet organized & parties are becoming inflamed," one diarist observed, with slavery issues disguising "the ambitious designs of demagogues." Finally, on the sixty-third ballot, the members agreed to abide by a mere plurality, and Cobb was elected Speaker by a margin of three votes. Cobb in turn named friendly moderate Democrats to the key chairmanships. But the chaos had hardly been resolved, and would break out anew once debate over the territorial question began in the Senate.

President Taylor, unruffled by southern talk of disunion and the impending southern rights convention in Nashville, presented his territorial plan in a special message to Congress in January 1850, calling for California's admission to the Union as a free state at once, and New Mexico's admission as soon as it was ready. Having once blamed Yankee abolitionists and Free Soilers as the instigators of sectional divisions, he was now persuaded that the greatest fault lay with "intolerant and revolutionary" southerners, led by Jefferson Davis. Taylor's fury fed the south-

erners' own, which persuaded even skeptical northern congressmen that their threats of secession were deadly earnest and
might well be made real at the Nashville meeting. Then, into the
fray, in one last effort to placate the South, stepped Henry Clay.

As ever, Clay had complicated motives. His desire to save the
Union was sincere. Equally sincere was his desire to save the
Whig Party by shoving aside the stubborn president and establishing his own dominance. On January 29, he presented his
alternative to Taylor's plan in the form of eight resolutions, six of
them paired as compromises between the North and South. In
the first pair, Clay called for the admission of California as a free
state and the organization of the remainder of the Mexican cession, including Brigham Young's Deseret, without "any restriction
or condition on the subject of slavery." The second set resolved
an existing boundary dispute between Texas and New Mexico in
favor of the latter—a pro-northern position that would reduce the
chance of a new slave state being carved out of Texas—while also
assuming outstanding debts contracted by the Republic of Texas.
Clay's third pair of resolutions tried to offset the resumed antislavery campaigns in the District of Columbia by appealing for
abolition of the slave trade, but not slavery itself, inside the District. The seventh and eighth resolutions were pro-southern,
denying congressional authority over the interstate slave trade
and calling for a stiffened federal law for the recovery of fugitive
slaves, in reaction to the personal liberty laws enacted by the
northern states.

Superficially, Clay's compromise tilted in favor of the South.
Its rejection of the Wilmot Proviso principle was sufficient to
enrage and permanently alienate the most committed antislavery
northerners. When he first proposed his resolutions, Clay said he
was asking the North to make the "more liberal and extensive
concession." Yet beneath the surface, and at times explicitly, Clay,
the Border South moderate, also repudiated what had become
the political axioms of the Deep South: that slavery was a benevolent institution which deserved to expand along with the rest of
the country, and that a belligerent Yankee minority had risen up

to oppress the slaveholders. Much as he had in the debate over congressional powers during the Missouri crisis thirty years earlier, the Kentuckian was speaking heresy to pro-slavery hardliners. Once broken out of their "pairing" formula, Clay's proposals handed all of the truly important decisions about the territories—the admission of California and the adjustment of the New Mexico–Texas border—to the North. Although Clay opposed, on grounds of prudence, the abolition of slavery in the District of Columbia, he insisted that Congress had the full power to do so if it chose—a sticking point with the South since the abolitionist petition campaigns of the mid-1830s. Even in the supposedly pro-southern fugitive slave proposal, Clay backed the guarantee of jury trials to decide on individual cases—a sop to the North that was certain to undermine any new process of returning runaways to their masters. In a five-hour follow-up speech commending his compromise, Clay not only failed to defend slavery; he charged that over the previous fifty years, the South had exercised a "preponderating influence" over national affairs and should now display forbearance and statesmanship before the citizenry and Almighty God.

Clay's two greatest surviving colleagues presented lengthy replies in the Senate. On March 4, the dying John C. Calhoun sat at his desk, wrapped in flannels, his eyes blazing from behind pale and hollowed cheeks, as his friend Senator James Mason of Virginia, chief sponsor of the new bill on fugitive slaves, read aloud his prepared remarks. Here was hard-line pro-slavery incarnate, grim and unyielding. The primary reason for the current discord, Calhoun's text asserted, was Congress's long-standing and systematic promotion of national legislation favorable to the North. The Northwest Ordinance and then the Missouri Compromise had prevented the South from occupying vast new tracts of land. Tariffs and internal improvements had enriched northern business at the direct expense of the South. The oppression would end only if the North ceased its aggression. The South must have equal access to western territories; all criticism of slavery must cease; a new law had to be enacted providing for the swift return of runaway slaves to their owners; and the nation had to ratify a constitutional amendment that, according to Calhoun's vague description, would "restore to the South, in substance, the power she possessed of protecting herself before the equilibrium between the two sections was destroyed."

Calhoun almost certainly envisaged, as the heart of any constitutional amendment, a proposal he had developed in his manuscript "Discourse on the Constitution and Government of the United States" (which, like his "Disquisition," would not be published until after his death) institutionalizing his concept of the concurrent majority by establishing two presidents, one northern and one southern, each with the power to veto congressional legislation. The proposal was as far-fetched as the rest of his speech was devious. One would never guess from Calhoun's syllogisms of oppression that he had supported not only the Missouri Compromise but also, early on and emphatically, the kinds of tariff and improvement legislation he now denounced as evil. One would never guess that anybody lived in the South except for slaves and slaveholders—and that the majority of white southerners, slaveless, were not barred from taking one bit of their property into the western territories. One would never guess that if any portion of the Union enjoyed an artificial subsidy of federal power, it was the slave states, whose representation in the House, the Electoral College, and the parties' national nominating conventions was greatly inflated thanks to the three-fifths clause—an arrangement which, in turn, had helped ensure that eight of the first twelve presidents of the United States, including the incumbent, were slaveholders. None of these evasions was new—but Calhoun's urgency and disunionist hints gave his remarks a foreboding power. The choice was simple, Calhoun said: were California admitted as a free state, either under Taylor's plan or Clay's, the southern states could no longer "remain honorably and safely in the Union."

Four days later, Daniel Webster, delivered the nationalist address many expected of him. In a low even voice, Webster announced that he wished to speak "not as a Massachusetts man, not as a Northern man, but as an American." Having once opposed the Mexican War and supported the Wilmot Proviso, Webster changed his position, turning on the Proviso with special contempt as "the Wilmot"—a gratuitous measure, he now said, designed merely to "taunt or reproach" the South. For the Union to endure, such northern attacks must end, and some law was required to guarantee the return of fugitive slaves to their masters, just as the Constitution's framers had intended. Likewise, southerners had to appreciate the North's alarm at the gradual rise of pro-slavery views and cease their blustery talk of disunion. By the time Webster finished, it was not entirely clear whether he favored Taylor's territorial plan or Clay's compromise proposals—which may very well have been Webster's intention. But with that ambiguity, and coming so soon after Calhoun's effort to draw a line in the sand, Webster's speech bolstered the view that some sort of compromise was required to keep the nation from falling apart.

Four days after Webster spoke, the freshman senator William Henry Seward presented the antislavery northerners' counterpoint to Calhoun's speech. Condemning out of hand Clay's compromise, and any such sectional deal, Seward attacked slavery as an oppressive and undemocratic institution—in "natural alliance with the aristocracy of the North, and with the aristocracy of Europe"—that should be hastened to its demise and not encouraged with craven bargaining. In Seward's view, Congress unquestionably had the constitutional power to exclude slavery from the territories. Even then, he continued, senators had to recognize that "there is a higher law than the Constitution," the law of nature's God, who had created all persons equal. Seward's claims were reprises of and variations on a theme antislavery northerners had advanced as early as the Missouri crisis in 1819 and 1820—that the egalitarian Declaration of Independence, with its invocation of the Creator, was the legal and moral basis of the Constitution. The bulk of Seward's speech concerned itself not with transcendent good and evil, but with a dense legalistic explication of why slavery was incompatible with the letter as well as the spirit of the Constitution, another familiar line of antislavery argument. Yet to some, Seward's reformulations of old contentions seemed to be asserting a new and unnerving radical claim, that the godly forces of antislavery were above the law. Reinforcing that impression was Seward's insistence that slavery was doomed, and that the only thing left to determine was the manner in which it would be destroyed—either peaceably, gradually, and with financial compensation under an intact Union, or violently, immediately, and utterly if the Union were dissolved.

Reaction to Calhoun's, Webster's, and Seward's orations was instant. Hannibal Hamlin, the antislavery Maine Democrat, rose in the Senate to counter what he regarded as Calhoun's inflammatory speech. Many southerners praised Calhoun's fire and brimstone, although some, like former president John Tyler, considered it "too ultra." Calhoun found much to praise in Webster's speech, which he thought showed "a yielding on the part of the North" that would discredit Clay, but antislavery New Englanders condemned Webster as a turncoat factotum for the cotton-manufacturing aristocracy and its slave-mongering allies. (One enraged Yankee, John Greenleaf Whittier, dashed out an angry poem, "Ichabod," blaming Webster's fall on "the Tempter"; the Free Soil Whig Congressman Horace Mann read the work in full before the House of Representatives.) Seward's speech made the South howl; Clay denounced it as "wild, reckless, and abominable"; and President Taylor, already furious at Clay and Webster for what he saw as a concerted effort to undermine him, now unloaded his wrath at Seward, whom he had heretofore considered and consulted as an ally. Yet in the antislavery districts of New England and greater New England, Seward was suddenly a hero.

While the speeches captivated the reading public, more mundane political efforts proceeded inside the Capitol's committee rooms. A special Senate committee, chaired by Clay, offered a long bill that incorporated several elements of Clay's proposed compromise: admission of California as a free state; the organization of two new territories, New Mexico and Utah (which had applied for admission in March), without reference to slavery;

and a ten-million-dollar compensation to Texas in exchange for Texas's recognition of New Mexico's boundary claims. The committee's bill helped to dampen the radical disunionist fervor in the South, where the Nashville Convention—boycotted by Louisiana and North Carolina as well as most of the Border South states—transpired in June with only minor incident. Yet as debate over Clay's bill continued on into the summer, its chances for passage dwindled. Clay's prickly demeanor and his obvious distaste for the Taylor White House did not help his cause, but the major problems were arithmetical. With all of his prestige, Clay could muster only about one-third of the members of each house to support the measure (now mocked at by President Taylor as the "Omnibus"). Taylor and most northern Whigs stuck to the president's original plan of admitting California only, with no acquiescence in allowing New Mexico or the rest of the Mexican cession opened up to slavery. Whigs and Democrats from the Deep South would not agree to any bill that admitted California as a free state. Even if, by some parliamentary miracle, Clay were to find the necessary votes, it was no longer clear that the incensed Taylor would abide by his campaign promise not to exercise his veto power.

Matters worsened in late June when word arrived that a small convention in New Mexico had drafted and won ratification of a free-state constitution. Taylor immediately called for New Mexico's admission along with California's; southern outrage flared to new heights; and the state of Texas vowed to secure its claims to all of New Mexico east of the Rio Grande, by force if necessary. Taylor ordered the federal garrison at Santa Fe to prepare for combat. By early July, it looked as if civil war might break out, pitting the United States against southern volunteers determined to secure greater Texas for slavery.

Fate intervened, as it had in 1841. On a blazing July 4, President Taylor spent much of the afternoon at the site of the unfinished Washington Monument, listening to patriotic speeches. Through the rest of the day and evening, he gorged himself on raw vegetables and cherries, washed down with pitchers of iced milk. The next day, he fell severely ill, and on July 9, he died of acute gastroenteritis. The ex-general who had become a southern Whig with northern feelings was suddenly replaced by a northern Whig with southern feelings, the conservative New Yorker Millard Fillmore.

Fillmore's accession was the turning point in the crisis. Immediately, the new president defused the Texas–New Mexico conflict by laying aside New Mexico's application for statehood and throwing his support behind Clay's bill. Instead of obstruction from the White House, the Great Compromiser could now count on complete support, with the added advantage that the obstreperous Seward, Fillmore's foe in New York politics, would be rendered more marginal than ever. Yet Fillmore could not save Clay's proposals in their Omnibus form. After a month of Byzantine negotiations, the anticompromise blocs in the Senate, North and South, sent the bill down to defeat at the very end of July. Clay, depressed and feeling every one of his seventy-three years, withdrew to Newport, Rhode Island, to recover. Other, younger men stuck it out in sweltering Washington, determined to maneuver some sort of agreement through Congress. They were led by the thirty-seven-year-old senator from Illinois, Stephen A. Douglas.

Personally and politically, Douglas epitomized the moderate to conservative nationalist Democratic politicians who had emerged in the North in the 1840s, at odds with Barnburner Jacksonian radicalism. Born in Vermont, he had moved to Illinois, where he prospered as a self-made lawyer and politician and married the daughter of a wealthy North Carolina planter (receiving, at his father-in-law's death, the title to a large and thriving Mississippi plantation). With ties to and sympathies for every section of the Union, Douglas believed that all sides were blowing the slavery issue out of proportion. A lifelong Democrat—he had gotten his start in politics as a teenager in Vermont, ripping down anti-Jackson handbills during the 1828 election—he had no truck with southern disunionist heresy, and he thought Wilmotism was an attack on the democratic rights of territorial settlers to determine their own form of government. Having rapidly ascended the political ladder by dint of his oratorical and back-room skills and his commanding presence (packed into a stumpy five-foot four-inch frame), the so-called Little Giant was chiefly interested in encouraging railroad construction and other internal improvements—traditional Whig aims that Douglas and others now associated with Democratic expansionism. His chief vice (though in politics this could be a fraternal virtue) was a fondness for whiskey that, along with his Polkian addiction to hard work, would kill him before he reached the age of fifty.

An implacable partisan infighter but with a cool political intelligence, Douglas had never admired Clay's Omnibus strategy; indeed, Douglas remembered, as Clay seemed to have forgotten, how Clay himself had manufactured the Missouri Compromise thirty years earlier. The day after the large bill failed, Douglas began breaking it down into its parts and engineering their separate passage. The strategy was simple: start with the foundation of pro-compromise votes that did exist, and then add on sectional minorities large enough to pass each measure one by one. Northern Democrats and Whigs thus joined with border-state Whigs to approve the admission of California, the abolition of the slave trade in the District of Columbia, and the adjustment of the Texas–New Mexico dispute along the lines Clay had originally proposed. Conservative and moderate northern Democrats joined with southern Democrats and Whigs to pass a new, stronger fugitive slave law (which would help recover long-gone as well as recent runaways), and to organize New Mexico and Brigham Young's Deseret, now called Utah, without reference to slavery. Behind the scenes, President Fillmore prevailed on enough northerners to abstain from the floor votes on the latter two bills to ensure their passage. By the end of September, all of the measures had passed both congressional houses. President Fillmore would proudly declare that Congress had achieved "a final settlement" of sectional discord.

Washington erupted in jubilation. Crowds chanted, "The Union Is Saved." The major government buildings were illuminated. According to one account, word spread that it was the duty of every patriot to get drunk. "[E]very face I meet is happy," wrote a friend of James Buchanan's. Happiest of all were the main protagonists, above all Stephen Douglas, who had made a name for himself during the two months he had brokered the truce. "If any man has a right to be proud of the success of these measures," noted the defeated Jefferson Davis, "it is the Senator from Illinois." Henry Clay, absent for most of the final heavy lifting, arrived back in Washington from his vacation in time to help pull the District of Columbia bill through the Senate and then bask in the adulation that came his way as the initiator of the bargain. "Let it always be said of old Hal," Douglas generously remarked, "that he fought a glorious & patriotic battle. No man was ever governed by higher & purer motives." Daniel Webster was elated and relieved. "I can now sleep anights," he wrote an associate (having long suffered intense bouts with insomnia). "We have gone thro' the most important crisis, which has occurred since the foundation of the Government; & what ever party may prevail, hereafter, the Union stands firm."

Behind the intoxicated glow, there was reason enough for satisfaction among political moderates. The crisis of 1850 was real. Southern secessionist fervor had overtaken even mainstream politicians like Robert Toombs. William Seward's "higher law" antislavery enjoyed substantial popular support in the North. By late summer, the congressional impasse had defeated Henry Clay's best efforts, and its resolution required industry and finesse. That resolution would serve as a patriotic bulwark of antisectional politics for years to come, emboldening moderates in the North and South, shoring up the political center much as the Missouri Compromise had thirty years earlier.

But 1850 was not 1820, when the politics of antislavery had seemed to arrive out of nowhere. The Free Soiler Salmon Chase came closer to the truth than the revelers when he said that "the question of slavery in the territories has been avoided. It has not been settled." As part of the price of getting the Utah and New Mexico bills passed, Congress had consciously omitted including any stipulations about whether slavery would be permitted in these territories before they applied for statehood. The issue was instead left to the Supreme Court to decide—a decision that never came, as no relevant case ever arose out of either territory. In other portions of the as yet sparsely settled West, the evasions of 1850 would come back to haunt political leaders soon enough. Nor had the apparent triumph of pro-Union centrism in Congress halted the gradual erosion of the political system. The factionalism that plagued both parties now tended more than ever to run along alarming sectional lines. Slavery and its extension were, as ever, the core issues.

Throughout the proceedings, the gaunt Calhoun, and then his ghost, haunted everyone. After showing up at the Senate one last time to hear Webster's nationalist oration, Calhoun died on March 31. Friends and even foes eulogized him as a brilliant leader of his cause. "[O]ne of the great lights of the Western world is extinguished," the conservative New York Whig Philip Hone, who disliked Calhoun's politics but admired the man, wrote in his diary. Southern moderates and Unionists were less charitable, calling his death, in one South Carolinian's words, "the interposition of God to save the country." Calhoun's old adversary Benjamin Perry said it was "fortunate for the country" and claimed that "the slavery question will now be settled." But Calhoun's passing did not lay the slavery question fully to rest any more than did the evasive truce of 1850. The spirit of Calhounism lived on, in an even more radical disunionist form, picked up by a new generation of unswervingly pro-slavery Deep South Democrats. "He is not dead sir,—he is not dead," said Thomas Hart Benton, who refused to speak at the official congressional obsequies. "There may be no vitality in his body, but there is in his doctrines."

For the Calhounites and the more fiery southern disunionists, there was no question that the North's irresponsible form of democracy was ruining the country, just as there was no question among antislavery northerners that the Slave Power's perversion of democracy was ruining the country. William Yancey and his

fellow extremists sounded less and less extreme to many southerners. Early in the post-truce session of Congress, a series of
resolutions arrived from the Vermont legislature, calling slavery
"a crime against humanity, and a sore evil in the body-politic,"
and denouncing "the so-called 'compromises of the Constitution.'" Jefferson Davis, appalled, announced that he had long
trusted "in the intelligence and patriotism of the masses," but
that now, in the North, demagogues and their dupes had "raised
a storm which they cannot control . . . invoked a spirit which they
cannot allay." Others went much further, to denounce democracy itself as the root of all evil, in need of responsible checks
by responsible slaveholders. The Virginian Muscoe R. H. Gar-
nett looked back with dismay at the general drift "in the direction of Democracy" across the nation for the previous fifty
years. "*Democracy, in its original philosophical sense,*" he wrote,
"*is, indeed, incompatible with slavery, and the whole system of
Southern society.*" For the moment, moderates and Unionists
had the upper hand in southern politics, both in Washington
and at the state level. (A second disunionist Nashville Convention, held in November to denounce the truce, was even less
well attended and effectual than the first.) But among slaveholders, especially in the Deep South, John Calhoun's shade
was finally displacing Andrew Jackson's.

Within two months of the settlement of 1850, the clash of
southern and northern ideas of democracy would break out anew,
over that portion of the truce called the Fugitive Slave Act. Once
again, as in the 1820s and 1830s, Americans at the very bottom
of political society would help instigate the conflict. Although its
immediate effects did not dispel the flush of amity created by the
truce of 1850, the conflict prefigured the truce's undoing.

THE POLITICS OF FUGITIVE SLAVES

On October 25, 1850, two slave-catchers named Hughes and
Knight arrived in Boston to apprehend the fugitive slave cabinet-

maker William Craft and his wife, Ellen, and bring them back into bondage in Georgia under the terms of the new Fugitive Slave Law. The Crafts were antislavery celebrities. Two years earlier, using money that William had saved up from odd jobs as a hired-out slave, they had escaped from Macon, Georgia, to the North by train and steamboat, with Ellen (her hair cut short and her skin fair enough to pass for white) posing as a sickly planter, accompanied by a man-servant—her dark-skinned husband. The couple settled in Boston, amid other fugitive slaves, where the story of their audacious flight became, in the columns of Garrison's *Liberator*, the most famous runaway saga since Frederick Douglass's. The commotion surrounding the Crafts quickly caught the attention of their owner, who, as soon as the Fugitive Slave Act became law, sent his agents off to recapture them. The two slave-catchers, emboldened by the new requirements that compelled federal authorities and private citizens to assist them, swore that they would complete their mission even if they had to bring reinforcements from the South.

Boston's abolitionists swung into action. An emergency meeting at the African Meeting House, in the black neighborhood on the back side of Beacon Hill, had already formed a group called the League of Freedom, pledged to protest the new Fugitive Slave Law, and ten days later, the group merged with Boston's revived, black-led Vigilance Committee. As soon as Hughes and Knight showed up, Ellen and William Craft went into hiding with the help of the Vigilance Committee—she winding up at the home of the Transcendentalist minister Theodore Parker, whose church the couple had joined, and he taking refuge at the home of a black abolitionist, Lewis Hayden. (The latter turned his place into a veritable fortress and promised to blow it sky-high rather than relinquish a single fugitive.) The Vigilance Committee, meanwhile, posted handbill descriptions of the "man stealers" all over the city, harassed and vilified them wherever they went, and had them detained on a charge of slander. After five days, the agents gave up and returned home.

Although Hughes and Knight had departed, the local federal

marshal still held a warrant for the Crafts' arrest, which he was now legally bound to execute. President Fillmore, enraged by the Bostonians' lawlessness, assured the Crafts' owner that he would have the pair apprehended, if need be by sending in federal troops. All the while, the veteran Garrisonian Samuel May, in contact with his English abolitionist friends, plotted out an escape route that took the Crafts to Portland, Maine, then to Halifax, Nova Scotia, and finally to Britain, where they connected with another well-known fugitive slave, William Wells Brown, and continued their antislavery work. Back in Boston, Theodore Parker sent a derisive note to Fillmore: "You cannot think that I am to stand by and see my own church carried off to slavery and do nothing to hinder such a wrong."

The Craft affair was one of the first in a burst of spectacular episodes in late 1850 and 1851 involving resistance to the Fugitive Slave Law. The following February, also in Boston, agents seized a runaway slave-turned-waiter, Frederick Minkins, who had taken the name Shadrach, and rushed him to the federal courthouse, where he was held under the guard of some deputy federal marshals. Much as in the George Latimer drama eight years earlier, an angry crowd gathered—only this time, a group of black protesters overcame the marshals, snatched Shadrach, and spirited him to Canada. Conservative Bostonians called the incident an outrage, and at President Fillmore's insistence, local officials, including prominent Democrats, indicted and tried four blacks and four whites, but juries refused to convict any of them. Shortly thereafter, in April 1851, a show of force involving hundreds of U.S. troops as well as armed police deputized as federal marshals was sufficient to secure the reclamation of yet another fugitive in Boston, seventeen-year-old Thomas Sims. But later that same year, a runaway cooper in Syracuse, New York, named William Henry (familiarly known as Jerry) escaped across Lake Ontario and into Canada thanks to a plan devised by Samuel May and Gerrit Smith, who happened to be in the city attending an antislavery convention. A local grand jury duly indicted twelve blacks and twelve whites for rioting, but nine of the blacks had already fled to Canada. Only one person was convicted, a black man who died before he could appeal the verdict. Other rescues were reported in places as far-flung as Cincinnati and Ypsilanti, Michigan.

The struggle reached a bloody crescendo on September 11, 1851, in the town of Christiana, Pennsylvania, near the Maryland border. Christiana was a Quaker settlement that welcomed fugitive slaves headed north, and reportedly two long-gone escapees were holed up there, hiding in the house of a free black. A posse consisting of a Maryland slaveholder, Edward Gorsuch, several of his relatives including his son, and three deputy marshals arrived in search of the pair and found them—surrounded by two dozen black men armed with clubs, corn cutters, and a few old muskets who were determined to send the slave-catchers packing. A pistol shot rang out, and in the melee, the slaveholder Gorsuch was killed and his son was severely wounded. The black resisters melted away into the countryside and their three leaders later turned up in Canada. "Civil War—The First Blow Struck," one Pennsylvania newspaper exclaimed.

President Fillmore, still smarting from the Shadrach and Jerry fiascos, directed a large force of federal marines and marshals to Christiana. They hauled in nearly forty prisoners, more than thirty of them black. The administration, determined to end the northern resistance once and for all—and in blood—then had the arrested men indicted for treason, a capital offense, which led to the largest treason trial in all of American history. But by the time the government mounted its case, its high-handed strategy had backfired. Guilty as the accused might have been of riot or even murder, few could take seriously the idea that a band of a few dozen, poorly armed men, including several Christiana Quakers, had seriously intended to wage war on the United States of America. ("Blessed be God that our Union has survived the shock," one of the defense attorneys mocked.) After the first defendant was cleared, the government dropped its charges against the others.

Various myths still cling to the fugitive slave disturbances of

1850–51. The greatest of them—originally propagated by irate southerners, and since given currency by Americans in search of abolitionist heroes—is the romantic image of what came to be known as the Underground Railroad. To hear some southerners at the time, one would imagine that the fugitive bondsmen presented a clear and present danger to the survival of slavery, abetted by a large and highly sophisticated conspiracy of northern whites who smuggled slaves to freedom. (One Virginia pamphleteer claimed that more than sixty thousand slaves had escaped to the North between 1810 and 1850, a figure Gamaliel Bailey called a "ridiculous perversion of facts.") In truth, the numbers of runaway slaves who were not returned to their masters within twelve months appear to have numbered several hundred annually, perhaps as many as a thousand, by the early 1850s—an embarrassment to southerners who claimed the slaves were perfectly content, but hardly enough to threaten a system of more than three million enslaved persons. Of the permanent runaways, a large number, possibly a majority, remained in the South, especially in coastal and river cities where they could blend in with free black populations. The preponderance of all runaways, especially in the Deep South, had no plan to escape completely from slavery, but would "steal away" from their masters for a short period of time, in anger at a rebuke, in respite from abuse, or simply in search of relief from backbreaking toil.

A related myth is that the Fugitive Slave Law actually created an effective machinery for recapturing fleeing slaves. The law did have harsh, even draconian aspects. It brought a major expansion of federal authority to track down runaways—an ironic consequence insofar as it showed, more than ever, that even the most doctrinaire state-rights slaveholders were perfectly willing to invoke robust federal power to protect slavery. Various provisions in the law—including the denial of jury trials to the apprehended, and a clause giving federal commissioners a ten-dollar payment if the captive was remanded to his or her owner, but only five if the captive was set free—were plainly weighted toward the slave-catchers. Runaways who were seized were almost certain to be returned South. But relatively few were actually caught under the law, just over three hundred between 1850 and 1861—roughly 5 percent of all runaways during the period. For most slaveholders, the sheer cost of undertaking capture and prosecution in order to secure the return of an uncooperative slave hardly seemed worth it, either financially or psychologically. (It was estimated that the recovery of Thomas Sims cost his master three thousand dollars and the federal government more than five thousand dollars.) Some observers freely conceded that the real point of the law had never been to recapture slaves but to test the North's sincerity over the truce of 1850. "The number of slaves escaping from the South is inconsiderable," one Wilmington, Delaware, paper observed in 1851.

Refutations of the myths surrounding the fugitive slaves can, however, themselves be exaggerated. The idea of the Underground Railroad certainly mattered, then and now, as a beacon of promise and possibility to slaves and free blacks, and of shame to slaveholders. Most successful runaways escaped in a haphazard manner, relying more on their own wits and planning than on other people's organizing—acts of extraordinary courage that may have done more than anything else to instill a hopeful endurance among southern slaves, and that later eulogies to (mostly white) abolitionists occluded. Some of the escapees, the most famous being the ex-Maryland slave Harriet Tubman—repeatedly and successfully dipped back down across the Mason-Dixon Line to help bring others to freedom. Neither "underground" nor secret, the black abolitionist vigilance committees, which had declined in the 1840s, sprang back to life after 1850, goaded by panic among northern blacks that now they were all, even the free-born, more vulnerable than ever to being kidnapped into slavery. In Chicago, seven divisions of six men each took turns patrolling the city and "keep an eye out for interlopers." Blacks in New York passed resolutions condemning the Fugitive Slave Law and appointed a secret committee to assist runaways. Boston's Vigilance Committee, which played an important role in keeping Ellen and William Craft free, claimed a membership of two hundred. Far from Boston, some white abolitionists strategically well placed near the border slave states—most famously the Quaker Levi Coffin, first in Newport, Indiana, and later in nearby Cincinnati—rendered valuable assistance in hiding and dispatching northward large numbers of refugees. No vast, well-oiled conspiracy, the Underground Railroad did, nevertheless, exist as a loose congeries of determined resisters, with free blacks doing most of the work and taking most of the risks.

The political and symbolic dynamics of the fugitive slave controversy were equally important. Of all the bills that made up the truce of 1850, the one on fugitive slaves stirred the least debate in the South. As originally proposed by Senator James Mason in January, it had appeared to some southerners as too weak, but by summer's end the dissenters managed to win tougher rules for the bill's enforcement. Not a single southern representative in Congress—Democratic or Whig, from the upper South or the Deep South, in either house—voted against the final proposal. For border-state men of both parties, it was the one issue in the compromise debates that truly hit home, as the vast majority of runaways came, not surprisingly, from areas neighboring the free states. For Deep South men, it was a grave matter of honor surpassing any economic considerations, an assertion of slaveholders' rights against Yankee extremists. "The loss of property is felt," Senator Mason would later remark, "the loss of honor is felt still more."

The northern resistance, especially in William Lloyd Garrison's Boston, not surprisingly incensed the southern extremists, increasingly known as fire-eaters. ("[R]espect and enforce the Fugitive Slave Law as it stands," one pro-slavery editor warned the North. "If not, WE WILL LEAVE YOU!") But southern Unionists likewise took offense at the abolitionists' lawlessness. In several states, pro-Union southerners, following the example of the so-called Georgia Platform, passed by a special state convention in December 1850, pledged to abide by the 1850 truce as "a permanent adjustment of this sectional controversy," but only if the North also did its duty, including "a faithful execution of the *Fugitive Slave Law*." The embodiment of Border South Whig moderation, Henry Clay, charged that "except for the whiskey rebellion, there has been no instance in which there was so violent and forcible obstruction to the laws of the United States."

The disturbances' impact on northerners was more complex. Radical immediatists gained the most within the antislavery camp. For more than a decade before the enactment of the Fugitive Slave Law, abolitionists, black and white, had been giving aid and comfort to escapees and then publicizing their travails—ranging from the famous story of Frederick Douglass to that of Henry "Box" Brown, who escaped Richmond ingeniously in 1849 by hiding in a small crate that was shipped to Philadelphia. Overshadowed by the political abolitionists, the Garrisonians made the most of the stream of runaways. "If Ohio is ever abolitionized," the immediatist leader Samuel May wrote, "it will be by fugitive slaves from Kentucky: their flight through the State, is the best lecture,—the pattering of their feet, that's the *talk*." The Fugitive Slave Law was an unintended political gift to the radicals, made more emphatic by their claim, now seemingly endorsed by William Seward—no abolitionist, but something of a fellow traveler—that a divine Higher Law could even take precedence over the Constitution.

The controversy posed a conundrum, however, about the radical abolitionists' philosophy of nonresistance. Garrison never wavered in his pacifism; but to others, even before the affray at Christiana, the idea of throwing a human being back into bondage without a physical fight was too much to bear. Black abolitionists in particular became disenchanted with nonviolence. "The only way to make the Fugitive Slave Law a dead letter," Frederick Douglass snapped, "is to make half-a-dozen or more dead kidnappers." Newspapers in several places reported that local blacks were buying lethal weapons to protect themselves from the slave-catchers. Some white abolitionists, too, were persuaded that armed resistance was now in order. While Theodore Parker hid Ellen Craft from her would-be captors, he kept a loaded revolver at the ready on his desktop. More ominously, a still-obscure, Bible-reading wool merchant and abolitionist named John Brown, in Springfield, Massachusetts, organized under his command a small band of armed black resisters that he called the United States League of Gileadites.

Among less radical antislavery northerners, the Fugitive Slave Law refocused attention on the Slave Power's alleged willingness to abrogate basic civil and democratic rights to get its way. The new law was not, to be sure, the first of its kind. The Constitution itself explicitly guaranteed to slaveholders the right to recover their fugitive property, under Article IV, Section 2. The Fugitive Slave Law of 1793 further guaranteed slaveholders' rights to cross state lines to do so. But enhancing those guarantees as it did, the new Fugitive Slave Law compelled ordinary northerners to participate in slave recoveries, on pain of fine and imprisonment, and placed heavy penalties on any found guilty of aiding runaway slaves—in effect turning the entire northern population, black and white, into one large slave patrol. By denying the fugitives jury trials, it attacked the most democratic aspect of American jurisprudence—one that, according to the lawyers who defended the fugitives, brazenly violated the Fifth Amendment's due process clause. The law carried across state lines, and by federal fiat, the full legitimacy of an institution still alive in the North in 1787, but since banned—restricting the prerogatives of the free states while edging toward declaring slavery a national, and not a local, institution. Why should federal power be extended, critics asked, to protect one special form of property to the exclusion of all others? Even if the idea of a fugitive slave law had constitutional legitimacy, did not this one go too far? The law's attacks on civil liberties and individual conscience, and its extraterritorial implications, seemed, at least momentarily, to awaken new concerns about northerners' rights. "The treason trials are making a great deal of talk here now," one of Joshua Giddings's associates wrote late in 1851, with reference to the Christiana affair, "and thousands are ready to listen who have long been indifferent."

Antislavery advocates of all camps emphasized how the law was symptomatic of a moral as well as a political evil. Horace

Greeley called it "a very bad investment for slaveholders" because it "produced a wide and powerful feeling among all classes averse to the institution itself." Official repression visited on white men as well as black men was bad enough: the sight of blacks who had lived in freedom for years being hauled in chains back into slavery also placed slavery's harsher realities in a glaring light, and punctured once again the slaveholders' argument that the slaves were content. "Our Temple of justice is a slave pen!" the Free Soil writer and lawyer Richard Henry Dana wrote during the Thomas Sims affair, adding that Massachusetts law had been silenced "before this fearful slave power wh. has got such entire control of the Union." In Concord, Ralph Waldo Emerson, infuriated by what he considered an immoral and therefore illegitimate law, wrote a lecture counseling disobedience. (In the one active election effort of his career, he delivered the lecture several times on behalf of John Gorham Palfrey's unsuccessful Free Soil congressional campaign in 1851.) "The Fugitive Slave Bill has especially been of positive service to the anti-slavery movement," Frederick Douglass claimed, because it at once dramatized the "horrible character of slavery toward the slave," exposed "the arrogant and overbearing spirit of the slave States toward the free States," and aroused a "spirit of manly resistance" among northern blacks.

Despite all the drama, however, the antislavery forces made far less headway in the North than they hoped or expected. The majority of northerners regarded the Fugitive Slave Law, if only reluctantly, as the necessary price of sectional peace and regarded those who violated or obstructed it irresponsible troublemakers. "The law in question may be defective . . . ," one Illinois newspaper asserted, in a typical editorial. "But, so long as it shall remain on the Statute book of the United States, it will be the bounden duty of every good citizen to interpose no resistance to its execution." In the spring and summer of 1851, a counterreaction gained momentum, turning the fugitive slave controversy into a temporary victory for the forces of order and political stability. In Boston, Mayor John Prescott Bigelow (the Cotton

Whig Abbott Lawrence's brother-in-law) allowed local police to be deputized as federal marshals during the Thomas Sims struggle, thereby assuring slaveholders and anti-abolitionists that the city's law-abiding gentlemen were still in charge of the city. In other northern cities, upright commercial associations and leaders of both major parties sponsored public meetings that drew huge crowds and passed resolutions supporting the Fugitive Slave Law. ("It is treason, treason, TREASON, and nothing else" to obstruct the law, a defiant Daniel Webster declared in Syracuse, considered an antislavery stronghold.)

Evangelical as well as mainline Protestant clergymen denounced the agitation as, in the words of one Illinois minister, the product of "wicked principles" upheld by men "in rapid progress, in qualification, either for the penitentiary, or the lunatic asylum." One merchant frankly told the immediatist leader Samuel May that northern businessmen would not stand by and see their profits threatened by a sectional rupture: "We mean, sir, to put you abolitionists down, by fair means if we can, by foul means if we must." In 1851, the legislatures of Indiana and Iowa (followed, two years later, by Illinois) enacted laws barring the settlement of any blacks, slave or free, within their borders. Reflecting the racist sentiments of many southern whites who had migrated to the southernmost portions of these states, the laws were also intended to reassure the South that the presence of fugitive slaves would not be tolerated. So were a string of resolutions passed by the legislatures of Connecticut, Delaware, Illinois, Iowa, New Hampshire, and New Jersey, approving all of the measures enacted in 1850, including the law on fugitive slaves.

The counterreaction worked. Even before the violence at Christiana in mid-September 1851, agitation against the Fugitive Slave Law had begun sputtering, and by midautumn, it was over. Moderates and Unionists rejoiced at the North's rejection of anarchic antislavery radicalism—a blow as well, as they saw it, against the disunionist southern hotheads. Sectional peace was holding, an elated Henry Clay announced in October; resistance was abating, "and the patriotic obligation of obeying the Constitution and the laws, made directly or indirectly by the people themselves, is now almost universally recognized and admitted." The fight had hardened the nerves of combative antislavery northerners and deepened their bitterness at the Slave Power. But on the surface, at least, it seemed as if the truce of 1850 was turning into a genuine compromise.

"THOU JUST SPIRIT OF EQUALITY"

During the lull that followed the brief storm, two extraordinary novels appeared, both reflecting the debates of 1850 and the controversy over the Fugitive Slave Law—and affirming that literature can tell as much about underlying political realities as speeches, resolutions, and elections can. One novel had broadly Democratic origins; the other came from the heart of northern Whig evangelical antislavery. One was philosophical and demanding, doubting the existence of God and then pondering those doubts; the other was sometimes mawkishly sentimental and conveyed no doubt whatsoever that God not only existed but was a constant, redemptive presence. One was a complete commercial failure at the time but is now widely considered one of the greatest American novels; the other enjoyed the greatest commercial success of any work by an American writer in the nineteenth century, but is now thought of mainly for its historical interest. And both warned that no proclamations of compromise and nationalism could dispel the destructive forces that were overtaking the Union.

Herman Melville, disappointed at the critical failure of his political allegory *Mardi*, wrote a pair of potboiler novels to support his new family, then withdrew his household to Pittsfield, Massachusetts, in 1850, to be closer to his idol, Nathaniel Hawthorne, and to complete a romantic narrative he had begun about whaling. Against the backdrop of the compromise debates in Washington, Melville labored furiously over his manuscript as if in a trance, revising drastically even as he drafted it, enriching its language in Shakespearean cadences, and turning its details about whales and whalers into promptings for much darker and mysterious reflections. On September 10, 1851—the day before the Christiana riot—Melville sent the long-delayed manuscript to his British publisher, Richard Bentley, who published it in London five weeks later as *The Whale*. A month after that, the Harper Brothers' firm published the first American edition under *Moby-Dick; or The Whale*.

Although still nominally a Democrat, Melville was no simple party man, and in its political implications, *Moby-Dick* was no simple moral fable. It was an assault on simple moral fables. (In apparent reply to abolitionists who would have northerners feel the oppressions of slavery, Melville has his odd narrator Ishmael climb to rougher metaphysical ground: "Who ain't the slave?" he asks.) Instead, Melville spun a twisted yarn of the whaling ship, *Pequod*, evoking a Connecticut tribe massacred by the Puritans two centuries earlier. The ship's crew members came from all over the globe, and in their presence, Ishmael can invoke "thou just Spirit of Equality" and the "great democratic God . . . who didst pick up Andrew Jackson from the pebbles; who didst hurl him upon a war-horse; who didst thunder him higher than a throne!" Yet the *Pequod* is bound on no ordinary, orderly voyage of slaughtering whales but on a diabolical quest—ruled by a chewed-up, peg-legged monomaniac who brandishes a harpoon staffed with hickory, who draws power from his black, red, and brown harpooners, and who secures loyalty with a promised reward of a piece of gold nailed to the ship's main mast. The Quaker first mate Starbuck protests to the mad Captain Ahab, but Ahab is master and he presses on, smashing his quadrant, plowing into the Pacific. There the *Pequod*—a ship of the "old school" dating back to the Revolution, but now much changed with the acquisition of grisly trophies, its hull freshly sealed with caulked hemp from the compromiser Henry Clay's Kentucky—would be smashed to bits by its prey and swallowed up in a vortex.

There was no stable set of correspondences between Melville's characters and the nation's actual political leaders, although critics and historians have tried to find them. ("I had some vague idea while writing it, that the whole book was susceptible of an allegoric construction, & also that *parts* of it were," Melville said.) The book contains no reference to fugitive slaves or the Fugitive Slave Law that would have been obvious to most readers, beyond the ambiguous person of the cabin-boy Pip, who may have been born free in Connecticut or may have been born a slave down South. ("[A] whale would sell for thirty times what you would, Pip, in Alabama," the second mate Stubb tells the boy after saving him from drowning when he leaps overboard. "Bear that in mind, and don't jump any more.") Melville moved by indirection. It is in the general ambience and pile-up of references that his prophecy of America's destruction, propelled by the politics of 1850–51, acquires its force. Yet *Moby-Dick*'s philosophical puzzles were not enough to impress readers and critics, who for the most part found the book impenetrable.* They were far more absorbed by another novel that had begun appearing in serialized form in Gamaliel Bailey's *National Era* in June 1851, and that would be published in book form, to a stupendous response, in March 1852.

Uncle Tom's Cabin; or Life Among the Lowly was not Harriet

---

* One who might not have was the Boston doorkeeper, bill-poster, and confidential agent of the city's Vigilance Committee, Austin Bearse, who used his sloop—which he launched six months after the book appeared, and named the *Moby Dick*—in at least one successful rescue of several captured fugitive slaves in 1853. As Melville invented the name Moby Dick, it is beyond dispute that Bearse named his craft after the book, although it is unclear whether Bearse actually read it. Bearse could have picked up the name from Richard Henry Dana Jr., a prominent member of the Vigilance Committee and a good friend of Melville's, with whom the author corresponded about the book during its composition, and who certainly did read it. At all events, Melville's white whale wound up symbolically embroiled in the fugitive slave controversy. See Bearse, *Reminiscences of Fugitive-Slave Law Days in Boston* (Boston, 1880), 34–37; Sidney Kaplan, "The *Moby Dick* in the Service of the Underground Railroad," *Phylon*, 12 (1951): 173–6.

Beecher Stowe's first successful piece of writing. In the early 1830s, she won a short-story prize from the *Western Monthly Magazine* and eventually published a well-received collection of her stories. Later, she contributed regularly to more prominent periodicals, including the premier magazine of American Victorian womanhood, *Godey's Lady's Book*, and in 1850 alone, she published four antislavery pieces in the *National Era*. But if Stowe was an experienced professional author, nothing could have prepared her, or the public, for the success *Uncle Tom's Cabin* would enjoy. The daughter of renowned New England evangelical Lyman Beecher, she had accompanied her family to Cincinnati in 1832, when her father took up the presidency of the future abolitionist hotbed, Lane Seminary, and two years later she married Calvin Stowe, a professor of biblical literature at Lane. There, while mothering six children and writing stories to help supplement her husband's meager professorial income, Stowe was surrounded by evangelical antislavery enthusiasm, reinforced by the actual presence of slavery across the Ohio River in Kentucky—although, like her father, she was more tempered and even elitist in her Christian antislavery views than the immediatist radicals.

Scenes of human torment—a family being separated at the auction block, escapees on the run uncertain of whom to trust—lodged in Stowe's imagination for future use. (If Melville's Ishmael claimed a whaling ship as his Yale College and his Harvard, Stowe had Lane Seminary and the ex-Lane man Theodore Dwight Weld's detailed exposé, *Slavery as It Is*.) But it took the Fugitive Slave Law—enacted after she had moved back to New England with her family—to inspire her greatest literary ambitions. "Now Hattie," her sister-in-law told her after Congress acted, "if I could use a pen as you can, I would write something that will make this whole nation feel what an accursed thing slavery is." This Stowe did, in her own trancelike state—induced, she would later say, by the Almighty, but helped along by the rigors of having to write late into the evening by candlelight, after her mothering and household chores were done.

With its episodic construction and sudden, implausible plot twists, *Uncle Tom's Cabin* can be difficult to take seriously as literature. (Stowe herself, who never claimed great literary gifts, described it as merely a "series of sketches," and its original appearance in installment form may have marred its composition, as it did not the serialized writings of Balzac or Dickens.) As social analysis, beyond dramatizing slavery's moral horror, the book is saturated in the prejudices and the idealism of Stowe's Yankee milieu. Stowe presented upper-class slaveholders—the tortured Arthur Shelby, the problematic, romantic Augustine St. Clair—as essentially kind, respectable men who want to do right but who are driven to misdeeds by financial misfortune or by ultimate failure in their search for God. The most upright white character of all, apart from the angelic Little Eva, is Shelby's deeply religious wife, Harriet, a model of Yankee female rectitude disguised as a plantation mistress. The darkest villains (other than St. Clair's wife, a symbol of self-centered southern womanhood driven mad by slavery) are godless, money-grubbing plebeian white men, above all the alcoholic transplanted Vermonter, Simon Legree—a tyrannical slave driver who, because he can never win the respect of his social betters, brutalizes his slaves and forces them to grovel in his presence. As for the slaves, the cruelest among them, Legree's assistants Sambo and Quimbo, are vessels of misery whose hearts are finally opened to Christ's love by the surpassing forgiveness and tender example of Uncle Tom. An antislavery novel above all else, *Uncle Tom's Cabin* can also be read as a temperance tract, an ode to evangelical womanhood, a witness of God's uplifting charity, and an appreciation of restrained Whiggish gentility.

None of the book's contrivances could detract from its transforming power. Previously, the testimony of escaped male slaves forced northern audiences to confront the horrors of captivity, yet projected with the manly, unforgiving bearing of a Joseph Cinque or a Frederick Douglass, often burning with contempt for their oppressors. Stowe's gripping scenes—of the quadroon slave Eliza Harris escaping across the ice floes in the Ohio River, or of the

Christ-like Tom enduring and, finally succumbing under, Legree's savage beatings—deepened readers' sympathies by completely shifting the emotional focus. Stowe had her readers identify chiefly with defenseless mothers, little girls, and pious old men, whose unearned suffering and Christian redemption rendered their stories all the more moving—and rendered slavery all the crueler. More than that, by making the novel's slaves, above all Uncle Tom, the chief agents of Christ's redemption, Stowe broke through the racism of white America as no one, even the uncompromising Garrison, had done—a point too easily lost on some modern readers who can only see her portraits of black meekness and patience as racist caricature. The immense cultural resources of Whiggery in its Yankee evangelical, antislavery, self-reforming variant, raised to transcendent heights, drove the writing of *Uncle Tom's Cabin*. Together, they made Stowe's book the best-seller that *Moby-Dick* could never be in the 1850s. Fittingly, the most powerful Whig text of all time was neither a work of political philosophy, nor a speech, nor an official state paper, but a sentimental antislavery novel composed by one of the first daughters of the Second Great Awakening.

Uncle Tom's Cabin insisted that slavery was a national sin, to be eradicated only when Christ's love and higher law triumphed over men's customs, economics, and legislation. The connection with the Fugitive Slave Law controversy was direct, for the controversy destroyed once and for all any pretense that slavery was a purely sectional concern and that the North was not actively involved in slavery's perpetuation. It mattered not at all, in Stowe's ethical universe, if the number of fugitives tracked down was small: the moral stain and complicity in sin of just a handful of captures, or even one, could not be evaded. By making her novel's most hateful villain, Legree, a Yankee, Stowe chastised the nation, and not merely the South, for its depravity. (She did the same, more subtly, with the character of Ophelia, the oppressively prim and principled northern visitor to Louisiana who, lacking love, cringes at the idea of touching black sin.) And in the human conscience, Stowe found the surest instrument for erasing immoral laws. In an early chapter, an Ohio legislator named Bird—a sworn enemy of "these reckless Abolitionists"—arrives home having just cast a vote in favor of a state fugitive slave law. His pious wife upbraids him, and he scoffs at her political naïveté—yet when confronted with an actual, living, suffering runaway in the person of Eliza, Bird heeds his conscience and helps Eliza make her getaway. Stowe hoped to force her readers into making the same moral reckoning.

The magnitude of *Uncle Tom's Cabin's* impact was and is difficult to gauge. Within a year of its release, the book version sold more than three hundred thousand copies in the United States—comparable to a sale of more than three million copies today. Countless other Americans were captivated by Stowe's "sketches" in the numerous stage adaptations of *Uncle Tom's Cabin* mounted quickly after the book's publication. Looking back, critics said reading it was a transforming experience. The book reviewer, writer, and Union army officer John William De Forest would, in 1868, proclaim it as close as anyone had ever come to writing "The Great American Novel" (despite its "very faulty plot"). In the South, where the book flew off the booksellers' shelves, critics vehemently denounced what they called its inaccuracies and fabrications, and described its author as a monster. Pro-slavery propagandists replied with several novels describing the misery of wage earners in the North, in contrast to the idyll of plantation slaves.

Yet if the fugitive slave controversy and then Stowe's riveting book kept the slavery issue alive, their immediate political effects were muffled. Stowe, although deeply antislavery, had had little involvement in organized antislavery politics, and she strongly believed in the value of uplifting the bondsmen and in voluntary colonization. Garrisonians and other radical abolitionists found various gradualist themes in the book objectionable—above all, at story's end, the decision by its most rebellious protagonist, the ex-slave George Harris, to migrate to Liberia. At the other end of politics, the reaction against the antislavery resistance, spearheaded by officeholders and politicians determined to keep sectionalism at bay, dampened antislavery spirits. Outside Boston and a few other smaller northern cities, most northerners wanted to believe that the territorial and slavery issues had been resolved once and for all. In the South, Unionist moderates now held the political initiative in state politics, having staved off disunionist challenges in Georgia, Alabama, Mississippi, and even South Carolina. Northern Free Soilers tried to build on their revolt of 1848, sometimes in coalition with one of the major parties, but they found their influence dwindling drastically in the early 1850s. Pro-compromise mass meetings passed resolutions and deprecated extremism, as if the Union could be saved by an act of collective will. Melville's prophecy would take time to unfold, just as it would take fresh sectional struggles before Stowe's sermon sank in with northern voters.

Mainstream party leaders remained confident that they could contain the slavery issue by adhering to the truce of 1850 and asserting the old partisan bonds that united Americans across the sectional divide. Thus encouraged, Democrats and Whigs alike approached the presidential election of 1852 with high hopes of victory. The Democrats would, in the end, succeed; the Whigs would fail badly. Yet both parties would also find themselves further entangled in what was becoming a brutal paradox: all efforts to shore up the political center eventually wound up worsening the clash between North and South.

LAST STAND OF THE OLD PARTIES

The Free Soil uprising of 1848 persuaded Salmon Chase that the antislavery insurgents could take over the northern Democratic Party. Old-line Hunkers, he believed, had learned a painful but valuable lesson from Lewis Cass's defeat. Now, cut off from national patronage, they would "cast a wistful eye toward the Buffalo platform," sever their ties with the South, and merge with the Free Soilers behind the "great cardinal doctrine of equal rights" once propounded by Jacksonian radicals. Chase's hopes could not have been more misplaced. But that he held them at all bespoke not so much his own myopia as the confused state of antislavery politics during the Taylor and Fillmore presidencies.

What were the lessons of 1848 for the most dedicated members of the Free Soil Party? For some, notably Joshua Giddings, the result proved that both the Whigs and the Democrats were hopelessly corrupt, and that third-party efforts had to continue. Others, like Chase, came to a very different conclusion, that only by building broader coalitions could the antislavery men actually achieve power. "I fear that this world is not to be redeemed from its ten thousand self inflicted curses so easily as we flatter ourselves at the outset of any reform enterprise," Chase wrote to Charles Sumner. To win, antislavery advocates had to take a more realistic approach, and be "much in contact with the [political] machinery behind the scenes."

Coalition efforts brought mixed results from 1849 through 1851. In Massachusetts, the Conscience Whig Charles Sumner, increasingly persuaded by radical Democratic economic ideas, helped arrange a Free Soil–Democratic alliance that elected him to the U.S. Senate. A similar coalition in Maine reelected Senator Hannibal Hamlin. But in the House, Free Soilers suffered a net loss of seven seats in the 1850 elections, which brought the defeat of, among others, Joshua Giddings's future son-in-law, the ex-Whig George W. Julian. In Ohio, the alliance of Free Soilers and Democrats that elected Chase to the Senate and ended Ohio's black code also embittered ex-Whig Free Soilers, who had hoped to win the Senate seat for Giddings. Even in places where the coalitions were successful, battles over patronage, partisan advantage, and personal ambitions kept the coalitions from winning anything close to what Chase had envisaged, while it sapped the more stubbornly independent Free Soilers of supporters and morale.

The most telling effects of the coalition efforts appeared in New York, where prominent Barnburner Free Soilers began their drift back to the Democracy only weeks after the 1848 election was over. At first, the Barnburners—claiming they had revolutionized the party but needed to give the Hunkers time to adjust—remained zealous in their support of the Buffalo principles. Leading Hunkers (eager, for their own reasons, to complete a reunion) encouraged reconciliation by insisting that they, too, opposed the extension of slavery into the territories. By the late summer of 1849, however, the old factional differences over slavery reemerged. Under intense pressure, the two sides ran a joint state ticket but adopted a cautiously worded platform that allowed for "the free exercise of individual opinion" about slavery in territories "among members of the Democratic family." The Barnburners, hungry to reclaim party spoils from the Whigs, talked themselves into believing that they had not abandoned their principles, and that they were the Democratic dog wagging the Hunker tail, when it was the other way around. Only too late did thoroughgoing antislavery Democrats such as Preston King understand what had happened. In the aftermath of the truce of 1850, the now reunited New York Democracy formally repudiated the Wilmot Proviso and ran a mild conservative, Horatio Seymour, as its candidate for governor.

Free Soil Democrats who had either rejoined the party or formed coalitions with it at the state level were just as confused and disorganized in national politics. Most of these antislavery Democrats had accepted the truce of 1850 as necessary for national peace. Yet as they looked to the presidential election of 1852, they recoiled at the idea of supporting any Democratic nominee who had formerly supported the expansion of slavery into the territories—the only kind of nominee the South would accept. The trouble was that the antislavery forces lacked a plausible alternative. Martin Van Buren, now seventy, had retired to Lindenwald and rejoined the Democracy, still antislavery in principle but persuaded that the sectional issues had been settled. Many Free Soilers were drawn to the old Jacksonian Thomas Hart Benton, still an active and influential presence in the Senate. But Benton's criticisms of the Slave Power and John C. Calhoun ("the prime mover and head contriver," Benton called him) had cost him dearly among Missouri's slaveholders, led by Benton's adamantly pro-slavery Democratic rival David Atchison, and Benton lost his Senate seat in 1850. Thereafter, Benton stuck to his declaration that he had no desire to be president. Other possibilities were floated—Benton suggested Justice Levi Woodbury, who was at least uncommitted on slavery—but none of the names mentioned raised much enthusiasm. (Woodbury died, anyway, in 1851, reducing the field to practically no one.)

Antislavery Whigs likewise seemed to have lost their edge. The forestalling of the slavery issue in 1850 and the collapse of the resistance to the Fugitive Slave Law emboldened Cotton Whig conservatives to believe that they could now lead a common front of the sensible gentlemen of property, North and South, against all sectionalists—and particularly against the radical Free Soilers. One self-styled "Northern Conservative," writing in the Whigs' *American Review*, even courted southern Democrats. The erstwhile northern Democratic friends of the South, the writer charged, had declared war on "everything that is firm, established, and just." Differences remained between Whigs and southern Democrats, especially on economic issues, but the writer insisted that these could be ironed out once slaveholders understood that their interests would be better protected by Whigs than by "the hot, wild, reckless body that is organizing out of the loco-foco and abolition elements in the North and West." The alliance of the Money Power and the Slave Power that Thomas Morris had warned of a dozen years earlier was exactly what the more candid of the dominant northern Whig conservatives had in mind.

As ever, some Whigs looked to Henry Clay as their standard-bearer, especially after his successful return to the Senate. If anyone could unite the splintering party, it was he. But Clay had never really recovered from the strain of his efforts in 1850. By the late spring of 1852, he was spitting up blood and suffering heavy chills. Old friends and adversaries stopped in for one last visit to his Washington hotel room. There he would die of tuberculosis at the end of June, barely a week after his party chose its presidential nominee.

Daniel Webster, named by Fillmore for a second stint as secretary of state in 1850, had no less fire than ever in his ambition for the presidency—even though he, too, was silently wasting away. Encouraged by the Unionists' successes in the South, Webster spent much of 1851 trying to organize middle-of-the-road opinion in the northern states, beginning in New England. Building on his reputation from his Seventh of March speech, Webster hoped that a broad majority of pro-compromise, pro-Union moderates would carry him into the White House. But Webster had rivals. The New York conservative President Fillmore, thanks to his vigorous enforcement of the Fugitive Slave Law, had become a favorite of southern Whigs. And poking their noses around Whig meetings were the friends of the also-ran general of 1840 and 1848, Winfield Scott—a Virginian but not a slaveholder, with no record on the truce of 1850, whose nationalist credentials some Whigs thought could rescue the party. Even antislavery Whigs like Horace Greeley seemed resigned to support the pretentious, officious Scott as the only available candidate who might win the votes of northern Whigs. "I suppose we must run Scott for President, and I hate it," Greeley wrote in February 1851.

What was left of the independent Free Soil Party battled on. In September 1851, a convention of the Friends of Freedom met in Cleveland "to let the country know that we are not disbanded and do not intend to disband." The persistent delegates, led by Giddings, Julian, and Lewis Tappan, included former Liberty Party supporters who had balked at supporting Van Buren's nomination in 1848. While it unfurled once again the Free Soil banners, the meeting also passed resolutions condemning the Fugitive Slave Law, denounced both major parties as morally and politically bankrupt, and appointed a committee to arrange for the coming presidential campaign. The most radical delegates wanted to push even further and commit the group to abolition in all of the states, but the convention hemmed in that proposal at the last minute.

As the battered remnants of the American 1848 struggled to survive, the politics of the European 1848 suddenly entered into domestic politics, with telling effects. In December 1851, Lajos

Kossuth, the exiled hero of the failed Hungarian revolution, landed in New York to a tumultuous public response. A dazzling if diminutive figure, and a brilliant speaker, Kossuth embodied the spirit of European popular radicalism at war with reactionary monarchy. Dubbed the "noble Magyar," Kossuth elicited special warmth from spread-eagle, expansionist Democrats who had identified with Young America, but so great was the mass enthusiasm that elements from across the political spectrum (except for some southern Whigs and wary Hunkers) tried to align themselves with him. Daniel Webster retrieved a letter he had written to the Austrian ambassador late in 1850, refuting charges that the United States was improperly intervening in the Hungarian revolution,   and upholding America's interest in "the movements and events of this remarkable age" that expanded popular constitutional rights. ("Webster has come out for Kossuth and must no longer be regarded as an 'Old Fogy,'" the *New York Herald* remarked.) William Seward, presumed by many to be backing Winfield Scott, along with other antislavery men went out of their way to praise Kossuth. President Fillmore's supporters arranged for an official invitation to the White House.

The unanimity did not last. Kossuth demanded that the American government side with his cause and abandon official neutrality and nonintervention, which was bedrock American foreign policy. The more he did so—deciding, when rebuffed by Washington officialdom, to take his cause to the country in a public speaking tour—the more he wore out his welcome. Fillmore, seeing the danger, nearly rescinded Kossuth's White House invitation. Southerners, meanwhile, became extremely nervous that Kossuth's agitation for self-determination and universal liberty implied condemnation of slavery and could stir up slave rebellions. Kossuth in fact took great precautions in his speeches to avoid the slavery question, a reticence which rankled the Garrisonian abolitionists, but after 1850, any public mention of freedom in any context provoked dire inferences. In Washington, southerners led by Alexander Stephens made clear their displeasure at the Kossuth phenomenon. Under pressure from fellow southerners, Senator Henry Foote withdrew a formal resolution he had introduced (at his ally Webster's suggestion) welcoming the revolutionary to the nation's capital. Most antislavery men, however, took delight in the Hungarian's appearances no matter how cautious his remarks on slavery: "Every speech [Kossuth] makes is the best kind of Abolition lecture," Benjamin Wade of Ohio remarked. The truce of 1850 was more fragile than mainstream party leaders wanted to admit. Efforts to remind Americans of the democratic political beliefs they supposedly held in common ran the risk of exposing how divided they actually were.

At their national conventions in 1852, held a month before Kossuth returned to Europe, the Democrats and Whigs did their utmost to keep the divisions submerged. The Democrats met in Baltimore on June 1 and settled into a protracted four-way struggle among William Marcy (who had stepped back from the New York Hunkers and enjoyed the Barnburners' backing), Lewis Cass and Stephen Douglas (rival western proponents of popular sovereignty), and the southerners' favorite, the ever-malleable Pennsylvanian, James Buchanan. None of the northerners except Buchanan was acceptable to the South; Buchanan was unacceptable to the North; and for forty-eight ballots, the delegates deadlocked. Finally, the convention settled on the ex-senator and party stalwart, Franklin Pierce of New Hampshire. After declining an offer to serve as Polk's attorney general, Pierce had served with distinction in the Vera Cruz campaign during the Mexican War, then returned to private law practice in Concord, where he remained active in party affairs and warmly supported the truce of 1850. As a Yankee nonslaveholder from a traditionally Democratic state, a former doctrinaire Jacksonian (and antinullifier), and a military hero, Pierce was tolerable to northern delegates. As an outspoken antiabolitionist, nemesis of the Free Soiler John Hale, and pro-compromise candidate, Pierce looked even better to the southerners, including one South Carolina fire-eater who reflected that "a nomination so favorable to the South had not been anticipated."

The Whigs convened two weeks later, also in Baltimore, for a

marathon of their own, pitting General Scott against President Fillmore. (Webster's campaign, caught in the sectional switches, had
faltered badly.) The contest was paradoxical: northern delegates,
led by the New York Seward faction, backed the Virginian Scott,
while southerners backed the New Yorker Fillmore, and many of
the Whigs who had opposed the Mexican War now backed one of
the top military commanders of that war, just as they had supported Zachary Taylor in 1848. The opposing forces agreed to a
compromise over the so-called Compromise of 1850, by adopting a
platform that called for "acquiescence in" the bargain as a final settlement of the slavery controversy. It took fifty-three ballots, and a
last-minute defection of a handful of southern moderates, for Scott
to win a narrow victory. Yet party unity was shaky, and it became all
the shakier when the nominee's latitudinarian acceptance letter
expressed only tepid support for the party's pro-truce platform.
Immediately, nine southern Whig congressmen, including the
influential Georgians Alexander Stephens and Robert Toombs,
announced that they could not support Scott's election. Scott's
nomination all but precluded the Whigs from running their usual
pro-slavery campaign in the South.

The most unified of the nominating conventions—though, in
the short run, the least effective—was the Free Soilers', held in
Pittsburgh in August. John P. Hale agreed to let his name be put
forward, and he was nominated on a ticket with George Julian.
Ohio delegates paraded around the convention hall carrying a
banner declaring, "NO COMPROMISE WITH SLAVEHOLD-
ERS OR DOUGHFACES"—an attack on the backsliding Barnburners. The convention adopted a platform that deepened the
antislavery appeal of the Buffalo manifesto by denouncing slavery
as "a sin against God and a crime against man," and dropping, by
implication, disavowals of congressional interference with slavery
where it existed. The delegates also repudiated the Fugitive Slave
Law and called for official diplomatic recognition of the black
republic of Haiti. Whereas Frederick Douglass had been treated
gingerly at Buffalo, he was chosen a secretary at the Pittsburgh
convention and took his seat to loud applause. And whereas

Douglass had given grudging support to the Van Buren–Adams ticket in 1848, he exulted in the Hale-Julian campaign.

On slavery questions, the new Free Soil platform marked a return to the spirit of the Liberty Party, but on other issues, it sounded even more strongly Democratic than the Buffalo platform had been. The intensification was signaled by the convention's official change in name from the Free Soil Party to the Free Democratic Party, and it turned up explicitly in the platform's policy program, which included one plank demanding "that the funds of the General Government be kept separate from the banking institutions" and another calling for strict construction of the federal Constitution (a blow against the Fugitive Slave Law). In part, the shift was tactical, since, following the major party conventions, Pierce the Democrat loomed as the greater of the two mainstream pro-slavery evils. Stressing Jacksonian affinities was one way to attack Pierce's northern base and, some Free Democrats hoped, deal the Democracy another national defeat that would push mainstream northern Democrats closer to antislavery. But the shift also bespoke the greater success Free Soilers had enjoyed in forging coalitions with Democrats than with Whigs after 1848, as well as the importance of Salmon P. Chase, Charles Sumner, John M. Niles, Gamaliel Bailey, and other pro-Democratic thinkers, including candidate Hale, in the political antislavery milieu. On matters of principle as well as pragmatics, the independents endorsed firm antislavery ideals while they promoted a general political orientation closer to that of radical Jacksonian Democracy than to Whiggery.

There was an irony, though, to the Free Democrats' Jacksonianism, for by 1852 many of the ancient economic and constitutional issues that long divided mainstream Democrats and Whigs had become virtually irrelevant in local and national debates. President Polk, by reestablishing the independent treasury and obtaining the Walker Tariff, had killed off the Whig political economy of centralized, privately run national banking and government protection for the foreseeable future—and still, to the Whigs' vexation, the economy was soaring, aided by large treasury surpluses that ended up replenishing state banks' specie reserves, and fed by the California gold strikes and British investment in railroad stocks and bonds. The independent treasury system, neither a second Declaration of Independence nor a subversive catastrophe, had a usefully sobering effect on the economy by restricting the banks' power over the currency. The railroad boom, meanwhile, undercut old Jacksonian suspicions of government-supported internal improvements, especially when those improvements promised to aid their home districts. As the nation pushed westward to the Pacific Ocean, Democrats' ideals of expansionist Manifest Destiny demanded the kinds of projects, preeminently railroad construction, that required federal, state, and local government support. Whigs and Democrats would fight fiercely, especially in state legislatures, to ensure that their backers received the most pork from the barrel. But the denunciations of bank aristocrats or Loco Foco lunatics, although still heard from time to time to rouse the old party faithful, had become anachronistic rituals. "[Q]uestions of mere economy, those which pertain to banks, to internal improvements, or protective tariffs, no longer occupy the public mind," Joshua Giddings would observe a few years hence, but the effacement had been long under way.

With the old party antagonisms softened, and with both the Democrats and the Whigs pledged to uphold the truce of 1850, the election of 1852 would turn on operational matters: which side could do the better job of holding together its strained intersectional coalition, vilifying the other party's candidate, and getting its own voters to the polls. The Whigs faced the more daunting task. The southern Whig defections that began after the struggle with Zachary Taylor and then the release of Scott's acceptance letter became a mass flight in the summer and early autumn. In the North, the Free Democrats' campaign promised to siphon off any antislavery vote Scott might receive with his equivocal stance on the 1850 bargain. Nativist Whigs, offended by Scott's decision to reject anti-immigrant appeals, organized separate tickets pledged to Daniel Webster in the mid-Atlantic states. In New York, embittered pro-Fillmore Silver Grays threatened further sabotage, while Sewardites backed Scott but not the party's platform. To rally their troops, the Whig managers stepped up their personal abuse of Pierce, mocking both his military career and, cruelly, his alcoholic past by dubbing him "the Hero of Many a Well Fought Bottle." (The Pierce forces countered more loftily with the best-known campaign biography in American history, written by the nominee's old friend from his student days at Bowdoin College, Nathaniel Hawthorne.) The Whigs also intensely courted Catholic voters and, with Fillmore's approval, sent Scott on an "official" tour of Ohio, Kentucky, Indiana, and New York, which allowed him to campaign in person without formally breaking the customary ban on overt presidential electioneering.

No Whig maneuver could stave off disaster. In November, Scott carried only four states, Vermont, Massachusetts, Kentucky, and Tennessee (the last by a whisker), for a pitiable total of forty-two electoral votes. Of the twelve governorships at stake, the Whigs lost nine. In the House elections, Whig candidates won less than one-third of all contested races, representing a net loss of seventeen seats and giving the Democrats an unbreakable control of the lower chamber. Whig losses in state elections also threatened to worsen their minority status in the Senate, whose members were still selected by the state legislatures. Despite the enormous long-term political fallout from Texas annexation and the Mexican War, the nation once again faced the prospect of one-party Democratic rule of the federal government. "Was there ever such a deluge since Noah's time?" a despairing New York Whig asked William Seward.

The damage done to the Whig Party, and to the national political system, in 1852 was severe, but it was not of biblical proportions. With his 1.4 million votes, Winfield Scott gained a larger popular total than any previous Whig candidate. Pierce's portion of the popular vote, 50.9 percent, was not exactly a landslide. The Whigs ran reasonably well in a number of important states, including New York, Pennsylvania, and Ohio. Above all, antislavery politics, so distracting to northern Whigs, had not recovered from the reassertion of political centrism that accompanied the bargain of 1850 and the reaction against the fugitive slave controversy. The Free Democrats won less than half the proportion of the total vote that the Free Soilers won four years earlier, ran well only in Massachusetts, Vermont, and Wisconsin, and barely made a difference in New York. Most Barnburners and other antislavery Democrats remained loyal to their old party and the uninspiring Pierce. The Whigs, although badly wounded, could read the returns—or, at least, the northern returns—and reasonably imagine they had survived to fight another day.

The results in the South, especially the lower South, were more worrisome. In 1848, General Taylor had won half the popular vote in the Deep South, carried six slaveholding states, nearly carried Alabama and Mississippi, and achieved what looked like a consolidation of southern Whiggery. Four years later, General Scott won only 35 percent of the popular vote in the Deep South and carried only two slaveholding states, Kentucky and Tennessee. Whig gubernatorial candidates went down to virtually universal defeat in the South, while the southern Whigs' ranks in the new Congress would be miniscule. Whig leaders and voters did not, to be sure, defect en masse to the Democrats; Whig losses owed more to abstentionism than to party-switching. But southern Whiggery, if not down and out, was on the ropes, with the loyalty of its voters more tenuous than ever. The 1852 elections marked the beginning of the creation of a nearly solid Democratic South.

The southern results brought additional shifts in the locus of sectional power within the national parties. The collapse of southern Whiggery in congressional and state races in 1852 not only consolidated Democratic political hegemony in Washington; it made the South an even greater force within the Democratic Party—and the North an even greater force within what remained of the Whig Party. Democrats in Congress, more than ever, would find themselves unable to get much done without the support of their powerful southern bloc. The future of the Whig Party, if there was to be one, depended on which northern or border-state faction—pro-Fillmore Silver Grays, Cotton Whig Websterites, upper

South moderates, or antislavery Conscience Whigs—could gain the political initiative. And on the future of the Whig Party would hang the future of American democracy.

THE WHIGS' LAST GASPS?

On October 24, 1852, at his home in Marshfield, Daniel Webster died, foreclosing the Cotton Whigs' fortunes. A lifetime of hard drinking—an addiction that had worsened in his later years—had rotted away his liver, but he actually died from the delayed effects of a fall he had suffered the previous spring. With Henry Clay dead in June, the last of the old Whig giants were gone. Between them, Clay and Webster, more than any other figures, had defined the combination of conservatism, nationalism, and capitalist developmentalism so central to the anti-Jacksonian opposition. Both had adapted to the new-school Whig innovations of the late 1830s; both had wanted desperately to be president; both were undone by a combination of poor judgment, bad luck, and, above all, the erosion of sectional harmony. Yet even when they were past their prime, both had stood up for a kind of Unionism that they deemed as essential for the nation's well-being as it was for their personal political fortunes. Those efforts, especially in 1850, calmed the country as much as was humanly possible. With them, the South Carolinian James Henry Hammond wrote in his diary, died "the last links of the chain of the Union," as well as the last great upholders of Whig moderation on slavery issues.

The Union chain did not break, though, in 1852; neither did the Whig Party. The old partisan order—and the nation—had stood for one more round. The future of both hung on what kind of Democrat the new president, hailed by his admirers as "Young Hickory of the Granite Hills," turned out to be.

6

THE TRUCE COLLAPSES

Franklin Pierce entered the presidency mourning the death of his eleven-year-old son, Benjamin, who had been horribly killed two months earlier during a family trip when their railcar jumped its tracks and overturned. Pierce's pious wife, Jane, had never wanted her husband to return to the stresses and temptations of Washington, and she interpreted the tragedy as God's price for winning the presidency. She refused to attend the inauguration and withdrew into a seclusion at the White House that would last for the entirety of the Pierce administration. Her personable, determined, but also fragile husband, distracted by guilt and grief, inspired more apprehension than hope. Robert Toombs saw in poor Pierce "a man without claims or qualifications, surrounded by as dishonest and dirty a set of political gamesters as even Catiline ever assembled."

Pierce's unexceptional inaugural address praised the Union, upheld Democratic orthodoxy on limiting federal power, and proclaimed that "the laws of 1850, commonly called the 'compromise measures,' are strictly constitutional and to be unhesitatingly carried into effect." The speech's most vigorous passages concerned territorial growth, which Pierce proclaimed a self-evident national imperative. "[T]he policy of my Administration will not be controlled by any timid forebodings of evil from expansion," he announced. Along with his enforcement of the Fugitive Slave Law, Pierce's resolve to gain new territories, and to organize existing territories into states, would dominate his presidency—and blow the political system apart.

EMPIRES OF SLAVERY?: FROM CUBA TO KANSAS-NEBRASKA

Pierce's most ambitious territorial design was on Cuba, which along with Brazil and the American South was the last great slave society in the Western Hemisphere. The idea of grabbing Cuba was not new. In 1848, after the signing of the Treaty of Guadalupe Hildalgo, President Polk disclosed his desire to acquire the island from Spain, a proposal endorsed by southern Democrats who wanted to enlarge the number of slave states and send as many as fifteen new pro-slavery representatives to the House and Senate. The Whig presidential victory that autumn ended the official planning,   but not behind-the-scenes plotting. Led by a charismatic Cuban revolutionary patriot, Narciso López, pro-annexationists organized three unsuccessful invasion expeditions, the last of which, in 1851, led to López's capture by Spanish troops. Northern expansionists and southerners lamented the failures as a setback for anticolonial, democratic principles. Antislavery northerners condemned what Horace Greeley called "the Cuban foray" as "a crusade for the extension and consolidation of the Slave Power."

   The defeat of López's third so-called filibuster expedition (from the Spanish word *filibustero*, or "pirate") led to the execution by firing squad of fifty American mercenaries—and the garroting of López—in front of thousands of cheering Havanans. The killings touched off riots in New Orleans. For a time, a full-scale diplomatic crisis seemed imminent. The Fillmore administration, embarrassed by the affair, averted further conflict, and pro-slavery filibusterers started looking for a new president, friendlier to their cause, in 1852. With support from northern expansionists, they at first backed the nationalist Stephen A. Douglas. After Douglas's defeat for the Democratic nomination, they switched to Franklin Pierce. They celebrated the landslide in November under banners proclaiming "The Fruits of the late Democratic Victory—Pierce and Cuba."

Among the most belligerent of the filibuster enthusiasts was the erstwhile Jacksonian radical and champion of Manifest Destiny, John L. O'Sullivan. O'Sullivan had sold the *Democratic Review* in 1846, but remained deeply interested in Democratic politics—raising doubts about Polk's drive to war and supporting his old Radical Democrat friends in the Free Soil campaign in 1848, but endorsing the annexation of Mexican land. After the war, O'Sullivan became fascinated with Cuba, an interest that turned into a fixation after his sister married a Creole planter who was also one of the founders of a rebel exile group, the Consejo de Gobierno Cubano, headquartered in New York. The 1848 revolutions in Europe also stirred O'Sullivan's antimonarchical soul. O'Sullivan lobbied Polk hard to purchase the island in 1848. He then gravitated to Narciso López's filibustering efforts, which landed him a federal indictment on charges that he had violated American neutrality laws. O'Sullivan was acquitted (several leading Barnburners, including John Van Buren, testified as character witnesses) and continued his agitation by returning as editor to the *Review*, persuaded that the political party that annexed Cuba would prove itself "the true American party, the party entrusted by God and Nature with the mission of American policy and destiny."

O'Sullivan continued to think of himself as a radical, but his old friends flinched at his new jingoism. The original idea of Manifest Destiny rejected unprovoked war and armed conquest as repudiations of the worldwide spirit of liberty. It studiously avoided any endorsement of Calhounite pro-slavery heresy. But now Sullivan and the new *Review* (acquired in 1851 by a hotheaded Calhoun admirer, George Nicholas Sanders) had sunk into a strutting chauvinism, and seemed to be acting on behalf of land- and power-hungry slavocrats. Breaking ranks without breaking stride, O'Sullivan switched his targets and coarsened his rhetoric, in the service of a reborn Young America. The *Review* descended into shrill polemics against the "imbeciles" and "vile toads" who had the slightest misgivings about American expansionism. The Jacksonian heroes whose portraits and brief biographies had been regular features of the old *Review* now suffered denunciation as "old fogies." Only the spirit of revolutionary solidarity with Europe's oppressed had not fled. (The first issue of the new *Review* featured a celebration of Mazzini. Victor Hugo, in exile, would inscribe several novels to Sanders as his *concitoyen de la république universelle*.) But soon, even those ties would unravel, as southern Young Americans objected to Mazzini's and other Europeans' pointed condemnations of slavery. One by one, Democrats who had once identified with Young America, including David Dudley Field and Theodore Sedgwick III, dropped away, leaving O'Sullivan to consort with his new southern friends and aggressive northern expansionists like Stephen A. Douglas.

President Pierce endorsed this belligerent new Young American spirit in his inaugural address, and he tried to advance it during his early months in office. His conservative Democratic cabinet (notable for its inclusion of the Hunker William Marcy as secretary of state, Jefferson Davis as secretary of war, and ex-Cotton Whig Caleb Cushing of Massachusetts as attorney general) was united in its pro-expansionist views. Pierce also appointed as his minister to Spain the hothead French émigré and filibuster supporter Pierre Soulé. Soulé received instructions that, although the United States would remain neutral, it fully expected Cuba's release, by invasion or revolution, from Spanish rule—and that, should events "excite revolutionary movements in that island," Cuban émigrés to America would undoubtedly be involved. Soulé soon began plotting with Spanish republican revolutionaries. Back home, the former Mississippi governor John A. Quitman, a fire-eater and backer of Narciso López's expeditions, began planning (apparently with Pierce's encouragement) yet another filibuster, greater than any yet attempted. Several influential southern leaders, including Alexander Stephens, supported the plan. By the spring of 1854, Quitman had recruited several thousand volunteer troops and, through Cuban exiles, contacted insurgents on the island.

Quitman aborted his invasion plans when another, more urgent territorial issue distracted the administration. "The Nebraska question has sadly shattered our party in all the free states," Secretary of State Marcy wrote, "and deprived it of the strength which was needed & could have been more profitably used for the acquisition of Cuba." Early in 1853, Stephen Douglas had proposed to the Senate a House bill calling for the formal organization of the Nebraska Territory, which embraced most of the remaining portion of the Louisiana Purchase north of the Missouri Compromise line of 36°30'. Douglas's aim was to hasten the building of a transcontinental railroad. Instead, he threw national politics into the upheaval that the truce of 1850 had only delayed.

The railroad had become an important factor in the nation's continuing economic development in the late 1840s and early 1850s, and the idea of a transcontinental line to California had long spellbound Manifest Destiny men. The acquisition of much wealth and prestige would turn on whether the new road ran across one of the proposed southern routes—where the required contiguous land mass had already been fully organized, thanks to the bargaining of 1850—or across the North. Douglas the expansionist had been pushing the idea of a Pacific railroad since his early days in Congress. Now he wanted desperately to get the remaining lands north of 36°30' organized, beginning with the area known as Nebraska, to secure the northern route, which he hoped would begin in Chicago. Southern representatives consequently had every reason to delay the organization of Nebraska, or to exact a terrible political price to allow it to proceed. And four hardline pro-southern senators—who shared quarters in a rented brick rowhouse on F Street and nicknamed themselves the F Street Mess—had virtual control over territorial organization: James M. Mason and Robert M. T. Hunter of Virginia (chairmen, respectively, of the Foreign Relations and Finance Committees), Andrew P. Butler of South Carolina (chairman of the Judiciary Committee), and David R. Atchison of Missouri (president pro tempore of the Senate). Atchison was especially important. The death of Pierce's vice president William R. King six weeks after taking office made him, under the existing rules of succession, next in line for the presidency. He was also among the Senate's most ardent defenders of slavery and southern rights.

Democratic politics in Missouri had for some years revolved around the conflict between the bellicose Atchison and the anti-slavery Democrat Thomas Hart Benton. Apart from his detestation of the Calhounite influence in the Democratic Party, Benton (who had returned to Congress in 1852) wanted to halt the expansion of slavery and to keep the West, as far as possible, lily-white. Atchison feared that any restrictions on slavery's extension would spell the institution's eventual doom in Missouri. Surrounded by free soil, he supposed, Missouri would find itself under siege by the abolitionists, who would directly threaten the state's slave laws.

Profane and provocative, Atchison had mixed feelings about the Nebraska question, as pro-railroad interests in St. Louis wanted to organize the territory in the hopes that their city might become the terminus of the transcontinental line. Reluctantly, he supported Douglas's Nebraska bill. At the same time, he vowed he would see Nebraska "sink in hell" before allowing it to bar slavery—and so, in effect, he also damned to oblivion the Missouri Compromise and any Nebraska bill that did not repeal it. Atchison's southern mess mates on F Street would not give even tepid support to Douglas's proposal.

Douglas knew the score immediately. In March 1853, the House passed his Nebraska bill, but the Senate tabled it, with the senators from every state south of Missouri joining the majority. Lacking southern support, and especially the support of the F

Street Mess, Douglas's efforts were doomed, but to accede to the South and repeal the Missouri Compromise would, as he put it, "raise a hell of a storm in the North." With hell on everybody's mind, Douglas introduced a new bill in January 1854 that tried to finesse the southerners' demands by allowing the residents of Nebraska to decide the slavery issue upon its admission as a state or as several states. But Douglas's fallback to supporting the popular sovereignty idea did not satisfy the southerners, who forced him to include a provision explicitly repealing the Missouri Compromise. To mitigate the expected northern reaction, Douglas's new bill organized two territories, Nebraska west of Iowa (which seemed to mark it for free soil), and Kansas west of Missouri (which seemed to mark it for slavery). The storm came anyway, and was no less hellish for Douglas's efforts to dodge and pacify.

Even the eager northern expansionists at the White House had doubts about Douglas's bill, and the administration drafted an alternative that would have left the matter of slavery in the territories up to the Supreme Court. But the F Street Mess and Douglas, with the strong support of Secretary of War Davis, told Pierce that if he opposed Douglas's bill, he would lose the South. Not only did Pierce cave in to the pressure; he agreed to make support of what was now known as the Kansas-Nebraska Bill an absolute test of loyalty within the Democratic Party. The result was to provoke even further the northern Democrats, as well as Whigs, against what Thomas Hart Benton would call Douglas's "farrago of nullities, incongruities, and inconsistencies."

In Congress, the remaining Free Soilers, now known as Free Democrats, and their closest allies were well prepared for the fight. As early as April 1853, the antislavery press warned that the Missouri Compromise might be endangered, and well before Douglas hammered his final bill into shape, efforts were underway to organize petition campaigns against it. Salmon Chase, Charles Sumner, Joshua Giddings, and three other Free Democrats (including Gerrit Smith, who had been elected to the House) wrote a manifesto against the bill, designed to arouse antislavery opinion out of the quietude of the previous two years.

First published the day after the Kansas-Nebraska Bill's formal introduction, in the moderately antislavery *New-York Daily Times* and in Gamaliel Bailey's *National Era*, "An Appeal of the Independent Democrats in Congress to the People of the United States" attacked slavery and Douglas's "atrocious plot" with the South and propounded the principles for a revival of antislavery politics.

Sensing the breadth of the indignation against the bill, the authors of the "Appeal" reached out to northerners generally, as well as to every existing current of antislavery belief, with a blend of fierce demagogy and northern democratic idealism. The inflammatory conspiratorial language of the "Appeal" has too often overshadowed its substance, and how the authors braided together the different strands of antislavery opinion. Familiar Liberty and Free Soil Party arguments laid the foundations: that slavery was an abomination, and that the Founders had envisaged slavery's demise, only to have their intentions undermined by the Slave Power. The "Appeal" then enticed moderate Whigs by claiming that Douglas's handiwork threatened to destroy Henry Clay's statesmanship of 1820 and 1850. To attract wider Democratic constituencies, the manifesto charged that "immigrants from the Old World and free laborers from our own States" would be excluded from the new territories if the bill passed. The "Appeal" also addressed "Christians and Christian ministers" and reminded them that "their divine religion requires them to behold in every man a brother, and to labor for the advancement and regeneration of the human race."

The authors then presented their overarching theme: the crisis over the territories was a crisis of American democracy. The antislavery cause, the "Appeal" argued, had become the embodiment of "the dearest interests of freedom and the Union." Its opponents had described the antislavery men as reckless agitators, but the "Appeal" turned the tables: "Demagogues may tell you that the Union can be maintained only by submitting to the demands of slavery. We tell you that the Union can only be maintained by the full recognition of the just claims of freedom and man." If antislavery was the true nationalist cause, it was also the true democratic cause: "We entreat you to be mindful of that fundamental maxim of Democracy—EQUAL RIGHTS AND EXACT JUSTICE FOR ALL MEN. Do not submit to become agents in extending legalized oppression and systematized injustice over a vast territory yet exempt from these terrible evils." Old complaints about southern oligarchy became a powerful call to overthrow the despotic Slave Power.

The "Appeal" was a masterstroke of political strategy as well as powerful propaganda. The six authors plotted the timing of their manifesto as carefully as they did its language. (Just as Douglas was about to initiate the Senate debate over his bill, Salmon Chase nonchalantly asked for and received a temporary delay, purportedly to give him extra time to read the bill, but actually to give the *National Era* and the *Times* a few extra hours to get the "Appeal" printed.) By striking immediately, the Independent Democrats caught Douglas off guard and shifted the terms of debate onto their own ground. No longer could anybody pretend that the Kansas-Nebraska Bill was chiefly a railroad improvement project or a benign effort to bring new territories officially into the orderly national fold. It was a bill about slavery and democracy and would be contested as such.

Over the next four months northern anti-Nebraska feeling, molded by the "Appeal," turned into a popular conflagration. Hundreds of local meetings sent petitions to Congress denouncing the "Nebraska infamy" and demanding the bill's defeat. Nine free-state legislatures either excoriated the measure or pointedly refused to endorse it. (Illinois lawmakers backed the bill only after Douglas and his friends and agents exerted intense pressure.) Even some inveterate Hunker Democrats joined the protests. "The Nebraska peace measure is working as might have been expected," one New Hampshire Democrat wrote to his brother, a close friend of President Pierce's, soon after the congressional debate ended. "Everybody almost is ready for a rebellion."

Events outside Washington fortuitously deepened the crisis.

In March, a hired-out slave named Anthony Burns, in his early twenties, escaped from his Virginia master, stowed away on a ship in Richmond, and arrived undetected in Boston. There, Burns found a job working in a black clothes dealer's shop on Brattle Street, not far from where the radical political writer David Walker had had his own clothing shop a quarter of a century earlier. Burns, like Walker, was deeply religious (the result, in Burns's case, of a Baptist revival that swept through his master's district in the mid-1840s), and like Walker, his religious piety shaped his hatred of slavery. ("Until my tenth year I did not care what became of me," he later recalled, "but soon after I began to learn that there is a Christ who came to make us free.") Soon after his arrival, he wrote to his brother to tell him of his deliverance, and took the pains to arrange to have the letter mailed from Canada—but he dated the letter at Boston. His master, Charles Suttle, intercepted the letter. In May, as debate over Douglas's bill reached its conclusion in Washington, Suttle set off for Boston to retrieve his human property under the Fugitive Slave Law.

On the Senate floor, Stephen Douglas mounted an ingenious and disingenuous argument that the legislation of 1850, by opening up to popular sovereignty territory above and below the compromise line, had already nullified the Missouri Compromise. Antislavery northerners destroyed that claim by pointing out that the 1850 truce applied only to the Mexican cession and not to the Louisiana Purchase lands, and that everyone, including Douglas, understood so at the time. Douglas nevertheless prevailed in the Senate, with help from the White House, by a wide margin. The situation was much more difficult in the House, where mainstream northern Democrats, feeling strong pressure from their home districts, worked up the nerve to resist their party's establishment. Every northern Whig representative voted against the bill (just as every northern Whig senator had)—and nearly half of the northern Democrats either voted nay or were paired against the measure. Tellingly, only two in five New York Democrats backed the bill, despite Douglas's fierce efforts to

force them into line. Only because of the extra southern representation granted under the three-fifths clause did the bill pass
on May 22, by a margin of 113 to 100. "Nebraska is through the
House," the bill's southern Whig floor manager Alexander
Stephens exulted. "I took the reins in my hand, applied whip and
spur, and brought the 'wagon' out at eleven o'clock P.M. Glory
enough for one day."

Stephens's glory, however, spelled out his party's ruin. Many
New York Silver Grays and other conservative northern Whigs
had been offended by Douglas's measure, not for any antislavery
reasons but on the conservative grounds that a compromise of
more than thirty years' standing ought not to be destroyed. Yet by
seizing the initiative with their "Appeal," the antislavery men
crippled these northern conservatives' efforts to stake out their
own political position, and they pushed southern Whigs into supporting Douglas lest they look like traitors to their section. The
result was devastating to the Whig Party. "No man has . . . struggled as I have to preserve it as a national party," the conservative
Connecticut Whig Truman Smith wrote at the end of January,
but "I shall have nothing to do with any Southern Whig who joins
Stephen A. Douglas in introducing into Congress & into the
country another controversy on the subject of slavery." In the
final tallies, a majority of southern Whigs, in both Houses, did
exactly as Smith had feared. For all practical political purposes,
the national Whig Party died on May 22, 1854, *aet.* 21 years.

The Kansas-Nebraska Bill struggle also shattered the northern
Democracy. "All democracy left the democratic party," the veteran Massachusetts labor Jacksonian Frederick Robinson later
wrote of the reaction by anti-Nebraska Democrats, "and every
true democrat that was too intelligent to be cheated by a name
deserted its ranks." For some Democratic leaders, including Benton and Martin Van Buren, the ancient ties of party were strong
enough to endure even their indignation over the repeal of the
Missouri Compromise. But for many of the Barnburners and
other antislavery Democrats—including William Cullen Bryant,
Preston King, and David Wilmot—Kansas-Nebraska was the

final insult; other angry old Jacksonians including Benjamin Butler and Francis Blair were coming to the same conclusion. The
defections left the Democracy almost fully transformed into the
party of the slaveholders, backed by a sharply reduced number of
northern appeasers. Somewhere, John C. Calhoun's shade
smiled. Two Yankees, Stephen A. Douglas and Franklin Pierce,
under pressure from undaunted southerners, had turned the
Democratic Party that Calhoun had long distrusted into a reasonable facsimile of the pro-slavery party he had spent two decades
trying to create.

The explosive denouement of Anthony Burns's story in Boston,
beginning only two days after the Kansas-Nebraska Bill's passage,
worsened the parties' disarray. On May 24, a deputy federal marshal arrested Burns on a false charge of robbery and incarcerated
him under heavy guard in the federal courthouse. Boston's abolitionists responded much as they had in the earlier fugitive slave
captures. A group of blacks met in the basement of Tremont
Temple and decided to set Burns free. A much larger gathering at
Faneuil Hall, largely of whites, denounced the "Virginia KID-
NAPPER!," got word of the blacks' march on the courthouse, and
dispersed, with hundreds rushing off to join in Burns's liberation.
Armed with hatchets, pistols, and a battering ram, a small group
of blacks led by the young white abolitionist minister Thomas
Wentworth Higginson broke through the door, but were repulsed
by club-swinging marshals. Someone fired a shot; then one of the
deputies shrieked that he had been stabbed and he died several
minutes later. Burns remained in custody.

President Pierce reacted even more fiercely than Fillmore had
in the Thomas Sims case in 1851, ordering Secretary of War Jefferson Davis to send marines, cavalry, and artillery to Boston,
along with a federal revenue cutter that would await the
inevitable order and return Burns to slavery. At one point, Burns's
claimant, Charles Suttle, seemed willing to allow the abolitionists to purchase Burns's freedom, but the federal attorney
insisted on enforcing the Fugitive Slave Law. Burns's legal
defense, headed by Richard Henry Dana Jr., unavailingly tried to

stall for time. Finally, on June 2—three days after President Pierce signed the Kansas-Nebraska Bill into law—federal troops marched the manacled captive through the streets of Boston to the wharfside. A throng estimated at fifty thousand persons witnessed the procession, their emotions shifting between sorrow and outrage. From inside buildings draped in funereal crepe came hisses and shouts of "Shame!" and "Kidnappers!" City church bells tolled a dirge. The scene shocked even conservative Bostonians. "When it was all over, and I was left alone in my office," wrote one old-line Whig, "I put my hands in my face and wept. I could do nothing less." In New York, a disgusted Walt Whitman, on the verge of his breakthrough as a poet, composed "A Boston Ballad": "How bright shine the cutlasses of the foremost troops!/Every man holds his revolver, marching stiff through Boston town."

The Burns affair revived the fugitive slave frenzy and loudly punctuated the debates over Kansas-Nebraska. A federal grand jury indicted seven white and black abolitionists, including Higginson, for riot and incitement, but the government eventually dropped the cases, knowing that there was not a jury in Massachusetts that would vote for conviction. The New England states passed new personal liberty laws at variance with federal law, as, eventually, did the legislatures of Ohio, Michigan, and Wisconsin. It was as if Anthony Burns had finally completed Harriet Beecher Stowe's mission, arousing the northern majority against slavery and the Slave Power—including, Dana wrote in his journal, "[m]en who were hostile or unpleasant in 1851." To the delight of antislavery veterans, the outbursts over Kansas-Nebraska and Burns, coming one right after the other, finally dissolved party allegiances. "Thank God," one Bostonian wrote to Charles Sumner, "the chains that have bound the people to their old organizations, have been snapped assunder."

Yet if the old organizations and loyalties had broken down, it was far from clear what new political alliances would replace them. Would the antislavery Whigs, as William Henry Seward and others now hoped, reemerge as a sectional party to counter the slaveholder-dominated Democracy? If so, what would become of the antislavery Democrats and of the old-line conservative northern Whigs? What would become of the southern Whigs, some of whom had begun drifting over to the Democracy, but others of whom, especially in the border states, clung to their moderation on slavery issues? Much would depend on events in the new territories now open to slavery, and especially in the territory of Kansas. "Come on, then, gentlemen of the slave States," Seward bellowed three days after the Kansas-Nebraska Bill passed the House. "Since there is no escaping your challenge, I accept it in behalf of the cause of freedom. We will engage in competition for the virgin soil of Kansas, and God give the victory to the side which is strongest in numbers as it is in right." Discerning God's will would be a gruesome business.

BLEEDING KANSAS, NATIVISM, AND THE FORMATION OF THE REPUBLICAN PARTY

In February 1854, Eli Thayer, an educator, entrepreneur, and member of the Massachusetts legislature, came up with the idea of forming a joint-stock company to promote the settlement of New Englanders in the proposed Kansas Territory. Incorporated in April, and funded chiefly by the Whig manufacturer Amos Lawrence, the Massachusetts Emigrant Aid Society (soon renamed the New England Emigrant Aid Company) was a frankly profit-minded venture that hoped to make a nice return by finding inexpensive group fares for sending New Englanders west, and by then providing them with the means to begin constructing their own towns and villages. (The first of the new towns would take Lawrence's name as its own.) The company's social, political, and philanthropic assumptions, however, came through clearly in its announced determination to establish a Kansas newspaper as an "index of the love of freedom and of good morals, which it is hoped may characterize the State now to be formed." By extending greater New England to the prairie,

Thayer, Lawrence, and their investors appeared to intend, or at least to suppose, that Kansas would be free soil. By year's end, about 450 Emigrant Aid Company settlers had arrived at the site of Lawrence.

The Yankees initially found themselves outnumbered by thousands of pro-slavery Missourians who had crossed the border and set down stakes. Few of the Missourians or emigrants from other slave states actually owned slaves, but they despised the New Englanders for what they saw as their air of moral superiority and their sickly love of blacks. Mocked as "pukes" and "border ruffians" by the free-staters, the pro-slavery men were determined to harass the abolitionists out of Kansas by any means necessary. ("We will be compelled to shoot, burn & hang, but the thing will soon be over," the ever violent Senator David Atchison predicted.) In November 1854, when the newly arrived territorial governor, Andrew Reeder, scheduled an election for a delegate to Congress, Atchison led an invasion force of more than one thousand Missourians to make sure that the pro-slavery candidate prevailed. With the help of seventeen hundred ballots later discovered to be bogus, Atchison's choice won the seat. In Kansas, it seemed, democratic power would grow out of the barrel of a gun.

Back in the free North, a new antislavery political party, quickened by the Kansas-Nebraska fight, was struggling to be born. In the larger states of Pennsylvania, New York, and Massachusetts, where the tidal wave of 1852 had not completely wiped out the Whig Party, antislavery Whigs tried to pin the latest crisis on the Democrats. One party newspaper claimed that "the spreading of slavery over free territory is A LOCOFOCO MEASURE"; others, that northern Whig solidarity against the Kansas-Nebraska Bill had left the party stronger than it had been in years. William Seward and Thurlow Weed in New York were particularly insistent that the antislavery insurgency defer to the existing party of freedom—their own—and join it. Others, including Abraham Lincoln—deeply shocked by what Lincoln disparaged as "the spirit of Nebraska"—were less dogmatically partisan, but refrained, just yet, from abandoning their Whig loyalties.

Anti-Nebraska Democrats, Free Democrats, and even some antislavery Whigs had other ideas. What was the point, Democrats and Free Democrats asked, to pledge allegiance to leaders of a party they had opposed for so long? For some antislavery Democrats, opposition to Whiggery had been the one last fiber attaching them to the Democracy. Why should they now genuflect to the Whig master manipulator Thurlow Weed? And what did Whiggery even amount to, now that the southern portion of the party had helped the Democrats destroy the Missouri Compromise? "I have ceased to expect wisdom from the Whig party," the liberal Whig editor Horace Greeley wrote to Schuyler Colfax early in 1853, before the Kansas-Nebraska fight pushed him over the edge. "It is like the duelist whose brains *couldn't* have been injured by the bullet through his head—'cause if he had had any brains, he wouldn't have been in any such predicament." Only a new party combining all antislavery northerners, along the lines sketched out by the "Appeal of the Independent Democrats," would satisfy the growing insurgency.

The anti-Nebraska fusion movement began taking shape three months before Douglas's bill actually passed. On February 22, Michigan's Free Democrats convened in Jackson and nominated a former Democrat for governor and two former Whigs for lesser offices. Six days later, antislavery Democrats and Whigs joined with Free Democrats in Ripon, Wisconsin, and resolved that, should the Kansas-Nebraska Bill pass, they would form a new "Republican" party (its name a tribute to the Jeffersonian Republican Party of old) to fight slavery's expansion. Larger state conventions, under various labels, named fusion slates. The most radical of them followed the Ripon example by calling themselves Republicans, and adopted resolutions based on the Free Soil platform of 1848 and the Free Democratic platform of 1852. More hesitant meetings (under titles such as "Union," "Fusion," "People's Party," "Independent," and "Anti-Administration") adopted narrower programs opposing repeal of the Missouri Compromise.

The anti-Nebraska outrage was fearsome, but by the time the

1854 elections began in earnest, nothing approaching a coherent antislavery party was in place. Compounding the antislavery men's difficulties, the northern nativist impulse, long dormant within the Whig Party, had resurfaced as a conservative political alternative for disaffected voters.

Nativism—or, to be more precise, anti-Catholicism—had had a curious political career since the urban rioting and local anti-immigrant election campaigns of the 1830s. After 1845, the numbers of new immigrants skyrocketed, fed by people propelled from their homes by political unrest and agricultural disaster, and attracted to the United States by cheap steerage fares and a booming economy. The new immigrant wave of the 1840s and 1850s—nearly three million new arrivals between 1845 and 1854, representing the greatest proportional arrival of foreign-born in American history—was also markedly poorer and more Catholic than previous streams of newcomers. Roughly two in five of the immigrants came from famine-ravaged Ireland, and nearly as many came from distressed, heavily Catholic regions of Germany.

Yet the cycles of migration and American political reaction seemed out of sync. The hard times of the late 1830s and early 1840s had inflamed ethnic and religious hatreds. Tensions between Protestant and Catholic workers degenerated into destructive and lethal rioting, most viciously in Philadelphia. In 1844, a nativist American Republican party, led by wealthy and middle-class evangelicals and by old-school Whigs, elected the wealthy publisher James Harper as mayor of New York City and won three congressional seats in Philadelphia. But then, just as the Irish famine immigration began, the nativist political movement stalled. In New York, the staunchly antinativist Seward Whigs reasserted control and cut off Whig support for the American Republicans. More broadly, recovery from the prolonged depression that had begun in the late 1830s alleviated the desperation in urban working-class districts; the war with Mexico (in which the pro-Catholic northern Democrats pushed for absorbing portions of a Catholic country into Protestant America) blurred ethnic and religious divisions; and anti-Catholic animus receded into more conventional channels within the Protestant churches and certain conservative precincts of the Whig Party. Among the latter was a New York fraternal group, the Order of United Americans, founded by a conservative Whig engraver and Harper supporter, Thomas R. Whitney.

The sudden revival of nativism in the 1850s had political as well as social origins. The new immigrant wave reached its peak between 1850 and 1855, at a level five times greater than a decade earlier. (By 1855, an absolute majority of New York City's population had been born abroad, almost all of them recent arrivals from Ireland and Germany.) The fresh influx settled into urban immigrant districts that were already overcrowded and scraping by in an overstocked market for unskilled and casual labor. Crime rates and demands on public and private relief rose precipitously, which nativists blamed on the immigrants themselves—especially the Catholic Irish, spiritual captives of a church that, with its exculpatory rituals, supposedly encouraged dissolution. The immigrants' Catholicism, one nativist pamphleteer wrote in 1855, "had lowered the standard till it was beneath the average level of human nature."

The fierce official Catholic reaction to these charges heightened the tensions. Most outspoken was New York's Archbishop John Hughes, Seward's ally during the school-funding controversies more than ten years earlier. Hughes not only refused to cower from the nativists' blasts; he conjured up their worst nightmares, declaring in one address that his church's great mission was "to convert the world,—including the inhabitants of the United States,—the people of the cities, and the people of the country . . . the Legislatures, the Senate, the Cabinet, the President, and all!" Hughes's defiance appeared in line with the crusading papacy of Pius IX (begun in 1846), which, with its staunch opposition to the European revolutions of 1848, made the Church among the most virulent opponents of liberalism and reform in the Western world. Hughes's and other prelates' equation of Free Soilers and abolitionists with the socialists and "Red

Republicans" of Europe estranged him from American liberals, including Seward, but the sight of a new Church militant did even more to antagonize the established forces of conservative nativism.

Divisions within American politics, and especially among the Whigs, also contributed to the nativist resurgence. The evangelical temperance movement begun in the 1820s had worked wonders through its combination of moral suasion and shaming. By 1850, alcohol had been virtually purged from northern middle-class homes where it had once been a mainstay. But the new immigrant Irish and German populations proved far less adaptable. To shut down the offensive saloons and *Biergartens* proliferating in northern cities, temperance advocates switched from coaxing to legal coercion. Their first breakthrough came with the passage in Maine of a strict prohibition law in 1851 (pushed by Portland's Whig mayor, the veteran total-abstinence campaigner Neal Dow). Over a dozen northern states adopted similar coercive laws over the next five years. The direct effects were uneven: nonenforcement of the prohibition laws was widespread; few who wanted to drink actually went dry; and in a quick counterreaction, most "Maine law" states repealed their antiliquor laws in the later 1850s. Still, the controversy reinforced the growing anxieties about the immigrant presence, just as it complicated divisions within the Whig Party. Whereas Democrats in the state legislatures generally opposed the temperance law drive, Whigs were divided between uncompromising "drys" and those who equivocated, still hoping to win over immigrant voters.

The Whig divisions over nativism had worsened during the 1852 presidential campaign. With encouragement from the anti-nativist Seward, the Whig nominee, General Scott, tried to suppress the party's conservative legacy and court the Catholic vote. But eight years earlier, hoping to advance his political fortunes, Scott had published a letter (under the pseudonym "Americus") denouncing ignorant foreigners and their growing political influence, and demanding that naturalization be made contingent upon two years of military service. Scott's managers in 1852 tried to spin the "Americus" letter into a pro-immigrant declaration, but failed. Nor could they render credible Scott's vapid pronouncements during his "official" tour about how he simply loved "that rich Irish brogue." The result was doubly disastrous for Scott: repelled Irish Americans voted in droves for the colorless Democrat Pierce, while many conservative northern Whigs, offended by Scott's pro-immigrant appeals, sat out the election. For these conservatives, the clear political lesson was that the Whigs, and the nation, could be saved only by restricting the political rights of the papist Democratic hordes.

By 1854, the anti-Catholic, antiliquor, and anti-immigrant zeal had produced a vast upsurge of organized nativism in the North, which contributed substantially to the Whig Party's collapse. Whitney's Order of United Americans (OUA)—with prominent New York Silver Gray Whigs including James Barker and Daniel Ullmann now in its leadership—claimed a membership of thirty thousand in New York State alone, as well as chapters in fifteen other states. In 1852, Barker and others began joining a smaller nativist organization, the Order of the Star Spangled Banner (OSSB), and incorporated it into the OUA to serve as a kind of political auxiliary, with Barker at the helm. Early in 1854, even before the Kansas-Nebraska Bill had been passed, Manhattan's leading Silver Gray newspaper joined the OUA-OSSB fold, and by year's end, ex-President Fillmore, though disturbed by the most strident anti-Catholic nativists, was privately urging reluctant Whig conservatives to do the same. The energetic Barker, meanwhile, organized hundreds of OUA-OSSB lodges around the country, pledging to vote only for native-born Protestant candidates for public office. Members were instructed to handle any questions about the group's activities with the curt reply, "I know nothing." The phrase caught on, and according to reliable estimates, there were at least one million "Know-Nothings" at the movement's height—a formidable political power, especially in and around the immigrant-packed northern cities.

As it edged into electoral politics, Know-Nothingism represented a rebirth of conservative Whiggery as an independent force, with a revamped program and a newfound, heterogeneous popular base. The movement's most prominent leaders were ex-Whig capitalists and other sectional conciliationists who had strongly backed the truce of 1850. Self-made businessmen like Harper were particularly conspicuous. The movement's mass following cut across class lines but consisted disproportionately of middle-aged and young urban men, in their thirties and forties, who worked in white-collar or skilled manufacturing jobs, or were successful small merchants or manufacturers: more petit bourgeois than working class. These were white natives who had escaped the debasements of early industrialization, who prided themselves on their elevation over the masses of sweatshop workers and day laborers—and who blamed the immigrants for the destruction of a fancied golden age before mass poverty, crime, and class strife. Nativist organizers reached out with particular skill to respectable, propertied, but anxious men at the border of middle-class life and just above it—men who came of age after the political struggles of the 1820s and 1830s and who pined for a supposedly pristine, preimmigrant past. It was this top-down populism—appealing to native skilled workingmen and shop-keepers as "the great bulwark of freedom and the foster-mother of liberty" while tapping into their social prejudices and insecurities—that primarily brought nativism its popular support. But it would also change the movement into a broader political coalition, focused less on Catholic immigrants than on corrupt politicians and the entire party status quo.

Beneath nativism's original nostalgic rhetoric lay undemocratic aspirations of a kind that had been in abeyance in northern politics since the advent of the new-school Whigs in the later 1830s. Distrust of foreigners, and especially Catholics, had, of course, been a feature of American conservative thought dating back at least to the Federalists and the alien and sedition laws. But while it turned traditional conservative disdain into an explicit attack on Catholic immigrants, nativist ideology also retrieved the broader old-line Federalist and early Whig contempt for partisan democratic politics—and, at times, for democracy itself.

Know-Nothings despised the established political parties as corrupt dispensers of patronage, interested more in gaining power and distributing spoils than in governing for the common welfare. Their own aim, as one Ohio nativist newspaper declared, was to "free our government from the . . . hordes of political leeches that are fattening their bloated carcasses in the people's money." The Democratic Party was the chief malefactor, having bought off its solid bloc of Catholic supporters with party jobs and drink and flattery. But the Know-Nothings' original mission to redeem the nation's politics advanced a deeper antidemocratic animus as well. "If democracy implies universal suffrage, or the right of all men to take part in the control of the State, without regard to the intelligence, the morals, or the principles of the man," OUA founder Thomas Whitney proclaimed, "I am no democrat." Whitney had a way of expressing nativism's political id, saying frankly what others tried to cloak, and he was also the revived movement's most prominent spokesman. By 1854, the proliferating Know-Nothing lodges were ready to pick up on Whitney's plan, which he had announced three years earlier, to establish a "great American party," a "conservative party, taking its cue from the doctrines set forth by the Order of United Americans."

Hastily, they nominated their own candidates to run against the Democrats and the anti-Nebraska men. Yet as the movement grew, it absorbed voters of far less conservative views than Thomas Whitney and the OUA founders. Antislavery Democrats frustrated by the failures of their own fusion efforts in 1850 and 1851, but still suspicious of the Whigs; humble country farmers and shopkeepers resentful of the political power wielded by city machines and men of great wealth; voters simply fed up with mainline parties that had dropped their old ideological appeals and appeared to be nothing more than patronage and vote-gathering organizations—a diverse and contradictory array of alienated northerners found their way into nativism as an ill-defined reform party. Some came to nativism out of confusion and anger; others thought they could use the movement to achieve their own goals, described by one Massachusetts nativist

as "a state government, not under control of powerful corporations, and a senator who would wake up the echoes of freedom in
the Capitol of the nation."

The point about freedom would prove crucial. In forming an
alternative to the emerging antislavery fusionists, the Know-
Nothings had to clarify their own views on slavery. In doing so,
they articulated a vehemently anti-Nebraska position that has
tricked some historians into believing the movement embodied
the growing northern militancy over slavery and the Slave Power.
To be sure, most nativists expressed a dislike of slavery as a backward institution, economically inferior to northern wage-labor
capitalism—a blight, Whitney wrote, that discouraged "the
development of great enterprises." As champions of the truce of
1850, Know-Nothing leaders were aghast at the needless provocations of the Kansas-Nebraska Act. Large numbers of Know-
Nothings sincerely opposed the expansion of slavery, and the
nativists' reputation as antislavery men as well as upholders of virtuous government helps explain the movement's eventual expansion into smaller towns and even rural areas where immigrants
were scarce. On the other side of the divide, nativist-style contempt for Catholic immigrants was certainly an element in the
thinking of many anti-Nebraska fusionists, especially in Whiggish evangelical districts.

Yet there were limits to the nativist movement's antislavery
commitments. Nativist leaders expressed little of the moral indignation at human bondage or at slavery's threats to democracy that
propelled the Conscience Whigs, antislavery Democrats, and
Free Democrats. Whitney, for one, sneered at "the attempts of
Seward, Weed, Greeley, and Co., to engraft upon the Whig banner the doctrines of the abolitionists." To achieve sectional conciliation, nativist conservatives were prepared to yield a great deal
to the slaveholders (including, in 1850, the Fugitive Slave Law),
while they denounced Free Soilers as hateful dividers. What
most concerned Whitney and others about the repeal of the Missouri Compromise was that it would feed sectional discord and
give antislavery radicals additional fodder for their demagogy.

Former Whig conservatives like Millard Fillmore drifted into Know-Nothingism more out of their desire to block the anti-Nebraska movement and buttress the Union than to attack Catholic immigrants. Like many of the more dedicated nativist leaders, they wanted to bury Kansas-Nebraska as a prelude to burying the slavery question once and for all—a question, one OUA leader would write in 1855, "so intrinsically difficult that wisdom and true conservatism dictate perfect silence upon it."

More steadfast antislavery men immediately sensed the weaknesses in the Know-Nothings' antislavery views, and in any case regarded nativism as a distraction from the truly important issues. "Neither the Pope nor foreigners ever can govern the country or endanger its liberties," Horace Greeley's managing editor at the *Tribune*, Charles A. Dana, observed in 1854, "but the slavebreeders and slavetraders *do* govern it." Some even thought (confusing cause with effect) that the growth of political nativism was part of a Slave Power plot, "a well-timed scheme," George Julian later wrote, "to divide the people of the free states upon trifles and side issues, while the South remained a unit in defense of its great interest." Few foresaw how the nativists would complicate the already confused northern political situation in 1854.

The overwhelming message of that year's election results was the thoroughness with which northern voters repudiated the badly divided Democrats. In 1852, the Pierce-King ticket had won all but two northern states; two years later, the Democrats held control of only two northern state legislatures. Northern Democratic congressional candidates took a drubbing, slashing the party's free-state delegation in the House from 93 to 22 (compared to 58 southern Democrats in the new Congress). Northern Democratic losses were especially heavy in districts where the incumbents, initially cool or even hostile to the Kansas-Nebraska Bill, finally voted for it. The antislavery forces—coming to be known simply as the Republicans—could count on holding about 100 of the 234 seats in the Thirty-fourth Congress. Yet the antislavery victory was not at all clear-cut. In some states, old partisan tensions within the antislavery coalition resurfaced quickly after the elections, with unsettling consequences. Notably, in the antislavery-dominated Illinois legislature, anti-Nebraska Democrats blocked Abraham Lincoln, still nominally a Whig, from gaining the necessary majority for election to the Senate, until Lincoln, to prevent the election of an organization Democrat, gave way to the antislavery Democrat Lyman Trumbull.

More startling was the Know-Nothings' impressive showing, especially in New England and the middle Atlantic states. The most astounding nativist triumphs came in Massachusetts. A curious alliance of Cotton Whigs and Boston Irish Democrats had emerged in 1853 to defeat a referendum for a new state constitution that would have provided for, among other reforms, expanded rural representation. The constitutional struggle placed the anti-Nebraska men on the defensive and stirred up rural counties resentful at the immigrants' rising influence. Nativism suddenly caught fire, sweeping out of the western towns and consuming everything in its path. In a four-way race for governor, the Know-Nothing nominee, a hitherto obscure Boston merchant and former Webster Whig named Henry Gardner, won 63 percent of the vote. Nativists seized virtually unanimous control of the state legislature, and all of the state's members in the House of Representatives were now nativists. (They included the politically savvy Democratic congressman Nathaniel Banks of Waltham, a former factory worker and journalist known as "The Bobbin Boy," who defected to the Know-Nothings and was reelected.) The Democrats and the antislavery forces took a severe beating, but mainline Whiggery was reduced to the ultraconservative coterie who found the Know-Nothings demagogic. "Poor old Massachusetts!" Daniel Webster's former comrade Robert Winthrop moaned. "Who could have believed that the old Whig party would have been so thoroughly demoralized in so short a space of time?"

Would the Know-Nothings surpass the antislavery fusionists as the major political opposition to the Democracy in the North? The odds seemed to favor them after the 1854 elections, but much would depend on the struggle in Kansas, which was fast verging on civil war. Not satisfied with their victory in the congressional delegate election in 1854, pro-slavery Missourians, egged on by David Atchison, prepared for future invasions and ballot-stuffing campaigns. Atchison and his allies were convinced—or at least claimed they were convinced—that Thayer and Lawrence's Emigrant Aid Company would eventually flood Kansas with tens of thousands of abolitionists. The charge was nonsense: at most, the company dispatched slightly more than fifteen hundred settlers by the end of 1855, and although free-soiler migrants were beginning to outnumber the slave-state Kansans, most of the new free-state advocates arrived from Ohio, Illinois, and Indiana, as well as from nonslaveholding areas in the southern border states. Far from bearing any "philanthropic" sympathies, these settlers wanted to keep slavery out of Kansas in part because they wanted the territory free of all blacks, slave and free. Without the provocations of the pro-slavery men, the northern majority probably would have made Kansas into a pro-Democratic free state. But fearing for the future of the peculiar institution in Missouri, and whipped up by the rise of the Republicans back East, the pro-slavery men continued to display what future governor John W. Geary described to President Pierce as "a virulent spirit of dogged determination to *force* slavery into this Territory."

The territorial legislative elections in March 1855 turned into an even nastier and more corrupt proceeding than the delegate elections four months earlier. With Atchison once again the chief instigator, thousands of Missourians—some of them members of a new semisecret pro-slavery society, and many identified by a badge of hemp, the area's chief slave cash crop—poured over the border to vote illegally. "There are eleven hundred coming over from Platte County to vote," Atchison shamelessly exclaimed, "and if that ain't enough we can send five thousand—enough to kill every God-damned abolitionist in the Territory." There was no killing—although a group of about one thousand heavily armed Missourians did set up camp outside Lawrence on election eve—but there was plenty of intimidation, illegal vote counting, and other flagrant irregularities. The election, the prominent free-stater Charles Robinson reported, was "controlled entirely by Missourians" who had seized control of the polling places. The final count broke heavily in favor of the pro-slavery men, who elected thirty-six legislators to the free-soilers' three. Only later did a congressional investigation show that all save about 500 of the 5,427 pro-slavery votes counted had been cast illegally.

Governor Reeder was unaware of the full scope of the fraud, but his initial sympathies for slavery had by now been destroyed by border ruffians' threats on his life if he tried to interfere. Reeder ordered new elections in one-third of the territory's election districts, and free-staters prevailed in most of them. But when the legislature met at Pawnee City in July, it scornfully seated the original pro-slavery winners. The lawmakers then passed a set of laws that incorporated Missouri's slave code and inflicted heavy penalties against anyone who spoke or wrote against slavery. Reeder journeyed east to inform the citizenry of the antidemocratic farce on the prairie and to beg President Pierce to intervene. "Kansas has been invaded, conquered, subjugated by an armed force from beyond her borders, led on by a fanatical spirit," he told one audience. Pierce greeted Reeder at the White House warmly, said that he approved of all he had done, and remarked that Kansas had caused him greater distress than anything since the death of his son. But the president went on to blame the Emigrant Aid Company for the catastrophe and, at Atchison's urging, replaced Reeder with a less sensitive soul, the Hunker ex-governor of Ohio, Wilson Shannon. Shannon began implementing what northerners and Kansas free-soilers had begun calling the "bogus laws" passed by the territorial legislature.

Pierce's fecklessness contributed to a crisis of political legitimacy. Free-staters—who, by the fall of 1855, represented a majority of settlers—flaunted the legislature's laws and freely accepted crates of new-model, breech-loading Sharps rifles sent out by sympathizers in New England. In September, a convention of "all the Free State elements of Kansas Territory" met at Big Springs near Lawrence, denounced the border ruffians and the territorial legislature, formed a free-state party, and nominated ex-Governor Reeder to Congress. A month later, the organized free-soilers reconvened in Topeka, drew up a territorial constitution that abolished slavery after July 4, 1857, and called their own elections for governor and a new legislature. The pro-slavery men, not surprisingly, boycotted the elections. Thereafter, Kansas had two governments, the official pro-slavery one (which had moved its seat to Lecompton, closer to the Missouri border) and the free-state one in Topeka. With both sides armed to the teeth, it seemed only a matter of time before combat commenced.

The murder of Charles Dow, a pro–free-state settler, by a pro-slavery man on November 21 touched off a series of incidents that set the informal armies in motion. A force of Missourians, numbering well over twelve hundred men, crossed the border and tramped to the countryside outside of the Yankees' main stronghold in Lawrence, torching and pillaging farms in their path, with the eventual objective, one settler wrote, of burning down the city and driving out "all the *Dambd* Abilitionists." The Lawrence free-staters, a thousand strong, outfitted with their new rifles and a howitzer, and receiving a steady flow of reinforcements from the surrounding areas, dug in for a fight to the finish. Governor Shannon rushed to Lawrence and, with Atchison's help among the pro-slavery men, persuaded both sides to lay down their weapons. But Atchison's advice to the Missourians was more tactical than pacific. "If you attack Lawrence now, you attack as a mob," he told the irregular army, "and what would be the result? You could cause the election of an abolition President, and the ruin of the Democratic party. Wait a little. You cannot now destroy these people without losing more than you would gain."

Free-staters and slave-staters alike held their fire for a few months, over a harsh and disabling winter. In the interim, they and the rest of the country would reflect hard and passionately on the struggle's importance and where it might lead. The northern press thundered against the official Kansas legislature, and publicized the Big Springs convention's resolution that the despotic lawmakers had "libeled the declaration of Independence, violated the constitutional bill of rights, and brought contempt and disgrace upon our republican institutions at home and abroad." Southerners insisted that any attempt to block the admission of Kansas over slavery would compel the Union's dissolution. And while democracy seemed to dangle in the balance in Kansas, voters everywhere prepared for a national election with the major political parties in chaos.

1856: DRESS REHEARSAL FOR REVOLUTION

Among the most prominent northerners moved by the Kansas conflict was Reverend Henry Ward Beecher, the son of Lyman Beecher, brother of Harriet Beecher Stowe, and pastor of Brooklyn's Congregational Plymouth Church of the Pilgrims. Beecher opposed slavery, but, like his sister, he was not an abolitionist radical, and during the early stages of the Kansas controversy, he agonized over what a mere minister could do. During a trip through New England early in 1856, he discovered Yankee clergymen—including, to his lasting inspiration, his father—preaching against the Kansas outrages and backing a monster protest petition drive. In March, Beecher himself spoke at United Church in New Haven, where a group of sixty had formed an antislavery band bound for Kansas. Noting that previous northern settlers had traveled armed, Beecher said he hoped the present group would "lack for nothing." The aging Yale professor of chemistry Benjamin Silliman, a former slaveholder, immediately pledged twenty-five dollars toward the purchase of a Sharps rifle. United Church's pastor, Reverend Leonard Bacon, pledged the same, and soon Beecher, carried away by the spirit, declared that Plymouth Church would provide not twenty-five dollars but twenty-five rifles. In a few days, more than six hundred dollars was collected, and the rifles were shipped off (along with twenty-five copies of holy scripture) in a crate marked "Bibles." Beecher, back in Brooklyn, was embarrassed when critics called the rifle shipments "Beecher's Bibles" and his congregation "the Church of the Holy Rifle," but he stood by his claim that, in Kansas, "self-defense is a religious duty."

In early March, the Topeka free-state government formally convened, and in mid-April, a special House committee arrived in the territory to investigate the charges of fraud in the previous year's elections. Witnesses told the congressmen one shocking tale after another; the spring brought fresh arrivals of northern settlers; pro-slavery tempers cracked. "Blood for Blood!" screamed one pro-slavery sheet, *Squatter Sovereignty*. "Let us purge ourselves of all abolition emissaries." Pro-slavery judge Samuel Lecompte convinced a grand jury to indict the entire Topeka government—"men who are dubbed governors . . . men who are dubbed all the various other dubs"—on charges of high treason. The local federal marshal falsely claimed that various free-staters forcibly resisted being served with papers, and called on the law-abiding citizens of Kansas to gather in Lecompton to form a deputized posse that would help the militia round up the miscreants. Lawrence was an obvious target, as several of the free-state officials lived there and the grand jury had brought additional indictments against the town's two antislavery newspapers and the Free State Hotel. Atchison's Missourians took the hint and joined the encampment at Lecompton.

On May 21, the pro-slavery force of between five and eight hundred men, dragging with them four six-pounder brass cannons, lay siege to Lawrence. Reluctant to resist the federal government's authority, the free-staters stood aside, and the pro-slavery men went on a rampage, burning homes, ransacking shops, and smashing to bits the antislavery newspaper presses. By the time the marauding ended, the Free State Hotel was a smoldering ruin, and the home and farm of the free-state governor, Dr. Charles Robinson, had been torched. Atop the gutted offices of the *Herald of Freedom* flew a bright red flag with a star in its center, the slogan "Southern Rights" inscribed on one side and "South Carolina" on the other. Reporters on the scene from Republican newspapers wrote dispatches about "the Sack of Lawrence." The pro-slavery press in Kansas and in the South told a very different story: "Glorious Triumph of the Law and Order Party Over Fanaticism in Kansas," ran the headline of the Lecompton *Union*.

On the day before Lawrence fell, Charles Sumner concluded a two-day speech in the Senate that he would later entitle "The Crime Against Kansas." Sumner knew nothing of what was about to transpire out West, but he was already furious. For months, Congress had been debating rival bills admitting Kansas as a state, either with the Topeka constitution or with a new constitution to be drafted under the auspices of the Lecompton government. Since southern Democrats controlled the Senate and northern Republicans controlled the House, neither side could prevail. Instead, speakers used the floors of Congress as soapboxes, to score points against their opponents. Finally, Sumner could take no more of the southerners' defense of the pro-slavery Kansans. "I shall make the most thorough & complete speech in my life," he wrote to Salmon Chase. "My soul is wrung by this outrage, & I shall pour it forth."

"The Crime Against Kansas," delivered to a packed Senate gallery, was an overblown effort at classical oratory—carefully rehearsed, at times pompous and pedantic, but also unforgiving in its denunciations of slavery and the Slave Power. The alleged crime that was its centerpiece was "the rape of a virgin territory, compelling it to the hateful embrace of slavery," for which Sumner held the entire Pierce administration guilty of complicity. Squired by the Sancho Panza of Slavery, Stephen Douglas, the rapists had set loose assassins and thugs in Kansas—"[h]irelings, picked from the drunken spew and vomit of an uneasy civilization"—and established a fraudulent legislature that passed a slave code unsurpassed in "its complex completely of wickedness." Sumner defended the Emigrant Aid Company as a group of sober conservative businessmen, and commended William

Henry Seward's bill for the admission of Kansas as the only reasonable response to the Slave Power's attacks on God and the Constitution. Yet despite its flashes of polemical brilliance, there was nothing new in the substance of Sumner's speech, while its heavy ballast of historical references, extended metaphors, and gratuitous classical allusions at times threatened to capsize it.

Sumner's performance did manage two feats. As if to shame his Democratic opponents, he reached back to recent history and explained how the ideas of Jacksonian Democracy favored a free Kansas, not a slave Kansas. He drew a parallel between the Topeka free-state constitution and the case of Michigan, where, in the mid-1830s, a popular convention, working at odds with an existing territorial legislature, drafted a constitution for statehood—which Jackson and the Democrats (including then-Congressman Franklin Pierce) accepted. The true principle of democratic popular sovereignty could not be clearer than as expounded by Thomas Hart Benton during the Michigan controversy twenty years earlier: "The sovereign power to govern themselves was in the majority, and they could not be divested of it." The most intense opposition to this claim, Sumner noted, came from John C. Calhoun, who supported legalistic authority over the people, but Jackson and the Democrats overcame him. Yet two decades later, Sumner declared, the nation was supposed to reject the majority's will and respect "the fantastic tricks now witnessed in Kansas" instead of legitimate democracy. "No such madness prevailed under Andrew Jackson," Sumner declared, while glaring at some of Jackson's leading acolytes and would-be successors, including Stephen Douglas.

Sumner also insulted the Slave Power, personified by the white-maned South Carolina senator Andrew P. Butler of the F Street Mess, in the vilest possible terms. Butler had given a speech that denounced the free-staters as fanatics, and Sumner, early in "The Crime Against Kansas," attacked Butler as Don Quixote to Douglas's Sancho Panza, tilting against antislavery "with such ebullition of animosity" that he had to be shown up for who he really was. And so Sumner exposed him as an old man "who has chosen a mistress to whom he has made his vows, and who . . . though polluted in the sight of the world, is chaste in his sight—I mean the harlot Slavery." The next day, Sumner singled out Butler once again, as one who had discharged "the loose expectoration of his speech" in defense of South Carolina, a state wallowing in its "shameful imbecility from slavery." Cass and Douglas immediately launched counterattacks on Sumner's insults. Republican newspapers, although pleased by the speech's substance, thought its rhetoric excessive and counterproductive. For southerners, Sumner had committed an unpardonable offense that deserved the meanest sort of punishment.

Two days later, Sumner was sitting at his desk on the Senate floor after adjournment, attending to his correspondence and franking copies of his controversial speech. Out of nowhere, he heard a voice address him, and he looked up to see a tall man whom he did not recognize looming directly above. "I have read your speech twice over carefully," said the stranger. "It is a libel on South Carolina, and Mr. Butler, who is a relative of mine." As he spoke these last words, the man crashed a hollow gold-headed cane across Sumner's head, which knocked Sumner blind, then hit him again and again, until Sumner (his legs trapped beneath his desk, which was bolted to the floor) rose with such force that he wrenched the desk from its moorings. Still the blows rained down, twenty or more, snapping the cane into pieces, until Sumner lurched forward and fell to the floor senseless, his head gushing blood. A few senators tried to stop the assault but were held at bay by another cane-wielder, one of two men who had accompanied the assailant into the chamber. Other senators, including Douglas and Robert Toombs, watched in silence (Toombs with complete approval) and offered no assistance to their colleague. Finally, Ambrose Murray, an antislavery Whig congressman who happened to be there, seized the assailant. Sumner's friends helped the victim to his feet and guided him to a sofa in the Senate lobby.

The attacker turned out to be the second-term congressman Preston Brooks, a South Carolina cousin of Butler's. (His accomplices were Congressmen Laurence Keitt, also of South Carolina, and Henry Edmundson of Virginia.) A staunch pro-slavery Democrat, Brooks had already declared that the fate of the South would be decided in Kansas, but now, honor as well as interest demanded instant vengeance. ("I went to work very deliberately . . . ," Brooks later said in a speech to the House, "and speculated somewhat as to whether I should employ a horsewhip or a cowhide.") The severity of the attack, and Brooks's pride in it, incensed even those northerners who had bridled at Sumner's excessive address. "Has it come to this," the old Jacksonian William Cullen Bryant asked in the *Evening Post*, "that we must speak with bated breath in the presence of our Southern masters? . . . Are we too, slaves, slaves for life, a target for their brutal blows, when we do not comport ourselves to please them?"

Southern celebrations of Brooks and his deed deepened the shock. "Our approbation, at least, is entire and unreserved," the *Richmond Enquirer* announced. "We consider the act good in conception, better in execution, and best of all in consequences. The vulgar Abolitionists in the Senate are getting above themselves. . . . They must be lashed into submission." Brooks claimed that his admirers were begging for fragments of his cane "as *sacred relicts*." The House voted to expel him, but the southern members blocked the required two-thirds' majority. Brooks, defiant, resigned nevertheless and returned to South Carolina, determined to win vindication through reelection (which he would). The only punishment he would ever receive was a three-hundred-dollar fine assessed by a local court. Sumner, traumatized mentally and physically, would not return to steady work in the Senate for another four years. During his convalescence, the Massachusetts legislature reelected him, turning his repaired, empty desk in the Senate into a silent protest against the Slave Power's savagery.

News of "Bleeding Sumner" hit "Bleeding Kansas" hard, especially coming so soon after the attack on Lawrence. A reliable witness said that one free-stater, in particular, went "crazy— *crazy*" upon hearing of Sumner's caning—the would-be guerrilla warrior John Brown. Brown, aged fifty-five and the father of twenty children, had left behind the quiet strains of wool growing and merchandising back in Springfield, Massachusetts, to become an avenger against slavery. His League of Gileadites, organized during the fugitive slave controversy, had come to nothing, as had a plan, backed by Gerrit Smith, to establish a colony for free blacks in the Adirondack Mountains of New York. In the summer of 1855, Brown followed six of his sons to Osawatomie, a small settlement near Pottawatomie Creek in eastern Kansas. The sons had come to make a new life for themselves; Brown became more interested in fighting slavery. He was named captain of the Pottawatomie Rifles company of the free-stater Liberty Guards, and in May, he and his men were among the antislavery forces who rushed to the aid of besieged Lawrence, only to learn en route that the town had been leveled. A day later came word of Brooks's attack on Sumner.

"Something must be done to show these barbarians that we, too, have rights," Brown declaimed—and he conceived a plan of retaliation for the caning of Sumner and the murders of free-staters over the previous year. On the night of May 24–25, Brown, four of his sons, and three other men, carrying broadswords, ambushed the farm of James Doyle, an anti–free-stater but not a slaveholder. They dragged Doyle and his two grown sons from their house and hacked them to pieces, sparing Doyle's wife and fourteen-year-old son. Then the band moved to the Wilkinson farm and abducted and killed the law-and-order man Allen Wilkinson before ending their attacks at the home of James Harris, where they split the skull of another pro-slavery partisan, William Sherman. Brown and his sons eluded capture; pro-slavery men destroyed the Brown homestead; and the massacre, combined with the Lawrence affair, touched off escalated violence all across the settled portions of the territory. Two hundred men (including Brown's son Frederick) died in the renewed combat. Brown himself fought on uncaptured until the autumn, when he headed back East to raise money to provide fresh supplies, hard cash, and more Sharps rifles to the Kansas warriors. "You know what I have done in Kansas . . . ," he cryptically told a group of abolitionist sympathizers in New York. "I have no other purpose but to serve the cause of liberty."

Northern reaction to Brown's atrocities was divided. While some antislavery editors idolized him as "Old Osawatomie Brown," others looked away. Stories even began circulating that Brown had not been involved, or had acted in self-defense. Brown, for his own part, would become cleverly evasive whenever questioned about what had happened along Pottawatomie Creek. In any event, dispatches about the subsequent bloodshed in Kansas soon enough overshadowed Brown's massacre. And by summer's end, when the prairie fighting temporarily died down, public attention had switched to the confusing presidential campaign.

"A VICTORIOUS DEFEAT": THE 1856 ELECTIONS AND THE CONSOLIDATION OF THE REPUBLICANS

The most surprising development in national politics during the Kansas excitement had been the precipitous decline of the Know-Nothing movement. The resurgence of the slavery issue played some role in diverting attention away from nativism, and so, too, did a sudden diminution of immigration after 1855—especially from Ireland, whose ruined population was nearly depleted of migrants. But the chief causes of the Know-Nothings' difficulties were internal to the movement and involved sectional issues.

In part, the nativists were the victims of their own success and ambition. After the party's strong showing in 1854, Know-Nothing organizers believed they could look southward and build a national party, as the antislavery men could never do. The nativists' greatest appeal was in the Border South among former Whigs who abjured the disunionist southern Democracy, but there was also substantial nativist sentiment in southern cities, where the immigrant presence had grown. In 1855, Know-Nothings won a large majority of seats in the Maryland house of delegates, took control of the Tennessee legislature, ran well in Kentucky, and, overall, performed better than the Whigs had in any election since 1848. Some nativists were persuaded that with an enlarged vote in the South in 1856, their party could actually win the presidency for ex-President Fillmore, who was by now a Know-Nothing devotee.

Instead of nationalizing nativism, however, the Know-Nothings' expansion caused an implosion. In June 1855, newly christened as the American Party, the Know-Nothings met in Philadelphia to draft their platform—and sectional divisions cracked wide open. Some northern statewide conventions had already adopted antislavery resolutions, while others had deferred to the South. New Englanders, led by newly elected Massachusetts Governor Henry Gardner, insisted on pragmatic grounds that without some sort of renunciation of the Kansas-Nebraska Act, the party would be doomed east of the Hudson. Southern delegates, joined by the conservative New York Silver Grays and the Californians, repudiated any such move as sectional and un-American. Able to agree about tightening naturalization laws and otherwise fighting the "aggressive policy and corrupting tendencies" of Roman Catholicism, the delegates split over slavery. When a majority report from the platform committee upholding Kansas-Nebraska passed the convention, a large majority of the northerners, including all of the New England and the Old Northwest delegations, formally repudiated the platform and boycotted the rest of the proceedings. The division was dually ruinous, not only pitting northerners against southerners but also dividing northern conservative Unionists in New York and the other middle Atlantic states against the rest of the northern nativists.

A second factor was also spoiling the Know-Nothings' prospects: the manipulative efforts by antislavery men in the party who were either fed up with appeasing the South or had intended all along to capture the movement for the antislavery cause. The Massachusetts Know-Nothings, and their most out-spoken antislavery leader, newly elected Senator Henry F. Wilson, exemplified what was happening. A former journeyman cordwainer from Natick, born in poverty, Wilson had risen to become a shoe manufacturer, entered politics as a new school Whig, and in 1848 helped to form the Free Soil Party. In 1854, when conservative Massachusetts Whigs, still certain they could dominate the state's politics, refused to fuse with the emerging Republicans, Wilson won the anti-Nebraska nomination for governor in 1854. Yet Wilson, whose background made him thoroughly familiar with the popular nativist milieu, sensed the Know-Nothing upheaval that was about to overtake the state's politics, and he signed up with the nativists, hoping to win their nomination as well.

Not wanting to appear creatures of the free-soilers, the Know-Nothings spurned Wilson and chose instead Henry Gardner. But Wilson was not done. Knowing that the nativists could not afford to ignore the antislavery vote, he agreed to drop out of the governor's race and support Gardner if the nativist leaders would support him for the U.S. Senate seat soon to be vacated by Edward Everett, who had decided to retire. Some antislavery leaders accused Wilson of betrayal, but at least one old-line Whig conservative, Robert Winthrop, figured out his real intentions and how they had changed the political calculus. "Our K.N. lodges," he wrote a friend, "have been controlled by the most desperate sort of Free Soil adventurers." The newly elected Know-Nothing legislature elected Wilson to the Senate, where he paid little attention to nativist issues and became a stalwart Republican. In the House, the former Democrat Nathaniel Banks, elected to a second term as a Know-Nothing, likewise threw in his lot with the Republicans. (The House Republicans, in turn, elevated Banks to the Speakership of the new Congress after a taxing two-month struggle early in 1856.) The new Massachusetts legislature, more antislavery than nativist, also adopted a resolution condemning the Kansas-Nebraska Act, approved a new personal liberty law, and added a law banning racial segregation in the state's public schools—the first of its kind in the nation.

In February 1856, the American Party met, once again in Philadelphia, to nominate its national ticket—and once again failed to mend its divisions over slavery. One Virginia delegate declared that the northern wing of the party was composed of abolitionists, that the party was a failure, and that the convention might as well disband. He exaggerated—there was still a strong complement of anti-abolitionist northern conservatives in the party—but every effort to finesse the slavery issue backfired. The convention adopted a prolix new plank that endorsed popular sovereignty in the territories, but was so confusing, one delegate remarked, that the election would be over before the people figured out what it meant. The convention nominated Millard Fillmore for president, the southerners' and New York Silver Grays' favorite, but totally unacceptable to New England and the Old Northwest. The northern malcontents withdrew, issued a protest demanding the repeal of Kansas-Nebraska, and called for a new convention of what would become known as the North American Party. The bolters agreed to meet in New York just prior to the scheduled Republican Party's Philadelphia convention in early June.

The North American Party's stated objective was to nominate an antislavery nativist in the hopes that the Republicans, holding their first national convention, would feel the pressure to choose the same man. But the stealthy antislavery men had different plans: instead of converting the Republican Party to nativism, they would convert the North American Party, such as it was, to the Republicans. Their plotting centered on the new House Speaker, Nathaniel Banks, who had been careful to keep up good relations with his Know-Nothing backers. A strong contender for the North American presidential nomination, Banks allowed his name to be put forward, but with the quiet intention of standing down as soon as the Republicans named their ticket, and supporting the Republican candidates. The plan worked like a charm. The North Americans (with Thurlow Weed, Preston

King, and other Republicans hanging around, quietly meeting with delegates) nominated Banks—and then the Republican Party took center stage.

The Republicans had been organizing their gathering since the previous Christmas, when a small group of influential antislavery fusionists met at the home of the old Jacksonian warhorse, Francis Blair, just outside of Washington. The planners included Nathaniel Banks, Charles Sumner (Brooks's attack on him still five months in the future), Preston King, Salmon Chase, and Gamaliel Bailey—all men with either strong past Democratic links like Blair or Democratic affinities. They discussed the names of prospective nominees—including Blair's favorite, the California explorer and Bear Republic hero John C. Frémont—but left the matter to rest until a larger informal national meeting to be held early in the new year. The second meeting, held in Pittsburgh in late February, gathered antislavery radicals and moderates from across the North and from five slave border states as well, to plan for a nominating convention and draft a party platform. The meeting's tone and the platform it approved were purposefully temperate—firm on issues that united the disparate antislavery movement like Kansas-Nebraska, but circumspect on others, including nativism and the Fugitive Slave Law. ("There is not a single warm and living position, taken by the Republican party," Frederick Douglass complained, "except freedom for Kansas.") The more radical delegates, like the now aging Joshua Giddings, checked their chagrin and prepared for the truly important national nominating convention, scheduled to open in Philadelphia on June 17.

In the interim, the sack of Lawrence and the attack on Sumner hardened the antislavery men's views, and ensured that the Philadelphia convention would be forceful. The platform committee, chaired by David Wilmot, produced a document that, without offending moderates, sounded radical, by reaching back to the Buffalo Free Soilers, citing the egalitarian principles of the Declaration of Independence, and denouncing slavery along with Mormon polygamy as "twin relics of barbarism." The platform also stressed the obliteration of legally protected rights in Kansas and arraigned the Pierce administration for committing an impeachable "high crime against the Constitution, the Union, and humanity" by permitting the Kansas outrages. Ultimately, however, the convention's work would be judged on whom it nominated for the presidency. Two men—William Henry Seward and Salmon P. Chase—loomed largest, yet neither was acceptable to important constituencies, including the antislavery nativists. Far better was Blair's original choice, John C. Frémont.

Raven-haired, adventuresome, and charismatic, Frémont had earned his romantic heroic nickname, "The Pathfinder," with his exploits mapping the Oregon Trail, the Sierra Nevadas, and the Pacific coast in the 1840s. His marriage to Jessie Benton, daughter of Thomas Hart Benton and a formidable person in her own right, made him more acceptable to ex-Democrats, and conservative Republicans liked the fact that he had been born and raised in Georgia. Frémont's support for a free-soil California in 1850 and his opposition to his father-in-law's enemy, David Atchison, over Kansas established his antislavery bona fides. But Frémont had no strong previous party allegiances and had played no direct political role during the previous six years, which spared him the complaints that dogged Chase and Seward. He won the nomination decisively on the first ballot. After naming the New Jersey ex-Whig William Dayton as Frémont's running mate to pacify its conservative wing, the party took to the hustings enthusiastically, under an updated version of the Free Soil slogan of 1848: "Free Speech, Free Press, Free Men, Free Labor, Free Territory, and Fremont." The convention, one antislavery Indiana newspaper later exulted, had "organized the Republican party—a FREE SOIL PARTY in the fullest sense of the term, gave it a Free Soil baptism, and a Free Soil Platform, and sent it forth."

As expected, the North American nominee Banks abandoned his candidacy and supported Frémont. Some angry northern nativists, chiefly in New York, ended up supporting Fillmore—an unsatisfying move given that Fillmore had become a tribune for staggered southern Whigs and some Silver Gray northerners more interested in Unionism than nativism. But the biggest losers in the wake of the Republicans' absorption of the North Americans were the old-line conservative northern Whigs, including Robert Winthrop, Rufus Choate, and assorted other ex-Websterites, Cotton Whigs, and patricians. The heirs to a Federalist political tradition that had once ruled the nation, these men, on the political defensive for decades, had been rendered obsolete in 1856. Some, like Choate, a founder of the Massachusetts Whig Party, joined with Webster's and Henry Clay's sons in switching to the Democrats, hoping to kill off the Republican fanatics and believing that the slaveholders' party now embodied the last vestiges of respect for property, order, and the Union. "Whig principles!" Choate exclaimed. "I go to the Democrats to find them. They have assumed our principles, one after another, till there is little difference between us." Other conservative Whigs (now derided as "Old Fogeys"), unwilling to ally with the one-time party of Jackson, decided to back Fillmore, not out of any sudden enthusiasm for nativism but to warm themselves around the dying embers of conservative Whiggery.

Pro-administration northern Democrats were also mightily troubled. The Pierce White House, alternating between inertness and pro-slavery complicity over Kansas, had tried to revive the aggressive expansionism that had been President Pierce's strongest original commitment. Redoubling efforts to obtain Cuba, Pierce had reauthorized Minister Pierre Soulé in 1854 to approach the Spanish government with a deal and, if spurned, to direct the effort "to detach that island from the Spanish dominion." The hotheaded Soulé assembled the American ministers to Britain and France, James Buchanan and John Young Mason, in the Belgian city of Ostend and had them sign a memorandum stating that if Spain balked, then "by every law, human and Divine, we shall be justified in wresting it from Spain." News of the so-called Ostend Manifesto leaked to the press and raised such a row in Congress that the stunned White House finally forced Soulé to resign.

Undeterred, Soulé linked up with the American man of fortune, William Walker, who took control of rebel armies in far-off Nicaragua in 1855, defeated the standing government, and appointed himself de facto dictator. Walker opened the country to southern slaveholders and quickly received diplomatic recognition from the Pierce administration. Celebrated by southern newspapers as "the grey-eyed man of destiny," Walker would eventually fall out with Pierce, lose his revolutionary regime, and wind up executed in 1860 by a Honduran firing squad, but the episode came as one more reminder of how Manifest Destiny had decayed into pro-slavery adventurism. With the blessings of the American government, a self-proclaimed American liberator had promised to bring slavery back to Central America. "[A] barbarous people can never become civilized without the salutary apprenticeship which slavery secured," one New Orleans paper asserted, in support of Walker's project.

With freedom on the run from Kansas to Nicaragua, northern Democrats, having been soundly rejected in 1854, were splintered into rival factions, some dating back to the aftermath of the Free Soil revolt. The most bitter and confusing divisions arose, as ever, in New York, where the so-called Hard Shell Hunkers, longtime fierce opponents of the antislavery Democrats, had turned against the Pierce White House over lack of patronage consideration, which they believed had gone instead to their Soft Shell Hunker rivals. The returns in 1855 were devastating, plunging the northern Democrats' numbers in Congress into a trough in which they would stay for twenty years. The violence in Kansas and on the Senate floor in 1856 left what remained of the northern Democracy reeling—mocked, in a retrieval of John Randolph's old phrase, as the Doughface Democracy. Pierce became the emblem of the Doughface disaster. The president's own former secretary, B. B. French, wrote that he "is in rather bad odor, and will stink worse yet before the 4th of March next. The Kansas outrages are all imputable to him, and if he is not called to answer for them here, 'In Hell they'll roast him like a herring.'"

The situation was exactly the reverse for southern Democrats. One by one, the leaders of southern Whiggery outside of the border states had defected, Robert Toombs as early as 1853, his Georgia colleague Alexander Stephens in the wake of Kansas-Nebraska. And in bastions of patrician domination, Master Race democracy finally made breakthroughs that enhanced the Democrats' political prospects while augmenting the slaveholders' power. In Virginia, the mercurial, furiously pro-slavery, sometime Whig Henry A. Wise had led a redrafting of the commonwealth's constitution in 1851 that finally wiped away the old freehold suffrage, provided for popular election of the governor, and more fairly apportioned the lower house of the legislature. Failure to reform the old regime, Wise persuaded his colleagues, would endanger slavery itself by alienating the mass of white freemen: "Will you dare say," he asked the convention, "that you will balance 94,000 free white population, with all their interests, moral, intellectual and political, with their police and arms-bearing responsibilities, with a million even of your black serfs?" Southern-style democracy, its hegemony in the hands of the slaveholders, would not threaten the peculiar institution but strengthen it by tightening the bonds of racial solidarity. Five years later, in the spring of 1856, Wise made good on his predictions by coming out of political retirement to run for governor as a pro-slavery Democrat—and, with his convincing victory, to stall the momentum of crypto-Whig Know-Nothingism in the upper South. Wise's triumph, Pierce wrote to Douglas, "has put a new face upon the prospects of the Democratic Party."

Pierce and Douglas came to the Democratic nominating convention in Cincinnati as rivals for the presidential nomination, sharing support from southern delegates grateful for their aggressive roles in the Kansas-Nebraska turmoil. Yet while Pierce also had backing from his native New England, it was not enough to gain a majority, and Douglas, outside Illinois, was reviled for having caused the northern Democracy's tribulations. That left the candidate with the best organization on the convention floor: James Buchanan of Pennsylvania. Few delegates could remember a time when the sixty-five-year-old Buchanan had not played some part either in government or in the party. His public service dated back to the War of 1812, when he fought as a volunteer in the defense of Baltimore; thereafter, he had won five elections to the House, three to the Senate, and served as minister to Russia under Jackson, secretary of state under Polk, and minister to Great Britain under Pierce. A tall, heavy, large-headed bachelor, he cut a dashing enough figure until he spoke, when his high-pitched voice (which Henry Clay used to mock in Senate debate) gave added currency to rumors that he lacked virility. He also had a defect in one eye that caused him to tilt his head slightly forward and sideways in conversation, which some regarded as a sign of intensity and others as a sign of deceit. Above all, Buchanan had the reputation of a dutiful and able public servant, a conservative who never allowed great principles to obstruct his political career. "[H]e was, assuredly, . . . a cautious, circumspect and sagacious man, amply endowed with . . . clear perceptions of self-interest and of duties as connected with it," recalled Martin Van Buren, a connoisseur of caution.

Buchanan also had the advantage of having been largely out of the political line of fire over the previous four years. As minister to Britain, he had signed on to Soulé's inflammatory Ostend Manifesto, but unlike Pierce or Douglas he bore no stigma in the public mind from the struggle over Kansas. He was a political powerhouse in his native Pennsylvania, a swing state. Although lackluster, he seemed a safe and acceptable option compared to either Pierce, Douglas, or any Republican nominee—unobjectionable to the North and the South, and therefore a potential winner. Even Frémont's father-in-law, Thomas Hart Benton, found Buchanan suitable enough, "[n]ever a leading man in any high sense, but eminently a man of peace." After more than a dozen ballots at the convention, Pierce and Douglas withdrew, and on the seventeenth ballot, Buchanan was nominated. The delegates gave him a platform that endorsed popular sovereignty, denounced the Republicans as inciters of treason, and tried to stir up what was left of the old Jacksonian fervor, including one plank opposing the creation of a national bank.

As Frémont could expect virtually no support in the slaveholding states, the southern campaign became a battle between Buchanan and Fillmore. Given the Democrats' sectional strength, Buchanan's victory there was a foregone conclusion. In the North, the Republicans had a lock on New England, Michigan, and Wisconsin. Thus, the national contest came down to the battle between Frémont and Buchanan in a few key free states. Buchanan only needed to carry Pennsylvania and one other toss-up state to win the election. But in New York, Pennsylvania, and Illinois, the numerous conservative pro-Fillmore Whigs were potential electoral wild cards, and Ohio, Indiana, and New Jersey, each of which had voted Democratic in 1852, were now closely divided between Democrats and Republicans.

Not since 1840 had the nation witnessed the kind of riotous, impassioned electioneering that the Frémont Republicans mounted. The shock of the Kansas-Nebraska Act, and the rush of spectacular events earlier in 1856, along with the Pierce administration's apparent siding with the South, excited antislavery sentiment to a fever pitch. Pro-Frémont Wide-Awake Clubs appeared across the North, leading mass parades and carrying banners espousing the Republican cause. Pamphlets, books, and popular songsheets (including one ditty based on the minstrel-song writer Stephen Foster's "Camptown Races") flooded the market, celebrating The Pathfinder and excoriating his Democratic opponent, "The Old Public Functionary" Buchanan. Yet the boisterous Frémont campaign also had a moral seriousness and sense of impending cataclysm that the Whigs' Log Cabin campaign of 1840 had completely lacked. John Greenleaf Whittier wrote fervently of how, finally, the time had come, "When Good and Evil, as for final strife,/ Close vast and dim on Armageddon's plain." Writers who normally refrained from political speechmaking, including the stage-shy William Cullen Bryant, turned out in support of Frémont. The more practiced antislavery stump-speakers—Chase, Giddings, Hale—seemed to be everywhere at once. Abraham Lincoln—pushed by his more radical law partner William Herndon to drop his Whig label at last and join the Republicans—delivered ninety-odd speeches for Frémont.

In the swing states of the lower North, the Republicans had to fend off Democratic charges that they were out to destroy the Union and impose racial equality. (One group of Indiana Democrats organized a parade featuring young girls in white dresses holding banners that read "Fathers, Save us from nigger husbands.") To the claims about their disunionism, the Republicans responded much as the authors of the "Appeal of the Independent Democrats" had two years earlier, arguing that it was the southern bullies, always threatening secession, who actually denigrated the Union. In reply to the racist attacks, Republicans, notably the ex-Democrats among them, fell on the defensive, sometimes claiming that their true intention was to save white labor from having to compete with black labor. That maneuver in turn alienated abolitionists including William Lloyd Garrison, who denounced the Republicans as "a complexional party, exclusively for white men, not for all men."

Frémont's supporters also raised their own powerful charges, that the Democrats wanted to subvert American democracy in favor of an aristocracy based on human bondage. A Frémont victory, one meeting in Buffalo proclaimed, would guarantee "for our country a government of the people, instead of a government by an oligarchy; a government maintaining before the world the rights of men rather than the privileges of masters." As their prime example, the Republicans needed to look no farther than Kansas. Even voters who had tolerated southern demands for state rights were appalled by the Kansas events and switched to the Republicans. "[H]ad the Slave Power been less *aggressively insolent*, I would have been content to see it extend . . . ," one former Democrat wrote a friend, "but when it seeks to extend its sway by fire & sword, I am ready to say hold, enough!"

The Democrats' advantages were their superior campaign organization and huge campaign war chest, raised by well-placed supporters in New York, Philadelphia, and the South. Much of the money went into producing tracts, carefully aimed at the voters in the battleground states. Party speakers everywhere received copies of the *Democratic Handbook*, which laid out the strategy: attack the Republicans as Know-Nothings (to shore up the Catholic immigrant vote), as "Black Republicans" (to exploit racial animosities), and as disunionists (to appeal to moderate and conservative ex-Whigs). Personal criticism of Frémont was tailored to particular local constituencies. (Northwest Democrats bandied about a charge that Frémont was a closet Catholic, which hurt the Republicans in some pockets of evangelical piety.) Above all, the Democrats harped on the Unionist issue in deftly contradictory ways. In the North, they warned that the wild-eyed Republican fanatics intended to dissolve the Union; in the South, they promised that if the wild-eyed Republican fanatics were elected, southerners would be forced to choose, as a leading Louisianan declared, "immediate, absolute, eternal separation." Either way, Democrats could claim, a Frémont victory would seal the nation's doom.

As expected, Buchanan swept the South and Frémont won New England, Michigan, and Wisconsin. The antislavery voters in the northern portions of New York and Ohio turned out large enough majorities to carry those states for the Republicans as well. But the Democrats ran well in Pennsylvania, New Jersey, Illinois, and Indiana, topping the Republican vote by margins that, in the first two states, came close to 20 percentage points—and deciding the election. Buchanan's electoral vote total, although far reduced from Pierce's landslide four years earlier, was a comfortable 174 to the Republicans' 114 (with Fillmore carrying only Maryland's 8 votes). The Democrats also reclaimed the majority in the House of Representatives. Still, Republicans greeted the results as highly encouraging. "We are beaten," said Senator William Pitt Fessenden of Maine, "but we have frightened the rascals awfully. They cannot help seeing what their doom must inevitably be, unless they abandon their unrighteous ways."

A closer look at the presidential returns bears out Fessenden's optimism. In only two of the crucial lower North states did Buchanan win a bare majority of the popular vote—50.4 percent in Indiana and 50.1 percent in his home state of Pennsylvania. In both of those states, as well as in New Jersey and Illinois (where he won, respectively, 47.2 and 44.1 percent of the vote), unexpected large turnouts for the American Party accounted for the margins between the Democrats and Republicans. Although the American Party died in its very first national election, there still turned out to be a considerable old Whig vote in the lower North—Unionists intimidated by charges of Republican radicalism, yet not willing to go all the way and vote for the Democrats. (Fillmore also showed unexpected strength in the border slave states as well as in Louisiana, an indication of persisting political divisions within the seemingly solid Democratic South.) Although enough to win Buchanan the White House, the outcome was hardly a resounding endorsement of the northern Democrats. In every free state outside New England, the Democracy's vote declined from what it had been in 1852, including a drop of nearly 20 percentage points in New York. Meanwhile, the Republican Party had polled 1.3 million votes and carried eleven of the sixteen free states, in an election that saw northern turnout rise to more than 80 percent of the eligible voters—by any measure a stunning debut.

Still, if the Republican campaign had ended in what one of Charles Sumner's correspondents called "a victorious defeat," Democrats had sufficient reason to refuse seeing their victory as pyrrhic. They had retained the White House; they now controlled the Congress; and the Supreme Court, under Roger Brooke Taney, seemed favorable to their political views. Of the two great parties of the Jacksonian years, the Whigs, and not themselves, had disintegrated, leaving the Democracy standing as the only authentically national political party. Hard-line southern Democrats were especially elated, to the point of cockiness. Their threats of disunion had, they thought, once again been heeded. The Yankee fanatics had once again been laid low. If some southerners wished that the party had stuck by Pierce, the proven breaker of abolitionist mischief, there was every reason to believe that Buchanan would be just as noble, would eradicate Douglas's weak-kneed popular sovereignty doctrine, and would protect slavery in the territories—and thereby make southern secession unnecessary. "Mr. Buchanan and the Northern Democracy," one Virginia Democrat reflected after the election, "are dependent on the South. If we can succeed in Kansas, deep down the Tariff, shake off our Commercial dependence on the North and add a little more slave territory, we may yet live free men under the Stars and Strip[e]s."

"ON THE TIP-TOE OF REVOLUTION": THE REPUBLICANS AND NORTHERN DEMOCRACY

Early in the 1856 canvass, a Buffalo Republican wrote to William Seward that it appeared as if public opinion was "on the tip-toe of Revolution." A staggered Republican journalist was more emphatic: "the process now going on in the politics of the United States," he wrote, "is a *Revolution*." By November, such pronouncements seemed overblown. Despite all of the turmoil, and despite the Republicans' consolidation, the American government would look, in 1857, much as it had in 1854, with the southern-dominated Democratic Party in charge. The events of 1856 were instead a dress rehearsal for revolution. The revolutionary process was well underway, and by year's end, a crucial part of the process had been largely completed—the formation of a coherent Republican political ideology.

The Republican Party, like all successful American political parties, was a ragtag coalition. At its heart were the antislavery Whigs, antislavery Democrats, and Free Democrats who had begun abandoning the established parties long before 1854. In the wake of Kansas-Nebraska, that core was joined by Whigs and Democrats who could no longer stomach what they considered the aggression of the aristocratic, pro-slavery South in the wake of Bleeding Kansas and Bleeding Sumner. The new antislavery recruits came from all classes, from urban as well as rural areas, and (though less plentiful in New Jersey and Pennsylvania and the southern portions of Indiana and Illinois) from every northern state. The Republican coalition included former reformist

Whigs and former reformist Democrats, immigrants (especially Germans) and nativists, old Liberty Party egalitarians and old Barnburner and midwestern racists. All shared the conviction that slavery had become a blight on the nation—a relic of barbarism that, if allowed to spread, would block the advance of free labor, squelch American prosperity, and degrade the status of the vast majority of ordinary American citizens. Republican leaders proclaimed the virtues of northern free-labor society, which, they asserted, were under siege by the slaveholders and the Democratic Party—"[i]ts Democracy . . . a lie, a cheat, and a delusion," one Republican editor declared. Above all else, they presented the Slave Power as a forceful and growing threat, "an aristocratic oligarchy" which would force "the twenty millions of freemen [to] surrender their dearest privileges at the ipse dixit of 347,000 slaveholders."

The testimony of two very different Republicans—veteran partisans from clashing political backgrounds—illuminates how the party's democratic ideology merged aspects of radical Jacksonianism and the more liberal strands of new-school Whiggery from the 1830s. Francis Blair was a comparative newcomer and moderate within the Republicans' ranks, and at age sixty-five, his career as the consummate Jacksonian polemicist was largely behind him. But in the wake of Kansas-Nebraska, some of the old brimstone of his days at the *Globe* erupted. In a letter addressed to a public meeting in New York, which he entitled *A Voice from the Grave of Jackson!*, Blair lit into his old party for abandoning the democratic principles it had vindicated in 1832 and 1833. "To use a homely phrase," he exclaimed, *"the Democracy has been 'sold out'* to Mr. Calhoun's nullifying party." There was no question, in Blair's mind, that Jackson, were he alive, would have stood up to the "perfect Southern phalanx" that now threatened disunion; the only question, he wrote, was whether "the Nullifiers who have thus usurped the name and organization of the Democratic party, but who have no principles in common with it, shall be allowed to carry out their designs in such disguise." The "spurious Democracy," Blair charged, had "perfected its system in the Kansas act, and made it their test"—and against it, "I, as a Democrat of the Jefferson, Jackson, and Van Buren school, enter my protest."

The ex-Whig Charles Francis Adams, son of John Quincy Adams, had a much longer history than Blair in antislavery politics, though by 1856 he, too, was a moderate among Republicans. His temperament was much milder than the old Jacksonian Blair's. But Adams also blamed the crisis chiefly on the self-preserving tenacity of a small elite, which had rejected the axioms of "the great apostle of modern democracy, Thomas Jefferson." Adams calmly explained to a New York audience that "[t]his slave power consists, in fact, of about three hundred and fifty thousand active men"—a tiny minority that commanded fifteen states directly, materially affected five or six more, and, through its "numerous friends and dependents" elsewhere, controlled the national government. To sustain their power and "what they consider [their] property," against "the prevailing tendencies of the age" and "a large body of their own countrymen," these men found it impossible to escape "adopting a system of policy aggressive upon the rights of the freemen." The influence of the Slave Power was pervasive and unrelenting: "It never relaxes in its vigilance over public events. It never is turned aside by the temptation of an incidental purpose." At stake, Adams said, was the fate of free institutions and the rights of freemen as well as slaves.

Republican spokesmen and supporters repeated the theme constantly—that an oligarchic enormity had disfigured the Constitution and perverted the very word *democracy* into a cover for its own domination. Genuine democracy, according to these formulations, was a peculiar feature of free societies. At issue, as William Seward explained on the campaign trail, was "an ancient and eternal conflict . . . between the system of free labor, with equal and universal suffrage, free speech, free thought, and free action, and the system of slave labor, with unequal franchises secured by arbitrary, oppressive, and tyrannical laws." The conflict between true and sham democracy could no longer be stilled or postponed by compromise, Seward contended: "The slave-holders can never be content without dominion, which abridges the freedom as well as circumscribes the domain of the non-slaveholding freemen." Slavery was incontrovertibly aristocratic, both where it held sway and where it wished to do so. But the future was democratic and the Republican Party was devoted to preparing for it, against a Democratic Party that had thoroughly betrayed its name.

As Seward remarked, the events of the mid-1850s threw into sharp relief how two different democracies, shaped by slavery, had arisen within the same nation. Although some southern franchises and systems of representation were, in fact, more equal than oth-ers, slaveholders, and normally wealthy slaveholders, held a com-manding power in the courts and legislatures throughout the South. By contrast, power was more dispersed in most of the North, where ordinary farmers and even wage earners not only voted but also held state offices. Southern politics could brook no open criticism of slavery for fear of destabilizing the system; northerners were free to write and say whatever they wanted about any political subject. In Kansas, upholders of southern-style popular sovereignty had flagrantly rigged elections, violently seized control of polling places, and turned democracy into a mockery—and had gained federal sanction from a doughface Democrat bullied into compliance by Slave Power congressmen and cabinet members. When an elected northern Republican had the temerity to call the bullies to account, one of them cut him down and beat him mercilessly on the floor of the U.S. Senate.

The Republicans demanded a rebirth of American politics, to break, once and for all, the slaveholders' stranglehold over the nation's political institutions and to hasten tyrannical slavery's demise. And it was precisely as revolutionaries that the slavehold-ers regarded their new sectional foe. Who were these Yankees, they asked, to challenge the duly constituted authorities in Kansas? Who were they to preach democracy to states where every white man could vote, just like in the North? Who were they to declaim against slavery, what the *Richmond Enquirer* called "a social sys-

tem as old as the world, universal as man"? One Alabama newspaper editor said exactly who they were: "a conglomeration of
greasy mechanics, filthy operatives, smallfisted farmers, and
moonstruck theorists." To conserve all that was natural, moral,
Christian, and orderly in America, these degraded radicals had to
be put down now, put down hard, put down once and for all.

What remained to be seen, after the 1856 elections, was the
shape that the southern counterrevolution would take, and
whether the new administration, with its party in control of the
entire federal apparatus, would back it. And in this, the proponents of the southern-style slaveholders' democracy could count
on the sympathies of a significant number of northerners: ex-
Whig hard-line conservatives; seaport merchants tied to the cotton trade; Catholic workers (especially Irish immigrants)
offended by the Republicans' nativist tinge and empathy for black
slaves; and farmers and small townsmen all across the lower
North who preferred Stephen Douglas's version of popular sovereignty and white supremacy to the prospect of disunion and
"Black Republican" rule.

Buchanan's ascendancy boded well for the forces of resistance
in the southern Democracy—and it boded even better when the
new president began selecting a heavily pro-southern cabinet.
But that final conservative effort would end up wrecking what
was left of the Democratic Party, and then it would wreck the
nation. It began with a momentous judicial ruling about an
obscure Missouri slave, Dred Scott, who a decade earlier, with
his wife, Harriet, had begun fighting for his freedom.

7

A NIGHTMARE BROODS
OVER SOCIETY

As he walked to the crowded podium at the Capitol to deliver his inauguration speech and take the oath of office, President-elect James Buchanan stopped to have a brief private conversation with the man who would swear him in, Chief Justice Roger Brooke Taney. Everyone toward the front of the throng below could see the two huddle together. Buchanan then told the nation that a case pending before the Supreme Court would settle the outstanding issues regarding slavery and the territories. He bid all good Americans to submit "cheerfully" to the decision "whatever [it] may be."

Two days later, Taney and the court majority rendered their stern pro-slavery ruling in *Dred Scott v. Sandford*. Republicans immediately speculated that Buchanan, at the inauguration, had known precisely how the case would turn out because Taney had just tipped him off. Over the months to come, the conjectures hardened into a conviction that a long-maturing Slave Power conspiracy lay behind the case, the Court's ruling, and Buchanan's remarks. The "whisperings" at the Capitol, William Seward told the Senate, had allowed the new president to sound impartial and magnanimous, when in fact he knew that the Court was about to hang "the millstone of slavery" on Kansas—and, potentially, clear the way to force slavery on every state and territory in the Union.

Seward's case against Buchanan was speculative and circumstantial. Yet there was unquestionably an affinity between pro-slavery southerners and the new administration, which confirmed a decade-long trend toward slavery's expansion. And, although the evidence would remain hidden for decades, there actually was improper collusion in the matter of *Dred Scott*. Weeks prior to his swearing-in, Buchanan started receiving covert reports from his fellow Pennsylvanian, Justice Robert C. Grier, about the Court's internal debates, and Buchanan, secretly alerted by pro-slavery Justice James Catron, pressed Grier to side with the pro-slavery majority. Well before inauguration day, Buchanan was fully apprised of how the Court would rule, and in his address he disingenuously undertook an advance campaign to get the nation to accept it. Seward and the Republicans knew nothing of the contacts, and never would, but the gist of their accusations about the new president and the *Dred Scott* decision turns out to have been true.

Buchanan's prediction that the ruling would at last settle the sectional battle proved just as hapless as Millard Fillmore's similar prediction about the truce of 1850. To southern Democrats and their northern allies, that failure would be shocking. Although the principles of judicial review and supremacy had not yet been fully established in American law, there was a widespread presumption that the Supreme Court should be respected as the most informed arbiter on constitutional issues. As the pro-administration Washington *Union* observed, with measured cheer, "the judgement of the highest tribunal in the land" stood "elevated above the schemes of party politics, and shielded alike from the effects of sudden passion and of popular prejudice." Failure to comply with *Dred Scott*, the leading New York dough-face newspaper claimed, would amount to an endorsement of "rebellion, treason, and revolution." But instead of commanding respect, the *Dred Scott* decision thoroughly discredited the Taney Court among Republicans and persuaded them more than ever that the dictatorial Slave Power needed to be eradicated.

Once again, a much-hailed final settlement of the nation's sectional rift worsened the rift. The middle ground, still sought by Douglas Democrats, conciliatory northern Whigs, and southern Unionists, crumbled into dust; the Buchanan administration exacerbated the situation; and the Republican Party, the intended political victim of the Court's ruling in *Dred Scott*, grew stronger in response. As if the battles over slavery were not bad enough, the nation was rocked, in the summer of 1857, by a financial panic that briefly augured a general economic collapse—and that snapped the boom mentality that had captivated political leaders for more than a decade. "A nightmare broods over society . . . ," one northerner remarked in the wake of the panic. "God alone foresees the history of the next six months." The economy proved more resilient than was feared, but for the Union the nightmare was just beginning.

"TIMES NOW ARE NOT AS THEY WERE": THE POLITICS OF *DRED SCOTT V. SANDFORD*

Of all the black Americans who achieved prominence in the fight over slavery, Dred Scott is among the most enigmatic. We know what he looked like thanks to daguerreotypes made in the last year of his life—although his expression, somewhere between bemused and startled, raises as many questions about him as it answers. Other sources show that he was probably born in Virginia in the late 1790s, that he was slight in stature, and that he was illiterate. A St. Louis newspaper claimed, in 1857, that, although unlettered, Scott was "not ignorant" and that he commanded a "strong common sense." Along with his wife, he was plainly resolute about gaining their freedom, a determination possibly reinforced by the congregation of St. Louis's antislavery Second African Baptist Church, where Harriet Scott attended services in the mid-1840s—and which was pastored by the martyred Elijah Lovejoy's former typesetter, now Reverend John Anderson.* It is likely that Harriet had as much or even more to do with instigating the suit than her husband. Otherwise, the circumstances of Dred Scott's fame have left him a cipher—and at times an almost incidental participant in the events forever linked with his name.

Scott's whereabouts between 1830 and 1846—the key facts in his case—are known precisely. In 1830, Scott's Virginia owner, Peter Blow, resettled his family and his six slaves to St. Louis. Within two years, both Blow and his wife died. (Their children stayed in the city and married into prominent families.) At some point before 1833, either Peter Blow or his children sold Scott to an army surgeon named John Emerson, who took him from Missouri to posts in Illinois and at Fort Snelling in the newly created Wisconsin Territory. While at Fort Snelling, Scott married Harriet Robinson, a teenage slave who was also Emerson's property. Over the next six years, the Scotts returned to St. Louis (where they lived in the custody of Emerson's wife) and spent time with their master in Louisiana and Iowa, before winding up, after Emerson's death, in St. Louis once again, inherited by Emerson's widow and working as hired-out slaves. (During these travels, Harriet had given birth to a daughter in free territory.) Finally, on April 6, 1846, Dred and Harriet filed separate petitions at the St. Louis District Court, charging Emerson's widow, the former Isabella Sanford, with false imprisonment, and claiming their freedom on the basis of their previous residency in Illinois and

---

* Anderson was in Alton when the mob killed Lovejoy in 1837. Grief-stricken, he returned to St. Louis, where he took up a Baptist ministry, claiming that Lovejoy's martyrdom had been his spiritual inspiration. Although not an outspoken abolitionist, Reverend Anderson was known quietly to give slaves seeking their freedom needed moral and financial support—an invitation to extreme danger in St. Louis in the mid-1840s. It is difficult to imagine that he did not have some influence in instigating the Dred Scott case, through his parishioner, Harriet Scott. See Kenneth C. Kaufman, *Dred Scott's Advocate: A Biography of Roswell M. Field* (Columbia, MO, 1996), 135–48.

Wisconsin Territory. Members of the Blow family provided the couple with legal and financial assistance.

The Scotts had a strong case. For decades, Missouri courts had ruled that slaves taken by their masters to free states were automatically emancipated. Although the Scotts lost at their first trial on a technicality—there was no record to prove that Mrs. Emerson actually held them as slaves—a much-delayed second trial, held in 1850, clarified the record. On instructions from the judge, the jury found for the plaintiffs. Mrs. Emerson's lawyers appealed, and the state supreme court agreed to hear the case, leaving no hint that it would fail to sustain its earlier rulings on such matters. But by the time the appeal came up for argument, the membership of the court had become marginally more pro-slavery, and the reaction to the truce of 1850 and the fugitive slave controversy had persuaded the court's majority, in the name of sectional peace, to overturn precedent. In March 1852, the court ruled against the Scotts, on the grounds that Missouri was not bound to recognize the laws of slavery of any other state or territory. "Times now are not as they were, when the former decisions on this subject were made," noted the majority decision, written by a pro-slavery Democrat.

Fortuitously—and for reasons that remain murky—Irene Emerson's brother, a wealthy New York businessman named John Sanford, then claimed ownership of the Scotts. The shift allowed the Scotts' lawyer, the Vermont-born antislavery Missourian Roswell Field, to take the matter into federal court. Field wanted to test federal law on residency and freedom. Although the Missouri Circuit Court agreed to hear the case—thus recognizing that Scott was a U.S. citizen—the jury, in mid-1854, affirmed the Missouri high court's decision. By then, it was a foregone conclusion that the dispute would wind up before the U.S. Supreme Court, providing the Court with an opportunity to resolve numerous troublesome constitutional issues about slavery in the territories.

Knowing that the case had become too high profile for him to handle, Field arranged for Francis Blair's son, Montgomery, a well-connected, pro-Benton, free-soil Missouri Democrat, to argue in Washington on Dred Scott's behalf. (Blair was later joined by George T. Curtis, a more conservative Massachusetts constitutional expert and the brother of Supreme Court Justice Benjamin Curtis.) Sanford engaged the services of Missouri's pro-slavery Whig senator, Henry Geyer, and a respected Unionist Whig and former attorney general, Reverdy Johnson. After some delay, the justices heard the case in February 1856 and allowed four days for argument, an exceptionally protracted span. The justices then held the matter over for reargument in the 1856–57 term, possibly to avoid having to render a decision until after the presidential election. Although it was still unknown to the broad American public, Court insiders now understood the case had acquired explosive potential.

The justices confronted three large questions. First, was Scott, as a black man, legally a citizen of Missouri and a citizen of the United States, and thus entitled to bring a suit against anybody? Second, was the Missouri Compromise constitutionally valid in prohibiting slavery north of 36°30', including Wisconsin Territory? Finally, had the Scotts' prolonged residence in a free state and a free territory earned them their freedom? Early in its deliberations, the Court appeared to be converging on a minimalist strategy by seizing on the last of these questions and ruling according to the precedent of its 1851 decision in the case of *Strader v. Graham*. Under *Strader*, individual states had complete power to decide for themselves if a slave who had lived in the North had been thereby freed. By applying that logic to *Scott v. Sandford*, the Court could summarily reject the Scotts' claims without having to touch any of the other delicate constitutional issues. In mid-February, the justices voted to follow precisely that course and gave Justice Samuel Nelson the job of writing the decision.

The compromise quickly came unstuck. The Court's five southern justices, including Chief Justice Taney, had hoped to hand down an expansive decision that declared the Missouri Compromise unconstitutional and banned any congressional interference with slavery in the territories. They agreed to the evasive minimalist strategy only to ensure that the two northern

Democratic justices, Grier of Pennsylvania and Nelson of New York, would join the majority. In late February, however, word circulated inside the Court that the other two northern justices, Curtis of Massachusetts and the aging ex-Jacksonian-turned-Republican, John McLean, planned to issue dissents that would declare congressional prohibitions of slavery in the territories constitutional and affirm the citizenship of blacks. The southerners hastily approved a motion that gave Taney the task of writing a majority opinion covering every outstanding issue. All the majority needed was for one northern Democrat to sign on in order to give the comprehensive ruling some bisectional protective coloration. Under pressure from President-elect Buchanan, Justice Grier consented; Justice Nelson, initially hesitant, also signed on; by early March, the Scotts' fate was sealed by a 7-to-2 margin.

Taney wrote a decision as imposing as any John Marshall might have imagined—ironically, given that Andrew Jackson's old confidant could not have been more ideologically unlike his Federalist predecessor. Taney's twenty-eight-year tenure as chief justice had been notable for some early decisions, above all his 1837 ruling in *Charles River Bridge Company v. Warren*, which had eroded the powers of special corporate charters that the Marshall Court had held beyond reproach. (Justice Joseph Storey thought Taney's opinion in the *Charles River Bridge* case so outrageous that he nearly resigned from the Court.) But beginning with the fugitive slave ruling in *Prigg v. Pennsylvania* in 1842, Taney's reputation became increasingly associated with defending slavery against northern troublemakers. Although he himself had sold off the slaves he had inherited from his Maryland tobacco-planter family, Taney believed that the integrity of southern life (which he revered) depended on slavery's survival. He privately railed against the "northern aggression" that he believed was out to slit slavery's throat. His four fellow southerners on the Court, Democrats all, shared his outrage. With their concurrence, Taney would attempt, at last, to place the full power and majesty of the Court behind the most resolute of pro-slavery views.

Reading his lengthy decision aloud in the crowded, dusky Court chamber, Taney, ill and a fortnight shy of eighty, spoke for two hours in a voice so tremulous that at times he could barely be heard—but his words were anything but feeble. Contending that Negroes had not been among the sovereign people who framed and ratified the Constitution—that they had, in fact, been held "so far inferior, that they had no rights which the white man was bound to respect"—Taney rejected the proposition that blacks, slave or free, were American citizens. In a few sentences, he then dismissed the assertion that Scott's residence in either the free state of Illinois or Wisconsin Territory made him free, even if Wisconsin were constitutionally deemed free soil. Finally, and at length, Taney rejected the claim that Wisconsin Territory had *ever* been free, on the shaky legal ground that the Fifth Amendment's protection of property superseded Congress's constitutional power to "make all needful rules and regulations" for the territories. Mere rules and regulations, Taney claimed, were not laws. Thus, he concluded, the already repealed Missouri Compromise had been unconstitutional all along, the Douglasite concept of popular sovereignty was equally unconstitutional, and slaveholders had the right to bring their slaves into whatever territory they pleased.

Taney's was the first Court ruling since *Marbury* to strike down (albeit retrospectively) an important federal law—a turning point in the rise of the doctrine of judicial supremacy that has since become a deep assumption in American politics and law. Taney's ruling was also filled with historical falsehoods and legal irrelevancies, a point that Justices McLean and Curtis were not shy in making in their dissents. When the Constitution was ratified, free black men had enjoyed many legal rights, including, in all but three states, the right to vote.* Black voters had participated in

---

* In 1790, free black men could vote on equal terms with whites in New Hampshire, Massachusetts, Rhode Island, Connecticut, New York, New Jersey, Pennsylvania, Delaware, Maryland, and North Carolina. Free black men were enfranchised in the new states of Kentucky in 1792 and Tennessee in 1796, although the right was removed in Kentucky in 1799 and in Tennessee in 1834. See Alexander Keyssar, *The Right to Vote: The Contested History of Democracy in the United States* (New York, 2000), Table A.3, 336–41.

the ratification process. That made them citizens not simply of their respective states but of the United States as well, under Article IV, Section 2 of the Constitution, which stipulated that "[t]he citizens of each state shall be entitled to all privileges and immunities of citizens of the several states." Concerning Congress's powers over slavery in the territories, numerous Framers—including later congressmen as well as Presidents Washington and Madison—had overseen congressional exclusion of slavery from various territories and raised no constitutional objections. Taney's assertions about the Missouri Compromise were utterly moot, as the powers of territorial governments regarding slavery were not at issue in Dred Scott's suit. Finally, to prevent a slaveholder from taking his slave into a territory did not deprive him of his property. If it did, what might prevent slaveholders from in the future asserting their Fifth Amendment rights and settling with their slaves in free states as well as in the territories?

Armed with McLean's and Curtis's dissents, Republicans denounced the decision as a politicized abomination, lacking precedent or standing. Much of their argument rested on the contention that Taney's opinion in *Scott* was "not binding in law and conscience"—and, in another turn of the screw, that the ruling consisted of *obiter dicta*, having no pertinence to the case at hand, and was thus irrelevant—a charge that, with respect to the Missouri Compromise, was certainly valid. "[F]ive slaveholders and two doughfaces," Horace Greeley's *New-York Daily Tribune* sneered, had handed down a decision "entitled to just as much moral weight as would be the judgement of a majority of those congregated in any Washington bar-room." Republican legislatures in several states, including New York, passed resolutions that attacked the Court for intruding on state rights.

Most of the remaining loyal northern Democrats reflexively supported the decision, but there were those who considered it too much to bear. "I feel quite mortified for the course of this Tawny Lion of Gen. Jackson—it is a great drawback on his fame," one New York Democrat wrote. In the Old Northwest states, some Democratic newspapers endorsed the Republican view that the decision was part of a conspiracy to elevate slavery nationwide. Thomas Hart Benton, in retirement, fired off a reply to Taney that ran to nearly two hundred pages (including appendices) denouncing the decision as an affront to the Constitution. Even Democrats, led by Stephen A. Douglas, who initially backed the Court came to understand that it had nullified their precarious doctrine of popular sovereignty. In a speech three months after the ruling, Douglas attempted to square the circle by claiming that although the slaveholders' right to property in slaves remained inviolate, it would prove "worthless" unless buttressed by "appropriate police regulations and local legislation" enacted by the territory's residents. For the moment, Douglas and his allies could retrieve this bit of middle ground. But what if *Douglas* was correct? Could the slaveholders, some pro-slavery Democrats wondered, fully protect their constitutional rights in the territories without additional federal legislation? Was Congress, declared by the Court as powerless to bar slavery in the territories, now compelled to pass new laws *guaranteeing* slavery in the territories—or even in all of the states?

At every point, Taney's decision raised questions and portents that heightened sectional tensions. Above all, it solidified the Republicans' claims that the Court had become a cog in a great conspiracy intent on nationalizing slavery. The fear turned up in private correspondence as well as in campaign speeches: if a slave could be brought into a free territory and his condition of bondage be left intact, what would then prevent Congress from foisting on the free states toleration of slavery within their own borders? Already, a case entitled *Lemmon v. The People* was wending its way through the New York courts, testing whether slaves brought temporarily to New York City were, as state law stipulated, freed persons. How would the Taney Court rule if it were to receive that case on appeal? Given *Dred Scott*, could it fail to overturn New York's freedom laws? What then would be left to prevent a slaveholder from "temporarily" enjoying his right to human property in a free state for months, or for years—or forever?

For the main participants in the *Dred Scott* case, who had

almost been forgotten amid the tumult, ensuing events brought poignancy as well as paradox. Two months after the ruling, John Sanford, who had fought for his purported property to the end, died in a New York City insane asylum. Title to the Scotts reverted to his brother-in-law, a Massachusetts Republican congressman named Calvin Chaffee who had married Irene Emerson—and who would soon resign his seat, forced out by the anger created by his unfortunate link to the case. Chaffee transferred title to Taylor Blow of St. Louis, the youngest son of Dred Scott's deceased original owner, who, as a Missouri citizen, had the power to manumit the Scotts. On May 26, 1857, the Scotts finally gained their freedom. Dred landed a job as a hotel porter, while Harriet took in laundry. Dred also became a minor local celebrity, fit to get his picture made at the daguerreotypist's— but his enjoyment was brief. On September 17, 1858, he died, in his early sixties, of tuberculosis. Within four years, both Harriet and their elder daughter Eliza also died. Irene Emerson Chaffee, the original defendant in the suit, lived on in a decent obscurity until 1903.

For the rest of the country, the decision deepened the crisis of American democracy. Pro-slavery southerners hailed Taney for vindicating the Constitution and slavery. "Southern opinion upon the subject of southern slavery . . . is now the supreme law of the land . . . ," the Augusta, Georgia, *Constitutionalist* declared, "and opposition to southern opinion upon this subject is now opposition to the Constitution, and morally treason against the Government." For antislavery northerners, the decision proved that an entire branch of the federal government had fallen into the Slave Power's clutches. Taney's opinion, according to the Ohio Republican state convention, was "anti-constitutional, anti-republican, anti-democratic, incompatible with State rights, and destructive of personal security." Justice Curtis, disgusted, resigned from the Supreme Court in September, on the transparent pretext that his salary was insufficient. Designed, as one New Orleans newspaper put it, to place "the whole basis of the Black Republican organization under the ban of law," the ruling backfired, reinforcing Republican resolve to win the White House in 1860, appoint new justices to the Court, and wipe away Taney's stain.

Among the northerners most exercised by the decision was the once-reluctant Republican of Illinois, Abraham Lincoln. A year later, Lincoln would make *Dred Scott* the chief issue in his campaign to unseat the man he considered the chief northern tool of the Slave Power, Stephen A. Douglas. But Lincoln's attack on *Scott*—and the worsening of sectional animosities—also reflected intervening events in Kansas and Washington.

"GENERAL JACKSON IS DEAD, SIR"

Once the initial astonishment at Taney's opinion had passed, it was unclear how *Dred Scott* would affect the inflamed political situation. For free blacks, certainly, the decision had dire implications. Yet unlike the Fugitive Slave Law or the Kansas-Nebraska Act, it did not demand immediate federal enforcement or force any reassessment among the chief political factions. For pro-slavery and antislavery partisans, the ruling did more to affirm existing views than to change any minds. Even Stephen Douglas, his principle of popular sovereignty now exploded, found ways, temporarily, to give the impression that the northern and southern Democracy remained united in principle. Fresh disturbances in Kansas soon destroyed such wishful thinking.

During the summer and fall of 1856, the situation in Kansas had seemed to improve dramatically. In August, President Pierce accepted the resignation of the disgraced territorial governor Wilson Shannon and replaced him with a no-nonsense Democrat, John W. Geary. Although unfriendly to the abolitionists, Geary, a fearsome man who stood six feet five inches tall, believed in law and order more than he did in protecting slavery. A hero of the Mexican War, he had enlarged his reputation for toughness as San Francisco's first mayor in the early 1850s, when he personally led the suppression of the city's endemic violent lawlessness. Directed to stop the Kansas border war, he did so inside of two months, skillfully deploying federal troops, disbanding the rival "armies," and showing no quarter to either side. Yet only four months later, on the day of Buchanan's inauguration in 1857, Geary quit his post over continuing abuses by the official pro-slavery legislature. First the pro-slavery men refused to consider his request to soften the harsh slave code that Governor Shannon had signed into law. Then they passed a new bill calling for a constitutional convention the following June, with the territory's flagrantly pro-slavery county sheriffs to oversee the election of delegates. The approved constitution would go into effect without any popular referendum. Stunned by the bill's audacity, Geary vetoed it, only to have it passed over his veto by what he would soon be calling the "felon legislature" in Lecompton. It was too much even for the formidable enforcer to bear.

Determined that Kansas would not break him the way it had broken Pierce, President Buchanan persuaded former Treasury Secretary Robert J. Walker of Mississippi to succeed Geary, with assurances that the administration desired a fair electoral outcome. Walker, a close friend of Stephen Douglas's (with whom he met in Chicago on his way to Kansas), was more of a partisan Democratic realist than a sectionalist. Surveying the territory's electorate, he estimated, accurately, that although most of the voters were Democrats, the majority were non-Yankee free-staters who wished to keep slavery out of Kansas in order to keep blacks out of Kansas. The only way to admit Kansas expeditiously as a safe Democratic state, Walker concluded, was to approve a free constitution. Accordingly, upon his arrival in Kansas in May, he tried to dissuade free-staters from their plans to boycott the imminent convention delegate elections. Coming after years of bushwhacking and bogus elections, Walker's appeals were useless. Pro-slavery men won every seat in the convention, which was scheduled to assemble in Lecompton in September.

Walker would end up just as sickened as Geary. A strict Jacksonian, he insisted that any state constitution be subject to a public referendum, which provoked an outcry from pro-slavery men in Kansas and Washington alike. In October, Walker threw out blatantly fraudulent returns from yet another legislative election and certified a free-state majority, prompting Jefferson Davis, Alexander Stephens, Robert Toombs, and other southern Democratic leaders to denounce him. (Some southerners also began expressing misgivings about Buchanan as, in one Georgian's words, Walker's "master who lives in the White House.") Finally, Walker squared off against the dubiously selected Lecompton constitutional convention. Declaring the rights of slaveowners to their human property as inviolable, the delegates' new constitution prohibited any future amendment abridging those rights. Ignoring Walker's warnings, the convention sent their constitution directly to Congress, accompanied by a petition for statehood.

Walker's complaints, and northern Democratic opposition on Capitol Hill, blocked the statehood maneuver, and in early November, the Lecompton convention acceded to a referendum to choose between a "constitution with slavery" and a "constitution with no slavery." But the choice turned out to be meaningless, since the "no slavery" version guaranteed the ownership of slaves already in the territory—in effect prohibiting the future importation of slaves while formally preserving slavery. The convention also gave oversight of the referendum to the same officials who had conducted the offensive convention delegate elections in June—an open invitation to rig the process. Northern Democrats as well as Republicans saw through the tricks and denounced them. Governor Walker called the convention's supposed compromise "a vile fraud, a bare counterfeit," and expressed certainty that President Buchanan would reject it. But Buchanan went along with the Lecompton arrangement, pleading that if he did not, the South would secede. Walker departed Kansas forever, to derisive pro-slavery charges that he had betrayed the cause and joined the blackest ranks of the "Black Republicans."

The Lecompton constitution controversy finally made Stephen Douglas snap. Douglas still wanted to be president, and he knew that if he were to swallow hard and support the pro-slavery Kansas legislature, the southern Democracy would probably support his nomination in 1860. But he knew equally well that doing so would ruin his chances in the North. The source of the difficulty, he concluded, was Buchanan. Bullied by the South, the president had betrayed his repeated claims that he wanted fair elections in Kansas. A consultation in Chicago with his friend Robert Walker helped convince Douglas that the only way to dissociate the national Democrats from southern extremism and stave off defeat by the Republicans was to force Buchanan to change course. On December 3, Douglas marched into the White House to assail the "trickery and juggling" of the Lecompton men and to try to get the president to listen to angry reason.

Buchanan frostily received the senator and heard him out. At stake, in their meeting, were the battered remnants and legacy of what had once been the Jackson Democracy—now, increasingly, the slavocrats' Democracy. The latest events in Kansas, Douglas charged, had made a mockery of popular sovereignty. If Buchanan persisted, he warned, the Democratic Party in the North was doomed. To prevent that, Douglas said, he would break with the administration and head the anti-Lecompton forces in Congress. Buchanan, the old functionary and quasi-Hunker, still lived in the mental universe of the 1830s and 1840s, when appeasing the South was paramount to keeping the Democracy in power. Douglas, for all of his own loyalties to the past, understood that times and men had changed. "Mr. Douglas," Buchanan responded smugly to Douglas's threat, "I desire you to remember that no Democrat ever yet differed from an administration of his own choice without being crushed." As if likening himself to Old Hickory, Buchanan told Douglas to "[b]eware the fate of Tallmadge and Rives," the party disloyalists of another era. "Mr. President," Douglas shot back, "I wish you to remember that General Jackson is dead, sir."*

The proceedings in Kansas followed a now-familiar course. In

---

* Buchanan's memory was selective: John C. Calhoun, whose legacy the president now appeared to be advancing, defied Andrew Jackson and, although defeated in 1833 over nullification, was not "crushed." Buchanan also underestimated Douglas, who was a far more formidable political leader than either Nathaniel Tallmadge or William C. Rives.

December, free-state voters stayed home during the sham referendum, and the "constitution with slavery" won overwhelming approval. (Leaving nothing to chance, pro-slavery men cast nearly three thousand fraudulent ballots.) The new free-state legislature would not let the vote stand and scheduled its own referendum on the constitution for two weeks later, in which voters could choose between the "with slavery" and "no slavery" versions or reject them both. Now it was the pro-slavery men's turn, once again, to boycott—and the result, as expected, was a nearly unanimous vote against both of the Lecompton constitutions. Immediately, southern politicians and officeholders pressured the White House to accept the first vote and send the pro-slavery constitution to Congress for its approval. Buchanan crumpled. Declaring the free-soil advocates "in a state of rebellion against the government," he pointed to *Dred Scott* as the ultimate confirmation that "slavery exists in Kansas by virtue of the Constitution of the United States," and concluded that "Kansas is therefore at this moment as much a slave state as Georgia or South Carolina."

Douglas proved as good as his word and threw every ounce of his strength into opposing Kansas statehood under the Lecompton constitution. Working sixteen hours a day, the Little Giant pushed himself to the center of every verbal fray on the Senate floor. ("The South never made a greater mistake than in provoking his opposition," the freshman Republican Senator James Dixon of Connecticut observed. "He will prove a terrible foe.") The urgency of his arguments sometimes made him sound heretical. On the final day of debate, Douglas objected to what he called an "authoritative" editorial in the Washington *Union*, which had declared property in slaves a natural right. "The attempt now," he asserted, "to establish the doctrine that a free State has no power to prohibit slavery . . . that slavery is national and not local, that it goes everywhere under the Constitution of the United States, and yet is higher than the Constitution . . . will not be tolerated." Without once mentioning *Dred Scott*, Taney, or Buchanan, Douglas had come dangerously close to sustaining the Republican charge that a plot was afoot to nationalize slavery.

Douglas's fury did not change a single vote in the Senate, which approved Kansas's admission as a slave state, 33 to 25. In the House, where the result was less certain, the debate led to violence. At two in the morning during one House session, the South Carolinian Laurence Keitt—one of Preston Brooks's accomplices in the attack on Charles Sumner—called another member a "damned Black Republican puppy," which touched off a donnybrook involving upwards of thirty congressmen. (Alexander Stephens, the floor manager for the pro-Lecompton side, claimed that had weapons been present, there would have been serious bloodshed.) Finally, after a week of nail-biting procedural votes and despite heavy administration lobbying, the Lecompton bill failed, by a margin of 120 to 112.

Congress's rejection of the Lecompton constitution did not bring peace to Kansas. Undaunted, the Buchanan administration attempted one last ploy—a kind of mass bribe—with a new referendum that would expand the size of the normal land grant to be offered settlers upon the territory's admission to statehood. No less transparent than any of the earlier pro-slavery schemes, this one went down to a resounding defeat in August 1858. By then, portions of Kansas had returned to open warfare. In the most spectacular incident, in May 1858—apparently timed to coincide with the second anniversary of the Pottawatomie atrocity—a group of slave-staters descended on the cabins of several free-staters, shot five of the residents to death, and wounded four others. Old John Brown, shuttling between fund-raising back East and hell-raising in Kansas, retaliated by taking his terrorists into Missouri, attacking two slaveholders and killing one, and carrying their horses and eleven liberated slaves up to Canada.

In Washington, however, the death of the Lecompton scheme looked like a turning of the political tide in Kansas. (Those perceptions would later prove accurate. After defeating the Lecompton plan once and for all, free-state Kansans would organize a Republican Party and control a new constitutional convention elected in 1859. Kansas would finally be admitted to the Union as a free state in January 1861.) Republicans rejoiced—as did the pro-Douglas, anti-Lecompton northern Democrats, who had provided twenty-two vital votes against the bill. "The agony is over," wrote one, "and thank God the right has triumphed!" Up on Manhattan, 120 guns fired off the Battery in an enormous celebration, one for every vote against the accursed constitution.

THE PANIC OF 1857: DEPRESSION, LABOR, AND SECTIONAL POLITICS

New Yorkers had additional reason to rejoice in the early spring of 1858—the lifting of a brief economic depression, sparked by the financial panic over the late summer and fall of 1857. The turmoil caused by the downturn had been mild compared to the civil war in Kansas. But it had been real enough, adding the specter of class warfare to the crisis over slavery, and forcing Democrats and Republicans in some key electoral battlegrounds to respond.

The origins of the crisis, as in 1837, were both foreign and domestic. The decade from 1847 to 1857 had witnessed a vast expansion of industrial development and railroad construction, funded largely by British and European investors and accelerated by the influx of newly mined California gold. In 1856–57, a sudden sell-off of American securities abroad, caused by a rise in foreign interest rates prompted by the Crimean War, depressed the value of American stocks and bonds. The war's elimination of Russian grain from the European market also fed a rapid rise in American grain exports and a speculation boom in western land. As American paper values sank and the land speculation bubble grew, investors turned jittery, looking for the smallest signal for them to liquidate their assets. An isolated episode in late August—the suspension of specie payments by the New York branch of an important Ohio bank, after one of its cashiers embezzled its funds—proved the trigger. Investors pulled their money out of banks; banks were forced to call in loans; and overextended businessmen, especially in the North and West, went under in droves. By mid-October, virtually every bank in the nation had suspended specie payments, and the fearsome phrase "hard times" appeared everywhere. "As to the hard times, it has wrought wonders—banks breaking and failures of many persons, business stopping, and labourers thrown out of employment," one Indianapolis resident related. Stephen Foster, no stranger to penury despite the popularity of his songs, authored a grim new composition: "'Tis a dirge that is murmured around the lowly grave,/Oh! hard times come again no more."

The depression hit New York City especially hard. "[B]ands of men paraded in a menacing manner through the streets of the city demanding work or bread," the British consul reported to his superiors. Local relief agencies were swamped during the fall and winter; unemployment, especially among the poorest classes of day laborers and sweatshop workers, skyrocketed; and on November 10, soldiers and marines under the command of Winfield Scott had to be dispatched to lower Broadway and Wall Street to keep a large and angry crowd from breaking into the U.S. Customs House and the subtreasury and stealing the twenty million dollars in their vaults. Similar if less spectacular unrest unfolded in smaller northern and western cities. Trade union organizing picked up its pace, and through the following year labor unrest continued in textile towns and railroad camps from New England to Pennsylvania.

The panic focused attention on the plight of northern wage-earners as nothing had since the economic collapse of 1837, but the rediscovered working class was very different from its Jacksonian forerunner. The proliferation of large textile mills and elaborate put-out clothing operations in New England had turned the pastoral dreams of an industrial utopia into a grimmer reality of stretched-out hours and tightened pay. Increasingly, the industrial labor force consisted not of farm daughters in temporary jobs but families resigned to being mill workers for life. The immigrant waves after 1845 had, in turn, profoundly changed working-class demographics, creating a workforce in the large cities and in the mining and railroad camps that consisted overwhelmingly of newcomers (above all Irish and German Catholics) and their children. That remaking deeply affected labor politics in the 1840s and 1850s, leading to the disturbances of 1857, which had important implications for national politics.

There had been some continuities between the labor movements of the Jacksonian period and those of the succeeding twenty years, but the most important activities involved newly arrived immigrants as well as natives in innovative efforts. Unskilled day laborers and craft workers built unions, cooperatives, and protective associations. Smaller, more radical political associations, like the Befreigundsbund, a secret revolutionary society founded in 1847 by the German émigré Wilhelm Weitling, arose in the immigrant neighborhoods. The new organizations attempted to create unity among skilled and unskilled workers, efforts that bore fruit in 1850 with the formation, in New York, of the national Industrial Congress. Although internal factional warfare soon divided the Congress, individual craft and laborers' unions persisted and led a wave of strikes in 1853–54, halted only by a brief financial panic (a prelude to 1857) in late 1854 and 1855.

Accompanying these union activities were various broader efforts at labor reform, preeminently the land reform movement headed by the former Working Men's Party leader George Henry Evans. Evans, exhausted, had retreated from his Manhattan base to the New Jersey countryside in 1835. When he returned to radical agitation in 1841, he was a thorough convert to the proposition that the wage slave would be freed only if he could obtain a patch of land. Followers of various utopian writers (including Albert Brisbane, the leading American champion of the French visionary Charles Fourier), as well as of British Chartist land reformers, found their way into Evans's fold. Constituted as the National Reform Association, the land reformers invented a snappy slogan, "Vote Yourself A Farm!," encouraged local movements like the New York state Anti-Renters, and developed blueprints for neo-Jeffersonian townships to be built out West—the building blocks of an America of free and independent labor.

While they spoke of equality and economic justice, these new labor movements had developed renewed tensions with the anti-slavery movement. A strong sense of rapport did arise in many quarters, especially in New England where urban skilled workers, factory hands, and trade unionists had been active abolitionists since the 1830s. In Boston as well as smaller cities, workingmen's mass meetings condemned southern aggression, and labor organizers helped elect Free Soil Democrats to local and national office in the early 1850s. William Lloyd Garrison's *Liberator* enthusiastically covered these developments and supported trade union strikes by journeymen (including journeymen printers) over wages. But there were also labor leaders (including Evans, who always hated slavery and preached racial equality, and who denounced anti-abolitionists) who came to regard the slavery issue as, at best, secondary to the emancipation of northern labor. "[R]eform should begin at our own firesides . . . ," Evans declared, "and philanthropists, if they would have an influence, must no longer confine themselves to *color*." Others argued that the living conditions for northern wage workers were no better and maybe worse than those of southern slaves—precisely the argument that slaveholders used to defend their system. Although workingmen's denunciations of "white slavery" always implied a hatred of all bondage—"the sin of slavery," one New Hampshire anti-abolitionist labor paper called it—they could also suggest that whites deserved better consideration from society than blacks. Antislavery radicals responded that no matter how just the workingmen's cause, equating northern labor's conditions with slavery was, as Garrison wrote, like "magnifying mole-hills into mountains, and reducing mountains to the size of mole-hills."

Alienation from the antislavery movement was particularly severe among the newly arrived Irish immigrant workers packed inside the slums of Boston, New York, and Philadelphia. The Irish sometimes found themselves in sharp competition with blacks for jobs at the nether end of the big-city workforce, and they feared that an end to slavery would only bring more blacks north. Antislavery also carried with it, many Irish believed, all the nativist prejudices of Yankee Protestantism—regarding papist Celts as a lower form of life, uncomprehending of the suffering the Irish had endured during the Famine years and after, magnanimous when it came to faraway black slaves but indifferent, even hostile, to the new immigrants. To be held by some in even greater contempt than blacks, in a nation whose highest tribunal had declared that blacks had no rights the white man was bound to respect, provoked sharp ethnic and class resentments among the Irish against abolitionists and Republicans—and an even more lethal hatred of blacks. The Irish were not monolithic: in the dance halls of the poorest slums, in some trade unions, and in private life, there was abundant evidence of toleration, cooperation, and even deep affection between blacks and Irish immigrants. But in the swirl of insecurity and resentment that buffeted Irish American working-class life in the 1850s, two conservative pillars loomed to many newcomers as the safest sanctuaries: the Catholic Church and the southern-dominated (and immigrant-friendly) Democratic Party. The Democrats, in particular (like the conservative anti-abolitionists of the 1830s), exploited and enlarged Irish working-class racism with the crudest kinds of Negrophobic propaganda.

The panic of 1857 and ensuing depression strengthened those political realities. In the eastern cities, local Democratic politicos leapt into the breach and came to the immediate aid of the unemployed. Leading the way was New York City's mayor, Fernando Wood, a strong-arming, pro-southern conservative with a penchant for public works and civic reform. Wood called himself a man of honor, protector of the poor, and "true friend of the Irish." He churned the political waters early in 1857 when, in trying to stave off the imposition of a Maine-style liquor law in Manhattan and preserve home rule of the city's police force, he helped provoke several days of mob violence. After the panic hit, he devised a bold relief plan in which the city would provide food and coal to the poor and hire the unemployed to work on a string of public improvement projects, including construction of the new Central Park. The city's Common Council blocked Wood's proposal (although the park commissioners eventually hired thousands of jobless men), and a fusion movement of anti-Wood Tammanyites, Republicans, and Know-Nothings, alarmed at Wood's identification with what one patrician called "the *canaille*," unseated the mayor in a close election in November. To the city's polyglot labor movement, and its masses of immigrant workers, the maverick Wood stood prouder and taller than ever.

Republicans responded to the panic by taking very different positions aimed at aiding workingmen. In March 1857, the Democratic Congress had enacted some additional downward revisions of the Walker Tariff of 1846—and to protectionist-minded Republicans, notably Horace Greeley, there was a direct link between the changes and the economic distress. The pro-tariff argument was especially effective in Pennsylvania, where, supposedly, iron companies had been undercut by British iron imports unleashed by the recent tariff reductions. In making their pitch, Republicans revived the old Whig doctrine of the harmony of interests, calling protection for the iron masters a boon for their workers as well. A higher tariff, Greeley's *Tribune* declared, would employ thousands "who have languished for months in unwilling idleness." The campaign would help spike the Pennsylvania Republicans' totals in the autumn 1858 congressional elections, bringing them an unanticipated and highly encouraging rout of the Democrats.

Congressional Republicans also pushed hard for three extant land-grant proposals that they presented as pro-labor: a homestead bill to guarantee cheap land for settlers, a Pacific railroad bill, and a bill offering grants to the states to found publicly funded agricultural and mechanical colleges. The provenance of these efforts was complex. The homestead and school land-grant bills drew on the ideas of Evans's National Reform Association. The transcontinental railroad bill was, in part, an effort to complete the project that had prompted Stephen Douglas to propose the Kansas-Nebraska Bill, but to do so under Republican auspices. All three measures were designed to appeal to working-class Democrats around the country, especially in the Old Northwest. After the panic, Republicans expanded their claims, offering the bills as the means to rescue workingmen and their families from the latest economic catastrophe. Cheap land in particular, Gamaliel Bailey wrote, would "secure to all our large cities a safety-drain," elevate living standards, and promote social order for both the homesteaders and the working men who stayed behind.

The panic had additional cultural effects in the North, including an outpouring of revivalist religion more fervent than any seen since the 1830s. Whether or not the prayers worked, the depression lifted much more quickly than anticipated, thanks largely to resupplies of gold from California and Europe. New York banks resumed specie payments as early as December 1857, and the rest of the nation's banking system was back on its feet within months. Factories reopened; wages were restored to their former levels; and the jobless began finding work again. "There was never a more severe crisis nor a more rapid recovery," the London *Economist* observed. Although the suffering had been great, the social upheaval it had caused had been relatively short-lived and largely nonviolent.

Despite its brevity, the downturn had immediate political effects. By strengthening the connections between immigrant workers and the Democratic Party, it solidified an important constituency of the dwindling northern Democracy, especially in the key state of New York—one that was as hostile to blacks as it was to Yankee Republicans. The depression also exacerbated sectional divisions in national politics. The impetus given to the Republican tariff and land-grant proposals raised new complaints from the South about the arrogant, plundering North. Successful in killing the railroad bill, the southerners could not prevent sectional majorities from passing a land-grant college bill in 1859 and, in the succeeding session, a homestead bill, but President Buchanan vetoed both, further infuriating the Republican rank and file.

The panic also reinforced a growing confidence among south-ern slaveholders that their way of life and ideas about politics were far superior to the northern free-labor democracy. In sharp contrast to the depression of 1837–43, the downturn of 1857–58 was mainly a northern phenomenon. Relatively untouched by overinvestment in railroad construction and by overspeculation in stocks, bonds, and western lands, the plantation cotton econ-omy suffered only slightly and rebounded quickly once demand from the North and Britain resumed. At first, the panic caused southerners to wail at the latest disaster brought upon them and the nation by greedy Yankee bankers and capitalists, but their outrage soon gave way to smugness. The region's very backward-ness with respect to industrial and financial development had spared it from the worst. To numerous slaveholder politicians, this was a sign of southern social and political superiority.

That case was put most famously early in 1858 by John C. Calhoun's ex-protégé, James H. Hammond. In a speech to the Senate during the Lecompton struggle but also attuned to the panic, Hammond compared the current conditions of the two sections: "Cotton is king. . . . Who can doubt, that has looked at recent events, that cotton is supreme? . . . We have poured in among you one million six hundred thousand bales of cotton just at the moment to save you from destruction." If cotton was king, Hammond contended, slavery made it possible. "[T]he greatest strength of the South arises from the harmony of her social and political institutions. This harmony gives her a frame of society, the best in the world, and an extent of political freedom, com-bined with entire security, such as no other people ever enjoyed upon the face of the earth." Hammond emphasized that slavery produced the fairest and most secure form of political democ-racy. "In all social systems," he said, "there must be a class to do the mean duties, to perform the drudgery of life . . . It constitutes the very mud-sills of society, and of political government." For Hammond, the South's respect for the self-evident supremacy of all whites over all blacks stood in shining contrast to the absurd democracy of the North: "Your slaves are white, of your own race;

you are brothers of one blood. They are your equals in natural endowment of intellect, and they feel galled by their degradation. Our slaves do not vote. We give them no political power. Yours do vote, and being the majority, they are the depositories of all your political power. If they knew the tremendous secret, that the ballot-box is stronger than an army with bayonets, and could combine, where would you be?"

Hammond had no particular empathy for the "galled" proletarians of the North. The lessons of his class analysis were those of a landed gentleman: either the rulers in the North could emulate the South by giving all "mean duties" to enslaved and politically powerless blacks, or they would run the risk of expropriation by their own enfranchised white slaves. The offensiveness of Hammond's claims, both to the dignity of labor and to Yankee democracy, was not lost on northerners. Hammond's speech, Horace Greeley wrote, expressed "the sentiment of all aristocracies, and simply assert[s] the old proposition that the few were made to rule, and the many to be governed." But those implications were of less immediate importance to national politics than Hammond's confident view that the South had built the greatest society in history, and with the greatest government—"satisfied, content, happy, harmonious, and prosperous." It was a view long in gestation. It formed the foundations of a self-conscious southern democracy, fundamentally at odds with the northern democracy. And it was becoming increasingly ubiquitous among southerners, despite the abiding divisions and anxieties that afflicted the region's rulers.

DIXIE DEMOCRACY

On the evening of March 4, 1859, at New York's Mechanics' Hall, Dan Emmett, a five-string banjo player for the enormously popular blackface Bryant Minstrels, introduced a catchy new "walkaround" song about an adulterous weaver named Willum. A native of central Ohio, Emmett was an accomplished songwriter—credited with, among other compositions, "Turkey in the

Straw" and "Ol' Dan Tucker"—and he was an expert performer in the googly-eyed, part-contemptuous, part-envious blackface style that set young northern workingmen to roaring. Emmett had kept the tune in his suitcase for years, and some writers have speculated that he first picked it up from free black musicians. The song's hastily written lyrics—with the refrain, "In Dixie Land I'll took my stand/To lib and die in Dixie"—were an unexceptional mixture of nonsense and contrived nostalgia typical of the northern minstrel genre. What made the song special, like all of Emmett's best work, was its rousing melody. Thus, from a corked-up Yankee pretending to be a slave—singing about a "gay deceiver" before a New York audience of "greasy mechanics"—came what was destined to be filched and transformed, to Dan Emmett's horror, into the best-known pro-slavery southern nationalist anthem.

The appropriated, wishful, and self-ratifying qualities of the emerging cult of the South and southern nationalism cannot belie the genuine outrage and bitterness of the later 1850s. Nor can they belie the intellection and shared ethical assumptions, rooted in slavery, that helped make the improvised seem natural and all-embracing. The polarizing sectionalism in national affairs and the demise of southern Whiggery pushed southern political leaders toward an appearance of utter unity. But the political realities of the slave South remained, as they had always been, fraught with internal divisions and fears. Differences that might seem just noticeable to outsiders were difficult and contentious to clear-eyed southerners. Those differences owed as much to the mixed character of southern political institutions as they did to variations in class, geography, and traditional loyalties. Ironically, they would reinforce the plausibility of those in the fire-eater wing of southern politics who argued that, short of an assertion of solidarity and secession from the Union, slavery was doomed—an argument that initially resistant southern democrats came to share.

The aristocratic republic of South Carolina remained the seat of southern reaction but also a perplexity—matching, more closely than any other state, the undemocratic South conjured up by the Republicans, yet defying standard images of the Cotton Kingdom. The short-staple cotton economy of the South Carolina up-country still supported an elegant slaveholder elite, but both the land and its owners were showing signs of wear and tear. After supporting two generations of cotton planters, the soil was losing its nutrients, and many of the scions of the original fortune hunters had pushed on to the rich black soils of Alabama and Mississippi. Surrounding the great estates like John C. Calhoun's Fort Hill (its slaves and white-columned mansion house sold by Calhoun's cash-poor widow to their son, Andrew, at her husband's death) were the vacant houses and weed-covered lawns of plantations abandoned for better prospects out West. The planters who remained regarded themselves as refined patriarchs, more interested in making a life than merely in making a living. Yet as they sipped their brandy and smoked their Spanish cigars, their voluble self-satisfaction betrayed an unnerving suspicion that time was running out.

Low-country South Carolina elite life, centered in Charleston, was more rarefied and showy but also fraying at the edges. In stark contrast to the nouveau riche southwest, the rice and long-staple cotton plantations of malarial coastal Carolina had an almost antiquated look, worked on by masses of dark-skinned African slaves (who outnumbered whites by ratios five times higher than in Alabama) commanded by semiresident masters and their overseers. Charleston, where the low-country planters and their families took refuge all summer and whenever else they could, was gay and cosmopolitan, closer in spirit to London than to Boston. Yet for all of the learning and wealth on conspicuous display along the Battery where the Ashley and Cooper Rivers met, Charleston also had a slightly outdated air, its reputation as the self-styled Athens of America no longer what it once was, its skyline still dominated by the colonial spire of St. Michael's Episcopal Church, built from the designs of Sir Christopher Wren. An English visitor observed that Charleston's street names—King Street, Queen Street—were markers of a "polished and aristocratic" upper class that had "reminiscences of the 'old country' and is proud of them." "We like the old things—," William Grayson, the poet, ex-congressman, and chief customs collector in Charleston, remarked, "old books, old friends, old and fixed relations between employer and employed."

The state's politics were even more antiquated, but they showed little sign of fatigue. In the 1850s, as ever, a singularly united class of slaveholders ruled South Carolina through the omnipotent state legislature in Columbia. The legislature appointed the governor (who was replaced every two years and lacked the power of veto); it also picked the lieutenant governor, attorney general, state military commanders, court clerks, justices of the peace, sheriffs, and all presidential electors. Through gross malapportionment, the interests of the low-country squirearchy and its backcountry allies reigned supreme and unchecked. With statewide elections virtually nonexistent, political parties never really took root in South Carolina. Partyless politics in turn shielded local leaders from opposition while dampening popular interest and participation.

The system did not go completely untested. After the Virginia constitutional revision of 1851, democrats from the rugged, northernmost counties that brushed the Blue Ridge, where slavery was scarce, demanded similar reforms. South Carolina's government, wrote one angry pamphleteer, existed "to guard and secure the interests of the large rice and cotton planters. The interests of men who have to work with their hands are entirely unprotected." That autumn, defiant ultra-sectionalists, infuriated at the terms of the national truce of 1850 and at the collapse of the Nashville Convention movement, pushed for a secession convention in a rare statewide vote—and huge majorities in the mountain districts helped send the disunionists down to a crushing defeat. It was enough to cause the Beaufort grandee William Henry Trescot to predict that in South Carolina, democracy—a word, he said, that "has betrayed the South"—would kill slavery. But with the legislature firmly in control, only the most trivial alteration of election laws ensued from the brief mountain uprising. Although pragmatic anti-extremists might momentarily hold sway, they endangered neither slavery nor the state's peculiar oligarchy.

Unreconstructed South Carolina nourished the most extravagant forms of pro-slavery reaction, exemplified by Robert Barnwell Rhett. Born Robert Barnwell Smith in Beaufort in 1800, Rhett had changed his last name in 1837 to honor an ancestor who had been British governor-general of the Bahamas and to pump up his own aristocratic lineage. (Completing the makeover, he also preferred to be called Barnwell instead of his commonplace first name.) Overcoming an interrupted formal education, he had begun his career as a lawyer, thrown himself into the most radical currents of the nullification movement in 1832–33, then climbed the political ladder from state attorney general to the U.S. Senate, where in 1850 he filled the vacancy left by John C. Calhoun's death. Although closely associated with the Great Nullifier, Rhett had always been more fiery, less interested in political ideas than in political action. (In his reverential eulogy to Calhoun, he could not help noting that the departed had "pursued principles too exclusively.") Rhett would pursue power for the South in order to turn principles into reality, and by 1850 he had decided that the only path left open was resistance and disunion. Efforts at compromise, he told the Nashville Convention, merely inspired "the Northern people with the belief that we value a union with them more than we value the institution of slavery." Slaveholders, he proclaimed, "must rule themselves or perish."

Although dejected by the surge of southern moderation during the early 1850s (which led him to resign from the Senate in 1852), Rhett never wavered. After the Republicans' strong national showing in 1856, he wrote an open letter to Governor James H. Adams, charging that a "complete revolution" by the antislavery North had transformed the federal government into "a sheer despotism," and that the only honorable course was for the South to seize its "glorious destiny" as "a great free and independent people!" The following year, Rhett obtained control of the old Calhounite newspaper, the *Charleston Mercury*, when his son bought it and installed himself as editor. In a purely tactical move, Rhett then modulated his tone, reentered the national Democratic Party, which he had abandoned years before, and began praising such figures as James Hammond and Jefferson Davis—southern rights stalwarts whom he had long criticized as unreliable party hacks. His unannounced aim was to capture the Democracy from within and use it to complete what he would soon be calling the South's "high mission"—to create a magnificent independent slaveholders' republic larger in territory than all of Europe, producing the world's most valuable commodity, cotton.

"Rhettism" won over such luminaries as congressmen Laurence Keitt and William Porcher Miles (the latter an ex-mayor of Charleston). Elsewhere in the South, ex-Carolinians, and out-of-staters with close spiritual and political ties to Carolina politics, expounded their own versions of disunionist extremism. Edmund Ruffin of Virginia, thrice appointed South Carolina commissioner of agriculture, made a considerable reputation beginning in the 1820s as a proponent of scientific land reclamation, but he earned popular acclaim only in the 1850s when he abandoned his earlier doubts about slavery, laid aside his work on calcareous manures, and began expounding on southern greatness and disunion. In Alabama, William Lowndes Yancey, the up-country South Carolina-born lawyer and scourge of the northern Democracy, formed, at Ruffin's suggestion, the pro-secession League of United Southerners—a group, Yancey announced, that would crush "the mere political tricksters, who now make the slavery question subordinate to the Parties." In Texas, a young firebrand émigré from a wealthy up-country South Carolina family, Louis Trezevant Wigfall, emerged as the major political rival to the old Jacksonian and Unionist Sam Houston. There were important pro-slavery extremists from outside the Carolina connection, most conspicuously the startling Virginia scribbler George Fitzhugh, a down-at-the-heels descendant of an old Commonwealth family who declared slavery "the natural and normal condition of society." But South Carolinians and ex-Carolinians dominated the fire-eaters' ranks.

Philosophically as well as politically, the fire-eaters stepped beyond the nullifier hero, Calhoun. ("I think Mr Rhett the logical extension of Mr Calhoun," William Trescot observed in 1858.) For Calhoun, liberty and equality meant the preservation of slaveholders' rights. His attacks on democracy—or what, in his unpublished "Disquisition on Government," he carefully called "absolute democracy"—amounted to an attack on majoritarian government and the reign of what John Randolph had called King Numbers. Until the last months of his life, Calhoun had always thought of interposition and nullification as the means to secure southern rights short of disunion, and even in 1850, when he talked more about secession, his mind was full of ideas about radical reforms that might yet keep the South within the Union. The later pro-slavery extremists went further, aiming at nothing less than secession, vaunting liberty as the prerogative of the naturally superior few, and rejecting the concepts of equality and democracy altogether. Man, Calhoun's old ally William Harper came to observe in 1852, was "born to subjection," and civilization rested on the enforcement of inequality. Self-government through universal suffrage, another South Carolinian wrote, was "the most pernicious humbug of the age." No society, wrote yet another, had ever "commenced the march of social movement" as "a mass of unarticulated democracy." For the Rhettist militants, the racial inequality of southern slavery reinforced their belief in the inequality of all mankind. They wanted to establish their own government as a pure slaveholders' republic untainted by the egalitarian foolishness of the age.

The Virginian Fitzhugh confronted the matter with clarity and audacity in a direct attack on Thomas Jefferson. "Men are not," he declared, "born entitled to equal rights!" Jefferson, with his palaver about how the mass of men had not been created to be ridden like horses by other men, was utterly wrong: "[I]t would be far nearer the truth to say, 'that some were born with saddles on their backs, and others booted and spurred to ride them' . . . they need the reins, the bit, and the spur." Few would go as far as Fitzhugh and claim that most whites as well as blacks were best

SLAVERY AND THE CRISIS OF
AMERICAN DEMOCRACY

1. Lincoln-Hamlin campaign banner, 1860

Provided nest, as an express and fundamental Condition to the acquisition of any ~~additional~~ territory ~~and ~~not now~~~~ from the Republic of Mexico, by the United States, by virtue of any treaty which may be negociated between them, and to the use by the Executive of the monies herein appropriated, neither Slavery nor involuntary servitude shall ever Exist in any part of said territory, except for crime whereof the party shall be first duly convicted.

Wilmott to 1st & is C

5. Handwritten draft of the Wilmot Proviso, 1846

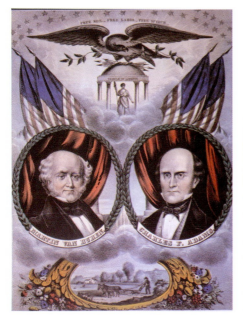

6. Free Soil Party campaign
engraving, 1848

7. Elizabeth Cady Stanton with her sons
Henry and Daniel, ca. 1848

8. The United States Capitol, ca. 1846

9. Henry Clay, between 1850 and 1852

10. Daniel Webster, between
1845 and 1849

11. William Henry Seward, 1860

12. John C. Calhoun, ca. 1849

13. Fugitive Slave Law abolitionist convention, Cazenovia, New York, 1850. Seated at the table, on the left, is Frederick Douglass; standing above him, hand outstretched, is Gerrit Smith

14. John Brown, ca. 1847

15. Anthony Burns, ca. 1854

2. Thomas Wilson Dorr, between 1844 and 1854

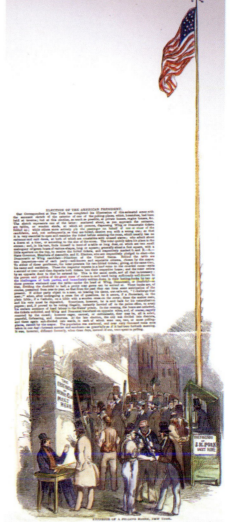

4. Polling booth in New York City, 1844

BULLETIN.

BY TELEGRAPH TO "UNION," WASHINGTON.

To the Editor of the Union :

NEW ORLEANS, Sept. 26, 1847.

SIR : The J. L. Day arrived here last evening from Vera Cruz. The news by her is important. The details are meagre, and something uncertain. The main points are, that the armistice has been concluded, without a treaty of peace ; and, after a considerable amount of hard fighting, the city of Mexico was captured, and our troops entered. Gen. Bravo was killed. Santa Anna was wounded, and has retired with his shattered forces to Guadalupe, about twelve miles from the city. The entrance to the city was on the 16th. The reports are that Scott lost from 1,000 to 1,700 men, killed and wounded.

Respectfully, yours, &c.

3. War bulletin, 1847

16. The caning of Charles Sumner, 1856

17. Dred Scott, ca. 1857

18. William Lowndes Yancey, ca. 1860

19. Robert Barnwell Rhett, ca. 1860

20. Alabama infantry flag, 1860

21. Abraham Lincoln, 1857

22. Wide-Awake Club and Band, Mohawk, New York, 1860

23. The inauguration of President Abraham Lincoln, March 4, 1861

fitted for slavery. But in the fire-eater mind, racial slavery was the cornerstone of a society that permitted the best men to rule over all the rest in virtuous harmony.

It all sounded slightly daft to most southern slaveholders. In the border states, where Unionism remained strong and where pro-slavery, though dominant, was still more equivocal than elsewhere, Rhettism seemed treasonous. Among Deep South planters, it was an affront to white solidarity. On certain essentials, most slaveholders could agree: slavery created an economy, society, and polity superior to the crass and cutthroat North; slavery was a benevolent, Christian institution which uplifted the slaves from the barbarism of their African ancestors; and the Yankees were determined to destroy all order, grace, and conservatism. But the transit from defending slavery to attacking some of the fundamental principles of 1776 seemed, outside South Carolina and among its extremist sons and admirers elsewhere, driven by unreal syllogisms. "Mr. Rhett is the most consistent of politicians," one Petersburg, Virginia, newspaper remarked in 1852. "He pushes his doctrines to their legitimate conclusions. He is rigidly logical, but remarkably impractical. He is something of a fanatic withal." And that was a friendly assessment. Farther west and south, the class-based, aristocratic, disunionist arguments clashed with ingrained white egalitarian assumptions. "Nowhere in this broad Union but in the slaveholding states," Albert Gallatin Brown of Mississippi proclaimed, "is there a living breathing, exemplification of the beautiful sentiment, that all men are equal." Brown immediately stipulated that by *men*, he meant "of course, white men," but with that vital exception, his own state and most others embraced the idea, enshrined in the opening passage of Mississippi's Declaration of Rights, that "all freemen, when they form a social compact, are equal in rights."

Master Race democracy of such an intense variety perforce insisted on black inferiority and on the indispensability of slavery to sustain white equality. Here, variations on the "mud-sills" theory propounded by James Hammond in 1858 largely displaced the antidemocratic conceits of the most reactionary fire-eaters.

All blacks, supposedly, were the moral, intellectual, and biological inferiors of all whites. Blacks were thus suited for servile drudgery without in any way demeaning their God-given limited capacities. By freeing superior whites from the mind-numbing tasks required of any society, slavery permitted the cultivation of a wise and advanced social leadership, not least in politics. But slavery also permitted the poorest white man to share social and civil privileges with his rich white neighbor, and to feel that basic political equality—"inspired," one pro-slavery man wrote, "with the just pride of a freeman, a sovereign." In the North, the exploited poor were held in contempt; in the South, the lowly white man enjoyed esteem and a basic equality with the richest planter. And slavery made it all possible, one Alabama convention declared, "by dispensing with grades and castes" among the free, "thereby preserv[ing] republican institutions."

These democratic defenses of slavery were shot through with their own contradictions. Did not the majority of slaveholders, working on small estates with fewer than five slaves, at least occasionally labor in the fields alongside their property? Did not the vast majority of white southerners, the nonslaveholders, lead lives full of hard labor and mental drudgery? Given the facts of life as opposed to the slaveholder's idyll, how truly egalitarian was southern slavery and the slaveholders' democracy for whites? Although white adult male suffrage was now universal, and men of humble attainment often filled local and county offices, did the slaveholders—and usually large slaveholders—not completely dominate the southern state legislatures, courts, and congressional delegations? How could slavery be justified on the basis of race when the actual labor performed by the great preponderance of whites and blacks was so similar? Master Race democrats blinded themselves to these questions, fixed on beliefs neatly summarized by the *Richmond Enquirer* in 1856: "[F]reedom is not possible without slavery."

Southern racist egalitarianism promoted an attachment to national political parties as well as to slavery. Outside South Carolina, southern Whigs and southern Democrats had long fought fiercely in local and statewide elections over which party would do the most to fend off the abolitionists. After the collapse of the Whigs in 1854, leaders of the southern Democracy remained assured that their command over the national party was so complete, they could have their way without leaving the Union. Contrary to the extremists who, like Yancey, believed that intersectional parties "preyed upon the vitals of the South" and deadened resistance to the Northern aggressor, southern Democrats believed that they had already achieved, within the Democracy, the Calhounite dream of a national party of slavery. Disunionists were not simply irrelevant; with their divisive antics in state politics and their attacks on solid, state-rights southern Democrats, they were a hindrance to southern domination of national affairs, which, at least through 1857, seemed to be growing ever stronger.

The clash between national Democrats and the fire-eater minority chronically disturbed southern politics. "As to the Rhetts, Yanceys &c.," the Louisiana Democrat John Slidell told Howell Cobb in 1852, "the sooner we get rid of them the better." Five years later, the venerable Democratic *Richmond Enquirer* attacked the "idle twaddle" of the extremist secessionists who seemed to consider themselves the "anointed defenders" of the South and slavery. The paper went on to single out the Rhetts' *Charleston Mercury* for its "editorial ravings" and "hopeless insanity." The Milledgeville, Georgia, *Federal Union,* having long criticized those who "wish to arouse the South by ringing in her ears the notes of preparation for battle," berated the fire-eaters' "excessive sensitiveness" on the subject of Southern rights. With a different kind of conservatism, the South's national Democrats insisted that the old ways really were best, that backroom deals, subcommittee struggles, and smoke-and-spitoon caucuses had served the South well—and that slavery was safe so long as the South could rely on what the *Federal Union* called "the magnanimity, good sense and prudence" of northern Democrats.

The divisions between fire-eaters and national Democrats were not, however, ineluctable. Some Deep South Democrats, including the Mississippians Albert Gallatin Brown and Jefferson Davis, flirted with extremist ideas. Even Robert Toombs of Georgia, a strong proponent of guarded moderation and Unionism after the truce of 1850, had been riled at times into embracing disunionism. The two sides could be pulled closer together by shared fears of Yankee aggression, as well by the chronic fears of slave insurrection and any signs of southern yeoman disloyalty to the slaveholders' regime. The last of these had flared up repeatedly in the border states, especially Kentucky, where, in 1845 and after, Henry Clay's antislavery cousin, Cassius Marcellus Clay, tried to stir the nonslaveholders out of their slumbers, and where, as recently as 1850, emancipationists had used the occasion of a state constitutional convention to push, albeit unsuccessfully, for slavery's gradual elimination. The fears flared again in 1857.

"Non-slaveholders of the South! farmers, mechanics and workingmen, we take this occasion to assure you that the slaveholders, the arrant demagogues whom you have elected to offices of honor and profit, have hoodwinked you, trifled with you, and used you as mere consummation of their wicked designs." So read *The Impending Crisis of the South: How to Meet It*, a new book published in New York but written by a North Carolinian of yeoman stock, one Hinton Rowan Helper. Soon the book was enjoying a respectable sale. More alarmingly, antislavery northern editors and orators, alerted by a lengthy and enthusiastic review in the *New-York Daily Tribune*, began spreading Helper's incendiary message. Might Helper's book prove that the southern nonslaveholders were not really as trustworthy and pro-slavery as the racist egalitarians assumed? Might Rhett and the aristocrats have been correct all along about the white lower classes of the South as well as the North?

Helper was an odd and determined fellow. Born and raised in rural Davie County, North Carolina, near the Appalachian foothills, the son of a poor blacksmith, farmer, and slaveholder, he had been educated at Mocksville Academy and, upon graduating in 1848, had moved down the road to Salisbury, where he found a job working for a storekeeper. Restless, he journeyed to New York in 1850, where he boarded a ship bound for San Francisco and the gold rush. After three disappointing years trying to strike it rich, he returned home to write an embittered narrative of his California experiences, *Land of Gold*, as a warning to any would-be prospectors. But as Helper surveyed the depressed condition of the Carolina backcountry, his mind turned to writing an embittered book about the South and what he would call "the bloodhounds of slavery." After moving to Baltimore, he completed a new manuscript two years later, but no southern firm would touch it, and so Helper went to New York once more. He finally acquired the services of a small publisher, A. B. Burdick, on Nassau Street.

The book was a mixture of roaring polemics and plodding statistics. Its basic argument was that slavery lay "at the root of all the shame, poverty, ignorance, tyranny, and imbecility of the South." Far from respecting the nonslaveholders as equals, Helper charged, slaveholders intentionally kept the ordinary folk ignorant by denying them a basic public education, thereby reducing their own tax burdens while making it all the easier to sustain their own political power over a semiliterate electorate. A tiny aristocracy—some three hundred thousand slaveholders out of some six million white southerners—ruled over what they fatuously called a democracy. "Slave-driving Democrats" regularly committed legislative outrages to keep the poor and middling white man down. Blacks, along with Indians and Chinese, were certainly inferior to whites, and Helper put no store by the insipid racial sentimentalism that he ascribed to the abolitionists. ("Yankee wives," he wrote, with Harriet Beecher Stowe clearly in mind, had provided "the fictions of slavery; men should give the facts.") Helper hated slavery in part because it contaminated a pure white America. But he also considered human bondage a moral abomination, and he wrote at length about how great southerners of the past had said as much. He then piled on row upon row of statistics culled from the 1850 federal census to prove that the South lagged far behind the North economically, socially, and intellectually—all because slavery degraded labor and left a despised people to wallow in material and mental poverty. The book concluded with an eleven-point program for emancipation without compensation to the masters, coupled with the resettlement of the freed blacks to Africa.

Much of Helper's racist emancipationism had been anticipated in earlier border-state and backcountry diatribes against the slaveholders. But Helper attacked the underlying myths of southern democracy with an unprecedented clarity and harshness—and he collaborated with a Yankee publisher. In the poisonous climate of 1857, that was sufficient to get the book noticed and to require its refutation. In his "mud-sills" speech early in 1858, James Hammond went out of his way to impugn Helper's statistics (without deigning to mention Helper's name) as taken from "trashy census books, all of which is perfect nonsense." Book-length rebuttals appeared under titles like *Helper's Impending Crisis Dissected* and *Review and Refutation*. Finally, taking no chances, several southern states made it a crime to circulate *The Impending Crisis*—laws that eventually led to at least two indictments. In North Carolina, anyone caught distributing the book faced a public whipping and a year in jail for the first offense, and hanging if caught again.

The attack on Helper's book only brought the book more attention—and seemed to confirm Helper's criticisms of the stunted southern democracy. By the late 1850s, every southern state save Kentucky had passed some sort of legislation infringing upon freedom of speech and of the press, to curtail the distribution of antislavery works. The chief motivation behind these laws was to stave off incitements to slave insurrection—fears which, despite the long peace that followed Nat Turner's rampage, loomed ever larger to slaveholders with the rise of the Republicans. To slaveholder democrats and antidemocrats alike, the abridgements were perfectly rational responses to Yankee aggression. Antislavery northerners regarded them as further proof that slavery and democracy could not coexist. To Republicans, the ban on *The Impending Crisis* marked the latest escalation in the struggle over free speech that stretched back to the

1830s. It also gave at least some of them the impression that the South was filled with whites who (as one young Pennsylvanian wrote) were "emancipationists at heart, and free-soilers secretly"—and that the oligarchic Slave Power was more vulnerable than ever.

By thus emboldening the Republicans, the controversy over *The Impending Crisis* drew the slaveholders closer together. Southern Democrats remained at least cautiously confident that Helper himself was an eccentric who would gain little support from the yeoman South. Fire-eaters were less sanguine. But nobody could deny that the "Black Republican" fanatics had emerged as the major opposition to the Democrats in the North—and that Helper was aiding their cause. As their exploitation of *The Impending Crisis* showed, those fanatics posed a clear and present danger to the stability of Dixie democracy. If they were ever to seize federal power—which, if they won the White House in 1860, they would take an enormous step toward completing—then in most of the South, the slaveholders' disagreements would dissolve, the fire-eaters would gain momentum, and secession would be the agenda.

What remained to be seen was whether the northern Democracy, rattled by the Lecompton tumult, could pull itself together and preserve its tenuous southern alliance, and whether the Republicans could unite behind a plausible presidential ticket. For clues, the nation turned its attention, during the summer and early fall of 1858, to a sensational election in Illinois.

POPULAR SOVEREIGNTY AND THE COMMON RIGHT OF HUMANITY: THE LINCOLN-DOUGLAS CAMPAIGN

As he approached his reelection campaign in 1858, Senator Stephen A. Douglas knew he would be in the fight of his political life. His break with the Buchanan administration over Lecompton had been costly. President Buchanan knew that Douglas held him in contempt personally as well as politically, and to many southern Democrats, Douglas's defiance showed the senator's utter unreliability. A militant southern clique within Buchanan's cabinet, consisting of Howell Cobb, John Floyd of Virginia, and Jacob Thompson of North Carolina, pressed for a purge of the recusant. In May, the pro-administration *Union* announced that Douglas would henceforth be treated as a pariah. Quietly, Douglas's foes within the party, including his detractors in Illinois, helped arrange for a separate slate of pro-administration legislative candidates in the 1858 canvass in order to kick him out of the Senate—even if it meant electing a Republican in his stead.

Douglas, who still longed to be president, did what he could to be conciliatory. He would not repudiate his revolt over Lecompton—doing so would be political suicide in the North—but he hoped to bring about a general agreement among the national Democrats over a diluted form of popular sovereignty, and to convince all sides to let bygones be bygones. In that effort, he had some important southern pro-slavery allies of his own in Washington, including Vice President John C. Breckinridge of Kentucky, Robert Toombs and Alexander Stephens of Georgia, and the ever-voluble Governor Henry A. Wise of Virginia. Douglas's home-state supporters, meanwhile, were convinced that, thanks to his fame and their financial resources, they could defeat the administration threat in Illinois and force the national party to come to its senses. Returning home to start his campaign in early July, Douglas affirmed his attachment to popular sovereignty, berated his vengeful Democratic foes as well as the Republicans, and vowed "to fight that allied army wherever I meet them." But Douglas had an additional problem. Three weeks earlier, a Republican convention in Springfield had nominated the opponent he feared above all others.

At age forty-nine, Abraham Lincoln enjoyed only modest renown outside Illinois, in marked contrast with the lightning-rod Democrat Douglas. Apart from political aficionados who recalled the one-term congressman, "Spotty" Lincoln, most Americans had little to go on about the man. Lincoln had certainly evolved in the 1850s. After returning home from Washington, he emerged, alongside his partner William H. Herndon, as one of the most skilled and respected lawyers in the western states and won the clientage of various large railroad and business corporations. The shocks and aftershocks of Kansas-Nebraska rudely reawakened his political interests and pushed him into the Republican Party. Yet while Lincoln's ambition remained, as Herndon would later recall, a "little engine that knew no rest," his political hopes had been thwarted more often than they had been fulfilled. President Zachary Taylor had rejected his application to be commissioner of the General Land Office in 1849; Lincoln was offered instead the governorship of Oregon Territory, a booby prize he wisely declined. Although he had gained a certain stature when he graciously gave way to Lyman Trumbull in the state legislature's selection of Illinois's junior U.S. senator in 1854, Lincoln had still been the loser.

More arresting than Lincoln's political résumé was his persona. Standing six feet four inches tall, a gigantic height for the time, thin but muscular, with a craggy face, outsized, slightly jugged ears, and striking gray eyes, he looked an ungainly popular leader—but a leader nevertheless. His background and early experiences—as the grandson of a migrating Virginia country democrat murdered by Indians in Kentucky, as the son of an uneducated, log-cabin farmer who had taken the family up to Indiana, as a young Illinois store clerk, ferryboat hand, and indifferent militiaman—were hardly extraordinary. But Lincoln's ability to connect those experiences to politics in simple prose, by turns humorous and icily logical, was rare. His speaking style, in the courtroom and on the political stump, was to begin in perfect stillness (his hands clasped behind his back), followed by emphatic head jerks, his semikempt hair flying, as he kindled to his argument, followed by waves of indignation, all punctuated with a sudden glowing gravitas. His tenor voice was sometimes shrill, even "unpleasant," his law partner Herndon reported, especially at the start of his speeches, but he learned how to hurl his remarks hard enough to reach to the farthest reaches of the crowd. The combination was quirky but arresting enough that both the Whigs and later the Frémont Republicans had made ample use of Lincoln's talents in their presidential campaigns.

Even more dangerous, from Douglas's standpoint, was Lincoln's mixture of seemingly preternatural moderation, hard-nosed political realism, and sincere conviction. Having entered politics as a new-school Whig, Lincoln's first political hero had been Henry Clay, and at least until 1854, his views on national issues connected with slavery ran much closer to Clay's than to those of Whig radicals like Joshua Giddings. (In a eulogy to Clay, delivered in Springfield in 1852, Lincoln's most striking remark was his ringing endorsement of the American Colonization Society.) His switch from guarded support to vocal opposition over the Mexican War, though not exceptional among northern Whigs, did require some political courage for a congressman from central Illinois. Otherwise, whenever Lincoln had had to choose between political alternatives—including, in 1848, siding with Zachary Taylor for the Whig presidential nomination—he usually took the more moderate, even safe political course. After he joined the Republicans, the Kentucky-born Lincoln eschewed polemics against the South, supported the Fugitive Slave Law, and remained open to the possibility of sectional reconciliation over slavery. Douglas would find it difficult to portray him as a crusading fanatic.

Yet neither could Lincoln be dismissed as merely a clever lawyer and political striver. For all of his restraint, his hatred of slavery ran deep, as did his certainty that Douglas's revised position on popular sovereignty was politically dangerous and morally bankrupt. The Kansas-Nebraska controversy had, for Lincoln, changed everything. Although still formally a Whig, he campaigned hard in 1854 for anti-Nebraska candidates—and twice confronted Senator Douglas. He forthrightly denounced "the monstrous injustice of slavery itself" and cited all of the by-now-familiar claims that the Founding Fathers had intended to see it eventually disappear. "The spirit of seventy-six and the spirit of Nebraska, are utter antagonisms," he declared in one widely publicized reply to Douglas at Peoria. "Let us re-adopt the Declaration of Independence, and with it, the practices, and policy, which harmonize with it." Although repeated acts of political compromise had permitted slavery to coexist with freedom, the thrust of American policy, he insisted, had been to confine slavery and prepare for its extinction, not to expand it. The great "moral wrong and injustice" of Douglas's Kansas-Nebraska Act was that it reversed that process and placed the accursed institution "on the high road to extension and perpetuity."

Three years later, the *Dred Scott* decision redoubled Lincoln's fury—and, once again, he directed it against Douglas, in a speech delivered in Springfield. Carefully noting that he favored no outright resistance to Taney's ruling, Lincoln proclaimed that the decision was "based on assumed historical facts which are not really true," and thus was not truly binding, as Douglas supposed it was. In the past, he noted, the Supreme Court had overruled its mistaken decisions, "and we shall do what we can to have it to over-rule this." Lincoln then quoted from Andrew Jackson's Bank Veto message on the duty of each public servant to support the Constitution "'*as he understands it*.'" He also quoted, once again, from the Declaration of Independence, charging that its egalitarian words, in 1776, were "held sacred by all, and thought to include all," and calling it "a stumbling block to those who in after times might seek to turn a free people back into the hateful paths of despotism." Taney and Douglas—the self-professed carriers of the Jeffersonian and Jacksonian traditions—had actually betrayed those traditions.

Lincoln returned to these lines of argument in his campaign for the Senate against Douglas in 1858, but he also sharpened them to fit the requirements of a rough-and-tumble political campaign. In retrospect, the contest has been viewed as a series of high-minded debates over grand American political principles. The impression is true but incomplete. Although the candidates engaged some of the most difficult and abiding problems of American democracy, the campaign, like any other, was a political fight in which each side sought to exploit the weaknesses of the other for maximum advantage. Douglas's political difficulties within his own party, after *Dred Scott* and Lecompton, could not have been more obvious. Lincoln thought hard for weeks prior to the state Republican convention about how he could divide Douglas even farther from pro-administration Democrats while stirring up his own Republican supporters. By the time he gave his first speech of the campaign, immediately following his nomination, he had found the words he needed.

Addressing a jacketless, sweating crowd inside the state Capitol, Lincoln opened with his main point. For five years, he charged, the federal government had followed an avowed policy of ending agitation over slavery, only to stir that agitation even more: "In *my* opinion, it *will* not cease until a *crisis* shall have been reached, and passed. 'A house divided against itself cannot stand.' I believe this government cannot endure, permanently half *slave* and half *free*. I do not expect the Union to be *dissolved*—I do not expect the house to *fall*—but I *do* expect it will cease to be divided. It will become *all* one thing, or *all* the other." Lincoln left no doubt that he also expected freedom would prevail against slavery and its northern abettors like Stephen A. Douglas.

What would forever after be known as Lincoln's "House Divided" speech was both a political preemptive strike and a call for fresh Republican boldness. Its main objectives were to destroy Douglas's benign view of the *Dred Scott* decision and to link Douglas to the grand designs of the Slave Power. First, Lincoln charged, Douglas's Kansas-Nebraska Act opened the national domain to slavery; then the Democrats interpreted the 1856 elections as a mandate to inflict slavery on Kansas; then Taney prohibited Congress and local legislatures from barring slavery in any territory. Reflecting the conspiratorial thinking that was abroad in Republican circles, Lincoln claimed that it was "impossible not to *believe* that Stephen and Franklin and Roger and James all understood one another from the beginning." The next step, Lincoln suggested, would be a Supreme Court decision prohibiting states as well as territories from keeping slavery outside their borders. And Lincoln would fight such an outcome with all his might—unlike the "*caged* and *toothless*" incumbent.

Lincoln's personal attack was demagogic, not least because it slighted Douglas's principled break with the administration over Lecompton. Yet its political value lay not so much in smearing Douglas as in forcing him, even before he had begun his campaign, onto his shakiest ground. Anything less than a stout defense by Douglas of his diluted popular sovereignty idea would rattle moderate Illinois voters who had admired his break with Buchanan. But that defense would further inflame pro-administration Democrats, especially in the southern portions of the state, and it would all but foreclose any chance of Douglas's winning his party's presidential nomination in 1860. For exposing his flank to Lincoln's offensive, Douglas had no one to blame but himself and his past entanglements with the Slave Power, and Lincoln intended to make him pay for it. At the same time, Lincoln wanted to rouse the Republican base and Democrats of goodwill with the stark image of a house divided that he believed, to the depths of his soul, was accurate. After *Dred Scott*, he had decided, it was no longer possible to rest the Republican case solely on the prohibition of slavery in the territories, as some of the more cautious Republicans preferred. It was now imperative to state candidly that halting slavery's expansion was one way to put slavery "in the course of ultimate extinction"—a prerequisite for preserving American freedom.

Douglas saw vulnerabilities in Lincoln's position. In his home-coming speech in Chicago on July 6 (delivered after he had sportingly shaken hands with his opponent, who sat just behind him), Douglas avoided any mention of his quarrel with Buchanan but still attacked the Lecompton constitution as a "monstrosity." He then defined his differences with Lincoln. Why could the United States, a diverse nation in so many respects, not tolerate both slavery and freedom? What evidence was there to support Lincoln's assertions that the nation was bound to be all slave or all free? The Founding Fathers whom Lincoln quoted so blithely believed no such thing. On the contrary: "The framers of the

Constitution well understood that each locality, having separate and distinct interests, required separate and distinct laws, domestic institutions, and police regulations adapted to its own wants and its own condition." Lincoln's rash declarations about slavery and freedom portended certain war between the North and the South; Douglas preferred peace. Lincoln, furthermore, had refused to abide by the authority of the highest court in the land—a refusal, Douglas charged, that arose from Lincoln's nauseating belief in racial equality as well as in abolition. Pugnacious as ever, Douglas would reject the extremism of the Lecompton supporters and of the "Black Republicans" alike, and sustain the proven American principles of Union, expansion, and democracy—above all the latter, "the right of the people in each state and territory to decide for themselves."

Lincoln, the underdog, took to following Douglas along the campaign trail, and in late July he proposed that they debate each other formally all across the state. Knowing how formidable Lincoln would be, but never one to back down from a challenge, Douglas cut Lincoln's suggested list of nine debates to seven. In a staggered schedule, the candidates would appear in easily accessible towns from the Wisconsin border down to the southernmost counties known collectively as "Egypt." Public interest, in and out of Illinois, was intense by the time the two met for the first contest in Ottawa, on August 21. Thence began one of the most stirring pieces of sustained political theater in all of American history. Trainloads of supporters traveled to the debate towns in banner-bedecked passenger cars, accompanied by brass bands. Local farmers and shopkeepers clogged the roads surrounding the debating grounds with their horses, wagons, and buggies. Newspaper reporters took down the verbal cuts and thrusts on the podiums and instantly relayed the news by telegraph to the rest of the nation. (The *New-York Daily Tribune*, along with numerous Illinois papers, printed verbatim transcripts, while reporters from Charleston and New Orleans, as well as from all over the North, covered the events.) In the middle of it all were the principals, both experienced debaters—one an absurdly tall, leathery shambler whose stovepipe hat and ill-fitting coat made him look all the odder, but who never lost his self-control; the other an exquisitely tailored bulldog who emanated prestige as well as stamina, but who had a tendency to bark his words and, if pushed too hard, to snarl.

The reporters in the crowd were swept up in the show, and described the seven contests as packed with suspense and revelation, like champion prizefights. And so the Lincoln-Douglas debates have become lodged in the national memory. In fact, the candidates said little of substance that they had not already said before the debates began. Lincoln mainly stuck to the themes of his "House Divided" speech, asserted that Douglas had departed from the designs of the Founding Fathers, and repeated that the nation could not forever stand half slave and half free. Douglas countered that the Founders (including the slaveholder Jefferson) had left the establishment of slavery up to the individual states, that Lincoln's talk of slavery's ultimate extinction was "revolutionary" and would ensure civil war, and that his distortions of American political principles were driven by the monstrous heresy that "the Almighty . . . intended the negro to be the equal of the white man."

Even the debates' supposed apex, during the second clash at Freeport, replicated well-established positions. Under the rules of this particular debate, the candidates were permitted to direct questions at each other, and Lincoln asked Douglas whether the people of any territory could "in any lawful way" exclude slavery if they wished to do so. Lincoln knew exactly what Douglas's reply would be, since Douglas had in effect been giving it in public speeches for more than a year—that a territory's citizens could, in accordance with *Dred Scott*, exclude slavery since, in the absence of supporting local laws from a territorial legislature, slavery could not exist. Republican newspapers hyped the exchange as a devastating body blow by Lincoln, and ever since, Douglas's enunciation of the so-called Freeport Doctrine has been remembered as a pivotal moment not just in the debates but in American history. But Lincoln's question merely recapitulated his efforts to strike at the contradiction between *Dred Scott* and popular sovereignty and thereby divide the Democratic vote. Douglas's reply would have been remarkable only if it had been any different from what it was.

If either candidate was thrown on the defensive during the debates, it was Lincoln, over the questions of racial equality and abolition. Douglas repeatedly charged, most ferociously in the central and southern portions of the state, that Lincoln's objections to *Dred Scott* arose from his unstated wish to confer full citizenship on the Negro. While his partisans cheered, Douglas hammered away, inviting all those who wished to see emancipated blacks flood into Illinois and become citizens equal with whites to vote for Lincoln and the "Black Republicans." Douglas even claimed (at the Jonesboro debate, deep in "Egypt") that he had spotted a carriage at Freeport, driven by its white owner, carrying "Fred Douglass, the Negro" who was "sitting inside with the white lady and her daughter," all part of the Republican coterie that "advocated negro citizenship and negro equality, putting the white man and the negro on the same basis under the law." ("Never, never," the crowd shouted.) Lincoln tried humorously to deflect the attacks. "I do not understand that because I do not want a negro woman for a slave I must necessarily want her for a wife," he jested at the next debate in Charleston, but Douglas's barbs hit their mark. Lincoln was reduced to explaining that he opposed equal rights for free blacks, and that physical differences "will for ever forbid the two races living together on terms of social and political equality." Likewise, when Douglas alleged that Lincoln's "House Divided" statements were just a cover for his disunionist, abolitionist designs, Lincoln responded, weakly, that he had no plan for slavery's elimination, only a certainty that it would one day occur.

The peril, for the moderate Lincoln, was that Douglas would push him to endorse prevalent racial prejudices to the point where he would antagonize more radical Republicans. No less than his opponent, the Democrat knew how to play wedge-issue politics. But in the concluding debate, in the downstate town of

Alton (where a mob had killed Elijah Lovejoy more than twenty years before), Lincoln eloquently regained the offensive. Whether he wanted to "make war between the free and the slave States" or introduce "a perfect social and political equality between the white and black races," Lincoln declared, were "false issues, upon which Judge Douglas has tried to force the controversy." The real issue was whether slavery should be viewed as wrong: "That is the issue that will continue in this country when these poor tongues of Judge Douglas and myself shall be silent. It is the eternal struggle between these two principles—right and wrong—throughout the world. They are the two principles that have stood face to face from the beginning of time; and will ever continue to struggle. The one is the common right of humanity, and the other the divine right of kings. It is the same principle in whatever shape it develops itself. It is the same spirit that says, 'You work and toil and earn bread, and I'll eat it.'" Loud applause interrupted Lincoln's remarks, followed by cheers at his conclusion. Douglas replied that the enemies of popular sovereignty were the real Tories, to more rousing cheers; and with that the debates ended.

In the balloting less than three weeks later, Lincoln's side narrowly won the most votes, but Douglas's side won the election. The geographical split was pronounced: Democrats swept virtually all of the southern counties and Republicans virtually all of the northern counties. The legislature had not, however, yet been reapportioned to account for the rising numbers of voters in the pro-Republican counties, and, by a quirk, most of the seats not up for election in 1858 were held by Democrats. As a result, although Republican candidates statewide won about four thousand more votes than the Democrats (out of roughly a quarter-million cast), the Democrats held a clear majority in the legislature and Douglas was thereby reelected to the Senate. For Douglas, it was a major vindication, not only because he had defeated Lincoln but because only a handful of voters, about five thousand in all, had supported the pro-administration Democratic candidates. In his first electoral test since the Lecompton schism, Douglas had affirmed his position as a leader—perhaps *the* leader—of the northern Democrats, and fortified his bid for the presidential nomination in 1860.

Yet who won the debates? The historical consensus favors Lincoln, although that conclusion is colored by hindsight. Certainly Douglas's views on the Founding Fathers and slavery had merit. No matter what the Northwest Ordinance said, slavery had been permitted to expand beyond the limits of its existence in 1787 into areas where it could flourish. Prior to the Missouri crisis, challenges to the rights of new southern states and territories to decide for themselves about slavery got nowhere. At the end of his life, Thomas Jefferson had explicitly opposed the antislavery agitation that led to the Missouri Compromise. Nor was Lincoln always the more high-minded or persuasive debater. Although Douglas cheapened the political currency with his misrepresentations and racist pandering, Lincoln's jibes about "Franklin and Stephen and Roger and James" and his purposeful effacement of the differences between Douglas and the Buchanan administration were hardly fair. His refusal to engage in any discussion of how he foresaw emancipation, although politically wise and necessary, also left an air of vagueness hanging over his arguments. Lincoln never lost his wit or his parables, and always had his claque, but Douglas's fierce style appears (from the reports of the cheering and shouting) to have played better to the crowds.

Still, merely by holding his own against the renowned incumbent, Lincoln won a huge personal triumph. And on the issues that mattered and were coming to matter, Lincoln got the better of his opponent, especially when his sentiments were read in cold print—an achievement that, although no substitute for actual victory, counted for a great deal. Douglas, his popular sovereignty solution ripped apart by the Taney Court, offered no shred of convincing evidence that unfriendly local legislation alone could halt slavery's expansion. The Court, after all, had ruled that Dred Scott was a slave even during his residence in a territory that lacked pro-slavery policing regulations. "[T]here is vigor enough in slavery to plant itself in a new country even against unfriendly legislation," Lincoln concluded during the debate at Jonesboro; Douglas never provided a persuasive rebuttal. More obliquely, but also importantly, the fact that the debates barely made mention of tariffs, banks, internal improvements, or anything other than slavery sustained Lincoln's basic contention that slavery was the one great issue that had divided the country and continued to divide it, despite repeated assertions that the issue had been settled.

Above all, Lincoln captured the moral high ground without sacrificing his moderate standing within the Republican Party. If he would not endorse the radical idea that the black man was his perfect equal, he did insist that the black man was entitled to freedom—and with it the rights to life, liberty, and the pursuit of happiness. As Lincoln put it in the first debate, "[I]n the right to eat the bread, without leave of anybody else, which his own hand earns, *he is my equal and the equal of Judge Douglas, and the equal of every living man.*" Among Republicans, it was a principled yet hardly outlandish sentiment, but Lincoln's insistence on proclaiming it in the face of racist invective arraigned Douglas's view of "equality" as mean and morally bankrupt. In doing so, Lincoln proved that a centrist western Republican could forcefully clarify the fundamental differences between his own party and the northern Democrats. He thereby began turning himself, despite his loss, from a provincial party leader into a national party hero.

The theatrics of the Lincoln-Douglas debates, and the intense coverage they received in the press, also created a new political reality which overwhelmed the fact that both candidates were largely repeating themselves. Although a crucial Senate seat was in play, both sides knew that even larger stakes were involved, and they conducted the debates accordingly, with the hope of influencing elections elsewhere and setting the stage for 1860. For the pro-Douglas Democrats, the Illinois contest was crucial to halting the Republicans' momentum and to establishing that they, and not the toadies of the Buchanan administration, were in charge of the northern Democracy, without alienating reasonable southern Democrats. For the Republicans, it was a matter of building on their stunning victories in 1856 and enlarging their attacks on a Slave Power that, in their eyes, had confirmed it would stop at nothing to enlarge its despotism. And here, Lincoln may have understood the new campaign realities better than his opponent, delivering speeches and ripostes that, as read in the newspapers around the country rather than heard by the local campaign crowds, carried greater moral and logical weight.

Lincoln's party was certainly the greater beneficiary. Outside Illinois, the Republicans, capitalizing on *Dred Scott* and Lecompton, succeeded beyond their wildest expectations in 1858. Democratic congressional candidates lost in droves, handing control of the House of Representatives to the Republicans. In the lower northern battleground states that had carried Buchanan to victory two years earlier, the Republicans won 52 percent of the vote, an increase that augured extremely well for 1860. The Douglas Democracy did secure its home base, including victories in five of Illinois's nine congressional elections, despite opposition from the administration—success that offered strong clues about where, between Douglas and Buchanan, the northern Democrats' best political interests lay. Yet even Douglas's victorious campaign was a mixed blessing for the Democracy and, in time, for Douglas. By the summer after his defeat, Lincoln was back on the stump, invited to speak on behalf of Republican candidates in Ohio and Wisconsin. In time, cheap editions of the complete text of the instantly famous Lincoln-Douglas debates appeared—edited and corrected by Lincoln himself, issued by the Ohio Republican Committee, and publicized by, among other newspapers, Greeley's *Tribune*. Growing numbers of Republicans were determined to see their new hero Lincoln have another go at Stephen Douglas—but this time for the presidency.

"ANOTHER EXPLOSION WILL SOON COME"

Abraham Lincoln knew how volatile the political situation remained late in 1858. The *Dred Scott* decision, the continuing war in Kansas, and the Democrats' division over Lecompton had deepened the sectional divide, amplified the differences between northern and southern democracy, and made slavery and its expansion the overriding issue in national politics. The Republican victories in 1858 outside Illinois ensured that brutal new struggles would precede the 1860 elections, although Lincoln could only guess at where and how they would arise. "The fight must go on," he wrote to a consoling supporter shortly after his defeat. "Douglas had the ingenuity to be supported in the late contest both as the best means to *break down*, and to *uphold* the Slave interest. No ingenuity can keep those antagonistic elements in harmony long. Another explosion will soon come."

Eight months later, a man calling himself Isaac Smith rented a small, secluded Maryland farm near the Virginia border from the heirs of a doctor named Booth Kennedy. All summer long, men, white and black, arrived at the place, at least once carrying heavy crates labeled "Hardware and Castings." A daughter and daughter-in-law of the mysterious Smith, both aged sixteen, did the men's cooking and cleaning and kept on the lookout for any prying neighbors. Suddenly, in September, the young women vanished, and the men began their final phase of preparations. Smith's visitors turned out to be a ragtag army; Smith turned out to be John Brown.

8

THE FAITH THAT
RIGHT MAKES MIGHT

The years from 1859 to 1861 marked the fortieth anniversary of the Missouri crisis, and brought the final defining of the two American democracies. In the South, hardline pro-slavery politics had come to prevail, and disunionism was gaining momentum. For the most intense of the fire-eaters, the conflict loomed over the legitimacy of democracy itself. "It is obvious that two distinct and antagonistic forms of society have met for the contest upon the arena of this Union," wrote the South Carolinian L. W. Spratt:

> The one assumes that all men are equal and that equality is right, and, forming upon that theory, is straining its members to the horizontal plain of a democracy. The other assumes that all men are not equal, that equality is not right, therefore, and forming upon this theory, is taking upon itself the rounded form of a social aristocracy.

More mainstream southerners prized political equality for white men, but insisted that true democracy required the mudsill system of racial slavery. And the more southern slavery seemed endangered, from within and without, the more the pro-slavery Master Race democrats converged with the planter aristocrats against the alien Yankee democracy.

In the North, the few surviving antislavery veterans of the Missouri crisis, including Marcus Morton, as well as older leaders of the Republican Party, could look back at the previous four decades with enormous satisfaction. The political antislavery movement had grown far beyond the temporary alliance of northern Jeffersonian Republicans and surviving Federalists that backed James Tallmadge in 1819. The moral and constitutional arguments against slavery's extension raised by Tallmadge and others had been sustained and enlarged. Salmon P. Chase remarked with astonished gratitude that the good old doctrine— "denationalization of slavery entire"—was now seriously contending for national power. "The feeble cause I espoused at Cincinnati in 1832," Henry B. Stanton later recalled, had come to rest "on the broad shoulders of a strong party which was marching on to victory." After the crack-up of the southern-dominated Democratic Party over Lecompton, that victory looked increasingly certain—and with it, the consolidation of a revolutionized northern democracy that would vindicate the Declaration of Independence by checking and, in time, overthrowing the Slave Power.

Uncompromising radical abolitionists, preeminently William Lloyd Garrison, took a more ambivalent view of developments since the Missouri crisis. The radicals could, with justice, claim they had changed the terms of antislavery politics by renouncing gradualism and colonization in the 1830s. The antislavery views advanced by the Liberty men and upheld by the Republicans had certainly been formed in the crucible of the American Anti-Slavery Society's early campaigns. But the radicals of the 1850s also berated more conventional antislavery advocates for their toleration of anything short of speedy emancipation and full racial equality. On July 4, 1854, Garrison, in response to the Kansas-Nebraska Act and the

Anthony Burns affair, publicly burned a copy of the Constitution, which the Republicans had pledged to uphold, calling it a pact made in Hell with the Devil. Among some hard-core radical abolitionists like Parker Pillsbury and Abby Kelley Foster and her husband Stephen, idealism curdled into sectarianism. Pillsbury called the Republicans' watered-down antislavery "more dangerous to the cause of liberty" than the Democrats' forthright oppression. Wendell Phillips, the brightest new radical star, scrutinized the rising antislavery politician Abraham Lincoln and denounced him as a "huckster" and "The Slave-Hound of Illinois."

In their frustration, the radical abolitionists also confronted anew their dedication to nonviolence. The warfare in Kansas had further weakened the hold of pacifism, even among some of Garrison's friends and loyalists. Gerrit Smith, who had been an officer in the American Peace Society, declared that the Kansas crisis had prepared him "and ten thousand other peace men" to have the Slave Power not just repulsed with violence "but pursued even unto death with violence." In November 1856, Thomas Wentworth Higginson, who had led the attack to free Anthony Burns, devised plans for a fighting force drawn from all of the northern states "for resisting the U.S. Government in Kanzas, and sustaining such resistance everywhere else." A year later, Higginson's supporters met in Cleveland and adopted a resolution extolling slave uprisings. The politics of insurrection would take precedence over fruitless efforts at moral suasion and over the hopelessly compromised politics of democracy.

To the consternation of Republicans, the new militant mood among the radicals had come to condone and even design violent efforts to overthrow the Slave Power—efforts, the Republicans feared, that would discredit their own democratic resistance and return the Democrats to power in 1860. But Higginson and his frantic friends alone could not get plans for insurrection off the ground. An experienced killer would carry the war directly into the American Egypt.

JOHN BROWN AND THE POLITICS OF INSURRECTION

John Brown never had to break with any previous commitment to nonviolence. Born in Torrington, Connecticut, in 1800 and raised chiefly in Ohio, he had been trained by his devout parents in the old Congregational Calvinism, with its adherence to pre-destination and divine intervention. Other antislavery activists had been moved by the evangelical promise of spiritual rebirth in Christ's merciful bosom. Brown, as comfortable in the Old Testament as the New, worshipped an angrier God and the Jesus of Matthew 10:34, who came not to send peace but a sword. As Brown grew older—wandering through Ohio, Pennsylvania, and upstate New York, following up one business failure with another—his hatred of slavery and his projected kinship with abused blacks hardened. Finally, in Kansas, he killed his first Philistines. To some who met him, the unforgiving, hatchet-faced Brown, with his fondness for speaking in pseudo-biblical epi-grams, was plainly a crazy man, laboring under religious delusions. To his admirers, he was a reborn Cromwell, a Puritan who would dare to do God's will when others merely talked about it.

On Washington's Birthday in 1858, Brown met with Smith at the latter's grand estate in Peterboro, New York. They were joined by Franklin B. Sanborn, a young Harvard graduate, school-teacher, and protégé of Ralph Waldo Emerson who had been helping Brown in his fund-raising activities for more than a year, and, possibly, by Captain Charles Stuart, an Anglo-American abolitionist. Brown laid out a plan for an attack on the South at some undisclosed spot, which would touch off a gigantic slave rebellion. To their protests that the proposal was mad—"an amazing proposition,—desperate in its character . . . ," Sanborn later wrote, "of most uncertain result"—Brown replied that he would carry on with or without their support. Awed by Brown's self con-fidence, and by the possibility that even if the plan failed, it might hasten a civil war, Smith and Sanborn agreed to help. With four other abolitionist radicals—Higginson, Parker, the physician and reformer Samuel Gridley Howe, and George L. Stearns, an affluent pipe manufacturer—they formed a secret advisory and fund-raising committee. Over the coming months, Brown and the so-called Secret Six quietly informed other radicals, including Frederick Douglass, of the plot.

Brown had become fascinated with the guerrilla tactics of the Spanish resisters against Napoleon's armies during the Peninsular War. His plan centered on a raid into mountainous western Virginia, followed by a hit-and-run campaign that would extend into Tennessee and the Deep South, picking up rebel slaves along the way. He expected that free blacks would, from the start, compose a large contingent in his band, and serve as further encouragement for the slaves to rise up. In early May, before his final journey to Kansas, Brown and eleven white men arrived at a community of former slaves in Chatham, Ontario, near Detroit, and secretly met with a group of more than thirty. Brown announced that he had completed a plan of action, and the assembled approved it along with the constitution for a provisional freedmen's republic. They also named Brown the new government's commander-in-chief, granting him unchecked powers to wage war. Brown left with the impression that blacks from Canada would join him en masse. "Had a good Abolition convention," he wrote to his family. He arranged to have plenty of copies of the provisional government plan printed up for when he made his strike.

After a year more of preparation, Brown was ready to go in the summer of 1859. Yet once his recruits had assembled at the rented Kennedy farm in Maryland (and received pikes and rifles in disguised crates), Brown's "army" amounted to a pitiful twenty-one soldiers, only five of them black. With radical free blacks backing away from the venture and some members of the Secret Six growing jittery, Brown appealed to Frederick Douglass, an old friend in the antislavery struggle, to join him. More than anyone, Douglass would legitimize that venture among free blacks, and he would be the ideal organizer of the slaves whom Brown expected would swarm to join in after the first blow had been struck. But at a secret meeting of the two in August at a quarry in Chambersburg, Pennsylvania, Douglass refused. Brown had determined that his guerrilla war would begin with an assault on the federal armory in Harpers Ferry—a plan that Douglass warned was suicidal and "would array the whole country against us." Brown carried on anyway, deeply disappointed at Douglass's demurral and at the failure of his other black supporters to show up for slavery's Armageddon. He hoped that the slaves living in and around his target would prove more receptive and steadfast.

Douglass's military instincts proved sound. Harpers Ferry, five miles from the Kennedy farm, was situated on a tip of land formed by the Potomac and Shenandoah rivers and surrounded by imposing cliffs—a "perfect steel-trap" as Douglass called it. Once inside the town, Brown's little force would be easy prey for a counterattack, which is exactly what transpired. On the evening of October 16, Brown's men marched out and easily captured the armory by overcoming its single watchman, and collected several dozen hostages. Brown had sent out a two-man patrol to spread the alarm and free slaves at the neighboring plantation of a distant descendant of George Washington; then he sat with his men and waited for the rebels to arrive. He had made no previous contacts with those neighboring slaves to prepare them; he had planned no escape route out of Harpers Ferry; and, even less explicably, he held a midnight train bound for Baltimore hostage for a few hours, but then allowed it to proceed—and bring word to a hostile outside world about what was happening in Harpers Ferry. The haphazardness of Brown's behavior suggests that by the time the raid began, he had realized it would be futile. But it is just as likely that he simply threw the dice and hoped that the slaves would join him—prepared, if they did not, to exchange the role of avenging commander-in-chief for that of martyr.

Less than a day and a half after it began, the raid was crushed. Brown's raiders did round up a number of slaves, but most appeared unmoved by what was happening and did not join in the fighting. Armed townsmen, not content to wait for the Virginia and Maryland militia, fired on Brown's volunteers, picking off eight of them while losing three men of their own. Brown, his surviving guerrillas, and some prisoners retreated inside a small but sturdy brick-walled fire-engine house. After nightfall, a company of federal marines, commanded by Colonel Robert E. Lee and Lieutenant J. E. B. Stuart, joined the militiamen on the scene and prepared for the final assault, using a battering ram and their bayonets in order to avoid killing innocent hostages. When the fighting ended, Brown, wounded in action, was taken captive. The combat had killed ten raiders (including two of Brown's sons), four townsmen (including the black baggage-handler at the railroad station, mistaken for a watchman), and one marine. Seven of Brown's men escaped, although two were later captured. One of the freed slaves was killed; the others were returned to bondage.

Defeated, Brown had a second drama to perform, which would prove perhaps more important than the first. In his jail cell in Charles Town, charged with treason, Brown recovered from his wounds, wrote letters, and gave interviews with an impressive solemnity. In his courtroom testimony, he claimed he had not intended to raise an insurrection against the United States, but only to arm oppressed slaves—a hair-splitting defense that made no impact on the judge and jury. (Having brought along copies of the provisional government proclamation from the Chatham meeting along with his war maps, all later discovered by his captors, Brown certainly looked like an insurrectionist.) But with his dignity and his uncowering remarks about slavery, he became a public sensation, and he saved his best for last. In his closing speech before being sentenced to hang, Brown eloquently appealed to the laws of God and expressed contentment that, in a just cause, he would "mingle my blood further with the blood of my children and with the blood of millions in this slave country." On the morning of his execution, December 2, he wrote out with a steady hand his final prophecy, that "the crimes of this *guilty land: will* never be purged *away*; but with Blood. I had *as I now think: vainly* flattered myself that without *very much* bloodshed; it might be done."

Governor Henry A. Wise, fearing an effort to free the prisoner, ordered fifteen hundred soldiers to Charles Town, which only heightened the tension. (Among the troops was John Wilkes Booth, a well-known actor who had enlisted in the Richmond Grays militia with the sole intention of seeing Brown die. Others in the hanging-day throng included the fire-eater Edmund Ruffin and Thomas J. Jackson of the Virginia Military Institute, who would one day earn the nickname "Stonewall.") Brown, taken to the gallows in a wagon, stared out over the Blue Ridge Mountains and remarked, "This *is* a beautiful country." After the deed was done and while John Brown's body dangled, a Virginia colonel intoned, "So perish all such enemies of Virginia! All such enemies of the Union! All foes of the human race!"

Southern reactions to the affair were varied, and swerved, within a matter of weeks, from alarm to reassurance to fury. While Brown's men exchanged gunfire with the citizenry of Harpers Ferry, exhilarated crowds lined the railroad tracks from Baltimore to Harpers Ferry to cheer the federal forces on their way. Then a wave of hysteria hit the slaveholding states. Early reports about the Brown raid and the captured materials suggested that the long-feared moment of reckoning had arrived, and that Brown's crimes in Kansas had been a mere prelude to massive uprisings on southern plantations. Well into the autumn, reports circulated about imagined black rebellions and about whole armies of abolitionists marching southward as reinforcements. Vigilance committees sprang to life; the South Carolina legislature passed several measures further restricting slave movement and augmenting military preparations. But when the rumors faded, and it became clear that no massive movement of slaves had joined Brown's insurrection or any other, relieved southerners momentarily calmed down. The insurrectionists represented only a small number of monomaniac Yankees. Some claimed that the events had actually vindicated slavery by proving that slaves everywhere were loyal and content. The raid itself, one Richmond paper had observed early on, was "a miserably weak and contemptible affair." Edmund Ruffin, who considered Brown an atrocious criminal and thorough fanatic, conceded that he was also "a very brave & able man." If the abolitionists would realize that the slaves were content, cease their mad plotting, and put their abundant energies to good use, there would be perfect peace in the valley. Only after the convict's execution, when northerners began their apotheosis of John Brown, did southern outrage revive.

Northern opinion passed through its own evolution. Initially, the acts shocked even some radical abolitionists—"misguided, wild, and apparently insane," Garrison said, though, as with David Walker and Nat Turner thirty years earlier, he would not renounce the guerrillas. But Brown's moving gallantry in defeat quickly led to the rise of a virtual religious cult of the man in antislavery circles. At the hour of his hanging, northern church bells tolled from Boston to Chicago. Ministers preached special sermons on Brown's sacrifice; mass meetings bowed their heads in worshipful silence. Well before execution day, New England abolitionists and intellectuals were already beside themselves: Henry David Thoreau wrote "A Plea for Captain Brown" and called him "a transcendentalist above all, a man of ideas and principles," and Ralph Waldo Emerson predicted that Brown would "make the gallows glorious like the cross." In New York, William Cullen Bryant said that Brown's name would go down in history "among those of its martyrs and heroes." The Boston patrician Charles Eliot Norton observed that "[t]he heart of the people was fairly reached, and an impression has been made upon it which will be permanent and produce results long hence." Illustrators churned out portraits of Brown and his exploits; hagiographies flew off northern presses. As the train bearing Brown's body to his last homestead in upstate New York pulled into Philadelphia, a gathering of free blacks greeted it, in a gesture of respect to the fallen hero.

The Christian imagery in so many of the northern outbursts revealed the emotional power of Brown's elevation. (It may also have reflected the impact, especially in New England, of the religious revival of 1857 and 1858.) In his letters from the Charles

Town jail, Brown himself encouraged comparisons between his fate and Christ's sacrifice, although he sometimes imagined himself as Peter taking a sword from Christ rather than as Christ Himself. Northern orators and ministers picked up the Christ comparison: Charles Town suddenly became Calvary; and Brown's execution would, supposedly, achieve the salvation of the enslaved and the nation's redemption. Yet unlike Charles Sumner, who had also suffered and been likened to Jesus, Brown could only be honored as an enraged savior, a killer as well as a victim. The switch from extolling Sumner to extolling Brown betokened a shift in radical antislavery sensibilities, following the Southern outrages that had begun in Kansas. Instead of holy meekness, the new mood projected manly fury, sending not peace but a sword.

Henry David Thoreau, the erstwhile theorist of nonviolent civil disobedience, summed up the new attitude in secular as well as biblical terms. "[T]here are at least as many as two or three individuals to a town throughout the North who think much as the present speaker does about [Brown] and his enterprise," Thoreau told the citizens of Concord. ". . . We aspire to be something more than stupid and timid chattels, pretending to read history and our Bibles, but desecrating every house and every day we breathe in." All of the speeches of the supposedly noble Republicans put together, he charged, "do not match for manly directness and force, and for simple truth, the few casual remarks of crazy John Brown, on the floor of the Harper's Ferry engine-house." The true day of reckoning really was coming, Thoreau warned the slaveholders, and slavery would be no more: "We shall then be at liberty to weep for Captain Brown. Then, and not till then, we will take our revenge."

Talk of avenging the crackpot killer and traitor infuriated white southerners even more than Brown's raid had. How, one Baltimore newspaper asked, could the South any longer "live under a government, a majority of whose subjects or citizens regard John Brown as a martyr and Christian hero?" To allay fears that Brown's sympathizers came even close to a northern majority, northern conservatives and businessmen sponsored their own public meetings condemning Brown and any who would trample on the Constitution. Democrats, North and South, tried to tie Brown around the neck of the Republican Party, singling out William Henry Seward—widely considered the most radical Republican—as Brown's instigator. Alarmed Republicans hastily distanced themselves from Brown. Seward announced his approval of the execution. Abraham Lincoln, more sensitive to the new militant mood, said that although Brown "agreed with us in thinking slavery wrong," this alone "cannot excuse violence, bloodshed and treason." Drawing similar distinctions between Brown's motives and his actions helped Republicans win several important victories in the off-year 1859 elections. But to the white South, expressions of even a modicum of sympathy with Brown's purposes affirmed their worst fears about Republicans and northerners generally.

What, then, was John Brown's achievement and significance? Tested against his original plans, his final attack was full of unintended consequences. Although rightly labeled, then and now, as a terrorist for his Kansas murders—John Wilkes Booth called him a "terrorizer"—Brown aimed at Harpers Ferry not to wreak terror but to ignite a revolution, and he failed. In that failure, Brown had succeeded, first, in shocking the South, but then in allowing white southerners to affirm that their slaves were perfectly content—the farthest thing from what he had hoped to do. Northern free blacks, who had long been the combative mainstays of abolitionism, showed little interest in joining a doomed mission, no matter how much they admired its leader's courage. Nor did Brown, a white man, stir the loyalty of the slaves his men temporarily freed. The paradoxes played out in national politics. By putting the perceived radical Republicans such as Seward on the defensive, Brown's attacks gave further political credibility to more moderate men within the party like Lincoln—an encouragement of restraint that Brown did not foresee and would have detested, but that would eventually strengthen the Republicans' political hand.

Most of these ironic ramifications were far from evident over the winter of 1859–60, when the Harpers Ferry attack stirred up nothing but strife. Above all, southern outrage at Brown's glorification created a pervasive mood of panic and fury at the end of 1859 that brought on what the British consul in Charleston, John Bunch, likened to a reign of terror. New military companies and vigilance committees sprang up to resist an expected abolitionist onslaught. Fresh reports of slave uprisings and abolitionist terrorism arose at the least sign of trouble, and sometimes at no sign at all. Southern state legislatures appropriated new funds for military preparations and expressed solidarity with their sister slaveholding states. The lawmakers of Louisiana considered a proposal affirming that if any Republican were elected president, it would be reason enough to dissolve the Union. There were numerous reports of random, unprovoked violence against northerners, including several confirmed lynchings.

These shocking scenes reinforced northerners' dismay at the slaveholders' democracy and greatly encouraged the southern fire-eater minority. Looking back, Herman Melville, who, disheartened at his continued failing career, had turned to poetry but still claimed no prophecy, would find in Brown's dangling body a portent:

> Hidden in the cap
> Is the anguish none can draw;
> So your future veils its face,
> Shenandoah!
> But the streaming beard is shown
> (Weird John Brown),
> The meteor of the war.

Throughout 1859, disunionists had been hatching and acting on plots of their own, to win over less strong-willed pro-slavery Democrats and destroy whatever chances a northerner like Stephen Douglas might have of winning the Democratic presidential nomination. After Brown's attack, and over the following winter, secessionist efforts accelerated. "If you can only urge our

Carolina view in such a manner as to imbue Virginia with it . . . ," Barnwell Rhett's ally Porcher Miles wrote to the Charleston lawyer and educator Christopher Memminger in early January, "we may soon hope to find the fruits of your addresses in . . . a Southern Confederacy." Thus began the political struggle of 1860.

THE REVOLUTION OF 1860 AND THE POLITICS OF DEMOCRACY

Memminger's mission was to persuade the Virginia legislature to send delegates to a fire-eater convention, planned by the South Carolina militants, which would discuss how best to protect slaveholders' rights and property—a not so thinly veiled appeal for disunion. "[T]here must be new terms established," he would tell the Virginians, "or a Southern Confederacy is our only hope of safety." Memminger spoke for three and a half hours and impressed his audience, but he failed to persuade—"Virginia is not prepared to do anything"—as his allies failed to do elsewhere. Only Mississippi heeded the fire-eaters' convention call: the rest of the South, despite the John Brown hysteria, still held out hope that slavery could be vindicated without dissolving the Union. Temporarily frustrated, the disunionists moved on to the next stage of their campaign.

Southern belligerence gravitated to two causes: reopening the African slave trade and enacting a federal slave code to guarantee slavery's protection in all national territories. After its initial law of 1807 forbidding the importation of Africans, Congress had acted unsteadily, sometimes reinforcing the ban with fresh legislation, but sometimes pulling back from efforts to enforce it. Proposals to end the ban completely began in the early 1850s in South Carolina, as an effort to begin reversing all of the federal restrictions on slave trading that had begun during the presidency of Thomas Jefferson. Advocates knew all too well that the exclusions of slavery from the territories, from the Missouri

Compromise's 36°30' line through the Wilmot Proviso, had as its implicit goal ending slavery. The same, they argued, held true for federal laws restricting the supply of slaves dating back to 1807, which had had the additional effect of stigmatizing slave labor as a form of plunder. After the Kansas-Nebraska Act's repeal of the Missouri Compromise, pro-slave traders became more frankly expansionist, insisting, as one of their spokesman asserted, that to survive, "[s]lavery must spread in power and area," which required fresh supplies of Africans. The dashed dreams of the pro-slavery filibusterers returned as a planters' utopian vision of a reborn New World slavery.

By 1859, the argument had broadened to include the claim that, with more slaves available, slavery would be made more efficient and profitable, while ordinary southern farmers would enjoy widened opportunities to be slaveholders. Hierarchical fire-eaters were learning how to both overcome concerns about a restive yeomanry and appeal to Master Race democrats. "Remove the restrictions upon the Slave Trade," wrote one Georgia yeoman (or a writer who claimed to be a yeoman), "and where is there a poor man in the South who could not soon become a slaveholder[?]" In 1859, the annual meeting of the Southern Commercial Convention voted to demand the repeal of all state and federal laws restricting the international slave trade. Soon after, a new organization appeared, the African Resupply Association, headed by an influential economic improver and budding southern nationalist, the Charleston-raised James D. B. De Bow of *De Bow's Review* (George Fitzhugh's chief literary forum and the most widely circulated southern periodical). William Yancey, not surprisingly, favored reopening the slave trade, but so did Alexander Stephens and Jefferson Davis. The latter charged in July 1859 that an 1820 law declaring overseas slave trading a capital crime had been enacted "under the false plea of humanity" and was an insult both to the South and to the U.S. Constitution.

The demand for a federal slave code arose directly out of *Dred Scott* and Stephen Douglas's revision of the popular sovereignty idea, although it had long been implicit in southern demands for equal access to the territories. For Senator Albert Gallatin Brown (now leaning heavily to the fire-eaters), it was a matter of upholding transcendent right, as affirmed by the Taney Court, against the meddling of a territorial majority. "What I want to know," Brown inquired of the Senate in February 1859, "is whether you will interpose against power and in favor of right; or whether you will stand by . . . refusing to interpose your authority to overthrow the unconstitutional and tyrannical acts of your creature—the Territorial Legislature." In a July 4 speech, Barnwell Rhett declared that without a federal slave code the South would secede. Yancey, using the Montgomery *Advertiser* as his mouthpiece, said much the same.

To judge from the reactions of other southern leaders, and much of the southern press, the fire-eaters' political offensive did not convert the mass of voters. "Is there any sane man living in the broad land," the *Montgomery Confederation* asked, "who believes that the laws prohibiting the African slave trade can be repealed?" Senator James Hammond, who wavered on the fire-eaters' campaigns, wrote his friend William Gilmore Simms that the slave code demand was "as absurd to ask for as a railroad to the moon (and everybody knows it)." Yet the fire-eaters were gradually gaining momentum, especially in the Deep South. In 1857, Rhett had long emphasized the disunionists' need to cultivate capable and established leaders with popular influence. By the summer of 1859, armed with their new issues, they had won the sympathies of several Democratic eminences, including Jefferson Davis, Howell Cobb, and John Slidell. The Deep South fire-eaters also fared well at the polls. In the autumn state elections, one disunionist won the governor's race in Mississippi and another was reelected governor in Alabama. The governor of South Carolina, William Henry Gist, was already working hand in glove with the Rhett-Ruffin-Yancey forces. The upholders of southern aristocracy were gaining power through the southern democratic ballot box.

The fire-eaters' next goal was to disrupt the Democratic Party, the last intersectional redoubt blocking their path. In September

1859, a weary President Buchanan affirmed his decision, announced in his inauguration address, not to seek reelection. The worst possible result, from the southern disunionists' standpoint, would be for the party to turn to another northern Democrat in 1860—worst of all Stephen A. Douglas, his prospects brightened by his victory over Abraham Lincoln. If Douglas ran with the backing of southern Democrats, he might actually win the election, thereby severely setting back the secessionist cause. If he did not—and if a southerner ran—a Republican would probably win enough northern electoral votes to win the White House, and thereby (disunionists calculated) trigger secession. The first step was to ensure that the Democratic ticket in 1860 firmly endorsed hard-line positions on the slave trade and the slave code. Late in 1859, Albert Gallatin Brown made it plain: "The South will demand . . . a platform explicitly declaring that slave property is entitled in the Territories and on the high seas to the same protection given to any other and every other species of property and failing to get it she will retire from the Convention."

The struggles among the sectional and intraparty factions carried over to the new Congress in December. Selection of the Speaker of the House had been an arduous process for several sessions, and the two-month battle that commenced in December 1859, only days after John Brown's execution, would prove nastier still. The proximate cause of the turmoil was not Brown's raid, but Hinton Helper's *The Impending Crisis*. Earlier in the year, Republican publicists, spearheaded by the old Jacksonian Francis Blair, had compiled a shortened, slightly toned-down version of Helper's work and distributed it by the tens of thousands around the country. Over sixty Republican congressmen signed a circular endorsing the book, among them the moderate former Whig John Sherman of Ohio—the man whom the Republican caucus, back in the majority, favored for Speaker. Guilt by association with *The Impending Crisis* was enough to block Sherman's elevation, on ballot after ballot. The rhetoric on both sides in both the House and Senate became so vicious, James Hammond remarked, that "the only persons who do not have a revolver and a knife are those who have two revolvers." After forty-four ballots, but before any shooting started, Sherman withdrew in favor of a bland Republican New Jerseyan who had supported the Fugitive Slave Act in 1850 and whom the upper South deemed safe enough.

Thereafter, inside and outside Congress, hard-liners and their sympathizers raised the stakes and exerted enormous pressure on southern Democrats. On January 18, 1860, Albert Gallatin Brown laid before the Senate resolutions calling for a territorial slave code to protect "property recognized by the Constitution of the United States." Two weeks later, Jefferson Davis presented an even more elaborate set of proposals, backing a slave code while also pronouncing all interference with slavery by any state government as well as the federal government a breach of the Constitution. In March, the Democratic Senate caucus approved Davis's resolutions, and pushed by the southern cabinet faction headed by Treasury Secretary Cobb, the Buchanan administration did the same. The Alabama Democratic Convention, which Yancey and his allies took over, voted to bolt from the party's national convention unless the platform supported a territorial slave code. The other Deep South Democratic organizations quickly followed suit.

In 1856 at Cincinnati, the Democratic National Committee, hoping to provide "an incentive to Union," selected Charleston over New York for its convention site in 1860. Hard to get to (the rail journey from Washington required ten changes of train), and lacking adequate accommodations for a national convention, Charleston was an unfortunate choice—and by late April 1860, it had become a disastrous one, especially for Stephen Douglas. By the flickering of gaslights, as sweltering northern delegates crammed into their overpriced hotel rooms, fire-eater orators addressed the street crowds, demanding honor and threatening disunion. Douglas men, headquartered at Hibernian Hall, were aghast at the hatred that their mere presence provoked among the southern delegates. The scenes so frightened the ex-Whig and staunch southern sympathizer Caleb Cushing that he decided to work for the nomination of some northern candidate—perhaps, he thought, ex-President Pierce would do—as a compromise between Douglas and one of the more hard-line southern favorites like Jefferson Davis.

Push came to shove over the platform. In the platform committee, where each state had one vote, a 17 to 16 majority supported a plank on the slave code similar to the Davis resolutions approved earlier by the Senate Democrats. Yancey, a superb speaker, led the floor fight for the majority report, proclaiming slavery a positive good and warning the northerners of the "great heaving volcano of passion and crime" that would erupt if they insisted on imposing their will. But the North, holding a three-fifths' majority of delegates in the general convention, could not be denied, and after two days of fierce tussling, the convention adopted the minority plank, which reaffirmed the 1856 convention's endorsement of popular sovereignty. Fifty southern delegates, led by the Alabamans, immediately walked out; those who remained denied Douglas the two-thirds' majority of the original delegate count of 304 required for nomination. After fifty-seven ballots, the delegates gave up and scheduled a second convention to meet six weeks later in the less combustible city of Baltimore.

The rescheduling merely delayed the inevitable rupture. Douglas enjoyed some support in the South, from unswerving Unionists such as Benjamin Perry of South Carolina and from moderate ex-Whigs like Alexander Stephens (who had recently tempered his views). In June, the Douglas men in the Deep South named state delegations to the Baltimore convention. But Douglas's southern foes, adopting what Stephens called a "rule or ruin" strategy, also showed up in Baltimore, and when the delegates approved a credentials committee report awarding seats to both pro-Douglas and anti-Douglas men, the Deep South recalcitrants walked out, joined by most of the border-state delegates and a small group of pro-slavery northerners. The schismatics immediately reconvened in Richmond and named Douglas's erstwhile friend, Vice President John C. Breckinridge, as their presidential candidate. The northern rump of the Democracy joylessly nominated Douglas. Once he had recovered from a drunken rage, the nominee said with more hope than assurance that he thought the bolters would see the light and return to the party before it was too late to save the Union.

Apart from Douglas's wishful scenario, there was one other possible way to prevent a Republican victory. If northern and border-state conservatives drew substantial numbers of votes away from the Republicans and the southern extremists, they might throw the election into a fractured House of Representatives, which in turn could elevate a sane compromise candidate to the White House. Toward that end, a group calling itself the Constitutional Union Party began organizing late in 1859, and a few days after the Democrats' Charleston debacle ended, the new party held its own nominating convention in Baltimore. Hopes for the enterprise ran high early on, within its own ranks if nowhere else. The core membership consisted of border-state ex-Whigs who, running as an opposition movement against the southern Democrats, had registered some impressive victories in 1858 and 1859. They were joined by some of the most venerable former old-line northern conservative Whigs, including Edward Everett, Amos Lawrence, and Robert C. Winthrop. The Constitutional Unionists' political program was simple: banish the slavery question from national affairs and uphold the Union. If high-toned respectability and good intentions had been reliable predictors of electoral success, the forces of sectional compromise—faintly echoing the old nationalist moderation of Henry Clay—might have immediately established themselves as a major force.

But the party had the vices of its virtues, and other vices as well. Many of its most prominent members—above all its most active promoter, seventy-year-old John Crittenden of Kentucky—were so aged and august that they gave the party the air of an over-the-hill gentlemen's club. Although pledged to end sectional strife, the party was beset by tensions that pitted southern ex-Know-Nothings against northern and border-state ex-Whigs. (The former wanted to nominate Sam Houston for the presidency, but the northern and border-state men prevailed and selected the ex-Whig Unionist slaveholder John Bell of Tennessee, age sixty-three, alongside the vice presidential nominee, Edward Everett, age sixty-six.) However noble, the party's brief pledge "to *recognize* no political principle other than *the Constitution of the Country, the Union of the States, and the Enforcement of the Laws,*" sounded at once pious, evasive, and antediluvian. Finally, the party's success would hinge on the outcome of the Republican convention in Chicago, scheduled to commence a few days after the Constitutional Unionists' convention ended. If the Republicans nominated one of their radical leaders—above all William Henry Seward—then the Whig gentlemen might stand a chance of winning over timid Republican sympathizers. If the Republicans nominated a moderate, the Constitutional Unionists would almost certainly prove irrelevant.

The early odds strongly favored Seward. Although never as extreme as his opponents described him, Seward personified the evolution of the reformist, new-school liberal Whiggery of the late 1830s and 1840s into Republicanism. His stands in favor of black education and against nativism had forever marked him as more egalitarian than most of his Whig colleagues. His uncompromising antislavery position long predated the Kansas-Nebraska controversy, and it had only hardened over the years. With his unfussy, at times rumpled dress, his addiction to cigars, and his outgoing manner, Seward defied the stereotype of starchy Whig propriety. He also had an impressive political operation at his disposal, headed by his eternally loyal wire-puller, Thurlow Weed. Over the months before the convention, Weed's lieutenants were everywhere, soliciting funds for Seward's campaign and rounding up public support from figures as different as Nathaniel Banks (now governor of Massachusetts) and Archbishop John Hughes.

The political intelligence that came back to Seward and Weed was unsettling. Support for Seward in New England as well as New York was solid, but elsewhere Republican leaders found him troubling. In the mid-Atlantic and Old Northwest states, Seward's radical reputation on slavery and race alienated the party's more conservative ex-Whigs and racist ex-Democrats. In those same states, his repudiation of nativism would make it difficult for the Republicans to attract ex-Whig native Americans, who had voted in such surprisingly large numbers for Millard Fillmore in 1856. Although his home state had named a delegation pledged firmly to him, intraparty feuding over the years had made enemies out of influential New Yorkers, above all Horace Greeley of the widely read *New-York Daily Tribune*. Seward also had a whiff of corruption about him, made stronger by the recent awarding of lucrative franchise grants by the New York legislature to his political friends. A string of stunning Washington scandals involving Democratic graft and bribery under Pierce and Buchanan was just coming fully to light, and the Republicans planned to exploit them in the fall campaign. Nominating the suspect Seward would make that more difficult.

But who could stop Seward and Weed? Republican managers from the lower North preferred four candidates with strong regional appeal: Governor Salmon P. Chase, the ex–Free Soiler from Ohio; Senator Simon Cameron of Pennsylvania, a former state adjutant general who had risen through the ranks first as a Democrat, then as a Know-Nothing; Edward Bates of Missouri, an aging ex-Whig backed by the Blair family, Horace Greeley, and various border-state delegates; and the great debater from Illinois, Abraham Lincoln. Chase was the best known but was deemed by some, even within his own state delegation, as too radical. Cameron could win his crucial home state, but his party-switching career and his fondness for dispensing patronage made him seem unprincipled. Bates had his imposing supporters, but he was also nearing seventy, had once been a slaveholder, and in 1856 had supported Fillmore and the Know-Nothings. Lincoln, although impressive in person, had not won an election since 1846.

Lincoln alone, however, had taken important steps before the convention to improve his chances. Although he lacked an experienced top political manager like Weed, he assembled an extremely talented group of political advisers, all from Illinois, including circuit court judge David Davis, Norman Judd, the chairman of the Illinois Republican Party, and Joseph Medill, co-owner of the *Chicago Tribune*. In 1859, Lincoln delivered political speeches all across the mid-western states, and he followed that up in February 1860 with a major address at New York's Cooper Institute and a speaking tour of New England. Without seriously threatening Seward's northeastern base, Lincoln's appearances won over a few Republicans completely, and established him as a viable alternative to Seward should the New Yorker's drive for the nomination falter. More important in the long run, his performance at the Cooper Institute laid out a powerful case not just for himself but for the Republican Party.

The previous September, Douglas had published an essay in *Harper's New Monthly Magazine* that, while candidly describing the rifts within the Democracy over the territories, attempted to vindicate popular sovereignty yet again with a labored discussion of federal and local law. Lincoln prepared his Cooper Institute speech as a rebuttal to Douglas, citing from the historical record to prove (once again) that the Framers had given Congress the power to bar slavery in the territories, and that the founding generation had marked slavery for extinction. Less than a week before Lincoln's scheduled address, Seward announced that he would deliver a major speech of his own on the Senate floor, formally to propose the admission of Kansas as a free state but with the obvious intention of laying out his claim on the Republican nomination. Lincoln's speech was bound to be compared to Seward's, and Lincoln knew it. Lincoln also knew that his New York audience would include dozens of influential Republican supporters and the most important press corps in the country.

Inside the cavernous, subterranean Great Hall of Peter Cooper's two-year-old institute, Lincoln put on a show that superbly conveyed his peculiar combination of political moderation and moral firmness about slavery. The first half of the speech, directed against Douglas's article, provided a point-by-point refutation that was far better informed and reasoned than Douglas's original. But it was in the second half, ostensibly directed at the South, that Lincoln bowled over his distinguished audience. In a calm and even conciliatory way, he declared the southern people just and reasonable, repudiated John Brown, and emphatically urged Republicans to show restraint in the face of southern provocations. Yet he would not concede an inch on the main points in contention. At bottom, he declared (his momentum building), the raging controversy was a moral issue— whether slavery was right or wrong. Despite what he called the "sophisticated contrivances" of the Douglas men, there was no middle ground. Could men of good conscience stand by while those who thought slavery good tried to bring it to places where it had never been? "If our sense of duty forbids this," Lincoln declared in a rousing peroration, "then let us stand by our duty fearlessly and effectively. . . . LET US HAVE FAITH THAT RIGHT MAKES MIGHT."

When Lincoln finished, the Great Hall rang with exultation. The first newspaper reviews singled out his riveting speaking style as an unexpected sensation. ("No man," the *Tribune*'s rapturous reporter wrote, "ever before made such an impression on his first appeal to a New York audience.") But the words mattered as well, and although Seward's speech two days later also won effusive praise, Lincoln's was easily its match. In the short run, Seward's remarks—delivered on the floor of the U.S. Senate by a long-time national leader—garnered even more publicity and affirmed Seward as the front-runner for the Republican nomination. But with his Cooper Institute address and subsequent speaking tour of New England, Lincoln began in earnest his effort to overtake him.

Chicago proved as fortunate a choice of convention site for Lincoln's supporters as Charleston had proved catastrophic for Douglas's. Although Seward and Weed sent trainloads of supporters westward, well supplied with liquor, to cheer their man on, Lincoln had an entire city at his disposal for volunteers to pack the galleries. Amid the raucousness of the convention's hotels and spacious meeting hall (built especially for the occasion and dubbed "The Wigwam"), Lincoln's political team went to work, first to secure enough first-ballot votes to deny Seward an instant victory, then to gain enough second-ballot commitments to turn the tide. Who promised what to whom in the way of patronage remains unclear. Although Lincoln had righteously told his managers to make no binding commitments, there is no reason to believe that Davis, Judd, & Co. took him seriously. Lincoln's side also wielded a powerful practical argument: Seward would lose the lower North and thus, probably, the election; Lincoln would carry the lower North and become the nation's sixteenth president. And so Lincoln's side made special work of cajoling delegates from the battleground states. Indiana's decision to join with Illinois and support Lincoln on the first ballot was a signal victory for Lincoln's negotiators, as was Pennsylvania's agreement to abandon Cameron after the first ballot and give most of its votes to Lincoln.

Lincoln's strategy succeeded brilliantly. On the first ballot, Seward held a commanding lead but fell well short of the simple majority required to nominate, while Lincoln ran a strong second. On the next ballot, the bulk of the Pennsylvania delegation and a number of New Englanders defected to Lincoln, and Seward's lead melted to a mere three and one-half votes. With that, the gallery crowd of ten thousand, the vast majority of them Lincoln supporters, let loose a roar of anticipation. When the third ballot was totaled up, Lincoln was only a vote and a half from winning a majority—and when the Ohio delegation added four more votes for Lincoln, the noise literally shook the Wigwam's wooden rafters, the entire scene gripped, one reporter wrote, "with the energy of insanity." To assure party unity, the convention nominated for vice president Hannibal Hamlin, a former Democrat from Maine and a friend of Seward's. It had already approved a platform that condemned John Brown; opposed nativist changes in the naturalization laws; backed a homestead act, federal aid to internal improvements, and an upward adjustment of tariff rates; and, quoting the Declaration of Independence, asserted that the normal condition of all American territories was and always had been freedom.

The enthusiasm of the May convention sustained the Republicans for the rest of the campaign. As if in response to southern truculence, thousands joined the revived "Wide Awake" Clubs and marched in pseudomilitary regalia. To applause and laughter, one of Lincoln's supporters had hailed his nomination in Chicago by calling him "the man who knows how to split rails and maul [D]emocrats"—and fence rails became the popular emblem of "The Railsplitter." Although Lincoln followed the custom of not appearing publicly—he passed the summer receiving callers at the governor's room in the State House in Springfield—Republican leaders, including the disappointed Seward, campaigned hard. Governor Edwin D. Morgan of New York, chairman of the party's national committee, commanded the most efficient electioneering machine in the field.

With New England secure for Lincoln, and with their antislavery credentials unimpeachable to all except the most radical abolitionists, the Republicans paid special attention to attracting voters in the lower North and the West by stressing ancillary issues. The Buchanan administration scandals, stoked in June by the release of a large and damning report by a special House investigating committee, allowed Republicans everywhere to position themselves as the party of reform. In the western states, party spokesmen played up the homestead issue. In protection-friendly Pennsylvania, they dwelt on the tariff, which they presented chiefly as a pro-labor measure designed to shield workingmen's wages against competition from the "pauper labor" of Europe. Although the Irish working-class vote seemed well out of reach, the national committee worked hard to win over German immigrants. Headed by the radical émigré from the 1848 revolutions, Carl Schurz, German-speaking Republicans proclaimed Lincoln the true workingman's candidate in a string of German-language party newspapers—among them the *Illinois Staats-Anzeiger*, a small but lively sheet in Springfield that Lincoln himself had purchased in 1859 and handed over to a reliable Republican immigrant editor.

The campaigns of the pro-Breckinridge southern Democrats and the Constitutional Unionists were, by comparison, lackluster. Managed, essentially, out of the White House, the Breckinridge campaign could never quite decide whether its chief aim was to win the election or lambaste Stephen Douglas. Any serious chance that the southern schismatics would see the light and reunite with the pro-Douglas men, as Douglas had hopefully predicted, died early on. ("They do well to call us bolters," the pro-slavery New York Hunker Daniel Dickerson declaimed, "for we intend to bolt the door fast against all hucksters, auctioneers, and jobbers.") The sectional tensions evident at the Constitutional Unionists' convention resurfaced, as several of the party's southern leaders crumpled under fire-eater pressure and endorsed the call for a federal slave code, which in turn prompted some of the party's northerners to desert and announce for Lincoln. Late in the campaign, Jefferson Davis, probably with the White House's support, tried to broker a deal whereby Breckinridge, Bell, and Douglas would withdraw in favor of a pro-southern Unionist, but Douglas spurned the offer as impractical and said that, in any case, he would rather see Lincoln elected than collaborate with the southerners who had tried to destroy him.

Douglas campaigned furiously and courageously, both for himself and the Union. Although his health was nearly ruined by alcohol abuse and overwork, the Little Giant defied convention and campaigned in every region of the country, save only the Pacific West. At the outset, he offered himself to the voters as the only genuinely national candidate who could prevent the horror of secession. In late summer, when, to his surprise, he was virtually certain that Lincoln would win, he shifted gears and took his campaign southward—less in the hopes of overcoming Breckinridge than to confront what he was now convinced was a southern plot to stage a coup d'état in November or December. In the crucial border states, he warned darkly of what the Deep South extremists had in mind, and evoked the spirit of Andrew Jackson, declaring that the next president should treat all attempts at disunion "as Old Hickory treated the Nullifiers in 1832." If elected, he vowed, he would hang all disunionists "higher than Haman." After a speaking tour of the friendlier Old Northwest, he then plunged deep into Georgia and Alabama, encouraged by friends like Alexander Stephens and drawing larger crowds than expected. Near the campaign's end, Douglas stood on the steps of the State Capitol in Montgomery at midday and, facing down rowdies who tried to disrupt his speech, delivered a powerful attack on secession. A politician to his marrow, Douglas managed to become a stump-speaking statesman.

Not all of Douglas's campaigning was so lofty. In Illinois and the rest of the Old Northwest—where voter enthusiasm for him ran highest—Douglas and his supporters returned to his tactics of 1858 and baited the Republicans as champions of black equality. His supporters elsewhere were even nastier. In New York, where radical Republicans had placed a doomed equal male suffrage referendum on the ballot, pro-Douglas Democrats tried to label their opponents as advocates of "Amalgamation" and "Nigger Equality." A float in one Manhattan Democratic parade carried effigies of Horace Greeley and a "good looking nigger wench, whom he caressed with all the affection of a true Republican." Tapping into the racism and economic insecurity of Irish workers, as well as into their distrust of Republican Puritans, the pro-southern *New York Herald* claimed that "if Lincoln is elected you will have to compete with the labor of four million emancipated Negroes."

The racist attacks, mingled with charges that Lincoln's election would guarantee secession, caused the Republicans some headaches. If the national Breckinridge and Douglas forces were almost inalterably at odds, there was room for tactical alliances among northern Douglas Democrats, Constitutional Unionists, and unaffiliated ex-Whig conservatives. Here and there, particularly in New York and Pennsylvania, even Breckinridge and Douglas electors managed to bury the hatchet and dickered over forming a fusion ticket. Douglas repudiated any links with Breckinridge but he encouraged merging with the Bell forces, and for a time, it looked as if the alliances might prove just strong enough to affect the outcome—not least in New York City, where leading bankers and merchants had forged a united antisecession opposition. Could Manhattan's large anti-Republican Irish and silk-stocking vote knock New York out of the Lincoln column and throw the election into the House, where under the one-state, one-vote rule, Lincoln might well lose? How would the attacks of a combined opposition to Lincoln play in the closely divided lower North? Apart from the fusion threat, how could the Republicans respond to the Democrats' inflammatory racial charges and secure the lower North without alienating their antislavery base?

The Lincoln campaign had to come to terms with its basic political identity. Republican spokesmen in toss-up districts tried to deflect the wedge issues by describing themselves as a white man's party and by reemphasizing issues like the tariff, internal improvements, and Democratic corruption. Some alarmed conservative Republicans even begged Lincoln to issue a public statement to appease the South and renounce racial egalitarianism. But here Lincoln drew the line. His "conservative views and intentions" had long been crystal clear: although dedicated to slavery's extinction by halting its spread, he intended no direct interference with slavery in the states or the Fugitive Slave Law. What could be gained from stating this yet again? ("Why do not uneasy men *read* what I have already said? and what our *platform* says," Lincoln wrote to one alarmed supporter.) Southerners who hated him and his party were not likely to be converted. Courting uncertain northerners with soothing words, Lincoln wrote, would only permit "*bad* men . . . to fix upon me the character of timidity and cowardice." Better to stay the course—not, he said, "merely on *punctilio* and pluck," but on principles that were as plain as day.

Whatever suspense remained about the outcome evaporated in the small hours of the morning after election day, when word flashed along the telegraph lines that Lincoln had carried New York by a large majority. In the final tally, Lincoln won every free state except New Jersey (where his vote was large enough to earn him a share of the state's electoral votes), which was sufficient to give him a sizable triumph in the Electoral College. Although the Republican ticket won only 40 percent of the popular vote nationwide, it won 54 percent of the northern vote. Had all the northern votes for Douglas, Breckinridge, and Bell been combined for one candidate, Lincoln would still have won the election. Crowds cheered the result—in the secessionist South as well as in the antislavery North. "A party founded on the single sentiment . . . of hatred of African slavery," the *Richmond Semi-Weekly Examiner* reported, "is now the controlling power."

Overall, the election showed how polarized the sections had become over the slavery issue. Only one candidate, Stephen Douglas, won any appreciable support in all regions of the country, the last faint echo of the intersectional Jacksonian party system—yet Douglas managed narrowly to win the popular vote in only two states, New Jersey and Missouri. A large majority, 58 percent, of the popular vote backed either Lincoln or Breckinridge, the candidates with the least compromising views on the slavery question. That polarization in turn marked the collapse of old-line Whig conservatism in the North. In only three free states—Massachusetts, Vermont, and California—did the Constitutional Unionists receive more than 3 percent of the popular vote.

Some portions of the respective sections were more estranged than others. Aided, perhaps, by Douglas's pro-Union tour, the Constitutional Unionists carried the Border South states of Virginia, Kentucky, and Bell's native Tennessee, came within a whisker of winning Maryland, and ran well in North Carolina and Georgia. Even in the secessionist hotbed of Alabama, the Constitutional Unionists ran strong in the northernmost yeoman counties and won nearly one-third of the vote statewide. In Louisiana, the combined Bell-Douglas total was far *greater* than the vote for Breckinridge. The Republican victory in the North was similarly uneven. In New England and the upper Northwest, Lincoln's victory was gargantuan. But the Republicans barely carried 50 percent of the vote in Illinois and Indiana, and won an unimpressive 52 percent in Ohio. If Republicanism had become a virtual political religion in much of the North, in some areas— Illinois's "Egypt" counties, the Butternut areas of southern Ohio, the city of New York—it was anathema.

Still, on the election's crucial issue, the expansion of slavery, the nation was split in two. If northerners disagreed about the efficacy of Douglas's popular sovereignty idea, the returns showed them thoroughly united about the necessity to halt slavery's unchecked spread—and to resist forcefully any southern effort to secede. If southerners disagreed about secession, they were nearly unanimous in their repudiation of the northern candidates and of slavery's restriction, whether by "Black Republican" fiat or Douglas's obnoxious popular sovereignty plan. The political reality of 1860 was incontrovertible: a sharply divided nation had, by wholly constitutional means, decided in the North's favor. Charles Francis Adams could hardly believe it: "There is now scarcely a shadow of a doubt that the great revolution has actually taken place," he wrote in his diary, "and that the country has once and for all thrown off the domination of the Slaveholders."

"THE DEMOCRATIC PROCLIVITIES OF THE AGE"

The election of 1860 had ended exactly as Adams and his fellow Republicans had hoped but could only have dreamed of four years earlier. No less pleased, though, were the southern fire-eaters. As Adams considered the magnitude of Lincoln's victory, southern militants took the next step toward creating their slaveholders' republic.

The election campaign had aggravated the fears provoked by what southerners perceived as the North's embrace of John Brown. Pro-Breckinridge newspapers were filled with unconfirmed reports of arson and rape by slaves, along with notices about shady Yankees seen moving about the countryside. A string of suspicious fires in Texas, all of which broke out at about the same time, convinced some southerners that a huge insurrection plot was building—timed, it was said, to coincide with Christmas. Here and there, vigilantes assaulted and, on occasion, lynched alleged evildoers, including two suspicious men in Texas found to be holding copies of Helper's *Impending Crisis*. In every district of South Carolina, a semisecret organization of self-described "minute men" pledged to take up arms and march to Washington to prevent Lincoln's inauguration, and the volunteers began drilling and wearing blue cockades in their hats, the emblem of nullification during the crisis of 1832–33.

The slaves, by their very presence, also contributed to the pervasive sense of dread. Despite every effort by slaveholders and southern legislatures to cordon off the South from incendiary talk and reading materials, the slaves, even in the interior regions, appear to have learned a great deal about what was occurring, through the "grapevine way" that transmitted overheard talk and rumor to the slave quarters. As Booker T. Washington, then a young Virginia slave, later recalled, the slaves were remarkably informed "about the great National questions that were agitating the country." Word of John Brown's raid had been impossible to suppress; now, slaves from central Georgia to northeast Texas were hearing that a man named Lincoln would soon be president and set them all free. At least some of the rumors of slave revolts appear to have originated with the slaves themselves, in an effort to scare local whites. And the masters knew they were sitting atop a powder keg.

But the greatest fears, far from hysterical, had been building for years, and were finally realized on election day. These fears were not confined to fire-eater extremists or jumpy vigilantes. Over the long, hot, and drought-ridden summer of 1860—which killed off much of the cotton crop and made the South a literal tinder box—even temperate southern slaveholders stood horrified at the impending electoral victory of northern-style democracy and its ramifications. "The democratic proclivities of the age pervade our whole country—," one ex-Whig Unionist North Carolinian despaired, "nothing can arrest our downward tendency to absolute Government." The absolutism they feared most meant policies geared to eventual emancipation, and its genius was Abraham Lincoln.

9

THE ILIAD OF
ALL OUR WOES

The fire-eaters of South Carolina quickly made good on their secessionist threats. "[T]he revolution of 1860 has commenced," the *Charleston Mercury* bellowed as soon as Lincoln's victory was official. "On every lip is the stern cry la liberta!" The grand drama had arrived, and Charleston would play its crucial part, "as becomes her intelligence, her stake and her civilization." In liberty's name, and slavery's, the southern reaction was massing, to strike back at the North and secede from the Union before Lincoln could even take office.

Lincoln himself was hopeful, even confident, the secessionists would fail. They had badly misrepresented him, he said. He was not a radical abolitionist. He would not eradicate slavery immediately. Soon enough, the sensible people of the South would see through the extremists' lies, abide by the democratic results of 1860, and remain true to the Union. "Disunionists *per se*, are now in hot haste to get out of the Union," Lincoln wrote, ". . . With such '*Now, or never*' is the maxim."

The president-elect was utterly mistaken. His election, the culmination of the long-building crisis of American democracy, instantly turned many Deep South moderates and even erstwhile Unionists into secessionists. No misrepresentation was necessary to show that he and his Republicans wanted to put slavery on the road to extinction, which was enough to make him a tyrant in Dixie. There were differences among southerners, to be sure, about how secession ought to proceed, and in Lincoln's native Border South, his assumptions about Unionist sentiment had considerable merit. But from South Carolina southward, and then westward to Texas, the main question was now not whether to secede but when and how. And by the time he began composing his inauguration speech, Lincoln found himself forced to find the right words to address a nation ripped asunder.

SECESSION, SLAVERY, AND THE POLITICS OF COUNTERREVOLUTION

South Carolina, predictably, instigated secession. On November 5, the legislature met in Columbia to name the state's presidential electors, in accordance with the state's uniquely archaic system. The fire-eater governor William Gist duly informed the members that, in view of the impending Republican victory, they ought to stay in session and, if Lincoln won, call a state convention to consider disunion. On November 9, the secession convention bill passed, scheduling the election of delegates for January 8 with the convention to assemble a week later. The two-month wait would leave enough time to determine the desires of other states. But the Charleston hard-liners would brook no delay, and following a large protest meeting, the legislature moved the election back to December 6 and the opening of the convention to December 17. On December 20, the convention unanimously approved an ordinance (drafted by a committee that included Barnwell Rhett) tersely announcing that "the union now subsisting between South Carolina and other States, under the name of the 'United States of America,' is hereby dissolved." Over the next week, the convention approved two longer declarations justifying secession, one by Rhett, the other by the somewhat more moderate Christopher Memminger, both explicit in their defense of slavery. Rhett denounced how the American republic had degenerated into a "consolidated Democracy."

South Carolina's alacrity surprised neither friends nor foes of secession. (Upon hearing of the ordinance, the staunch, lonely South Carolina Unionist James Petigru is reported to have remarked that his state was "too small for a republic, but too large for an insane asylum.") But the swiftness with which the rest of the Deep South followed suit was breathtaking. On November 29, the Mississippi legislature passed its own secession convention bill, and on January 9, the Mississippi convention approved, by a huge margin, an ordinance similar to South Carolina's. The next day, Florida seceded, and the day after that so did Alabama, followed by Georgia on January 19, Louisiana on January 26, and Texas on February 1. "The time is now come," one delegate from Mobile told his state's convention, "and Alabama must make her selection, either to secede from the Union . . . [or] submit to a system of policy on the part of the Federal Government that, in a short time, will compel her to abolish African Slavery."

The upper South and border states resisted the trend; indeed, Unionists in Maryland, Virginia, North Carolina, Tennessee, Missouri, and Arkansas mounted a successful, explicitly antisecession counteroffensive during the early months of 1861. One former Tennessee governor told his disunionist Alabama cousin that the cotton states had no legitimate grounds for separating from the federal government, and warned that his state and Kentucky would never be "dragged into a rebellion that their whole population utterly disapproved." With larger nonslaveholder white populations than in lower Dixie, and with a stronger persistent Whig political organization (which produced the victorious turnouts for the Constitutional Unionists in 1860), the upper South contradicted militant proclamations about an imminent united southern nation. This gave hope to northerners (like the Kentucky-born Lincoln) that secession was a chimera, and emboldened those who believed that the slaveholders' democracy could be overturned by the white yeomanry and even by slave-holders who remained ambivalent about human bondage.

The Unionist counteroffensive, however, also had sharp limits. Portions of some of the most politically important reluctant states, especially the so-called Southside counties of Virginia and the Democratic plantation districts of North Carolina, seethed with southern rights discontent. And although the border-state Unionists included a large number of nonplanters—who, in places, even expressed antislavery opinions—their leaders came out of the same elite of comfortable slaveholders who dominated politics throughout the South. For these upper South gentlemen, secession, far from a necessity, looked suicidal for slavery, hand-ing the northern Republicans the grounds for destroying the institution even where it existed. The Union, they believed, gave infinitely greater protection to slavery than some fancied and untested new confederacy. Yet if they were willing to allow a for-mal ban on slavery's expansion in northern territories where they believed slavery would never flourish, all but the most flexible Unionist slaveholders also wanted to provide what one Virginian called "explicit *protection* of slavery" in the form of a federal code, to cover territories south of the old 36°30' Missouri Compromise line. If their hostility to secession obstructed the spread of dis-unionism, their allegiance to the Union extended only so far as it would preserve, protect, defend, and extend the slaveholders' democracy.

The Deep South's allegiance to slavery led to more pessimistic conclusions now that the Republicans had won the presidency. "Our people are calmly and fully determined never to submit to Lincoln's administration, or to any Compromise with the North-ern States," one Alabaman observed. The Deep South's solidarity confounded the Republican moderates' thinking about southern loyalty to the Union, and has puzzled historians ever since. Even in the cotton kingdom, the fire-eaters appeared, at first, to face considerable opposition. Outside of South Carolina and Texas, a substantial number of voters—at least 40 percent of the total—cast their ballots for convention delegate candidates who expressed reservations about the suddenness of secession, or about having their state secede independently of others. Support for the most extreme disunionists dwindled remarkably in those Deep South counties inhabited chiefly by nonslaveholders, as well as in traditionally Whig wealthy cotton counties and urban areas with strong commercial links to the North. In the conventions, opponents of immediate secession called into question not merely the fire-eaters' accelerated program but the legitimacy of the conventions themselves. In Alabama, for example, the convention was nearly evenly divided between supporters and opponents of immediate secession. On the third day of debate, Nicholas J. Davis of Huntsville, directly challenged the disunionists' leader, William Lowndes Yancey, by claiming that the convention was irregular, and that a plebiscite was the only proper way to ascertain the public's sentiment on so grave a matter as secession. Yancey, on the verge of his greatest victory and apoplectic at any sign of resistance, charged that resistance to secession was treason to Alabama. Davis shot back that the secessionists were acting like Tories, out "to coerce an unwilling people." Should Yancey treat those who opposed him as enemies of the people, Davis exclaimed, they would "meet him at the first of our mountains, and there with his own selected weapons, hand to hand, and face to face, settle the question of the sovereignty of the people."

These divisions led some writers to describe secession in the Deep South as a coup d'état by the fire-eaters, who pulled an unwilling white citizenry out of the Union. There is certainly reason to think the extreme disunionists in various states either helped rig the outcome of the convention elections or misled the public about the strength they enjoyed. The secessionists' victory in Louisiana—where the Unionist vote had been strong in 1860, and the actual vote count was suppressed for months—was particularly dubious. In Alabama, the heavy vote for immediate secession in Mobile and Autauga Counties, strongholds for Douglas and Bell only two months earlier, raised eyebrows. The holding of elections and conventions as quickly as possible, and a marked decline in turnout in the convention delegate elections compared to the presidential elections, looked like the products of extremist threats. "In South Carolina the people have little to do in politics but choose their own masters," one outraged Alabaman wrote. "And outside of South Carolina in the Cotton States politicians are trying the experiment of getting along without the people."

Yet these assessments slighted the slaveholders' long-standing domination of the very terms of debate within the Dixie democracy—and the popular revulsion that swept through the Deep South after Lincoln's election. Even in Alabama, where doubts about immediate secession ran high, slaveholders were elected to the state conventions out of all proportion to their numbers in the population, and tended to take a more militant posture than the nonslaveholders. More important, the hard reality of the Republican victory, and the threat it posed to the slaveholders' democracy, changed Deep South skeptics into secessionists. The prominent Mobile, Alabama, editor John Forsyth Jr.—son of Martin Van Buren's meddlesome secretary of state and a resolute Douglas man in 1860—typified the shift. With Douglas's defeat, Forsyth concluded, "the cause of the Union was lost," and he started to resign himself to secession and civil war lest the South be "stripped of 25 hundred millions of slave property & to have loose among us 4,000,000 of freed blacks." All across the Deep South, a pro-Douglas Georgia newspaper observed, "[t]he hopelessness of preserving the Union has made disunionists, since the election, of thousands of Conservative and Union men."

The Deep South debates over secession were mainly about means, not ends. In the secession conventions, the major fault line was never between Unionists and disunionists, but between two groups of disunionists: the conditional secessionists (sometimes called, a bit confusingly, "cooperationists") and the immediate secessionists. Conditional secessionists wanted to slow the chain reaction of state-by-state secessions. Some of them thought it wiser to organize a united southern confederacy first;

others wanted to deliver a list of impossible demands to Lincoln and then secede; and still others truly wished to test Lincoln's claims to moderation and await an overt act against the South before dissolving the Union. Although their ranks included a few leaders of great stature, including Alexander Stephens, few of the conditional secessionists had much faith that secession was avoidable, and virtually none thought that secession was illegitimate. Some refused to assent when secession finally came—residents of one Alabama county burned Yancey in effigy—but the great majority signed on quickly thereafter, either out of localist loyalty or determination to resist any Yankee interference. "I shall vote against the ordinance," Nicholas Davis told the Alabama convention. "But if Alabama shall need the strong arm of her valorous sons to sustain her . . . I say for myself and for my constituents—and I dare say for all North Alabama—that I and they will be cheerfully ready to take our part in the conflict." Stephens, who had argued for months that slavery was safer inside the Union than outside, backed the new sovereign state of Georgia as soon as it declared its independence.

More telling was a philosophical division within the disunionist camp over the constitutional theory of secession. The division was not sharply expressed in 1860 and 1861, in part because the immediate secessionists tried to soften it, in part because some major figures blew back and forth about it, and in part because the audacity of secession overwhelmed other considerations. But the division was real, and it conformed to the preexisting division between hard-core Rhettists and the majority of slaveholder Master Race democrats.

Fire-eater secessionists held the militant view that secession was perfectly legal and represented nothing radical. The core of their argument was the state-rights compact theory of the Union as it had been developed by John C. Calhoun and then made operative by the fire-eaters in the 1850s. The states, so the argument went, existed before the Union. The Constitution did not alter the states' powers and prerogatives as autonomous governments. By seceding, the states were merely reasserting the total sovereignty they had exerted in creating the Union in the first place. That assertion had been necessitated by a revolution undertaken by northern Republicans, who had abrogated the original constitutional agreement that left slavery undisturbed. "I am a secessionist and not a revolutionist," William Yancey explained. The Republicans, Barnwell Rhett concurred, were "the practical revolutionists and hatchers of trouble," opposed to the true southern conservatives. "*We* are not revolutionists," the pro–fire-eater editor James D. B. De Bow declared. The southern states, one secessionist leader announced, had left the Union "to preserve their old institutions" from "a revolution [that] threatened to destroy their social system."

Embodied in the militant fire-eater argument was a thorough repudiation of Jeffersonian politics, especially about equality and natural rights, in favor of what its proponents upheld as the natural differences among men. The new slaveholders' republic would stand as a living refutation of Jefferson's harebrained egalitarian doctrines, and of the anarchic vulgarities that had emanated from them and degraded the North. Fire-eater anti-Jeffersonianism did not, however, fully persuade the majority in the disunionist camp, including some like Jefferson Davis who had long been among the most forceful advocates of southern rights. The southern states, on this other view, had no more constitutional right to secede from the Union than the original colonies had to separate themselves from the British Empire. Instead, these secessionists draped themselves in the Jeffersonian natural right to revolution. Senator Alfred Iverson of Georgia put the matter squarely just before he departed Washington for good, insisting that although no state had the right to secede, "each State has the right of revolution, which all admit," when placed under burdens "so onerous that it cannot bear them." By this logic, the Republicans were the Tories, enlarging and then abusing the powers of the central government to strangle the liberties of the revolutionary southern patriots. Secession was a replay of the American Revolution, a new War of Southern Independence that aimed to vindicate, not repudiate, the struggles of the founding generation. Resisting "an unbridled majority, the most odious and least responsible form of despotism," Jefferson Davis intoned, echoing Calhoun, would "renew such sacrifices as our fathers made to the holy cause of constitutional liberty."

Where the two versions of secessionism firmly agreed, forging the ideological foundations of the Confederacy, was over the defense of a polity based on slavery and an insistence on preserving the slaveholders' liberty against northern despotism. Decades later, in what has turned out to be one of the most consequential acts of falsification in American history, secessionist leaders tried to deny this crucial fact. In a long, self-justifying memoir, Jefferson Davis asserted that "the existence of African servitude was in no wise the cause of the conflict, but only an incident." Secession, he said, was really prompted by sectional rivalry, political ambition, and the passions, prejudices, and sympathies fomented by the North. Alexander Stephens, the reluctant secessionist, put the matter in familiar but highly abstracted constitutional terms, as a battle not over "the policy or impolicy of African Subordination," but "between the supporters of a strictly Federative Government on the one side, and a thoroughly National one, on the other." Davis, Stephens, and others wanted their readers to believe that secession was the culmination of a political contest rooted in the clash between Federalists and Anti-Federalists in the 1780s, a clash that just happened to become attached to slavery.

It was all very different in 1860 and 1861, when the state secession conventions and secessionist leaders justified leaving the Union. There were, of course, southerners in the Unionist minority who claimed to support secession for reasons that had little or nothing to do with slavery. "I care nothing for the 'Peculiar institution,'" one wrote, "but I cant stand the idea of being domineered over by a set of Hypocritical scoundrels such as Sumner, Seward, Wilson, Hale, etc., etc." But for those who effected secession, including those in Davis's and Stephens's home states, slavery and the attacks on it by the northern democracy were the fundamental issues—and they declared as much to a candid world. The South Carolina convention's "Declaration of the Immediate Causes" was matter-of-fact: "an increasing hostility on the part of the non-slaveholding States to the institution of slavery" had led the North to assume "the right of deciding upon the propriety of our domestic institutions." Now that the free states had "denounced as sinful the institution of slavery" and encouraged slave runaways and "servile insurrection," they had released South Carolina from her obligation to the Union. "Our position is thoroughly identified with the institution of slavery," the Mississippi convention declared, "the greatest material interest in the world." (The Mississippians mentioned no other cause for secession.) The Georgia convention emphasized above all "the subject of African slavery," and the Texas secessionists declared themselves the defenders of "a commonwealth holding, maintaining and protecting the institution known as negro slavery—the servitude of the African to the white race within her limits." Even more moderate heads in the Deep South fully agreed: the fight to extend slavery, one cooperationist delegate to the Alabama convention asserted, was "'the Iliad of all our woes.'"

Alexander Stephens was no less direct in an extemporaneous speech he gave in Savannah two months after Georgia seceded. "The prevailing ideas entertained by [Jefferson] and most of the leading statesmen at the time of the formation of the old constitution," Stephens remarked, "were that the enslavement of the African was in violation of the laws of nature; that it was wrong in *principle*, socially, morally, and politically. It was an evil they knew not well how to deal with, but the general opinion of the men of that day was that, somehow or other in the order of Providence, the institution would be evanescent and pass away." But that cherished idea of Jefferson and the Founders was fundamentally mistaken:

> Our new government is founded upon exactly the opposite idea; its foundations are laid, its corner-stone rests upon the great truth, that the negro is not equal to the

white man; that slavery—subordination to the superior race—is his natural and normal condition. . . . This, our new government, is the first, in the history of the world, based upon this great physical, philosophical, and moral truth. . . . It is upon this, as I have stated, our social fabric is firmly planted; and I cannot permit myself to doubt the ultimate success of a full recognition of this principle throughout the civilized and enlightened world.

"Slavery, so called," as Stephens later termed it, was not incidental to secession; it was the summum bonum that united the secessionist cause.

Building a polity based on slavery did leave open questions about the loyalties of the nonslaveholding white majority. Helper's *Impending Crisis* had alarmed slaveholders sufficiently to cause them to suppress the book, lest it delude and arouse the yeomanry. Lincoln actually picked up more than twenty-five thousand votes in slaveholding border states, a tiny proportion of the total but disturbing enough to edgy extremists.* Even more disturbing was the concentration of anti–fire-eater opinion in upcountry districts with few slaveholders, especially noticeable in Georgia and Alabama. Leaving nothing to chance, the secessionists propagandized the interests of slaveholders and nonslaveholders as, in James De Bow's words, "in the present sectional controversy identical." First, they rebutted the charge that the slaveholders represented a privileged minority of white southerners. Most slaveholders, they noted (correctly), owned fewer than five slaves. Even in the largest slaveholding states, the proportion of landowners in the total free population was higher than in sev-

---

* Lincoln's name did not appear on the ballot in ten slaveholding states. He won a smattering of votes in Kentucky and Virginia, nearly four thousand votes in Delaware, as well as more than seventeen thousand votes in Missouri— roughly 10 percent of the state total—mainly in German-speaking districts in and around St. Louis.

eral New England states. And although, as De Bow conceded, "a very large class" of southern whites owned no slaves, they profited directly from slavery by providing goods and services to those who did. In many cases the nonslaveholders were themselves incipient masters waiting only for their chance to accumulate sufficient funds to purchase a bondsman. "This, with ordinary frugality, can in general be accomplished in a few years," De Bow wrote, "and is a process continually going on"—a slaveholders' version of the Yankee theme of prudent upward mobility, as well as of the overriding social harmony of interests.

Above all, the secessionists appealed to the nonslaveholders' white supremacist pride and fears, as well as to their local loyalties. Georgia's hotspur secessionist Joseph Brown—a humbly born, up-country ex-Democrat, nicknamed "The Ploughman"—made the racist argument with plebeian pungency, proclaiming that slavery "is the poor man's best Government." Abolition would eradicate this happiest of estates for the poor, and create particular hardships for nonslaveholders. "*[T]he slaveholders, in the main, will escape the degrading equality which must result by emigration*," De Bow wrote; the poor white, however, would "be compelled to remain and endure the degradation . . . unless, as is to be supposed, he would prefer to suffer death instead." Apocalyptic visions dominated the slaveholders' warnings about immediate emancipation followed by white submission of the most shameful sort. Beyond slavery and race, nonslaveholders, like many a hesitant planter secessionist, were also determined to resist any northern effort to crush secession by force, and to uphold what Nicholas J. Davis—William Yancey's harsh critic at the Alabama convention—called the South's "honor or the rights of her citizens."

Sealing the unity among slaveholders and nonslaveholders was the rush of militance that came with the final cast of the die. Alexander Stephens, before Georgia seceded, called it a kind of madness in which the people became "wild with passion and frenzy, doing they know not what." It was actually more of a catharsis—a release of outraged emotion that had been building for more than a decade, and had been exacerbated by the "reign of terror" that followed the trauma of Harpers Ferry, but now had focus and purpose. At mass gatherings in Charleston and Savannah and New Orleans, in country towns where new volunteer companies and vigilance committees of old men and young lined up on dirt roads, there appeared improvised and not so improvised elements of allegiance to a nation that did not yet exist: irregular uniforms; flags of numerous designs; heart-pumping songs, adapted from stage tunes, whose lyrics shouted, "Hurrah! Hurrah/For Southern rights hurrah!" In the wake of the threatening triumph of "Black Republicanism," southern nationalism began becoming something real.

The calculating politics and the emotionalism reached a crescendo in Montgomery in early February, when thirty-seven delegates from six of the seceded Deep South states assembled to draft a national constitution and establish a provisional government. A festive air surrounded the convention, which grew more intense as the deliberations continued. (After hearing a band play "Dixie," Jefferson Davis's wife, Varina, suggested that the song be adopted as the Confederacy's anthem.) But the delegates also worked with great seriousness and efficiency. Within four days, they adopted a preliminary constitution for the provisional government of the Confederate States of America. The next day, they unanimously chose Jefferson Davis as president of the provisional government and scheduled popular elections for the autumn. The convention then unanimously chose Alexander Stephens as vice president and set about debating a permanent Confederate constitution, which it finally approved on March 11.

On the evening of February 16, Davis arrived in Montgomery from his Mississippi plantation and gave a fiery impromptu speech, promising that all who opposed the new Confederacy would "smell Southern powder and feel Southern steel." Yet for the most part, the new government projected as moderate an image as possible, both to keep the ranks in Montgomery solid and to appeal to the upper South states still undecided about secession. Among the delegates, several leading fire-eaters, including Barnwell Rhett and Laurence Keitt, recoiled at the restraint and harbored doubts about the stalwartness of men like Davis and Stephens. Davis, after all, although pro-secession and at times something of a fire-eater fellow traveler, had participated in congressional efforts to defuse the crisis only weeks earlier. But friends persuaded the fire-eaters to suppress their distrust, lest they frighten off Virginia and other hesitant slave states. ("The man and the hour have met," Yancey famously declared to the crowds, with forced friendliness, after he had accompanied the newly arrived Davis to his hotel.) With the crucial support, sent from Richmond, of leading Virginia pro-secessionists, Davis had emerged as the best man, broadly acceptable for his strong record on southern rights and secession, his long military record, and his experience in the Senate and as secretary of state. Stephens's elevation to the vice presidency was both a sop to the Georgia delegation, disappointed that a Georgian did not get the presidency, and an affirmation of the new government's efforts to project calm reasonableness.

Davis's inaugural address, delivered two days after his arrival, reached out for a broad southern base. The new president asserted that the new government harbored no aggressive intent and issued a warm invitation to any states that might wish to join. Above all—and no doubt to the suppressed outrage of the fire-eaters—Davis explicitly linked the Confederacy to certain ideas and words of Thomas Jefferson, including the "inalienable" right to revolution. "Our present political position has been achieved in a manner unprecedented in the history of nations," he intoned. "It illustrates the American idea that governments rest upon the consent of the governed, and that it is the right of the people to alter or abolish them at will whenever they become destructive of the ends for which they were established." In establishing a new government, the convention, he said, promised a permanent constitution "differing only from that of our fathers in so far as it is explanatory of their well-known intent." Secession was a perfectly American revolution.

Yet if Davis's words were soothing, nothing could disguise the

Confederacy's overriding purpose, dear to Rhettist aristocrats and southern Master Race democrats alike: to create a republican government formally based on racial slavery. The new permanent constitution's scattered departures from the text of the U.S. Constitution left no doubt on these matters. The preamble, following the opening phrase, "We, the people," omitted the reference to creating "a more perfect Union"—a line that suggested that the Union was older than the Constitution—and eliminated the clause committing the government "to promote the general Welfare." It then explicitly endorsed the Calhounite compact theory of state sovereignty, proclaiming that each state was "acting in its sovereign and independent character." The rest of the document contained none of the semantic evasions about slavery (or, as the new constitution sometimes called it, "negro slavery") so carefully worked out by the Framers in 1787. In deference to Britain (whose official recognition the new government craved) and the Border South (which enjoyed a virtual monopoly on selling slaves to the lower South), the constitution prohibited the importation of slaves from abroad. But it protected the interstate slave trade and guaranteed the existence of slavery in any new territories the Confederacy might obtain. One departure from the U.S. Constitution stood out above all: Article I, Section 9, which stated that "[n]o . . . law impairing or denying the right of property in negro slaves shall be passed."

In other ways, the convention designed a central government with minimal powers, except with respect to protecting slavery and the slaveholders' supremacy. The Confederate plan at once weakened the executive branch (by limiting the president to a single six-year term) and strengthened it in order to curb congressional fiscal excesses (by giving the president a line-item veto over appropriations bills and by giving cabinet officers nonvoting seats in Congress). The constitution made difficult central government expenditures on anything other than national defense and delivering the mail. With a few notable exceptions about river and harbor projects (which planters needed to get their cotton safely shipped), government aid to "internal improvement intended to facilitate commerce" was banned. All congressional appropriations required a two-thirds' supermajority in both the House and the Senate. A tariff was permitted for raising revenue but not for protecting home industries, although the provision was worded so vaguely that the distinction would have to be worked out by later Confederate congresses. The constitution's suffrage and representation provisions basically replicated those in the U.S. Constitution, leaving broad latitude to the states, but with one exception—a formal exclusion, from both state and national elections, of all persons of foreign birth not citizens of the Confederacy. Suspicious outsiders would have no formal political voice.

The convention and its constitution codified what most secessionists meant when they spoke of liberty—the liberty of whites to own black slaves and take them wherever they chose, with only minimal obligations to the central government. With that core conviction, the southern reaction of 1860–61 brought about what would in time represent a momentous shift in American politics, away from the hierarchical conservatism of Federalism and old-line Whiggery, now all but vanished, and toward a southern hierarchical conservatism, based on the presumptions of white supremacy, the supreme political power of local elites, and the proclaimed virtues of "small government." But that long-term shift was not on Americans' minds in 1861: the fate of the country was. On Jefferson Davis fell the burden of forging a new nation out of seven sovereign states—and, if possible, expanding that nation to include as many additional slave states as possible. On Abraham Lincoln fell the task of stopping that expansion cold and deflating the secessionist movement.

"THIS GREAT TRIBUNAL, THE AMERICAN PEOPLE"

Lincoln departed Springfield for Washington on the same day, February 11, that Davis departed Mississippi for Montgomery.

Northern majority opinion had already lined up solidly behind Lincoln's position (identical to Andrew Jackson's in 1832) that the Union was older than any of the states, that secession was anarchy, and that in this current crisis hung the fate of constitutional democracy. The foremost principle animating the Union, Lincoln would reflect, "is the necessity of proving that popular government is not an absurdity," and on this point, even the outgoing President James Buchanan seemed to agree. Although sharply critical of the North for starting the slavery agitation, Buchanan had startled his southern patrons by declaring, in his final annual message in early December, that secession over Lincoln's election was illegitimate and that the Union's dissolution "would be quoted as conclusive proof that man is unfit for self-government." Yet if the outgoing president opposed disunion, he also believed that, under the Constitution, he lacked any powers to prevent it. With Lincoln not due to take office until March 4, 1861, and with members of the cabinet and the lame-duck Congress from the Deep South departing after their states seceded, the federal government was rudderless and adrift.

Buchanan did offer a compromise of sorts in his final address, whereby the northerners would cease criticizing slavery, support a constitutional amendment protecting slavery in all territories, and approve of renewed efforts to secure Cuba. Republicans instantly saw through this as capitulation. Some pledged to break secession even if it meant reducing the South to rubble. At all events, the Republicans argued, the government had to enforce the laws of the United States, including the collection of customs duties in southern ports, and stand up to the rebels just as President Jackson had to the nullifiers. ("Oh, for one hour of Jackson!" the Springfield *Republican* exclaimed.) Other Republicans, including Horace Greeley, declared that if the Union could be saved only by surrendering Republican principles, it would be better simply to let the South go and let it fester in its own backwardness. (Radical abolitionists, including William Lloyd Garrison and Frederick Douglass, agreed.) Still others, fearful that bellicosity would provoke the upper South to secede, tried to fashion a congressional compromise less one-sided than Buchanan's.

The most promising compromise plan emerged from the special Senate Committee of Thirteen in early December, before any state had seceded. Established to sift through the numerous compromises coming out of Congress, the committee included some of the ablest and influential men from all sides, among them William Henry Seward, Benjamin Wade, Stephen Douglas, Jefferson Davis, and Robert Toombs. Chief credit for crafting the committee's compromise proposal belonged to John Crittenden of Kentucky, the aging ex-Whig and, lately, prominent Constitutional Unionist. The plan called for a series of irrevocable amendments to the Constitution, the most important of which would revive the old Missouri Compromise line at 36°30', extend it all the way to the Pacific, ban slavery in all territories to its North, and protect slavery in territories (including any territories gained in the future) to its South. Although less offensive to Republicans than Buchanan's suggestions, the so-called Crittenden compromise was still one-sided. Yet some powerful Republican business interests were worried that secession might touch off a financial panic far worse than that of 1857, and they endorsed the idea. So did Thurlow Weed and (in more muffled ways) William Henry Seward.

In Springfield, President-elect Lincoln broke his determined silence in order to help kill the plan. The ironies of the situation were large. Seward, the supposed radical, was playing the conciliator, to the consternation of Republican radicals like Joshua Giddings and Charles Sumner. ("God damn you, Seward," one senator told him, "you've betrayed your principles and your party; we've followed your lead long enough.") It was left to Lincoln the moderate, whose political fortunes the insurrectionist John Brown had inadvertently improved, to stand by Republican principles. The Crittenden plan, Lincoln wrote to a few influential Republicans—most pointedly Seward and Weed—"would lose us everything we gained in the election," reawaken the South's lust for Cuba, and put the nation once again "on the high-road to a slave empire." More important, the plan repudiated the basic Republican proposition that slavery's expansion should be halted everywhere. At Lincoln's urging, all five Republicans on the committee voted against the compromise, and with Toombs and Davis also opposed, the measure failed. Crittenden brought the plan to the Senate floor anyway, but by the time it came to a vote in mid-January, senators from states that had seceded or were about to secede abstained, and the remaining Republican majority defeated it.

Other compromise schemes made the rounds in January and early February—although with one Deep South state after another declaring secession, efforts at mediation increasingly looked like stalling maneuvers until Lincoln could formally take over. The House counterpart to the Senate's special committee offered two measures that avoided violating Republican fundamentals and gained Lincoln's passive support: a resolution in support of the Fugitive Slave Law (which eventually passed on February 27) and a constitutional amendment prohibiting federal interference with slavery in the states (which also passed, much more narrowly, the following day). Seward also supported a self-described "peace convention," called by the Virginia legislature, that met in Washington on the same day that the Confederate convention opened in Montgomery. Chaired by the seventy-one-year-old former president John Tyler, the assembly looked even more antique than the Constitutional Union Party. After three weeks of deliberations, it offered a revised version of the Crittenden compromise, limiting the extension of the Missouri Compromise to the existing territories, and requiring majority votes of senators from both the free and the slave states before adding any new territories. The idea got nowhere.

Lincoln, while keeping tabs on these discussions and bolstering the Republican faith, applied all of his political skills to appointing his cabinet and preparing for his inauguration. Keeping his fractious Republican rivals in line—especially Seward, who believed that he should have been elected president—was extremely difficult. On the principle of keeping one's friends close and one's rivals even closer, Lincoln chose Seward as secretary of state, Edward Bates as attorney general, Simon Cameron as secretary of war, and Salmon Chase as secretary of the Treasury. When Seward objected to Chase's selection and threatened to withdraw, Lincoln persuaded him to stay. More unfortunate was Lincoln's decision to turn his journey to Washington into a twelve-day railroad tour of northern towns and cities. Not wanting to add fuel to the fire, Lincoln addressed the trackside crowds with platitudinous speeches which raised concerns that he really was the unexceptional provincial his critics had always claimed. As the train headed south, recurring reports about planned assassination attempts gained more credibility, compelling a sudden change of schedule that left the president-elect to arrive in Washington secretly and ignominiously in the predawn hours of February 23—"like a thief in the night," he ruefully remarked.

The situation in the capital was dismal. Since the election nearly four months earlier, almost half of the slaveholding states had seceded from the Union, formed their own country, and begun seizing federal property within their own borders. No clear policy had been established about the collection of customs duties in ports where the new Confederacy now claimed full authority, or about the disposition of what federal assets remained in Union hands—most auspiciously, Fort Sumter, perched on a man-made island in Charleston harbor. Yet Lincoln had some cause for hope. After buckling in the immediate aftermath of the presidential elections, Unionists had made a strong comeback in the Border South. Virginia and Missouri, as well as Arkansas, had elected Unionist majorities to their state conventions called to consider secession. Given the choice over calling a convention, voters in North Carolina (by a narrow margin) and Tennessee (by a four-to-one majority) rejected the idea. Lincoln's repudiation of the Crittenden compromise and the failure of the Virginia peace conference had somewhat undermined "conditional Unionist" sentiment in the upper South. Much like the conditional secessionists of the cotton states, large numbers of antisecessionists elsewhere would consider any armed intervention by the federal government an act of invasion. But short of taking any overt military action against the South, Lincoln still had some room in which to operate, and he thought that his inaugural address could well determine the outcome. With input from Seward and from a close Illinois adviser, Orville Browning, Lincoln tried to compose a message that would help preserve the Union without abdicating his duty to assert federal authority. At the very last minute, he revised his text, on Seward's advice, to emphasize conciliation.

March 4 dawned cold and gloomy in Washington, but a crowd estimated at twenty-five thousand turned up at the Capitol for the inauguration ceremonies, and bright sunshine broke through at noon, just as President Lincoln began his speech. Looking stately beneath a newly grown beard, Lincoln reversed the usual order and began the ceremonies by taking the oath of office from a man he considered an arch fiend (the feeling was mutual), Chief Justice Roger Brooke Taney. Then, with an eloquence that announced the lifting of the Pierce-Buchanan era's rhetorical fog, Lincoln developed a series of points and counterpoints about slavery and the Constitution, and defended the democracy that the southern disunionists had spurned and traduced.

As president, he said, he would refuse "directly or indirectly, to interfere with the institution of slavery in the States where it exists," but he would not countenance secession. He would enforce the constitutional obligation to return fugitive slaves, but he would also "hold, occupy, and possess the property and places belonging to the government, and . . . collect the duties and imposts." He would not deny "the very high respect and consideration" due Supreme Court rulings on constitutional questions (did Taney squirm at this obvious reference to *Dred Scott*?), but he would not allow "erroneous" decisions and their "evil effect" to fix irrevocably "the policy of the government upon vital questions, affecting the whole people." In a moving peroration, Lincoln pleaded with his native Border South and men of patriotic goodwill everywhere. "I am loth to close," he said. "We are not enemies, but friends. We must not be enemies. Though passion may have strained, it must not break our bonds of affection. The mystic chords of memory, stretching from every battle-field, and patriot grave, to every living heart and hearthstone, all over this broad land, will yet swell the chorus of the Union, when again touched, as surely they will be, by the better angels of our nature."

The speech was a blend of political cunning and bedrock idealism, a style of leadership that Lincoln had been mastering since 1858. On the crucial matter of reasserting the government's authority over forts, customs houses, mints, and armories appropriated by the Confederates, he remained purposefully vague. Anything more specific could easily be regarded as a provocation, which would undermine his efforts to keep the Border South from seceding. A shrewd courtroom and political strategist thrown into a national crisis, Lincoln understood that what he needed above all else was time, time to get his White House in order, to persuade the persuadable of his moderation, and, if possible, to permit the secession fever finally to break. He made the point explicitly in his address: "Nothing valuable can be lost by taking time."

Yet Lincoln did not rely simply on temporizing and artful ambiguity. The speech's evocations of the Union and "the better angels of our nature" were as lofty an appeal to nationalist principles as any since the days of Webster and Jackson. And above and beyond the slavery issue, Lincoln unflinchingly defended certain basic ideals of freedom and democratic government, which he asserted he had been elected to vindicate. There was, he said, a single "substantial dispute" in the sectional crisis: "[o]ne section of our country believes slavery is *right*, and ought to be extended, while the other believes it is *wrong*, and ought not to be extended." There could be no doubt about where Lincoln stood, and where his administration would stand, on that fundamental moral question. But regardless of that, the only just and legitimate way to settle the matter, Lincoln insisted (with a direct echo of Thomas Jefferson's first inaugural address), was through a deliberate democratic decision by the nation's citizenry:

> Why should there not be a patient confidence in the ulti-
> mate justice of the people? Is there any better, or equal
> hope, in the world? In our present differences, is either
> party without faith of being in the right? If the Almighty
> Ruler of nations, with his eternal truth and justice, be on
> your side of the North, or on yours of the South, that
> truth, and that justice, will surely prevail, by the judg-
> ment of this great tribunal, the American people.

The future of American democracy, the best hope in the world, would rise or fall on whether secession—"the essence of anar-chy"—succeeded or failed.

Reactions to the address encouraged the new president. Not surprisingly, most Republicans applauded its mixture of modera-tion and adamancy, while Confederates and their supporters denounced it, either as an outright declaration of civil war— "couched in the cool, unimpassioned, deliberate language of the fanatic," the *Richmond Enquirer* claimed—or as a cleverly Del-phic contrivance, "concealing dark designs, iniquitous and flagi-tious." But anxious Wall Street Republicans, and even some northern Democrats, who had pushed for conciliation found the speech reassuring. (One Wall Streeter named H. D. Faulkner reported to Lincoln that he heard almost unanimous praise from his friends, ranging from a Breckinridge Democrat who called the speech "first rate . . . and full of faith" to an old Silver Gray who thought it "splendid.") Moderates in the upper South worried over its lack of specifics, but hailed what the *Spectator* of Staunton, Virginia, called its "frank and conciliatory" tone. Con-trary to the secessionists' diatribes, they insisted, Lincoln's speech was *"not a war message"* and was "not unfriendly to the South."

More than Lincoln knew, however, time was running out. On inauguration day, Buchanan's departing secretary of war, Joseph Holt, received an alarming dispatch, dated February 28, from Major Robert Anderson, commander of the federal forces at Fort Sumter. Holt quietly put it aside for the incoming administration.

Anderson reported it would take a force of at least twenty thousand troops to fight their way into Charleston harbor and relieve the weary garrison. The Union, it seemed, could evacuate Sumter—repudiating Lincoln's vows on the Capitol steps—or it could initiate a war with a massive and bloody show of force that was bound to unite the entire South and divide the North.

The next morning, Lincoln walked into his White House office for his first full day's work as president and found Major Anderson's dispatch lying on his desk.

THE SLAVEHOLDERS' REBELLION

The back-and-forth scheming over Fort Sumter lasted for six weeks and pitted Lincoln against members of his own cabinet as well as against Jefferson Davis. Winfield Scott, now general-in-chief of the U.S. Army, told Lincoln and his advisers that there were not enough ships and men available to save Sumter and that the fort ought to be evacuated. All but Treasury Secretary Salmon Chase (who favored relieving the fort if it could be done without risking war) and Postmaster General Montgomery Blair (who wanted to hold the fort under any circumstances) agreed with Scott. Secretary of State Seward, carrying over both his conciliatory strategy with the South and his ambition to undermine Lincoln's authority, secretly advised a group of Confederate commissioners that the government would indeed abandon Sumter. Such an act of generosity and goodwill, Seward reasoned, would impress the Border South and encourage Unionists within the seceded states.

Northern newspapers, including some that were pro-Democratic, expressed outrage when reports of Sumter's imminent evacuation leaked out. Lincoln, under pressure, agreed with Blair that any display of charity over Sumter would only look like a sign of weakness and embolden the rebels. His position hardened after Blair's father, the old Jacksonian Francis Blair, paid a personal visit to tell him, heatedly, that a surrender of Sumter would be "virtually a surrender of the Union" and might even constitute treason. But the impasse within the White House only broke on March 28, when General Scott, overplaying his hand, urged the evacuation of both Fort Sumter and Fort Pickens in Pensacola Bay, and cited the political arguments favored by Seward as well as military considerations. Montgomery Blair accused the general of "playing politician," and most of the cabinet swung over in favor of resupplying Sumter.

Seward, isolated, switched his ground and told Lincoln that the abandonment of Sumter linked with a defense of Pickens would change the focus of the showdown from slavery to Union. After personally ordering a large ship bound for Sumter diverted to Pickens, the secretary of state sent an astonishing note to Lincoln, demanding, in effect, that he, Seward, be given command over the situation. Lincoln rejected the suggestions firmly, but not wanting to antagonize Seward and lose his services, he kept the exchange private. On April 4, at the chastened Seward's prompting, Lincoln met with a Virginia Unionist to discuss a deal whereby Sumter would be abandoned in exchange for adjournment of the Virginia secession convention. The meeting was fruitless, and Lincoln ordered that the Sumter resupply mission commence.

Plans for that mission had been evolving for weeks. Now, instead of trying to reinforce Sumter with an all-out assault, the Union would send unarmed supply boats out to the fort, with warships standing by in case shooting started. If the Confederates tried to halt the mission, they would bear the burden of having started hostilities—and if they did not, the Union would win a great symbolic victory. On April 6, Lincoln dispatched an envoy to Charleston to inform Governor Francis Pickens of the impending resupply effort, stating that if the mission was allowed to proceed unharmed, "no effort to throw in men, arms, or ammunition will be made, without further notice, [except] in case of an attack on the Fort."

The focus now shifted to Jefferson Davis's provisional presidential office in Montgomery. Weeks earlier, Davis had placed the newly commissioned Confederate General Pierre G. T. Beauregard in command of the thousands of militia in Charleston and of the harbor defense works that menaced the Yankee fort. On March 9, Beauregard received orders to prevent Sumter's resupply, on the premise that, once strengthened, the Union forces would rain ruin on Charleston. But now Lincoln had undercut that rationale with his humanitarian supply-boat scheme.

Like Lincoln, Davis was under tremendous pressure to act. The weeks of waiting had taken their toll, leading some southern newspapers to denounce the new government's "do-nothing" policy and to despair for southern independence. Veteran fire-eaters were especially vociferous, arguing that a show of military might was essential to the Confederate cause. Virginia secessionists told their Charleston allies that the surest way to bring the Old Dominion and the rest of the border states into the fold would be to strike a blow. "The shedding of blood," the extremist eminence Edmund Ruffin, now living in Charleston, wrote in his diary, "will serve to change many voters in the hesitating states, from the submission or procrastinating ranks, to the zealous for immediate secession." It mattered little which side fired the first shot, so long as the shot was fired. If only South Carolina and the Davis government would vindicate the South's honor, then all of the slaveholding states would rally to the Confederate banner.

The fire-eaters' predictions would prove accurate soon enough. Informed of Lincoln's resupply mission, Davis interpreted it as an attempt to relieve Fort Sumter by force. He at once drafted orders to Beauregard, instructing him to demand the fort's immediate surrender and, if Major Anderson refused, to reduce it. On April 9, Davis's cabinet endorsed the order; two days later, Anderson, as expected, turned Beauregard down, remarking in passing that if help did not arrive within a few days, he and his men would be starved out. Taking Anderson's remark as confirmation that the Yankee reinforcements would be arriving soon, Davis and Beauregard moved quickly. Final orders were telegraphed from Montgomery: confirm Anderson's commitment to abandon Sumter or else attack the fort. During the night of April 11–12, the Confederate forces moved into battle position. Anderson attempted to stall for time by telling Beauregard's aides that he would leave on April 15, but only if the Confederates agreed to a host of conditions. At 3:20 A.M. on April 12, the aides informed Anderson that his reply was insufficient and that Beauregard's mortars would open fire in one hour's time. Then the aides returned to their boat and went directly to one of the surrounding Confederate batteries on Fort Johnson, at the tip of James Island.

Might this showdown have been prevented or at least forestalled? With full knowledge of all that followed the events at Fort Sumter, Americans have sought to find some point where events might have taken a different course, and affix blame accordingly. Do not Lincoln and his Republican allies bear responsibility for defeating the Crittenden compromise, thereby ensuring secession by the Deep South? Had Alexander Stephens and other moderates taken a stronger and better-organized stand against disunion, might the fire-eater juggernaut have been slowed or even halted? If true statesmen, on the order of Clay and Webster, had been in command of events instead of sectional politicians, would not the Union have been saved once again?

Like most counterfactual inquiries, these questions are based on premises easily distorted by hindsight. Over the winter of 1860–61, few Americans had the slightest conception of the mass butchery that would follow secession. The more truculent southerners asserted that the pencil-necked mongrel Yankees would not put up a real fight, and that if they tried to, they would be quickly vanquished with little loss of life. "You may slap a Yankee in the face and he'll go off and sue you," one politician claimed, "but he wont fight!" South Carolina's Senator James Chesnut, husband of the subsequently famous diarist Mary Chesnut, said that he would personally drink all of the blood that would be shed as a result of secession. Northerners were no less certain that, by the grace of God, any war against the backward South would be short and glorious. (One exception, Harriet

Beecher Stowe, foresaw that the millennial "*last* struggle for liberty" would be "a long pull.") With this sense of what in retrospect looks almost like blitheness about the consequences of secession and of resisting it, there is little wonder that the pro-compromise forces did not exert more influence.

In any case, by 1861, no effort at compromise could have long bridged the chasm in the American political soul. That chasm was deep before 1856, when the Republicans with their revolutionary antislavery ideology emerged as the chief opposition to the pro-Nebraska Democrats and their southern allies. Subsequent polarizing events—*Dred Scott*, the struggle over Lecompton, the Democrats' sectional debacles—flowed directly from the Republicans' rise. So long as the Republicans expanded their following and stayed true to their basic principles—that slavery was morally wrong, that it was an oligarchic system that perverted democracy, and that its expansion had to be halted—the ultimate clash between North and South was unavoidable. In Abraham Lincoln, the party found a leader who would prove both popular and principled. Once Lincoln was elected president, there was, for the Deep South, no turning back from secession, which was well under way before any compromise proposals arose.

Fittingly, the crisis came down to a stand-off in Charleston, spiritual capital of the slaveholders' cause in its purest form, where for more than thirty years the ideals proclaimed by John C. Calhoun had evolved into ideals of the Confederacy. And, fittingly, a well-known survivor of roughly Calhoun's own generation was on the scene. In 1823, as a young Virginia state senator, Edmund Ruffin had refused to support Calhoun for the presidency, as Calhoun was too much the nationalist. Only in succeeding years did the South Carolinian, in Ruffin's eyes, see the light and emerge as a great spokesman for southern rights and slavery. At Calhoun's death in 1850, Ruffin joined with younger pro-slavery extremists who picked up the torch, and he emerged as one of the elder statesmen of the secessionist movement. In 1861, the glorious moment come round at last—Ruffin enlisted, at age sixty-seven, as a private in a Charleston militia company, the Palmetto Guards. At 4:30 on the morning of April 12, he stood at the east mortar battery of Fort Johnson, unmistakable with his long white mane, his homespun suit with a fresh insignia, and his hat with a rebel blue cockade. General Beauregard had selected the Palmettos to fire the first shot at Sumter, and the company in turn handed the honors over to Ruffin, who was "highly gratified by the compliment, & delighted to perform the service—which I did." Ruffin's shell exploded on Sumter's parapet; nearby Confederate batteries let loose their fire; and the War of the Rebellion had begun.

EPILOGUE

On the morning of June 17, 1865, Edmund Ruffin sat in his study at his Virginia estate, Redmoor, placed the muzzle of his loaded rifle into his mouth and, with the aid of a forked stick, forced the trigger.

After the attack on Fort Sumter pushed reluctant Virginia to secede from the Union, Ruffin had happily returned home to watch the war. But now all of the Confederate armies had surrendered; one of Ruffin's sons had been killed in action; Union soldiers had pillaged Ruffin's plantations; and all of his slaves had run away forever. Ruffin's health was failing, and he was nearly deaf—but worst of all, he wrote in his diary, he himself had been rendered, with the Union's victory, "a helpless & hopeless slave, under the irresistible oppression of the most unscrupulous, vile, & abhorred of rulers." For weeks, he had struggled with the Bible and finally concluded that suicide, unlike murder, was no sin. After writing out instructions to his family that his body be buried in hallowed South Carolina, he rose from his breakfast table, walked upstairs, and rigged his rifle.

Unexpected visitors at the front door interrupted him, and

Ruffin waited until they left. After making one last diary entry, he resumed his final task—but though the firing cap exploded, the bullet remained in its chamber. Hearing the noise, his daughter-in-law frantically fetched her husband, and the two dashed upstairs, as another shot rang out. Inside the study, they found Ruffin, his head blown to pieces, the rest of him seated bolt upright in his chair.

The final words in his diary read, "And now, with my latest writing & utterance, & with what will be near to my last breath, I here repeat, & would willingly proclaim, my unmitigated hatred to Yankee rule—to all political, social, & business connection with Yankees, & to the perfidious, malignant, & vile Yankee race. Edmund Ruffin sen. Kept waiting by successive visitors to my son, until their departure at 12.15 P.M." The man who had fired the first shot of the rebellion had fired the symbolic last shot as well.

The gruesome war that killed the Confederacy settled some of the basic issues that attended the rise of American democracy. Slavery was abolished. Secession was disgraced. A southern rural vision of formally equal and independent white men, their equality and independence made possible by the bondage of blacks, was destroyed. So was another, older southern vision, of superior, aristocratic slaveholders ruling virtuously and wisely over a grateful people, slave and free, black and white. The free-labor North with its very different democracy—denounced by southerners on the eve of the war as a motley throng of infidels, free lovers, and panderers who insisted that "equality is the right of man" and believed government should be run by "the heels" instead of "the head of the society"—had won the Second American Revolution. Out of that revolution emerged a transformed nation, no longer referred to as the Union or, as in common prewar parlance, in the plural sense—the United States *are*—but in the singular—the United States *is*. That is what President Lincoln had promised in his address at Gettysburg in 1863, when he said that the war would bring "a new birth of freedom" to a "nation, conceived in Liberty, and dedicated to the proposition that all men are created equal."

The paradox, of course, is that this second revolution, as well as part of the effort to halt it, had been inspired by the words of a southern slaveholder who had helped lead the first revolution. As he transformed himself from a Henry Clay Whig to a Republican to a national leader, Lincoln found himself pulled more than ever to the ideas and the figure of Thomas Jefferson. "All honor to Jefferson," he wrote in 1859, who in the midst of the War for Independence had had the "coolness, forecast, and capacity" to introduce the great truth of equality, "applicable to all men and all times," that would forever stand as "a rebuke and a stumbling block to . . . re-appearing tyranny and oppression." For all of his inconsistencies and hypocrisies, Jefferson had not only pronounced what Lincoln called "the definitions and axioms of free society," but, in the 1790s and after, had put them into practice, winning over, encouraging, and giving a measure of real political influence to the city and country democracies that had emerged out of the American Revolution.

That Jefferson also won over so many of his fellow slaveholding planters, with his Declaration of Independence later cited by Jefferson Davis, has confused later writers, and persuaded some that the protection of slavery was the hidden motive behind Jeffersonian democracy. But as the historian and biographer James Parton observed in 1867, Jefferson was no defender of slavery, and the paradox surrounding his politics was really a fateful ambiguity: "The Southern aristocrat saw in Jefferson the sovereignty of his State; the 'smutched artificer' of the North gloried in Jefferson as the champion of the rights of man." Parton was too constrictive. Some of those "smutched artificers" were southern whites who fought the "aristocrats" for widened political rights, just as some were blacks, slave and free, who fought to end American bondage. Females and males would champion the rights of woman as well as man. These Americans, taking Jefferson at his word, would expand the principles and practices of political democracy beyond what even Jefferson had envisaged.

Still, Parton's basic point holds. By the 1840s and 1850s, two distinctive democracies, northern and southern, had finally arisen out of the strivings of the city and country democrats of the infant republic. The southern democracy enshrined slavery as the basis for white men's political equality (except for those disunionists who recoiled at any sort of equality). In national politics, southern democrats proclaimed (when it was convenient) what they called the Jeffersonian idea of state sovereignty, but only as filtered through the writings of Jefferson's factional adversaries, the Old Republicans, through the refractory writings of schismatic Federalists, and then through the pro-slavery stalwart John C. Calhoun. The northern democrats thought slavery a moral abomination that denied the basic humanity of blacks and whose expansion threatened white men's political equality (to say nothing, as free blacks and a minority of whites charged, of full political equality for all men). They stood, forthrightly, for Jeffersonian ideas about the rights of man, including free speech, which southern democrats perforce had to curtail.

Neither of these democracies was fully formed at the nation's founding. Federalism's defeat at the hands of the Jeffersonian Republicans, along with a myriad of reform efforts at the state and local level, undid many of the prevailing hierarchical political assumptions that had survived the eighteenth century. Thereafter, the largest vehicle for expanding democracy became the flawed Jackson Democracy. Organized as a movement of reform to eliminate a perceived recrudescence of privilege, the Jacksonians combined the evolving city and country democracies into a national political force. They also created a new kind of political party, more egalitarian in its institutions and its ideals than any that had preceded it, unabashed in its disciplined pursuit of power, dedicated to securing the sovereignty that, as its chief architect Martin Van Buren observed, "belongs inalienably to the people." Yet Jackson and Van Buren's Democracy had its contradictions as well, which brought, initially, the great mass of southern planters into its ranks. Out of that revived coalition of "Southern aristocrats" and "smutched artificers"—what Van Buren called the alliance of planters and "plain republicans"— the Jacksonians believed that the "monarchical spirit" of established, monied privilege could be subdued.

Tensions within the original Jackson coalition quickly undermined its unity, leading to the departure of Calhoun and the nullifiers, and to the defection of northern conservatives and wealthy southern planters over Jackson's banking and currency policies. Yet the Jacksonians were hardly consistent egalitarians, nor did they encompass all of the democratic impulses that were breaking out in the 1830s. Above all, in order to preserve the spirit of the Missouri Compromise and their party's intersectional unity, the Jacksonians joined in the attack on the radical abolitionists and bent over backward to placate southern outrage, short of disunion, at attacks on slavery. The strategy was partly successful, but it could neither prevent a small number of northern antislavery Democrats from bolting the party in disgust, nor halt the defection of more southern planters once the Yankee Van Buren became the Democracy's standard-bearer. Nor could it halt the emergence of a new-style Whig opposition more reconciled to political democracy than old-guard conservatives, and adept at turning the programs of government-supported economic development that Jacksonians had held constitutionally suspect into manifestos for the common man. In the North, these new-school Whigs, combining secular humanitarianism and the moral imperatives of the Second Great Awakening, leaned more heavily than the Jacksonians to antislavery politics and to various crusades for moral reform.

Two factors—the expansionist pursuit of Jefferson's empire of liberty, and the extraordinary continued growth of plantation slavery thanks to the cotton revolution—upset the Democratic and Whig Parties that had formed by 1840, and hastened the growth of the antagonistic northern and southern democracies. Americans experienced the crack-up primarily as a political crisis, about whether slavery would be allowed to interfere with democratic rights—or, alternatively, whether northern tyranny would be allowed to interfere with southern democracy. Over those questions, which encompassed clashes over northern free labor and southern slavery, the political system began falling apart in the mid-1840s. First the Wilmot Proviso and the Free Soil revolt temporarily split the Democracy; then the Whig Party collapsed under the weight of sectional discord; and finally a new northern Republican coalition emerged—its name borrowed from Jefferson's old party—consisting of northern antislavery Whigs, Free Soil Democrats, and the long-beleaguered political abolitionists. After the demise of what remained of the Jackson Democracy over the struggles in Kansas in the late 1850s, Americans' differences became so profound that they could not be settled at the ballot box, but only on the battlefield.

Before his election in 1860, Lincoln looked back over this history to the time of the Federalists and Jeffersonians and likened it to a brawl between two drunks, in which one man manages to fight his way into the greatcoat of the other, and vice versa: "If the two leading parties of this day are really identical with the two in the days of Jefferson and Adams, they have performed about the same feat as the two drunken men." Like the old-line Federalists, and unlike the party of its supposed founder Jefferson, he explained, "the so-called democracy of to-day"—meaning the slaveholder-dominated Democratic Party—"hold the *liberty* of one man to be absolutely nothing, when in conflict with another man's right of *property*." On the contrary, he explained, Republicans "are for both the *man* and the *dollar*; but in cases in conflict, the man *before* the dollar"—devoted, as Jefferson was, "to the *personal* rights of men, holding the rights of *property* to be secondary only, and greatly inferior."

Lincoln then turned to the politics of his own time and observed that it would be difficult "to save the principles of Jefferson from total overthrow in this nation" when slaveholders and their apologists either pronounced them "glittering generalities" and "self-evident lies," or argued that they applied only to "superior races." These expressions had the same objective: "supplant-

ing the principles of free government, and restoring those of clas-
sification, caste, and legitimacy. They would delight a convoca-
tion of crowned heads, plotting against the people. They are the
van-guard—the miners, and sappers—of returning despotism.
We must repulse them, or they will subjugate us." Lincoln did
repulse them, and saved Jefferson's principles as he saw them—
though at the cost of more than six hundred thousand American
lives.

How would the victors define and implement democracy, now
that secession and slavery were crushed and the South's peculiar
democracy lay in ruins? Lincoln was murdered before he could
make his own thinking plain and test it against hard realities.
Other Americans, North and South, pressed ahead with their
own solutions.

One democratic proposal came from Garrison Frazier, a black
Baptist preacher in Georgia, who had been a slave for sixty years
before he purchased his freedom for a thousand dollars in 1857.
At an official meeting with Secretary of War Edwin Stanton and
General William Tecumseh Sherman in Savannah, after the city
was safely in Union hands, Frazier, speaking on behalf of a group
of twenty prominent local blacks, replied to questions about
bondage, freedom, the past, and the future. What was slavery?
"[R]eceiving by *irresistible power*, the work of another man, and
not by his *consent*," Frazier said. And freedom? Frazier defined it
as "placing us where we could reap the fruit of our own labor,
take care of ourselves and assist the Government in maintaining
our freedom." The minister unhesitatingly called the South "the
aggressor" in the war, given that "President Lincoln was elected
President by the majority of the United States, which guaranteed
him the right of holding that office and exercising that right over
the whole United States," after which "the South rebelled." Frazier concluded that the best way to ensure the ex-slaves' freedom
was "to have land, and turn it and till it by our own labor."

Hundreds of miles to the North, a now largely forgotten
Jacksonian-era labor leader read Frazier's remarks in a newspaper
and heartily approved—and hinted at the links between the

stripling democracy of the 1820s and 1830s and the politics of the postwar era. William Heighton had been the pivotal intellectual and political leader in the transformation of Philadelphia's old city democracy into an independent but broadly pro-Jackson labor movement. He had disappeared in the early 1830s, only to resurface in 1865, living across the Delaware River in rural Elmer, New Jersey. There the abolitionist and former member of John Brown's Secret Six, George L. Stearns, tracked him down and asked for his ideas about "the reconstruction of the social and political institutions of the Rebel States." Stearns immediately published Heighton's reply (alongside remarks by Wendell Phillips, Frederick Douglass, and other radical antislavery leaders) in a pamphlet entitled *The Equality of All Men before the Law Claimed and Defended*.

Heighton, now in his midsixties, had retained his old radical fire. He still railed against "money rule" and "MONOPOLIES," and the slavery of wages, and he upheld the doctrine that "[a]ll human beings have an *equal* right" to life, liberty, and "*property* in the common elements of nature—light, air, water, and the land." Yet Heighton also saw the connections between those older ideas and the challenge of what he, like others, had begun calling "reconstruction." Noting Garrison Frazier's "uncommon shrewdness and good sense," Heighton laid out a two-step plan for rebuilding southern democracy. First, fair and universal elections: "[a] corrupt use of the ballot-box is not Democracy, but an aristocracy (money rule) of the most odious kind." Second, the redistribution of land: "[t]he landed estates . . . of all the prominent and active rebels, the great chiefs, should be confiscated and broken up," a portion of it given to their heirs, and "an equal homestead should be apportioned to each colored family." The ex-slaves deserved the land, having cleared and improved it by their own labor, Heighton asserted. More than that, "[i]mmense landed estates in a few hands (baronies) the world over, are death to Democracy. If three or four men own a whole country, they will be its governors . . . even under republican forms."

Heighton's updating of his Jacksonian labor radicalism as

Reconstruction radicalism was but one democratic response to the postwar political situation. The Confederacy's defeat cracked open all sorts of ideas about how equality might best be expanded—or curtailed—in the new era, especially in the North. For Elizabeth Cady Stanton, an active Lincoln Republican in 1860, and her widening circle of allies, it was a signal to press harder for the cause that Stanton had helped ignite at Seneca Falls in 1848, in the cauldron of the Free Soil revolt. ("Suffice it, therefore, to say," the veteran radical abolitionist Lydia Maria Child would write, "either the theory of our government is *false*, or women have a right to vote.") For a Massachusetts machinist, antislavery campaigner, and trade unionist named Ira Steward, his newfound ally Wendell Phillips, and organized wage earners across the North, it was time to undertake the creation of a new labor movement, based on the charge that "something of slavery" persisted in the rapidly industrializing North. Opponents of these and other northern stirrings recoiled with horror at a democracy that seemed to be boiling over, and they began challenging, in essays, editorials, and proposed legislation, the most basic of democratic principles. Charles Francis Adams's son, Charles Jr., would sneer in 1869, in an article heavy with hostility toward the lowly, that "Universal Suffrage can only mean in plain English the government of ignorance and vice."

For the immediate future, the problems of southern Reconstruction were paramount—and deeply divisive. William Heighton's anti-aristocratic radicalism was one legacy of the old Jacksonian movement. So was the obstructionism of Andrew Johnson, an ex-cobbler and true-blue yeoman Democrat from East Tennessee who would prove that while he despised the planter oligarchy, he despised the freedmen even more. Among the ascendant northern Republicans, the fractiousness that Lincoln had handled so masterfully reasserted itself under President Johnson, dividing radicals like Thaddeus Stevens (who favored land distribution) against a panoply of northern moderates and conservatives. Within the South, alongside a small new class of black political and social leaders, old-line Whigs—men who had never fully adjusted to the democratizing trends of the prewar era—grabbed the mantle of Unionism, loyalty, and leadership. And everywhere in the fallen Confederacy there were southern whites, ex-slaveholders and ordinary farmers alike, who were no more reconciled to the new order than Edmund Ruffin had been, but who carried on anyway, in sullen detachment or in night-riding fury, vowing one day to redeem the South from Yankee "Black Republican" rule. "I hates the Yankee nation/And everything they do," ran one popular song ostensibly written by an ex-Confederate, "I hates the Declaration/Of Independence too/I hates the glorious Union—'Tis dripping with our blood/And I hates their striped banner,/I fit it all I could."

The collision of hopes and despairs that marked the development of American democracy after 1865 would take decades to settle, and in some respects, they remain unsettled 140 years later. Not long after the war ended, an aborted trial dramatized— and a photograph survives to illustrate—the enormous challenges that lay ahead.

On May 10, 1865, Jefferson Davis was captured by U.S. Army forces near Irwinsville in southern Georgia, as he tried to flee to Texas. Imprisoned under military guard at Fort Monroe in Virginia, Davis faced a charge of treason for levying war against the United States, but the government decided he would have to be tried by a civil court. After nearly four years of indecision and delay (two of which Davis spent behind bars), the case was finally dropped. Davis, who had wanted to use the trial to justify secession, would live for another twenty years, enough time for him to complete and publish his two-volume recollection, *The Rise and Fall of the Confederate Government*. Here, in what is still the most influential presidential memoir in American history, Davis blamed many others (but himself not at all) for the Confederacy's defeat and established the myth that slavery had nothing to do with secession—a crucial part of the larger, then-emerging myth of the Lost Cause.

Jefferson Davis got his say, though not his trial. Yet the federal court in Virginia had made full preparations for that trial, to the point of empanelling thirteen men to decide the case—twelve petit jurors plus one alternate, all respectable citizens of the Commonwealth of Virginia. Seven were black. Even today, the picture that was made of the twelve proud men startles, inspires, provokes. It affirms that the revolution caused by the rise of American democracy had created realities and possibilities scarcely imaginable five years earlier. Would those new realities endure and those possibilities flourish? On the outcome relied the fate of what Thomas Jefferson and Abraham Lincoln had called the world's best hope.

SELECTED FURTHER READING

This list of suggested readings is far from exhaustive. Readers interested in exploring particular topics in greater depth, especially concerning local and state politics, may wish to consult the relevant endnotes in the full one-volume Norton edition of *The Rise of American Democracy*, available in paperback.

Tyler Anbinder, *Nativism and Slavery: The Northern Know-Nothings and the Politics of the 1850s* (New York, 1992).

John Ashworth, *Slavery, Capitalism, and Politics in the Antebellum Republic, Volume I: Commerce and Compromise, 1820–1850* (New York, 1995).

Samuel Flagg Bemis, *John Quincy Adams and the Union* (New York, 1956).

Frederick J. Blue, *The Free Soilers: Third Party Politics, 1848–54* (Urbana, 1973).

Donald B. Cole, *Martin Van Buren and the American Political System* (Princeton, 1984).

David H. Donald, *Lincoln* (New York, 1995).

Jonathan H. Earle, *Jacksonian Antislavery and the Politics of Free Soil* (Chapel Hill, 2004).

John S. D. Eisenhower, *So Far from God: The U.S. War with Mexico, 1846–1848* (New York, 1989).

Don E. Fehrenbacher, *Prelude to Greatness: Lincoln in the 1850s* (Stanford, 1962).

———, *The Dred Scott Case: Its Significance in American Law and Politics* (New York, 1978).

Eric Foner, *Free Soil, Free Labor, Free Men: The Ideology of the Republican Party before the Civil War* (New York, 1970).

————, *Politics and Ideology in the Age of the Civil War* (New York, 1980).

William W. Freehling, *The Road to Disunion: Secessionists at Bay, 1776–1854* (New York, 1990).

Holman Hamilton, *Prologue to Conflict: The Crisis and Compromise of 1850* (Lexington, 1964).

Michael F. Holt, *The Rise and Fall of the American Whig Party: Jacksonian Politics and the Onset of the Civil War* (New York, 1999).

Robert Johannsen, *Stephen A. Douglas* (New York, 1973).

Alexander Keyssar, *The Right to Vote: The Contested History of Democracy in the United States* (New York, 2001).

William S. McFeely, *Frederick Douglass* (New York, 1991).

James M. McPherson, *Battle Cry of Freedom: The Civil War Era* (New York, 1988).

Frederick Merk, *Manifest Destiny and Mission in American History: A Reinterpretation* (New York, 1963).

Allan Nevins, *The Ordeal of the Union* (New York, 1947).

————, *The Emergence of Lincoln* (New York, 1950).

Roy F. Nichols, *The Disruption of American Democracy* (1948; New York, 1962).

Stephen B. Oates, *To Purge This Land with Blood: A Biography of John Brown* (1970; Amherst, 1984).

Merrill D. Peterson, *The Great Triumvirate: Webster, Clay, and Calhoun* (New York, 1987).

Norma Lois Peterson, *The Presidencies of William Henry Harrison and John Tyler* (Lawrence, 1989).

David M. Potter, *The Impending Crisis, 1848–1861* (New York, 1976).

Benjamin Quarles, *Black Abolitionists* (New York, 1969).

Joseph G. Rayback, *Free Soil: The Election of 1848* (Lexington, 1970).

Robert V. Remini, *Henry Clay: Statesman for the Union* (New York, 1992).

————, *Daniel Webster: The Man and His Time* (New York, 1997).

Charles G. Sellers, *James K. Polk, Continentalist, 1843–1846* (Princeton, 1966).

Richard H. Sewell, *Ballots for Freedom: Antislavery Politics in the United States, 1837–1860* (New York, 1976).

James Roger Sharp, *The Jacksonians Versus the Banks: Jacksonian Politics in the States after the Panic of 1837* (New York, 1970).

Joel H. Silbey, *The Shrine of Party: Congressional Voting Behavior, 1841–1852* (Pittsburgh, 1967).

Judith Wellman, *The Road to Seneca Falls: Elizabeth Cady Stanton and the First Woman's Rights Convention* (Urbana, 2004).

Charles M. Wiltse, *John C. Calhoun* (Indianapolis, 1944–51).

ACKNOWLEDGMENTS

I am deeply grateful to the John Simon Guggenheim Memorial Foundation and the American Council of Learned Societies for their financial support. An intellectually challenging fellowship year at the Woodrow Wilson International Center for Scholars in 1998–99 transformed my understanding of American democracy, for which I am indebted to the Center and its excellent staff. I am equally indebted to the Princeton University Research Board, the Shelby Cullom Davis Center for Historical Studies, and the Princeton University History Department for their generosity over many years.

Gerald Howard, then of W. W. Norton & Company, showed faith in this book and its author when he signed me up long ago, and he remains a steadfast ally. At Norton, I have been blessed to work with Drake McFeely, a friend for more than two decades and a wise editor, who also possesses the patience and fortitude of a saint. His assistant, Brendan Curry, offered me his energy, encouragement, and shrewd expertise. Mary Babcock's superb copyediting improved my prose and pushed me to omit large amounts of extraneous material. Thanks go as well to Starling Lawrence and Jeannie Luciano for their support. During the final stages, Nancy Palmquist, Anna Oler, Gina Webster, Don Rifkin, Bill Rusin, Louise Brockett, Elizabeth Riley, Sally Anne McCartin, and their staffs performed splendidly in turning out the finished book.

Tom Wallace of T. C. Wallace, Ltd., and Andrew Wylie of the Wylie Agency handled business matters with sagacity and efficiency.

Judith Ferszt, the manager of the Program in American Studies at Princeton, has helped me in matters large and small nearly every day for the past dozen years and given me the gifts of her singular intelligence and good cheer.

Amanda Ameer and Samantha Williamson put in many hard hours checking footnotes and quotations.

Numerous friends, loved ones, colleagues, students, teachers, librarians, research assistants, technical wizards, counselors, and confessors have helped me beyond measure, in everything from suggesting sources, locating documents, and reading drafts to making allowances for my exasperating distraction. To praise them here as they deserve would add many more pages to an already long book. I have thanked them, and will continue to thank them, personally. Above all, thanks go to my beloved and forbearing family, who make me wish I could have been a poet instead of a historian and said it all much better and quicker.

The dedication is a toast to essential companions and decades of companionship—and to decades more, through thick and thin.

CREDITS

1. The Granger Collection, New York
2. Library of Congress
3. Library of Congress
4. The Granger Collection, New York
5. Picture History
6. The Granger Collection, New York
7. Coline Jenkins / Elizabeth Cady Stanton Trust
8. Library of Congress
9. Library of Congress
10. Library of Congress
11. Library of Congress
12. The Granger Collection, New York
13. The Granger Collection, New York
14. National Portrait Gallery, Smithsonian Institution / Art Resource, NY
15. Library of Congress
16. Library of Congress
17. Picture History
18. Library of Congress
19. Library of Congress
20. Alabama Department of Archives and History, Montgomery, Alabama
21. Library of Congress
22. Picture History
23. Library of Congress

INDEX